DATE DUE

Imperial Projections

ARETHUSA BOOKS

Series Editor: Martha A. Malamud

IMPERIAL PROJECTIONS

Ancient Rome
in Modern Popular Culture

Edited by
Sandra R. Joshel, Margaret Malamud,
and Donald T. McGuire, Jr.

THE JOHNS HOPKINS UNIVERSITY PRESS
Baltimore and London

©2001 The Johns Hopkins University Press
All rights reserved. Published 2001
Printed in the United States of America on acid-free paper
9 8 7 6 5 4 3 2 1

The Johns Hopkins University Press
2715 North Charles Street
Baltimore, Maryland 21218-4363
www.press.jhu.edu

Library of Congress Cataloging-in-Publication Data

Imperial projections : ancient Rome in modern popular culture / edited by
Sandra R. Joshel, Margaret Malamud, and Donald T. McGuire, Jr.
    p. cm. — (Arethusa books)
  Includes bibliographical references and index.
  ISBN 0-8018-6742-8 (alk. paper)
  1. Rome—In motion pictures.   2. Rome—In literature.   I. Joshel,
Sandra R.   II. Malamud, Margaret.   III. McGuire, Donald T.   IV. Series.

PN1995.9.R68 I47 2001
700'.4237—dc21   00-054602

A catalog record for this book is available from the British Library.

Contents

Contributors

NICHOLAS J. CULL is a professor of American Studies at the University of Leicester in the United Kingdom. He has published widely on British and American film and political communication, and he is currently writing a history of the United States Information Agency and its propaganda during the Cold War.

WILLIAM FITZGERALD is a professor of classics and rhetoric at the University of California at Berkeley. He is the author of *Agonistic Poetry: The Pindaric Mode in Pindar, Horace, Hoelderlin, and the English Ode* (Berkeley 1986), *Catullan Provocations: Lyric Poetry and the Drama of Position* (Berkeley 1995), and *Slavery and the Roman Literary Imagination* (Cambridge 2000).

ALISON FUTRELL is an associate professor in the Department of History at the University of Arizona. She was recently an Ailsa Mellon Bruce Visiting Senior Fellow at the National Gallery's Center for Advanced Study in the Visual Arts, where she continued work on her current project, *Barbarian Queens: Paradoxes of Gender, Power, and Identity.*

SANDRA R. JOSHEL teaches at the New England Conservatory of Music. She is the author of articles on gender and slavery in ancient Rome and of *Work, Identity, and Legal Status at Rome* (Norman, Okla. 1992), and she is a co-editor, with Sheila Murnaghan, of *Women and Slaves in Greco-Roman Culture: Differential Equations* (New York 1998).

MARGARET MALAMUD is an associate professor of ancient history and Islamic Studies at New Mexico State University. Her current research and publications investigate the reception of classical antiquity and ancient Egypt in modern popular culture. She recently received an NEH fellowship and a research grant from the American Philosophical Association to support her research on the classical tradition in American popular culture.

MARTHA MALAMUD is an associate professor at the State University of New York at Buffalo. Her areas of interest include ancient epic, Roman literature, and late antiquity. She has also taught at the University of Southern California. She is currently the editor of the interdisciplinary journal *Arethusa* and the series editor for *Arethusa Books*. She is the author of *A Poetics of Transformation: Prudentius and Classical Mythology* (Ithaca 1989) and has published articles on Ovid, Lucan, Statius, Persius, Prudentius, Valerius Flaccus, and Virgil. She has received a Mellon fellowship, an NEH fellowship, and an ACLS fellowship, and she is a fellow of the American Academy in Rome.

DONALD T. McGUIRE, JR., received his Ph.D. in classics from Cornell University in 1985 and is currently a member of the Classics Department at the State University of New York at Buffalo. He works primarily on Roman imperial epic poetry. His book, *Acts of Silence: Civil War, Tyranny, and Suicide in Flavian Epic*, was published in 1998.

MARTIN M. WINKLER is a professor of classics at George Mason University. He has published articles on Roman literature, on the classical tradition, and on classical and medieval culture and mythology in film. His books are *The Persona in Three Satires of Juvenal* (Hildesheim 1983), *Der lateinische Eulenspiegel des Ioannes Nemius* (Tübingen 1995), and the Penguin Classics anthology *Juvenal in English* (London 2001). *Classics and Cinema*, a collection of essays he edited in 1991, is appearing in an extensively revised edition as *Classical Myth and Culture in the Cinema* (Oxford 2001). He has organized and presented two month-long film programs at the National Gallery of Art in Washington, D.C.: *Greek Tragedy from Stage to Screen* and *Hollywood's Rome*. He frequently lectures and teaches courses on classical literature and film.

MARIA WYKE is a senior lecturer in classics at the University of Reading. She has published widely on Roman love poetry and ancient gender, as well as in the area of classics and popular culture. She is the author of *Projecting the Past: Ancient Rome, Cinema, and History* (New York 1997) and co-editor, with Michael Biddiss, of *Uses and Abuses of Antiquity* (Bern 1999). She is now researching a book on the representation of Julius Caesar in American and Italian popular culture.

Imperial Projections

Introduction

Sandra R. Joshel, Margaret Malamud, and Maria Wyke

Late April 2000: the actor Russell Crowe in gladiator garb struts across television, movie, and computer screens and graces trailers, advertisements, and the covers of many magazines on the newsstand that announce the May 5 opening of Ridley Scott's *Gladiator*, a "sword-and-sandal epic of the kind they didn't make anymore until he did," comments the *New York Times* (28 April 2000). This advertising campaign, and the film itself, instance the experience of ancient Rome available to most Americans and Europeans in the twentieth century. They receive their principle contact with the ancient world through popular culture in its diverse manifestations: films and television programs, historical novels and plays, comic books and toys, advertising and computer games. The Romes created in popular culture are so pervasive and entrenched in the contemporary imagination that television programs purporting to present the "real" Rome use clips from Hollywood's historical epics to bring ancient Rome to life.

The film also exemplifies how ancient Rome is rediscovered and re-presented. The new "real" Rome in *Gladiator* is a pastiche of a seventeenth-century Spanish fort on Malta (rebuilt by Napoleon in classical style), pictures of classical buildings from all over Europe, and computer-generated effects. Thus its physical setting is formed by pasting together different Roman buildings in different places, an edifice redesigned by a European emperor who reprocessed ancient Rome for his own contemporary uses, and a twentieth-century imaginative sampling of the director and computer artists. These images, however, would seem to reprocess other pop-culture Romes. The bits and pieces shown to tantalize the ticket-buying public seem all too familiar from Hollywood epics: vi-

1

olence and sex, a beefy male and a lovely female, a noble slave and an evil emperor, and, of course, monuments and spectacles, now made more compelling by computer-generated effects. Ridley Scott's Rome, like earlier Hollywood Romes, is shaped not only by its popular predecessors but also by its own era, the turn of the century. Film as a medium involves a process of projection enhanced in this case by *Gladiator*'s content: the filming of the gladiator combats in the arena, for example, "mimic[s] the way modern-day sporting events are shown on television . . . to subliminally make them more real to today's audiences" (*New York Times*, 28 April 2000).

Imperial Projections investigates the utility and mutability of images of Rome for modern popular culture. The essays analyze how the legacy of Rome has been appropriated by diverse groups at different historical moments for varied ends—most especially, for debates, explicit and implicit, about politics and sexuality. The volume joins recent work that investigates popular recreations and interpretations of ancient Rome and the variety of ways ancient Rome has been used to articulate and address contemporary concerns (Bondanella 1987, Wyke 1997b, Edwards 1999, Wyke and Biddiss 1999). However, the texts and practices that it examines are more diverse, and the essays, taken together, explore the circulation of imaginary Romes on an American/British axis. Following an approximate chronology from the postwar 1950s to the close of the twentieth century, seesawing between the United States and Britain, and investigating an array of modern entertainments—historical novels, pornography, theater, cinema, television, and casino architecture and practices—the essays in *Imperial Projections* converge on a coherent account of the Roman empire as a peculiarly privileged instrument of popular culture.

The authors, classicists and cultural historians, investigate the ways in which Americans and Britons have used Rome to define themselves and to measure their own cultural, political, and material achievements. The volume takes as its point of departure the view that representations of the Roman past should not be judged by the ways in which they successfully represent a "real" text or past events; rather, they should be seen as complex and rich dialogues with the past whose value resides precisely in how the past is reformulated in the light of the present. We are particularly interested in the ways in which popular representations of Rome present different constructions of the metaphoric relationship between Rome and Britain and Rome and the United States, and how these constructions articulate and interrogate America's and Britain's own political, cultural, and sexual identities.

The "Imperial" and "Projections" of our title each play on doubled meanings. "Imperial" refers to ancient Rome and to modern empires: the geopolitical empires of Britain before the Second World War and of the United States after, as well as the cultural empire of Hollywood. "Projections" evokes two senses of the word: many Romes of popular culture are projections in the sense that images of an ancient empire are projected on the screen of the cinema or the television and, more figuratively, the ancient past itself becomes a screen for the projection of contemporary concerns in ancient garb—a sort of retrofitting of the past with the present. As the essays demonstrate, images of Rome are not stable: they shift in accordance with the political and social circumstances of particular historical moments, changes in generic and artistic conventions, the very technologies of different media, the ideological frameworks of individual writers, directors, and artists, and the aesthetic sensibilities and desires of their spectators and consumers. Collectively, the essays reveal multiple and sometimes highly provocative uses of ancient Rome and illustrate the continued relevance of the classical tradition in shaping and contesting matters of cultural and political significance.

Although republican Rome operated as a model for the United States, twentieth-century popular culture demonstrates little interest in the Roman republic. The Rome that emerges from American and British popular culture in the twentieth century is predominantly the Rome of the Caesars. On page, stage, and screen, Petronius, the sophisticated Roman writer of the first century c.e., may make an appearance, but it is the mad emperor Nero who really matters. The Roman empire, most often represented as brutal, militaristic, and hypersexual, is defined by its enjoyment of unrestrained power and moral corruption: Rome becomes, stereotypically and almost archetypally, a society characterized by might and vice (Winkler). Signs of this Romanness typically include armies on the march, triumphal processions, chariot races, gladiatorial games, Christian martyrdoms, banquets, and orgies. Against this Rome is set a diverse range of opponents, generally Christians but also Jews, slaves, and other non-Roman enemies. Most often, these opponents give us the only point of view on Romanness from inside Roman society, and these witnesses are the marginalized within Roman society or outsiders held in Rome by force. At the same time, modern audiences as external witnesses to these narratives of imperial ambition and lust are always positioned as more knowledgeable than the Romans themselves, permanently aware of the extinction to which history is leading them (Fitzgerald).

The Roman empire has been and continues to be an enabling device for comment on the present. By displacing contemporary concerns into a recognizable and familiar past and by projecting modern empires back onto an ancient one, popular representations allow audiences simultaneously to distance themselves from that past and to identify with it. Popular representations of the Roman empire can conveniently exhibit the greatest extremes of political power, material life, and sexual behavior. They can supply explanatory origins for modern social structures, validate or challenge their procedures, and make them the culmination of an ineluctable history, while audiences of these representations are shaped as knowing participants in a seemingly shared and prestigious cultural tradition.

Adapting History, Texts, and Other Popular Romes

Images and texts of Rome have been adapted and deployed in a variety of media to evoke and animate a Rome traditionally depicted as lying at the roots of Euro-American culture. Whether the project is to create a seemingly authentic rendition of Roman history, as in Colleen McCullough's novels, or to create an imagined Roman pleasure palace, as in Caesars Palace in Las Vegas, the process is subject to manipulation, distortion, and, at times, highly significant invention. Larry Gelbart, co-writer of the Broadway musical comedy *A Funny Thing Happened on the Way to the Forum*, summed up the process of adapting the Roman comic playwright Plautus for the American stage as: "digging around," "extract[ing]," "cribbing," and "fashioning a cat's cradle of a plot" (1998.207). Although the result here is specific—the transformation of Plautine humor into American vaudeville, Roman slave into Jewish comic, and Rome into Brooklyn—similar pastiches and metamorphoses shape many popular culture Romes, albeit with different results.

Some twentieth-century popular culture adaptations have lengthy histories that reveal the malleability and multivalence of figures from ancient Rome. The British film director Derek Jarman laid out an explicit history for his 1970s film adaptation of Saint Sebastian's martyrdom—from Renaissance paintings of an exquisitely beautiful youth, through the seventeenth-century sculptures that still adorn his catacombs, to more recent photographic exploitations of the saint's penetration by arrows—as a means for imaging homoerotic desire and identity (Wyke). Alison

Futrell explores a two-hundred-year tradition of adaptation of an event in Roman history: the Roman slave revolt associated with the gladiator Spartacus (73–71 B.C.E.). In 1760, the French playwright Bernard-Joseph Saurin adapted the historical accounts of the Roman slave rebellion to put on the stage an Enlightenment hero struggling for the natural rights of man; nineteenth-century abolitionists made the ancient Roman Spartacus into a Haitian Toussaint L'Ouverture; in 1810, the Austrian Franz Grillparzer attempted to turn him into a tortured Romantic poet; the American Robert Montgomery Bird saw him as an analogue for American colonists battling imperial Britain; and Howard Fast's 1951 novel *Spartacus* told a Communist parable that Hollywood had to tame to put on screen in 1960 against the backdrop of McCarthyism.

As nearly every essay makes clear, in the second half of the twentieth century, virtually every popular culture Rome is obliged to engage with or challenge Hollywood's canonic productions of ancient Rome. Most of Hollywood's Roman epics were ultimately based on nineteenth-century sources, ranging from historical novels to plays, paintings, circus shows, and many were indebted to the cinematic Romes of Italian silent films (Wyke 1997b). Most commonly, Hollywood translated late nineteenth-century novels and toga plays, like Wilson Barrett's *The Sign of the Cross* (1895), Henryk Sienkiewicz's *Quo Vadis?* (1896), and Lew Wallace's *Ben-Hur* (1880), into cinematic epics (Fitzgerald, Winkler; see also Wyke 1997b). Adaptation goes beyond turning novels into screenplays however. Cinema recycles its own celluloid Romes, so that American cinematic Romes of the 1950s tend to reproduce each other: William Wyler, for example, claimed to have studied earlier Roman films in order to get the right look for his 1959 *Ben-Hur* (Winkler).

Hollywood's Romes inform virtually every artifact of subsequent popular culture Romes, even those, like the British camp comedy *Carry On Cleo* (1964), that attempt to undermine its dominant images of imperial Rome. In its attempt to demolish the classical epic by parody, it necessarily inscribes Hollywood's Rome even as it attempts to subvert it. *Carry On Cleo* not only parodies the subject matter of the infamous Hollywood extravaganza *Cleopatra* (1963), starring Richard Burton and Elizabeth Taylor, it also borrows some of its costumes and props from *Cleopatra*'s elaborate sets (Cull). The difficulty of circumventing, let alone escaping, Hollywood's Rome is ironically evidenced in Richard Lester's 1966 cinematic adaptation of the 1962 Broadway musical comedy *A Funny Thing Happened on the Way to the Forum*. Lester wanted both to expose the seamy underside of Rome, highlighting its social and economic injustices, *and* to parody Hollywood film genres, particularly the historical epic and its images of ancient Rome. To create his sordid Rome, an authentic urban landscape and not Hollywood's shining marble surface, Lester turned to Jerome Carcopino's *Daily Life in Ancient Rome* (1940). Leaving aside the problems of Carcopino's vision of the authentic, we can observe Lester's tangible indebtedness to Hollywood practice in the resulting representation of the ancient city. Lester shot his film in Spain on the set used for Anthony Mann's *The Fall of the Roman Empire* (1964). He dirtied that set by covering it in mud, carting in rotting vegetables, and hiring Spanish peasants to play the poor of the ancient city. By recycling the set, Lester ensured that Hollywood's grand city remained like a palimpsest under his gritty, non-Hollywood Rome (Margaret Malamud).

Distancing: Romans as Others

Adaptation always involves a process of projection that fundamentally alters the Rome adapted. Imperial Rome provides a screen onto which concerns about contemporary international relations, domestic politics, and cultural and social tensions can be projected. Projection depends on two processes: distancing ("We are not the Romans") or identification ("We are the Romans"). But the alternatives are not limited only to distancing or identification; most often we encounter a complex and ambivalent projection in which the Romans are both self and other ("Might *we* be the Romans?").

When the weight is on distancing, the Romans have taken on the analogical role of an astonishing variety of oppressors and enemies: the *ancien régime* against *philosophes*; slaveholders against slaves and abolitionists; capitalists against exploited workers; colonizers against the colonized; and totalitarian regimes of the right and left against democracies. When the projected Rome is a society of might and vice, it might work to distance the audience from the Romans and to invite that audience to identify with Rome's victims or opponents. Perhaps the most significant and self-satisfied series of polarizations appeared on the screens of Hollywood in the 1950s. Hollywood's historical epics were structured around a polarization inherited from Victorian religious fiction that opposed Romans to embattled religious communities—primarily Christians and Jews (who are usually proto-Christians or the soon-to-be converted)—and sometimes even to slaves who, as in *Spartacus*, are framed in terms of a Christianity that has not yet arrived (Fitzgerald; Wyke 1997b.23, 71–72, 133–34; Wood 1975).

The religious distinction is mapped onto the political and ideological map of World War II and the Cold War (Wyke 1997b.23). Spectacles of legions on the march and Roman characters intoning the language of repression convey a tyranny associated with hyperbolic militarism. Martin Winkler focuses on the ways in which Romans become analogues for Nazis, yet these same Romans, Wyke shows, simultaneously become Italian fascists and Soviet Communists (Wyke 1997b.142–43, 145). They are deployed in an American rhetoric of the Cold War, initiated by President Truman in 1947, that universalizes a discourse of freedom and sets out a simple, mutually exclusive alternative: freedom or tyranny. The symbolic elasticity of cinematic Romans, who stand in for Mussolini, Hitler, and Stalin, projects into antiquity an American Cold War discourse that collapses fascism and Communism into one overriding totalitarianism that, reassuringly, will be defeated by the requirements of history. The absolute dichotomy between Roman and Christian on the narrative level obviates or at least alleviates American imperial concerns. If, in the 1950s, an American audience, relying on a polarized discourse of freedom versus tyranny, could say, "We are not the Romans," then it could also say, "We are not imperialists." In the toga epics, at least at the level of plot, the reality of the American empire and the runaway consumerism of the 1950s could be disowned, and the increasing militarism, materialism, and hypermasculinity of 1950s American culture could be pitted against its "true" heart: religious sentiment, the family, and "domesticating femininity" (Fitzgerald).

The political otherness of the Romans translated into religious terms makes the Romans either fanatics or cynics in a polity that should not or could not be reformed. In *Ben-Hur* and *Spartacus*, the fanatical devotion of the Roman villains to the state or the emperor shores up the identification of the Romans as totalitarian militarists whose excess of belief is invested in a repressive system (Winkler). Hollywood's imperial Romans can also appear as men who, unlike their Christian opponents, no longer have anything to believe in; they have lost their republican ideals and reject Christian ones (Fitzgerald). Yet the films disallow any reform or regeneration of the public sphere even by Christianity (Fitzgerald). Cynicism, too, affects the Romans of Robert Graves's novels: their hero, the emperor Claudius, denies the possibility of any reform or improvement in the "stagnant pool" that imperial Rome has become (Joshel). Thus, at two different postwar moments, 1930s Britain and 1950s United States, Rome becomes the name of an irredeemable polity.

Across a variety of media, the Romans, as opposed to the "us" of the audience, luxuriate in excess, material decadence, and sexual deviance. In Howard Fast's 1951 novel *Spartacus*, the Romans are cast as capitalists utterly devoted to commodification who purchase power, death, and pleasure in dizzying amounts (Futrell). From the socialist point of view, Roman expenditure, symptomatic of a warped economic structure, defines Roman political corruption. More often, Roman excess marks a moral otherness that complements Roman political tyranny. Although most Hollywood directors were probably unfamiliar with the ancient Roman moral discourse on *luxus* (the corrupting nature of wealth and luxury), that discourse, as Peter Bondanella and others have shown, has shaped popular views about the decadence and corruption that supposedly paved the way for the decline of Rome (Bondanella 1987.207–51). Some sort of orgy, or at least an excessively lavish banquet or spectacular, extravagant entertainment, became almost de rigueur in Hollywood epics, reaching an infamous pinnacle in the 1963 *Cleopatra* (Fitzgerald, Malamud and McGuire; Wyke 1997b).

Roman sexual otherness plays out in diverse directions. Audiences are made witnesses to excessive heterosexuality, often epitomized by leering emperors and lascivious empresses. Romans on screen have disordered family lives, and such images of family life gone haywire have important ideological and political resonances for twentieth-century audiences. Or, as in *Spartacus* (1960), the Romans are sterile and/or gay (Futrell). In contrast to the slave rebels, the Roman politician Gracchus avoids marriage and family; his enemy and the chief villain of the film, Crassus, tries to seduce his slave Antoninus in a notorious scene cut from the film's first distribution and restored in 1991. In his dialogue with Antoninus, Crassus encodes sexual preferences in the morally neutral choice between eating snails or oysters. Thus the film makes this Roman transgressive not only in his sexual preferences but also in his refusal to categorize desire within a system of ethics (Futrell). Hollywood's images of Romans as sexually deviant helped make Rome a natural setting for the sadomasochistic fantasies of gay eroticism and pornography (Wyke).

Often, in the context of American popular culture, political, moral, and sexual projections of ancient Rome rely on colonial projections in which the "we" of the audience identifies itself with the colonized of the Roman empire. What Wyke calls the "linguistic paradigm" of Hollywood cinema—the casting of British actors as tyrannical, evil, or decadent Romans and American actors as heroic Christians, Jews, or slaves—projects into antiquity British-American colonial history: in Michael Wood's words, "the colonies against the mean mother country" (Wyke

1997b.23, 132; Wood 1975.184). The colonial model further empowers the projections of postwar film epics that make the Roman empire stand in for the tyrannies of the decadent Old World from which the United States had delivered itself in the recent war and against which it will defend, in Truman's words, "all free peoples who are resisting attempted subjugation" in the Cold War (Fitzgerald). That an English accent in an American cultural context signifies any and every state that is perceived as both tyrannical *and* foreign depends on that accent's ability to signify the imperial power of Britain over its American colonies. The sound of cut-glass, theatrical English, the English of the elite expressed in the terms of high culture, identifies its speakers as external oppressors through a reduction of history, contemporary politics, and the relations of self and other to a colonial paradigm (cf. Wyke 1997b.139). The fate of the English accent in Hollywood's historical epics is somewhat ironic in view of both earlier and later *British* projections. In the 1930s, Robert Graves's novels of Roman corruption invited his British readers to identify with the ancient Britons as the colonized of a corrupt Roman empire. Yet when the BBC's adaptation of Graves (which cast English actors as members of the imperial family) was broadcast in the United States, the linguistic paradigm of Hollywood cinema asserted itself to enable American viewers again to identify themselves as the colonized of the British empire and, therefore, as not Roman (Joshel).

Romans as Self and Other

Most often, projection is complex and ambiguous because identification and distancing occur simultaneously. In Derek Jarman's *Sebastiane* (1976), the court of the emperor Diocletian and a military outpost of the Roman empire are celebrated visually as settings for highly pleasurable homoerotic spectacles. Imperial Rome becomes an ideal world of sexual liberalism, a place that revels in homosexual desire and the beauty of the male nude in contradistinction to 1970s Britain, where homosexual behavior was still being punished with social exclusion, while, on the level of narrative, the torment and martyrdom of Saint Sebastian in an army barracks is constituted as an assault on the British state and its repressive attacks on male expressions of homosexual desire. Audience comprehension of Jarman's critique is facilitated by the long-standing political association of the British with the Roman empire and by the tradition begun in the nineteenth century whereby ancient Rome was deployed to imagine and to legitimate male homosexuality (Wyke).

The medium of film can simultaneously allow for identification and distancing, owning and disowning, in a process that "allows the audience to have its cake and eat it" (Fitzgerald). Fitzgerald and Wyke highlight the intersection between the "educational, spiritually uplifting" narrative and "the opportunities for cinematic exhibitionism and spectatorial scopophilia" of the medium as it functioned in Hollywood (Fitzgerald; Wyke 1997b.28–29, 31–32, 130, 137). On the narrative level, the Romans become the decadent other, disowned from the early Christian point of view (with which view an American audience is invited to identify), but, at the same time, the audience can enjoy, on the level of the spectacle, the decadent power and extravagance of the Romans (Fitzgerald). The American technology and money expended to put Rome on the screen mirror the Roman imperial grandeur they work to produce, and the American viewer can take pleasure in and identify with this display of imperial self-confidence. Moreover, as Wyke has shown, these films "became showcases for the display of commodities," and the viewer is encouraged to participate as a consumer in the postwar economy (1997b.27). Here, the display and "the solicitation of a consumer gaze" that engage viewers and invite them to enjoy the spectacle are in conflict with the narrative that rejects the spectacle as a sign of foreign decadence (Wyke 1997b.27–28). This identification and distance play out "the conflict between pleasure and guilt that Madison Avenue identified as the main psychological feature of the young consumers of the fifties, more affluent than their parents and looking for the moral permission to have fun" (Fitzgerald).

Similarly, the films are a way of entertaining anxiety without experiencing it directly. Threatening concerns peculiar to the era in which the films were produced were projected onto the Romans, allowing the forbidden to be expressed by cloaking it in Roman dress. Fitzgerald shows how Hollywood's epics could display tensions and anxieties within mainstream American culture, the body politic, and the bodies of individual Americans which could not be raised directly or publicly in the fifties. Audiences could thus experience such internal American concerns as problems with masculinity, homoeroticism, and male alienation from the public sphere without having to own them fully or to acknowledge them as their own.

Identification: Romans as Self

Most popular representations of imperial Rome in the twentieth century have depended on a process of distancing or a complex amalgamation of distancing and identification. However, towards the close of that century, it is possible to discern a shift in direction away from the self-satisfied 1950s statement, "We are not the Romans," and the related anxious question, "Have we become the Romans of empire?" to a more confident imperative, "Be like the Romans!" In some of the most recent popular representations of imperial Rome, moralism is elided in an invitation to join a city of limitless power and fabulous parties.

When might and vice are translated into wealth and power, projection may work to create an acknowledged or desired identification between the Romans and "us." Colleen McCullough unequivocally claims that while she was writing her *Masters of Rome* novels, she *"was a Roman."* For McCullough herself and for her women readers, who find satisfaction in a fantasized identification with the author's public persona as a woman who has endured hardship to succeed in a man's world, the novels offer a chance to identify with the powerful instead of with the weak, and to indulge in imagined excesses of absolute power (Martha Malamud). Here, the "might and vice" that inevitably characterize Rome are translated into Roman power and wealth as a positive ground of identification.

Jay Sarno, the owner of Caesars Palace in Las Vegas, wanted to provide "a little true opulence" for guests, who are invited to emulate the supposed lifestyles of decadent Romans during their visit to the Roman pleasure palace (Malamud and McGuire). Although the original Caesars borrows Hollywood's imagery of Roman luxury and power, it, like McCullough, nurtures a different attitude towards it: where Hollywood narratives ultimately see decadence as destructive, the casino-hotel celebrates it (Malamud and McGuire). Caesars also picks up on the extracinematic commodification of imperial Rome begun by the 1930s Hollywood film industry: the economy of tie-ins and merchandising. It invites guests to become Caesar for a day, just as *Quo Vadis* (1951) once invited spectators to "make like Nero" through the purchase of *Quo Vadis* boxer shorts or pajamas. Caesars takes the politics and religion out of imperial Rome and displays it as a timeless city dedicated to fun and shopping. At the adjacent 1992 Forum Shops, a Roman-themed shopping mall, imperial Rome provides a landscape for consumerism and a showcase for commodities. At this spectacular temple to American consumerism, capitalistic enterprise and the pleasures of conspicuous consumption are given a veneer of classical culture, and spending money is made entertaining (Malamud 1998). Thus, in the United States of the 1960s and 1990s, an economy of spending is projected onto the Romans—here, the luxury-loving, big-spending, consumption-oriented Romans.

Projecting Imperialism

Different projections of empire are deployed in Britain and the United States at different imperial moments (Cull, Joshel). The loss of empire so important to the British identity in the post–World War I period, the expansion of American imperialism in the Cold War, and the predominance of Hollywood films and American cultural imperialism in the post–World War II period have all influenced the process of popular projection of ancient Rome. In imperial Britain, for example, ancient Rome served as a source of both identification and distance. The Roman republican heroes of Livy's history, whose duty and devotion built the state that forged an empire, were staples in the education of British administrators of empire (Stray 1998, Colley 1992, Edwards 1999). At the same time, images of Roman imperial decadence were also deployed to distinguish imperial Britain from Rome and to facilitate the identification of the ruling class of the modern British empire with its putative ancient ancestors. By presenting themselves as morally superior to the Romans, the British could avoid the attendant analogy with the decline and fall of empire.

However, in the wake of the decline of the British empire, the rise of the American post–World War II political empire, and the spread of Hollywood's media empire, Roman references have served to critique and parody a variety of empires, ancient and modern. In Britain, Hollywood's projection of American imperial concerns onto Rome becomes (or is perceived as) a laughable form of American cultural imperialism. In British camp comedies about Rome and in Richard Lester's 1966 cinematic adaptation of the Broadway musical comedy *A Funny Thing Happened on the Way to the Forum*, the tendency of Hollywood to make Americans Christians (or Jews or slaves) and Romans totalitarian imperialists who speak with upper-class English accents becomes the material for comic Romes that aim not at Roman history or literature per se but at elements of Hollywood's cinematic use of ancient Rome and the by now cliched mechanics of its representations. Images of orgies, spectacles of the arena, legions on the march, lavish costumes, and the authoritative claims to history of voice-overs and scrolling texts are parodied in *Carry On Cleo* (1964) and in Lester's film; both films offer critiques of Hollywood and its cultural hegemony (Cull, Margaret Malamud).

Joshel shows the range and complexities of interpretation and reception possible when the British representation of imperial Rome, the

BBC adaptation of Robert Graves's *I, Claudius* novels, crossed the Atlantic to be shown on American television in 1977–78. Reviewers in the American press took to heart the producer's and the director's statements that they had deliberately made Rome familiar, finding in the television serial immediate parallels to a post-Watergate America. But the old colonial model (Americans versus the "mean mother country") is also reinserted as a distancing mechanism to reduce the uncomfortable effects of identifying the United States with Rome. The reputation of Masterpiece Theatre for "quality" television and the British origin of its serials associate the program and its narratives with the former colonial rulers of the United States (Joshel). As noted above, the linguistic paradigm of Hollywood cinema that makes the rulers of empire speak in the cadences of the English theater allows American television viewers to distance themselves from the familial and political corruption of women and mad tyrants displayed in *I, Claudius* and to project it onto their own British colonizers.

Domesticating the Romans

Romans and the chronologically distant and culturally different empire they inhabit can be made familiar by domesticating them. By domestication we mean the process in projection by which or through which representations of politics, empire, and history in narratives about Rome devolve onto the family, personal relations, or romance. In what Futrell calls "domestic politicization," adaptations of the story of Spartacus encode politics "in symbolic interactions between individuals"; thus, in the 1960 film *Spartacus*, sexual relations especially become vehicles for displaying and evaluating social relations. In other novels, plays, films, and television programs, too, the domestic paradigm is given political priority over the public: ideal communities, whether of slaves, Jews, or Christians within a larger corrupt Roman world, are represented as families (Futrell, Fitzgerald), and, conversely, dysfunctional Roman families signal the corruption of empire (Futrell, Joshel).

Domestication defuses the public and political dimensions of power and reinscribes them in the private and personal sphere. Projections of the Spartacus story from the eighteenth century on use the ancient slave rebellion as the material for a critique of the hegemonic order and for an expression of egalitarian impulses. At the same time, these popular adaptations of the slave rebellion elaborate Spartacus's personal characteristics and his relations with others, especially his relations with family members and his beloved. In the process, the ancient gladiator is domesticated and the history of the slave rebellion subordinated to the personal and the familial. In short, the drama of personal relations and families swamps the political narrative of the slave rebellion or, at the least, becomes more compelling and memorable.

In Fitzgerald's analysis of the 1950s Hollywood historical epics, the private domestic sphere is a refuge and an escape from a corrupt, tyrannical public sphere, a world ruled by effeminate emperors or macho militarists. Although the Roman public sphere is depicted as incapable of regeneration, the individual Roman can achieve salvation through the love and faith of a Christian woman (Fitzgerald). Unlike the Roman who remains firmly in the public sphere or within a disordered and dysfunctional family, the newly family-oriented hero is no longer cynical, for, through his romance, he has found "something to believe in." Belief and regeneration in the domestic sphere seem to be the only outcomes possible when the public sphere is corrupt and tyrannical. Much of this cinematic scenario replicated what was happening on the American domestic front: "Clearly, in the early fifties, there are contemporary resonances in the theme of the rough-edged soldier returning from the wars and encountering a self-possessed woman who demands the domestication of his martial instincts" (Fitzgerald). We might add that women, who had been drawn into the workplace by the war effort, were pushed to return to the home. Cinema's projection of the postwar American scenario onto antiquity, where good women are depicted as domesticators and bad women as women with public power, naturalizes and gives the legitimacy of history to the domestic reassimilation of American women into their traditional roles as wife and mother.

In *Projecting the Past*, Wyke argues that Hollywood's narratives of Roman history make "romance . . . the point of the historical discourse—very often pagan boy meets Christian girl. History is contained within domestic conflict and provided with the perfection of a story and an end in the rescue or the death of the loving couple" (1997b.10). The political and social forces that shape history are thus subsumed into a simple narrative of an individual's or couple's inevitable destiny (Fitzgerald, Martha Malamud; cf. Kennedy 1999). In the television adaptation of Robert Graves's novels, empire itself is contained within the family and domestic space: the narrative of empire focuses almost exclusively on members of the imperial family and, with few exceptions, takes place within the imperial palace. Domestication in the television serial affects the representation of the conquered and colonized, who often are represented only as the topics of conversations that note Roman superiority and the willingness of non-Romans to be ruled. Their narrative role as the stuff of family talk "naturalizes imperial relations of exploitation and domination" and doubles the exploitation of conquered and colonized by reducing them solely to the material for clothing the personalities of the imperial family (Joshel).

Clearly, the process of domestication varies. According to Futrell, the film *Spartacus* turns the public into the private and the political into the personal. In Fitzgerald's broader analysis of Hollywood's epics, although the family becomes an idealized community, it is less a case of turning public into private than of opposing public and private. Here the private becomes a retreat from the public: in a tyrannical and decadent public space that admits no possibility of improvement, the private sphere, the family, becomes the only place for regeneration and moral existence. In television's *I, Claudius*, domestication is neither a retreat from public to private nor a metamorphosis of public into private; rather, public and private are conflated so that family becomes a metonymy of empire, and empire is contained within the family.

Gender Roles and Sexuality

Ancient Roman masculinity, femininity, and, especially, sexuality have been particularly rich fields for adaptation and appropriation in popular culture. In the dual and intertwined narratives of romance and religious conversion of the sexually conservative American toga films of the 1950s, good women are mates and converters, bad women embody Roman decadence and are featured in spectacles that cater to the scopophilic pleasure of the film viewer. In Howard Fast's 1951 novel and the 1960 film *Spartacus*, the depiction of Varinia, the heroine and Spartacus's beloved, depends on her familial roles as wife and, later, mother. Although she is the first to join Spartacus's community of slaves by telling him her name when they are both still under the control of their masters, the community itself becomes "a series of male family relationships: the gladiators become brothers, fathers, sons, and husbands" (Futrell). Participating in this community only as wife and mother, Varinia becomes a "container of meaning" or "an emblem of ideology," "isolated from the ideological process" itself (Futrell). Varinia's role in the narrative reproduces in Roman dress, and thus gives historical validity to, the roles advocated for women in 1950s mainstream American culture.

If *Spartacus*'s transposition of community into family results in a reduction of female agency, an excess of female agency is contrastingly produced when family becomes the empire in television's *I, Claudius*.

Like the fictional Varinia, women in this televisual Rome occupy the roles of wives and mothers; the domestication of empire, however, here enlarges rather than reduces the narrative role of women (Joshel). Although they act in a domestic setting, the women of the Julio-Claudian dynasty are untamed: scheming, corrupt, or lustful, they pursue their own desires, producing the familial disorder and disintegration that spells the corruption of empire.

In the context of popular representations of ancient Rome in postwar Anglo-American culture, lust and desire for power are the usual markers distinguishing bad women from good. Although Colleen McCullough's novels chronicling the last century of the Roman republic include a variety of women, the few women who show any strength are described in terms that make them monstrous or unnatural. Female sexual passion, in particular, produces disgusting images of Roman women as "sucking, devouring, wriggling, wet" (Martha Malamud). Aurelia, the mother of Julius Caesar, the ultimate hero of the series, is the exception that proves the rule. The most sympathetic female character of the series (whose death evokes great pathos in the fifth novel), she never displays the messy emotions typical of the other female characters: this passionless, distant, self-controlled paradigm is a "woman with the mind of a man" (Martha Malamud).

Popular culture Romes are filled with macho military men, effeminate emperors, infantilized elites, cynical courtiers, and pious Christian men who turn the other cheek. Each in his own way bespeaks a troubled masculinity. In the fifties and early sixties, cinematic projections that make Rome the tyrannical oppressor and the emblem of social decadence frequently display that oppression and decadence in a masculinity polarized between a cruel and often sadistic militarism and a mincing effeminacy or deviant sexuality (Fitzgerald, Winkler, Futrell). Televisual projections that map bad empire onto the disordered family in *I, Claudius* put on display not only evil rulers and their henchmen but good imperial patriarchs with family values and noble Romans with "republican" values blinded, manipulated, and murdered by desiring women (Joshel). In McCullough's novels, sadistic cruelty and "a style that frequently recalls the nursery" converge to represent history as "the result of the actions of strong-willed men, who are . . . nothing more than overgrown children, motivated by powerful but basic impulses of rage and desire" (Martha Malamud). As Malamud succinctly notes, "The Inner Child is never buried very far beneath the surface of these would-be world rulers."

While the effeminacy of cinematic emperors like the Nero of *Quo Vadis* (1951) constitutes one pole of a problematic male sexuality, its troubling implications are contained by its associations with Roman decadence. In the camp scenario of *Carry On Cleo*, where effeminacy, gags centered on impotence, and jokes about eunuchs belong to camp's subversive message, the issues of identity are less easily contained. Cull argues that assigned roles are twisted and challenged so that all gender roles become performances. Thus casting against role, the most powerful Romans are played by the most effeminate actors in the film (with the important exception of Sid James who plays Antony). Far from being manly barbarians, the ancient Britons in *Carry On Cleo* take a woman's traditional place as sexual object when they are sold as slaves to wealthy Roman women. In the first case, effeminacy translates the British upper-class sense of imperial loss into sexual terms. In the second case, assuming the place of woman and slave effects an equation of contemporary Britain with its former colonies: "both a reversal of the British treatment of the subjects of their own empire and a metaphor for the new reality of living in America's world" (Cull). Whether Roman or Briton, the identities open to the British male audience of this camp Rome frequently involve impotence. The narrative itself inscribes impotence in heterosexual terms in its particular intersection of spectacle and narrative: the film titillates the audience with a display of sexy, available women in skimpy costumes, but the plot includes almost no episodes of male sexual gratification. Thus, as Cull points out, "although such images reinscribe the female as an object, the male on the screen and the male viewer are positioned as eunuchs, forever looking and denied consummation." The film's exploitation of social class, however, leaves British audiences with some possibilities for pleasure. Against the upper-class cadences and effeminacy of Julius Caesar (or "Julie") played by Kenneth Williams, Sid James performs Antony (or "Tony") as a virile working-class hero who gets the girl.

In Derek Jarman's film *Sebastiane* (1976), the excesses and transgressions of ancient Rome are to be reveled in. Earlier, in Hollywood's Rome of the 1950s, enmity, violence, and sadism enwrap a beefcake display of the male body, and, despite the narrative focus on the heterosexual romance, "the most intense scenes, both physically and emotionally, tend to transpire between men" (Fitzgerald). Fitzgerald discerns in Hollywood epics the convolutions of a "homoeroticism [that] is there but not there." The homoeroticism that cannot be expressed in the earlier films is finally made explicit in Jarman's adaptation of the martyrdom of the Roman soldier Sebastian. In the film, the sexual violence of all-male barracks life at an outpost of the Roman empire is used to lay out a whole taxonomy of male eros, with homoeroticism given pride of place. In a play of domination and submission, both masculine military aggression and feminine religious passivity are explored as positions within a fluid masculinity.

Media Power

If, to twist Marshall McLuhan's famous dictum, the medium is not quite the message, medium shapes the Romes discussed in this volume and their relation to their audiences: celluloid Romes seen by spectators in the movie theater; televisual, soap opera Romes watched at home on a domestic appliance; written Romes read in private; tragic and comic Romes performed live on the stage; and material Romes in which the audience eats, sleeps, and, above all, gambles and shops (on McLuhan see Dienst 1994.133–34). Cinema, television, print, theater, and architecture produce their own particular "knowledges of 'Rome'": sensibilities about the present onto which Rome is projected and popular notions of history in general (Wyke 1997b.3). Maria Wyke's observation about film extends in differing ways to the other media considered here: "Cinema's historical narratives of antiquity have worked to interpellate spectators into their reconstructions of ancient Rome and have left their traces even on the subjectivities of those fascinated spectators" (1997b.8). Each medium has its own specific methods for drawing audiences into its reconstruction of imperial Rome and for impressing that Rome onto its audiences.

Films like *Carry On Cleo* and Richard Lester's *A Funny Thing Happened on the Way to the Forum* that use parody to critique Hollywood and its construction of Rome themselves reveal the power of the cinematic medium to shape the Rome experienced by audiences. In part, this is a matter of technology and Hollywood technique—sound, casting, editing, and *mise en scène*—and, in part, of economics. The intersection of casting and the technology of sound make possible the "linguistic paradigm," discussed above, that facilitates the identification of the Romans with the United States' enemies in World War II and the Cold War, a projection that ultimately relies on British-American colonial relations. The practice of continuity editing sutures viewers to the narrative of virtuous Christians, Jews, or slaves versus the tyrannical, cynical, decadent Romans. The cinematic spectacle, whether of scantily clad bodies, of legions on the march, of orgiastic banquets, or of mighty monuments, which offers viewers different pleasures and varied points of identification, depends on Hollywood's economic power to marshal material resources and purchase labor; its effects depend on the psychological dimensions of the projection of images onto the large, lit, wide screen before the spectator isolated in his/her seat in the dark of the movie theater. The Hollywood star system nurtures viewers' fascination and identification with Elizabeth Taylor's Cleopatra or Kirk Douglas's Spartacus. In addition, to the degree that stars and star images both reinforce "dominant values" and "embody social values that are . . . in crisis," they embody contemporary cultural discourses and thus project them on ancient Romans (Dyer 1986a.27–30 and 1986b.19–20).

Hollywood's productions of Rome display their own "imperiality" in the construction and decoration of lavish sets and employment of thousands of extras. Directors put on grand shows and become beneficent twentieth-century emperors: Cecil B. DeMille employed Americans out of work during the Depression in *The Sign of the Cross* (1932) and Joseph L. Mankiewicz, according to MGM press releases, distributed the uneaten food left from the banquets in *Quo Vadis* (1951) to Italian war orphans (Fitzgerald; Wyke 1997b.137 and 1994). As *Time's* review of *The Robe* (28 September 1953) makes clear, with the development of Cinema-Scope, film images acquire colossal and imperial dimensions (quoted at Wyke 1997b.29):

> In CinemaScope, which uses a wide-angle lens to throw its picture on a curved screen nearly three times the normal width, it all but overpowers the eye with spectacular movie murals of slave markets, imperial cities, grandiose palaces, and panoramic landscapes that are neither distorted nor require the use of polarized glasses. In CinemaScope closeups, the actors are so big that an average adult could stand erect in Victor Mature's ear, and its four-directional sound track often rises to a crescendo loud enough to make moviegoers feel as though they were locked in a bell tower during the Angelus.

Unlike cinema, television produces a domestic experience for its viewers and, correspondingly, the empire of the televisual Rome of *I, Claudius* differs from Hollywood's Roman empire. The domesticity of television, whose images are watched on a household appliance by the family in the home, mirrors the domesticity of the screen narrative that contains the Roman empire within a ruling family whose actions take place within the family home. The reduction of imperialism to family affairs in the televisual fictions of Rome repeats the practices of television news programs in the United States that domesticate other nations and peoples by representing them in the comfortable, familiar terms of American culture.

The development of the communications media themselves in the nineteenth and twentieth centuries cannot be disconnected from European and American empires. In the case of cinema and television, the very media that represent the Roman empire are themselves engaged in an imperialism that the ancient Romans could never have imagined. Wire- and wave-based communications technologies like radio and cinema "became surrogates for the industrialized nations, reaffirming their empires but also reconstructing them in economic and cultural manifestations, helping to confirm the proprietary rights the industrialized world believed it held over the poor regions of the world" (Schwoch, White, and Reilly 1992.110). It is especially American dominance in production and distribution, even over its former colonial rulers, that requires emphasis: the size of the domestic market in the United States, the cost of new technologies, the star system, and American cultural chauvinism maintain the United States' imperial position in the world audio-visual market and secure its own "resistance to colonization by foreign information goods" (Collins 1988.81, 89).

The rapid growth of the modern mass media has even been connected to the history of imperial Rome. During the course of the twentieth century, imperial Rome has regularly been deployed in apocalyptic critiques of popular culture. A system of parallels was established between the Roman empire and, in particular, the mass culture of the United States: America is to Europe as Rome was once to Greece. Failing to keep ablaze the civilizing flame lit by the older culture, both the American and the Roman empires have submerged themselves in rampant consumerism and decadent mass entertainments. Critics reserved the greatest distaste for television. It was a kind of Colosseum, exhibiting all the characteristics of mass spectacle to be consumed by passive spectators. Substituting an immediate visual experience for something more lasting and profound, a false for a genuine sense of community, appealing to sadomasochistic instincts in its exhibitions of sex and violence, television was the new "bread and circuses" and its audiences the new barbarians (arising this time within, rather than outside, the civilization they were set to destroy). In this view, we face cultural decline and extinction because we are all too like the Romans, enjoying our latter-day bread and circuses in the shadow of our mass media empire's imminent collapse (Brantlinger 1983).

In differing ways, the Romes of popular culture and the experiences of their audiences are shaped by a consumerism interwoven into the texture of the audio-visual and print media. Hollywood films as showcases for the display of commodities, their solicitation of a consumer gaze, and the organization of merchandising tie-ins with other consumer industries result in a commodification of the past and hence of ancient Rome. Cleopatra gowns, soaps, and cigarettes were marketed when Cecil B. DeMille's 1934 *Cleopatra* opened, and Ben-Hur merchandise, including toys, clothes, and even wallpaper, accompanied the opening of the 1959 *Ben-Hur* (Wyke 1997b.27–28, 97–98 and 1994). Mobil's (now Exxon Mobil's) sponsorship of Masterpiece Theatre is an example of the "commercialization of public television," leading one reviewer to call PBS "the Petroleum Broadcasting System" (Von Hoffman 1977). As Timothy Brennan observes, the "object, of course, is not always to sell a dirty little commodity. It is just as important to set the tone within which many commodities can be sold efficiently. An empire is a feel-good community" (1987.376).

Martha Malamud's comparison of the effect of the publisher's jackets of McCullough's novels with the author's "stated goal of authenticity" makes clear that the novels are not simply texts that reproduce ancient Rome in print but products for sale. In late twentieth-century consumer capitalism, this means they must participate in the construction and evocation of consumers' desires, in particular, the desires of women, who, especially since McCullough's romance *The Thorn Birds* became a hit television mini-series, are her primary audience. The cover of the first novel somberly evokes authenticity with an image of the Ara Pacis, Augustus's Altar of Peace, but the covers of the following novels display the iconography of a women's romance. If, on the first cover, the image of the Ara Pacis simulates authenticity with a monument that is ahistorical for the novel's time framework and is represented as more fragmentary than its actual condition, on the following covers, "the Roman content is almost entirely effaced" (Martha Malamud). Ironically, although the jackets become more transparently "pop," in contrast to McCullough's claims about the novels' authenticity and the seriousness of her purpose, they also increasingly bespeak the truth about the *Masters of Rome* series: it is a sort of Roman *Thorn Birds*. Thus, concludes Malamud, in McCullough's novels, "a rhetoric of historical accuracy and diligent scholarship plays itself out against a powerful appeal to fantasies of wealth, total power, and self-indulgence."

Las Vegas is perhaps the culmination of the shaping power of medium (Malamud and McGuire; Margaret Malamud 1998). Las Vegas celebrates empire. Monumental building projects are an expression of an imperial self, and the American investors, designers, and builders of Las Vegas's empire in the sands are implicitly associated with the ancient Romans who constructed edifices like the Colosseum and, more fantastically, with the spectacular sets of Hollywood's Romes. At Caesars Palace, the empires of Las Vegas and Hollywood are joined and conflated with the larger geopolitical American empire, and gamblers and guests revel in this celebration of empire. Architecture and interior design engage all five senses in a projection of Rome; the visitor is not simply a spectator but a participant in this projection. Shaped from other artifacts of popular culture's Romes, Las Vegas also collapses them. In Las Vegas's Roman pleasure palace, Hollywood's images of a lavish and decadent Roman empire become part of the patron's experience in a material way. The invitation to be like the Romans within the confines of the casino-hotel is mediated in part by an assimilation that identifies a Roman imperial elite with film and entertainment stars (Malamud and McGuire). Moreover, here, the typical association of imperial Rome with luxury and decadence translates into a particular economy of spending. Fully immersed in sights, sounds, and sensations, the patron/client participates in Roman conquest and luxury by spending money in the casino, dining rooms, and hotel. In effect, Caesars translates the conquest and wealth of empire into guests' own expenditures. The Caesars Palace complex is continually undergoing renovations and additions, including, in 1992, an opulent Roman-themed shopping mall (Margaret Malamud 1998). In Las Vegas, there is no sign of a decline of either the Roman or the American empires. Ridley Scott's film *Gladiator* also suggests that "imperial projections" will continue to thrive and ancient Rome may continue to serve the twenty-first century as it served the twentieth.

1 Oppositions, Anxieties, and Ambiguities in the Toga Movie

William Fitzgerald

Legions tramp across the screen and toiling slaves are lashed as a voice-over intones solemnly on the irresistible might of Rome: brutal, arrogant, and cruel, but destined to be overcome by a gentle faith that will blow away the curse of slavery.[1] The opening of a toga movie, with its combination of montage and voice-over, situates us firmly in the position of outsiders, even when, as in *The Robe*, that voice belongs to a Roman, the tribune Gallio (Richard Burton), speaking cynically and wearily about a Rome that has created its own gods and whose ruling class is now free to do just as it pleases. It is a perspective that has no use for culture and that implicitly dismisses the *Aeneid*'s version of Rome's beneficent imperialism with a scorn worthy of Tacitus's Calgacus ("Where they make a desert, they call it peace," Tacitus *Agricola* 30). As for literature, there is Nero, in terrible voice, singing while Rome burns, but Petronius's *Satyricon* is nowhere mentioned in the movie in which the great Roman novelist features so prominently (*Quo Vadis*). In the opening voice-over of *Spartacus*, the words of "the poet" about golden Rome are quoted ironically as we watch slaves toil under the lash while quarrying rocks on a steep mountain somewhere in Death Valley. There is room for only one book in this world: the good book, quoted in paternal tones by the ubiquitous Finlay Currie at the beginning of *Ben-Hur*. Heavy irony is squeezed from the Romans' failure to distinguish Christianity from any number of other "subversive" fads that will be forgotten in a matter of years. Roman soldiers, officers, and magistrates witness world-historical events without noticing them because they haven't read the Bible. But the (implied) audience has, and that is what provides our entry into the ancient world.

23

Take, for example, the beginning of *The Sign of the Cross*. After an introductory scene that plunges us *in medias res*—the burning Rome of 64 C.E., with Nero, lyre in hand, conceiving the plan to shift the blame onto the Christians—the smoke of the conflagration clears, a pastoral flute is heard, and we find ourselves on an ordinary Roman street. Two beefy and very hairy men are playing dice while discussing the prospects of snaring a Christian and pocketing the emperor's reward. An old man with a staff looks around him in a puzzled way; like us, he comes from out of town, dropped here, perhaps, by a time machine. He's looking for someone. Another old man with a staff comes our way; the first old man draws something in the dirt in front of him and the second completes it: the sign of the cross. They talk, and, after they part, we see the sign, trodden but not erased by the feet that pass on the street. We know where history is going better than the owners of those feet know what is going on around them.

In the toga movie, you know where you stand. But beneath the crude dualistic structures and oversized emotions of this genre, I argue, there are more complex and troubled negotiations in process, as we might expect given the transitional nature of the historical period within which most of them were made (1951–64). The basic "us and them" structure, pitting a decadent Old World against a healthy New World on the rise, holds up a mirror to postwar America as it stands poised for global leadership, but this structure also reveals a layered series of complementarities, antagonisms, and ambiguities *within* American culture itself. One of the antagonisms that I will be exploring is that between public and private, resolved in the romance of conversion when the Roman military man leaves a hopelessly compromised Rome with his new Christian wife. But after *The Sign of the Cross* (1932) and *Quo Vadis* (1951), the classic movies of conversion, this structure ceases to drive the narrative; instead, the main emotional force is generated by the unresolved and awkward intensity of homoerotic relationships between young men. I want to suggest that these impossible relationships, fostered by the cruel demands of the Roman father, contain utopian longings for a redemption of the public sphere.

Oppositions and Identifications

The world of the toga movie is structured around an opposition in which Rome is always one pole. The primary Roman/Christian opposition has its analogues in Romans and slaves (*Spartacus*), Rome and Egypt (*Cleopatra*), even Rome the metropolis and Rome the empire (*The

Fall of the Roman Empire); whatever the issue that organizes the opposition, the first term is always devalued in relation to the second. Of these oppositions, the most important, of course, is that between Romans and Christians, a theme that the movies inherited from Victorian fiction and drama: Edward Bulwer-Lytton's *Last Days of Pompeii* (1834), the international blockbusters *Quo Vadis?* (Henryk Sienkiewicz 1896) and *Ben-Hur* (Lew Wallace 1880), and the hugely successful play *The Sign of the Cross* (Wilson Barrett 1895). In these works, history is caught at some imaginary turning point, or anticipation of the turning point, between the Roman and Christian worlds; the Christians, a small minority with history on their side, are being cruelly persecuted by the decadent Romans. David Mayer (1994.13) has described how this opposition might reflect class tensions in the world of the audience, which was itself strikingly heterogeneous. The classical education of the upper classes was given short shrift as it ran up against the authority of the working-class classic, the Bible. Hollywood's casting of the toga movie tells a slightly different story: the Romans, at least the decadent or evil Romans, are generally played by English or European actors, and the Christians (or their equivalents) speak in the accents, and trade in the sentiments, of the New World (Wood 1975.183–84). We are left in no doubt about where the future lies. This model for the relation between the older and the newer culture has its ancient equivalent in the views that the Romans and the Greeks had of each other: to the Greeks, the Romans might appear boorish upstarts; to the Romans, the Greeks could be seen as the decadent products of a tired civilization that was too clever by half in the first place (Balsdon 1979.38–39, 161–62). In modern times, Europeans who saw their ascendancy waning comforted themselves on being Greeks to the upstart Americans' Romans, but, given the right spin, Americans might proudly agree (Hitchens 1990.22–37). After all, for the newly independent states after the American Revolution, republican Rome had been both an ideal and a model. But there was another Rome, the Rome of the Caesars, and its image was more volatile.[2] In the Hollywood toga movie, the Romans, in all their imperial decadence, now appear as the older culture and the Christians have the advantage of both history and righteousness.

The Romans-and-Christians scenario has other advantages for Hollywood. Mainstream American values, identified with Christianity, can be experienced as revolutionary: persecuted rather than persecuting, the possession of a plucky minority with history on its side. Insofar as "Christian" values unify a ragtag assortment of ordinary people, they can claim to offer the best hope of a common culture for a heterogeneous nation founded on opposition to tyranny (Mayer 1994.14). But the opposition between Romans and Christians serves, as we shall see, not only to establish a deep historical identity for a young nation, it also dramatizes oppositions *within* American culture. "Incidental" aspects of American culture (consumerism, entertainment, gigantism, hypermasculinism) can be pitted against its true heart (sentiment, the family, a domesticating femininity). In terms of its own historical context, too, the negative image of Rome has both an external and an internal application. In the period during which most of these toga movies were made, the United States was adjusting to its postwar status as leader of the "free" world and enjoying an extraordinary boom in affluence. The treatment of the Roman empire in these movies, at least until the 1964 *The Fall of the Roman Empire*, is universally negative: oppression is the only possible consequence of power. On the one hand, the Roman empire stands for the tyrannies of the decadent Old World that the United States had overcome in the recent war, but, on the other hand, it provides a monitory image of what the United States might itself become.[3] Meanwhile, the only kind of triumphalism that is openly celebrated is that of another world, the realm of the spirit rather than of secular power. For these movies, Christianity's triumph in the world still lies in the future.

Clearly, the postwar years that saw the resurgence of the Hollywood epic carried with them anxieties about empire and wealth that are reflected in the representation of imperial Rome. Is the alternative to isolation a corrupting imperialism? Can prosperity be enjoyed without it devolving into a runaway consumerism? For the most part, the movies do not probe these questions, and the stark polarity of Roman and Christian allows for little nuance. But there is a distinction to be made between the identifications that are encouraged on the narrative level and the thrills that are experienced on the level of spectacle, a distinction that allows the audience to have its cake and eat it, to be in two places at once.[4] This bilocation is one manifestation of the conflict between pleasure and guilt that Madison Avenue identified as the main psychological feature of the young consumers of the fifties, more affluent than their parents and looking for the moral permission to have fun (Halberstam 1993.506–07). The decadent power and extravagance of the Romans could be enjoyed, appropriated, and, at the same time, disowned from the early Christian point of view. In this, the toga movie reflects a strategy that itself has Roman roots, for Roman writers liked to represent the city of Rome as a palimpsest, in which the poor origins of a rustic community were overlaid by the magnificence of the imperial capital (Edwards 1996.31–43). The *locus classicus* is Aeneas's visit to the site of Rome "golden now, then rough with woodland thickets" (*Aeneid* 8.348), where Evander reads him a lecture on the virtues of poverty. Such passages create both pride in the difference between then and now and a sense of the underlying moral foundations of the golden city. Similarly, the toga movie both hearkens back to the War of Independence, when an emerging and righteous nation struggled against the oppressor, and conjures up a spectacle of power and splendor that accords better with contemporary realities and measures how far the nation has come.

This secondary, spectacular identification with Roman power is made clear in the original trailer to *Quo Vadis* (included on the video release), that promises that we will join with Rome's roaring multitudes as they greet their general. This was the year (1951) of MacArthur's recall and triumphant return from Korea, and, in those roaring multitudes, the American audience may indeed see its own image as crowds flock to the spectacle of Marcus Vinicius's triumph and enjoy the glorious Technicolor of it all. Rome is not only the decadent Old World about to be superseded, but also an aspect of the American self.[5] As Michael Wood argues, the awesome splendor of Rome is not so much represented in these movies as recreated by the power of American technology and money.[6] *Ben-Hur*, for instance, recreates a full-scale arena in Italy complete with 40,000 tons of sand. But this kind of recreation by duplication is not entirely new. In 1888, Sir Lawrence Alma-Tadema imported from the south of France, at enormous cost, massive quantities of roses for his painting *The Roses of Heliogabalus*, thus rivaling the extravagant decadence of his subject.[7] In fact, the power of recreation with which a newer civilization brings to life, even outdoes, the glories of the past, making visible and real what is otherwise known only through books, is the very power that was attributed by Martial to the imperial arena in ancient Rome. Pasiphaë mates with a bull before the eyes of the audience and the truth of the myth is vindicated (Martial *Book of Spectacles* 5): "Let aged antiquity cease to admire itself. Whatever Fame sings of, the arena makes real to [the emperor]." The recycling of this aspect of imperial self-confidence is itself one of the forms in which modern America, in the form of Hollywood, duplicates ancient Rome.

As Maria Wyke has vividly demonstrated, the very enterprise of filming the movies was sometimes represented as an imperial or military endeavor on a Roman scale. The press coverage of the making of *Quo Vadis* in postwar Italy assimilated the production team to an invading army (Wyke 1997b.142). Hollywood directors saw themselves, and were seen, as emperors, but they reflected a more benign version of the Roman emperor's power: DeMille gave work to thousands of ordinary people as extras in the Depression, becoming a positive version of his screen despot Nero in *The Sign of the Cross*. In postwar Italy, LeRoy does the same when he films *Quo Vadis*, giving the food left over from the orgies to charities for Italian children (Wyke 1997b.137, 145). To this tendency of moviemaking to duplicate, as well as to represent, Rome, one might attribute also the internecine struggles over the script of *Spartacus*. With its blacklisted author (Dalton Trumbo) and its sacked director (Anthony Mann, replaced by Stanley Kubrick), its endless rewritings and ideological wrangling, the making of the movie comes to mirror, in its complexity and animus, the political maneuverings at Rome over the rebellion itself (Cooper 1991a and b). During the making of the 1963 *Cleopatra*, the romance of Antony and Cleopatra was duplicated offscreen by the scandalous affair between its principals, Liz Taylor and Richard Burton, blown up by the press to the proportions of an epic saga (Wyke 1997b.101–05). The world of empires, palaces, and world-historical figures is duplicated by the world of global superstars.

If our position as the pampered "subjects" of Hollywood aligns us at times with the Roman subjects of Nero, the structure of the toga movie's world enables us to be in two places at the same time, to have an alibi. When the arena's endlessly varied bill of sadistic fare turns surfeit into nausea (for instance, in *The Sign of the Cross*), we can pretend that we have been waiting all along in the dungeon with the Christians as the transfiguring moment of truth draws near. And when Laurence Olivier's Crassus, watching the legions framed by the window of his magnificent villa (Hearst Castle), speaks of the insuperable might of Rome, we can thrill to his words and then claim that, like his slave Antoninus (Tony Curtis), we've already run away to join the rebellion. It is *Spartacus* that provides the only moment in a toga movie when the audience is actually *accused* of complicity with the Roman spectators who command the spectacle of men killing each other. When the gladiator Draba refuses to kill the defeated Spartacus and instead hurls his trident at Crassus and his entourage, the trident comes flying right at the camera; the fact that Draba is black only accentuates the disturbing parallelism between the slave-owning Roman spectators and the American moviegoers.

Belief

However much we may be implicated in the spectacular aspects of the Roman empire, everything about the presentation of the Romans on the narrative level suggests an effete, played-out, and corrupt civilization in which no one believes any more. This lack of belief, more than anything else, is identified as the sickness that is eating away at Rome. Readers of the *Aeneid*, with its sonorous endorsements of Rome's mission, will be puzzled. At the end of *Quo Vadis*, Nero has been deposed and the legions of Galba are entering Rome. Marcus and Fabius are discussing the task that Galba has before him. Rehearsing the succession of empires ("Babylon, Egypt, Greece, Rome"), Marcus wonders what will be next. "A more permanent world, I hope. Or a more permanent faith," says Fabius, to which Marcus adds, "One is not possible without the other." The emperor Claudius in *Demetrius and the Gladiators* says of the Christian Demetrius that he possesses what Rome has not had since the early days of the republic: something to believe in.

Though the Christian perspective on the Romans' lack of belief organizes the primary identification of an American audience with the Christians, the Roman perspective on the Christians provides an outlet for a down-to-earth, "show me" skepticism. When the Roman Marcus, having failed to dissuade Mercia from martyrdom, decides to walk up the steps into the arena with her in *The Sign of the Cross*, he declares passionately, "I believe in *you*, not this Christ." Mercia knows better, confident that Marcus's romantic instincts are now in line with his better self and that it is Christianity to which he is opening his heart.

Belief, in these movies, is whatever comes from the heart, but the possibility that belief might involve surrender of the self to some external authority has to be handled with care. Mainstream American culture of the Cold War period is conflicted about true believers and anxious about the specter of fanaticism that haunts the world of early Christianity. When *Ben-Hur's* Messala arrives in Judaea he is told that the Jews are "drunk on religion." The speaker is a Roman, and therefore suspect, but the Romans are not infrequently used to voice (maybe to exorcise) the concerns of the implied audience. Of course, when *Rome* is spoken of with religious fervor, belief begins to take on the lineaments of political extremism. The fanatical devotion of Crassus in *Spartacus* ("Rome is an eternal idea in the mind of God") comes across as more than a little deranged, glossed as it is by his speech to Antoninus, apropos the sight of the legions: "There, boy, is Rome—there is the might, majesty, the terror of Rome. There is the power that bestrides the known world like a colossus. No man can withstand Rome, no nation can withstand her—how much less a boy . . . There's only one way to deal with Rome, Antoninus: you must serve her, you must abase yourself before her, you must grovel at her feet, you must—love her." This speech has now acquired new resonances, coming as it does just after the recently restored "oysters and snails" scene in which Crassus tries to seduce Antoninus. It is indicative of the ambivalence of belief that, in *Spartacus*, the Roman antagonists of the fanatical Crassus are played by Charles Laughton (Gracchus) and Peter Ustinov (Lentulus Batiatus, the *lanista*), the Neros of *The Sign of the Cross* and *Quo Vadis* respectively. Here these erstwhile tyrants play pragmatic, fallible but ultimately lovable characters. When contrasted with the fanatical belief of Crassus, the childish self-indulgence of the emperor Nero appears as the attractive humanity of *l'homme moyen sensuel*.

It is not until the generically unorthodox *The Fall of the Roman Empire* (1964) that the word "Rome" conjures up an ideal that a decent person might reasonably believe in, a multicultural ideal eloquently expressed by Marcus Aurelius before a gathering of dignitaries from the corners of the empire at a frontier fort in Germany.[8] He holds out the prospect of "golden centuries of peace, a true *pax Romana*," promising that, "Wherever you live, whatever the color of your skin, when peace is achieved it will bring to all—all—the supreme right of Roman citizenship . . . A family of equal nations. That is what lies ahead." Johnson gave his "Great Society" speech in the year of this movie and, a year earlier, Martin Luther King, Jr., had addressed the march on Washington ("I have a dream").[9] The figure of Marcus Aurelius is just remote enough to stand for a conflation of the two. Later in *Fall*, the senator played by Finlay Currie (who played Saint Peter in *Quo Vadis* and the wise man Balthasar in *Ben-Hur*), explicitly raises the issue of belief when he declares that a civilization falls when people cease to believe in it. The casting of Finlay Currie, with its reference to two earlier Romans-and-Christians movies, makes the point that this one will not drain the secular, public sphere of the ethical weight that the genre usually reserves exclusively for religion.

But, in the Romans-and-Christians movies, the possibility that the Roman public sphere, in which no one believes any more, might be regenerated by the new religious belief is studiously avoided. To the Romans, Christianity itself may appear to be a subversive political creed, but any accusations of disloyalty to the state are stoutly and routinely denied by the movie Christians, who have no revolutionary ambitions. In

Barabbas, for instance, the eponymous hero, an outlaw saved from the cross by Jesus' crucifixion, tangles with the cruel machinery of Roman justice and encounters Christian converts at every turn. Stubbornly refusing the faith that he encounters in others, he is finally won over when he hears that the Christians are burning Rome, and he joins in with gusto. He is apprehended and thrown into prison with his "fellow" Christians who tell him he has got it all wrong: the rumor he has helped to confirm is false. No doubt some in the audience will share his disappointment. But, occasionally, the Roman perspective on Christian sedition chimes uncannily with contemporary political paranoias. After Tiberius in *The Robe* has heard Gallio's eyewitness account of the Crucifixion, he says, "When it comes, this is how it will start. Some obscure martyr in some forgotten province. Then madness, infecting the legions, rotting the empire, then the finish of Rome . . . Man's desire to be free. It is the greatest madness of all." This is not entirely ironic in the America of 1953, which saw itself menaced by a fanatical ideology predicated (like the United States itself) on freedom; it demonstrates clearly the uneasiness that lies at the heart of the genre's embracing of belief. Tiberius here speaks as the guarantor of political stability and, as such, he speaks for most of the audience. Because Christianity is no longer a persecuted, revolutionary movement, and because the United States is now a great power, "threatened" by a revolutionary movement infiltrating its fabric, the genre allows, even demands from the audience a certain mobility of identification between its polarities. But when Tiberius proceeds to ask Gallio to return to Judaea, investigate the Christians further, and bring him "names," shadows of McCarthyism deepen (Babington and Evans 1993.211). The belief of the early Christians, who, at this stage, have no stake in the status quo, is highly volatile when applied to the political world of the mid-fifties.[10] This volatility allows for a subversive subtext, but also calls for strenuous denial.

Quo Vadis, which contains the interchange quoted above on the need for a more permanent belief, is an instructive example of the problematic relationship between Christian belief and the public sphere. Probably the most complex figure in the toga movie genre is the Petronius of *Quo Vadis* (Leo Genn), an ironic and urbane observer who smiles at both the megalomaniacal antics of Nero and the fervent hopes of the Christians. His secular "Last Supper" before his suicide appears to be a more humane form of heroism in the face of death than that of the martyrs, and his Old World urbanity and aestheticism offer an attractive alternative to the contrasting drives for transcendence of Nero and the Christians.[11] And yet Petronius's noncommittal and evenhanded irony comes in for sharp criticism—from himself. Shortly before the final gathering of friends in front of whom he commits suicide, Petronius recants his detachment, accusing himself of being content, out of force of habit, to be an amused cynic: content to let others shape the world. In 1951, this may speak to contemporary American concerns about isolationism and the responsibilities that come with power, even if those concerns, coming as they do from a European sophisticate, may also conjure up *le trahison des clercs* under the tyrannies of fascism. But what are we to make of the movie's ending in the light of Petronius's regret that he had allowed others to shape the world? Our converted hero Marcus Vinicius, having watched the troops of Galba enter Rome and having delivered himself of the remark about the need for a more permanent world with a more permanent belief, proceeds to leave Rome with his beloved Lygia to start a family. As the troops march into Rome, he rides his wagon out. Now that Marcus is a Christian, his world has shrunk to the private sphere with which a generalized contemporary Christianity is associated.

Public and Private

Petronius's recantation does not conflict with the happy ending of Marcus and Lygia because the toga movie's dualistic structure (Romans and Christians, etc.) corresponds roughly to a compartmentalized separation of public and private in American culture itself. Rome in these movies is a cruel, oppressive, and ubiquitous presence, a fetishized name that represents for its subjects the unavoidable and the undefeatable.[12] Rome will indeed fall, but not yet, not in this movie. Prognostications and foreshadowings abound, most spectacularly the fire of Rome (*Quo Vadis, The Sign of the Cross*) and the eruption of Vesuvius (*The Last Days of Pompeii*), but more subtly in speeches like Tiberius's on the Christian threat in *The Robe* (quoted above). But Rome does not fall.[13] Here again, the genre allows the audience to have it both ways. We can dream, even actively will, the fall of the oppressor Rome under the comforting knowledge that it will remain there, at least for a century or so, preserving the status quo in all its spectacular glory but without commanding our respect or loyalty any more. We can cultivate our own gardens, or return to the plough, secure in the knowledge that there's nothing to be done and that eventually history will take its beneficent course. Meanwhile, "Render unto Caesar what is Caesar's . . ."

Ben-Hur's epic trajectory through the Roman world brings him back to the place where he began, his lavishly appointed house, embraced by mother, sister, and a family slave, about to become his wife. "Be wise, Judah. It's a Roman world," says Messala to his Judaean friend at the beginning of the movie, and even though his advice goes unheeded, our hero finds that he must come to terms with Rome. No one can get around the fact that it's a Roman world, but once that world has been successfully negotiated, the nuclear family can pick up with life. It is as if the whole of the movie fills in the bits that the fifties sitcoms leave out: what happens to father between the time he finishes breakfast and the moment he calls, "Honey, I'm home." In Lew Wallace's novel on which the movie is based, Ben-Hur, realizing that the Messiah does not call for a military struggle against Rome on the part of his followers, desists from the rebellion on which he has embarked and, instead, devotes his fortune to the building of the catacombs. The theme of rebellion appears in the 1959 movie only as the desire for revenge, from which Ben-Hur is dissuaded by the Christianized characters; his ex-slave and future wife Esther, for instance, warns him that he is becoming the very thing he set out to destroy. Nothing at the end of the movie suggests that there is work to be done outside the family home.

The refusal of power and the turn away from the public world to the private is not restricted to the Romans-and-Christians movies; it provides a striking ending to *The Fall of the Roman Empire*, practically the only toga movie that has no Christian presence.[14] Our hero Livius has killed the corrupt emperor Commodus in a duel and is offered the imperial throne, but walks away in disgust with his beloved Lucilla (Sophia Loren). As they leave together, we hear the prefect of the praetorian guard auctioning off the vacant position.[15] Throughout, Lucilla and Livius have been obliged to put their love in second place to their public duty, living out the legacy of Lucilla's father, Marcus Aurelius, the Stoic (and stoic) emperor. But now the public world has proven itself to be hopelessly corrupt and corrupting. Romance can at last flourish unimpeded by its demands. At the end of *Quo Vadis*, the newly converted Marcus Vinicius has deposed Nero and watched the legions of Galba enter Rome in the scene referred to above; he then leaves Rome in a cart with wife and child. If there is a future, it lies with the progressive spread of a Christianity identified with family values and not with a reformed center of power: the idealized communities of the rebel slaves in *Spartacus* and the barbarian settlers in *Fall* are both presented as big families, and the same is true of the Christians in *The Sign of the Cross*.

Supporting, or perhaps underlying, this turn to the private, is the pervasive fear that once you have killed the monster you may become him and that the very struggle may assimilate you to your enemy. The moment when Spartacus takes deliberate control of the rebellion he has sparked is a case in point. After the rebellion at Capua, the triumphant gladiators force Roman captives to fight to the death. Spartacus stops the fight with the words, "What are we becoming—Romans?" Earlier in the movie he had shouted at his superiors who were watching his encounter with Varinia through the grill of the cell, "I'm not an animal." Ina Rae Hark (1993.159) takes these two moments as defining the parameters of *Spartacus*'s problematic: "How does one escape animality, the purely material form of existence imposed upon the gladiators that constructed their masculinity in terms of bodily force and aggressive penetration, without becoming Roman, transcending materiality only by entrance into a system of desire and signification propped up by the objectification and oppression of the Other?" The problem, according to Hark, is not resolved, and it is perhaps symptomatic of this problem that *Spartacus* is the only toga movie where there is a suggestion of unresolved tension between the public and the private: the last scene produces a poignant splitting of the nuclear family, with the father hanging on the cross while mother and son drive away from Rome in a cart with the cowardly *lanista* Lentulus Batiatus, hardly a promising candidate for surrogate father. Varinia holds up Spartacus's son to the crucified father and tells him that he was born free. But Batiatus hurries her away from the cross before she gives away her identity to the watching soldiers.

Romance

The typical romance of the toga movie was one of the legacies of Victorian toga literature, lovingly parodied by Shaw's *Androcles and the Lion* (itself filmed in 1952 with toga stars Victor Mature and Jean Simmons). The plot line of the romance has the Roman soldier falling in love with the Christian girl and abandoning his loyalty to the Roman state under her influence. *The Sign of the Cross* and *Quo Vadis*, based on a hugely popular Victorian play and novel respectively, both conform to this type. The casting of the lovers bears an interesting relation to the Old World versus New World agenda of the Romans-and-Christians plot, betraying something of the cultural anxiety of the newer culture in relation to the old. The romance is usually cast against the grain: the Roman soldier who will convert is played by an American and the Christian beauty who will convert him by an English, or English-sounding, actress. This model works for the archetypal Romans-and-Christians movies *The Sign of the Cross* (Fredric March and Elissa Landi) and *Quo Vadis* (Robert Taylor and

Deborah Kerr). Where there is no conversion, for instance in *Spartacus* (both of the lovers are slaves), the woman is still English (Jean Simmons) and the man American (Kirk Douglas). If the Old World Romans are not men enough, the virile New World hero has some rough edges that the dignity and poise of the heroine will polish. When Spartacus cries out against his oppressors that he is not an animal, Varinia (Jean Simmons), the woman who has been allotted to him by the owner of the gladiatorial school, adds, "N*ee*ther am I."

The narrative trajectory of the earlier toga movies links the hero's conversion with his preparation for marriage. Both *Quo Vadis* and *The Sign of the Cross* have their heroes make their first entries as reckless charioteers, but end with thoroughly domesticated men who have rejected the advances of the seductive, and married, empress Poppaea. The Gallio of Richard Burton in *The Robe* is clearly something of a cad when he enters the forum at the beginning of the movie, but he finally walks down the aisle with Jean Simmons to his martyrdom. At the beginning of *Quo Vadis*, Marcus Vinicius, returning from the wars, drives his chariot wildly into Rome, upsetting all in his way. His initial approaches to the Christian Lygia, whom he takes at first for a slave, are marked by a similar brutishness. In the final scene, he is leaving Rome on a very sedate cart with Lygia and a Christian boy at his side and a slave bringing up the rear. From the bachelor sports car to the family station wagon![16] Clearly, in the early fifties, there are contemporary resonances in the theme of the rough-edged soldier returning from the wars and encountering a self-possessed woman who demands the domestication of his martial instincts.[17] The hypermasculine Roman, cynically sophisticated in 1932 (*Sign*), cruder and more explicitly sexist in the fifties (*Quo*), is gradually tamed by the calm steadfastness and faith of the Christian woman and finds something to believe in. The courtship of the lead couple is a negotiation between the sexes that revolves around the issue of what it is to be a man or a woman.[18]

Accompanying the progress of the hero towards a proper understanding of what it is to be a man in the new, Christian, sense, is the difficult confrontation of a young boy with the demands of manhood in the old sense. Each of these movies features a boy confronted with a standard of manhood that he is unable, or unwilling, to live up to and with conflicting role models or figures of authority. In *Sign*, the boy Stephan is sent on a dangerous mission by the stern elders of the Christian community, who remind him that he must be ready to die for "The Master." Captured by the Romans, Stephan is tortured and succumbs, betraying the location of the meeting.[19] He is tormented by the fact that he was unable to withstand this test, but when he is eventually faced with martyrdom he is still unwilling to take his place in the arena with his fellows. In the end, he derives the strength to go to his martyrdom from the maternal figure of the well-named Mercia, who has taken over leadership of the Christian community after the sterner old men have been killed. In *Quo Vadis*, the Christian boy, shell-shocked after surviving the fire of Rome, is told by Marcus to straighten up, "A man must be a soldier." "I don't want to be a soldier," he whines when Marcus is out of earshot, and leaves Rome in the company of the gentle Peter. But he will leave Rome a second time, as a member of the nuclear family headed by the converted, and domesticated, Marcus.[20]

Rome is the locus of manhood gone haywire, polarized between the cruel, but effete and effeminate emperor and a ruthlessly macho military (Nero and Tigellinus in *The Sign of the Cross*, for instance). The conversion of the lead Roman involves finding a masculinity that will avoid both of these extremes, while reassuring us that the ability to turn the other cheek is just that, an ability and not a necessity. One of the problems that the genre most inventively negotiates is the reconciliation of a "turn the other cheek" pacifism with epic heroism. The Christian Demetrius (*Demetrius and the Gladiators*), who promises to make a sorry gladiator given his refusal to fight, has a convenient temporary loss of faith during which he dispatches an impressive array of his fellows (and makes love to Susan Hayward's Messalina) before returning to the straight and narrow. He retires from the court scene with his girl, leaving Messalina and Claudius reconciled and the institution of marriage triumphant.[21]

Men: Friends and Enemies

In *Spartacus*, the conversion of Spartacus himself from solitary animal to domesticated family man is effected as much by his love for Antoninus (Tony Curtis), "singer of songs," as by his romance with Varinia; from *The Robe* (1953) onwards, the heterosexual romance fades beside the more intense relations between men. In these movies, moreover, it is the male, not the female body that is most prominently on display. Here again, the toga film deviates from its Victorian origins, since Victorian paintings of life in ancient Rome availed themselves of every opportunity to represent female flesh. But where Victorian bath scenes, for instance, feature naked women, the bath scenes of the toga movie are populated by well-oiled male bodies.[22]

The Sign of the Cross and, more modestly, *Quo Vadis* point back to Victorian painting in making a semi-naked woman the centerpiece of the sadistic spectacle of the arena. In later movies, it is scantily clad men who will be featured in scenes of physical torment and humiliation. One of the most striking of these is the scene in *Spartacus* where Kirk Douglas stands before his fellow gladiators, clad in an ancient version of bathing trunks, while the trainer, Marcellus, paints on his naked torso the target areas for the kill, the slow kill, and the maim. The scene is, first of all, a good example of the way this movie recycles episodes from the New Testament: Pilate's exhibition of the pathetic Jesus to the bloodthirsty crowd is here given a new twist. *Ecce homo*, in the form of Hollywood beefcake, becomes problematic for the modern male viewer, who might read the "homo" as English, not Latin. In the toga movie, the male body is spectacularized for an implicitly male audience; it is not only a body with which the male viewer identifies, but also the one that is presented as an object for his gaze, giving rise to an "unquiet pleasure."[23] The male look at the male body must be motivated in such a way that its erotic component is repressed, hence the sadism and violence connected with many of the scenes in which the male body is displayed. The ambivalence attending the subjection of male bodies to the gaze in the Hollywood movie is emblematized by the mixture of caressing adornment and murderous hatred in Marcellus's action. Kirk Douglas's stance expresses a perfect balance between proud self-display and humiliating exposure.[24] In this scene, the fictional audience is male: the other gladiators. Later in the same movie, the display of male bodies is safely corralled into a heterosexual context when one of the Roman ladies who is to be regaled with a private gladiatorial combat asks that the combatants be clothed only as much as decency demands. In *Demetrius and the Gladiators*, the heterosexual gaze is introduced through the figure of Messalina, who takes an unhealthy interest in gladiatorial combat and gladiators. The perverse pleasures of the aristocratic female spectator, a theme that dates back to Juvenal (6.103–13), feature prominently in Victorian toga literature and art.[25] In the Hollywood toga movie, the stereotype of the lascivious female spectator helps to reassure the anxious male viewer that the eroticism of the male body so abundantly on display is for the gaze of women.[26]

Recently the movie *The Celluloid Closet*, which examines Hollywood's treatment of gay and lesbian themes, revived an old controversy about *Ben-Hur*. In it, Gore Vidal repeats his claim that he persuaded William Wyler to instruct Stephen Boyd (Messala) to play the reunion of the boyhood friends as if they had had an earlier sexual relationship that Messala was eager to reinstate but which his friend now repudiated.[27] If you look at that scene, you will indeed see, as Vidal claims, that Boyd looks "like a man starving." But Wyler claims that he can't remember any such conversation and Charlton Heston (who, according to Vidal, was left out of the loop) is suing. Whatever the truth of the matter, it is interesting that denial is built into the scene itself when the two friends rehearse their boyhood motto, "Down Eros, up Mars."

In *Ben-Hur*, the romance between Ben-Hur and Esther takes second place to the relationship between the two principal men. Where the novel makes much of Ben-Hur's wavering between the good woman (Esther) and the bad woman (the Egyptian Iras), the movie reduces the love story drastically, eliminating Iras, to focus on Ben-Hur's relations with a series of men (Messala, Arrius, Sheik Ilderim, Balthasar). This reorientation is typical of the toga movie after *Quo Vadis*; not only is the male body put on display more than the female, but the most intense scenes, both physically and emotionally, tend to transpire between men.

Is there any relation between this homoeroticism and that of the ancient culture that is supposedly being represented? Gore Vidal reasoned that the Jewish Ben-Hur repudiated as an abomination the sexual relationship that the Roman Messala, with his very different sexual mores, was eager to reinstate. The bisexuality of the ancient, classical male was something of which much of the audience of these movies would have been, however vaguely, aware. But Hollywood is notably shy about recognizing this aspect of ancient culture explicitly. In the 1932 *The Sign of the Cross*, Nero's throne is flanked by Claudette Colbert's Poppaea and a naked, epicene youth, posing languidly, rather like Michelangelo's Adam, on the ground (illustrated in Wyke 1997b.138). But it is not until *Spartacus* (1960) that we get any explicit reference to ancient bisexuality in the famous, and censored, "oysters and snails" scene, restored for the 1991 re-release. There Crassus not only propositions Antoninus, but also makes the case that bisexuality is purely a matter of taste and morally indifferent.

For the most part in these movies, homoeroticism is there but not there. The overture of *Ben-Hur*, for instance, is played over a close-up of Michelangelo's *The Creation of Adam*, in which a languid, recumbent Adam lifts an arm towards God, flying in from the wings and reaching to touch Adam's finger. This Christianized version of a story from the Old Testament, painted in the style of classical antiquity, is certainly a good choice for a movie based on Lew Wallace's "Tale of the Christ" that follows the story of a Judaean prince and his struggle with Rome. But imagining the Creation as the coming together of two semi-nude male figures also provides a high-cultural gloss to Hollywood beefcake, as well as to the movie's foregrounding of quasi-erotic relations between men. The fingers of Adam and God are about to touch, but, in this painting, they will always remain frustratingly separated, and in the close-up of the opening shot, it is the fact that they are not touching that is emphasized. Much of the drama of the movie is generated by this gap, beginning with the reunion of the two boyhood friends whose love is now poisoned by the divisions of empire. Ben-Hur, magnificently realized by Charlton Heston (whose face seems to have been chiseled out of granite), is repeatedly shaken by tremors of violent frustration: he cannot embrace, or even reveal himself to his mother and sister when they become lepers; he must repress the rage that breaks out when Quintus Arrius lashes him in the galleys; he cannot kill the treacherous Messala when he has him in his power. The Michelangelo painting is an extraordinarily economical condensation of many of the movie's themes. I will come back to some of its other resonances later, but, for the moment, I would like to suggest that its homoerotic tinge injects the intensity and pathos of a (socially) impossible love into this image of frustrated touching.

In *Ben-Hur*, the Roman world tears the boyhood friends apart and separates the hero from his family, but it is the protagonist's relationships with Messala and with Quintus Arrius, the commander of the galley in which he rows, that explore most intensely the paradoxical emotions generated by the cruel realities of the Roman world. In movies after *Quo Vadis*, the conversion romance of Victorian toga literature is displaced as a focus of the clash between worlds and replaced by problematic relations between men. Already in *The Robe* (1953), the romance between Gallio and Diana is shadowed by the troubled relationship between Gallio and his slave, Demetrius (Victor Mature). The movie starts with a slave auction at which Gallio intends to buy a voluptuous pair of female twins, but ends up with a man (the "voluptuous" Mature),[28] for whom he pays twice the price. Although the relationship between Gallio and Diana spans the movie, transforming the womanizing Gallio into the husband who walks down the aisle to martyrdom and "the kingdom" with Diana at his side, it is Demetrius who converts him to Christianity, and it is the relationship between master and slave that encloses the real heart of the drama. Gallio first encounters Demetrius when the latter tries to run away at the slave market; Gallio knocks him down, but then proceeds to buy him (recklessly outbidding Caligula) and to display his trust by telling Demetrius to make his own way to his new master's house and report for duty. When Gallio is sent to Palestine (a "pesthole") by Caligula,

Gallio asks Demetrius to be less formal with him: they're both going to need friends where they are going. Demetrius replies sullenly that you can't buy a friend. But after Demetrius has run away, been tracked down by Gallio, converted his erstwhile master to Christianity, and finally been rescued by Gallio from Caligula's torture chamber, the two say farewell, exchanging the words "Goodbye, *friend*." This trajectory from slave and master to friends pivots on the scene in which Demetrius denounces Gallio and the Romans after his master has presided over the crucifixion of Jesus. The scene takes place in the driving rain, with Demetrius, face contorted with emotion, weeping as he rails against his master.[29] In later toga movies, such scenes of deep emotion and pain between men, scenes whose intensity expresses a mixture of love and hate, are common. Rome sets men against each other: as competitors, as enemies, or as master and slave. But the intervention of Rome in what is perceived to be the natural brotherhood of men only intensifies the emotional world of these relationships, so that the physicality through which enmity is expressed comes to express also the love that revolts against that enmity.

In the final scene between Ben-Hur and Messala, even more emotionally intense than the first, thwarted love has become thwarted hatred. Ben-Hur has defeated Messala in the chariot race and Messala, trampled by horses, is lying in the surgery where the doctor insists that they must amputate his leg immediately if he is to be saved. Messala, convinced that Ben-Hur will come to see him, refuses. He will not meet his enemy with his body less than whole. The doctor protests. "He will come," Messala replies. And, sure enough, Ben-Hur keeps his appointment. Messala pulls himself up by the straps above his bed, and, in a voice interrupted by spasms of pain, tells his enemy that his mother and sister (whom Messala had imprisoned) are not dead, as he believes, but lepers; "It goes on, Judah . . . the race is not over." This time it is Ben-Hur who is racked by a spasm of pain; the scene is dominated by the heavy breathing and groans of the two tormented, sweating, and scantily clad men. Their final reunion is a tortured consummation of what is implied in their first.

In *The Fall of the Roman Empire*, Stephen Boyd (Messala in *Ben-Hur*) returns as Livius to play out a similar love/hate relationship with Commodus (Christopher Plummer). The two friends are reunited at the beginning of the movie under the shadow of Marcus Aurelius's death, when Commodus arrives from Rome to visit the border fortress where Livius has been serving. They drink together, twining their arms in an echo of the toast of Ben-Hur and Messala, and then collapse drunkenly on each other. But their friendship is threatened by reasons of state, for Marcus has bypassed his son in favor of Livius, whom he wants to succeed him. The historical record is saved by Commodus's henchmen who murder Marcus and ensure that Commodus ascends to the throne.[30] The two erstwhile friends coexist uneasily for a while, but Commodus's excesses eventually lead to Livius's rebellion and a final showdown between the two, staged as a gladiatorial duel. When Livius stabs Commodus with a spear, Commodus collapses forward onto Livius and embraces him as he slowly sinks to the ground and dies, a reminiscence of their drunken collapse at the beginning of the movie.

Earlier in the same movie, Timonides (James Mason) is sent by Livius to talk to Ballomar, the captured German chief, whom Livius hopes to win over to friendly relations with Rome. Timonides finds himself alone with the German prisoners, who overpower him; Ballomar then tortures Timonides to test the power of the Roman gods. Applying a torch to some part of Timonides' body below the screen (and belt), Ballomar tells him that he only has to "touch Wotan"—a wooden pole representing the god—to stop the torture. Should he cry out and summon the Roman guards, the Germans will have the privilege of dying in battle; if he endures the ordeal, the Roman gods are stronger; if not, Wotan wins. Timonides does touch Wotan, but he does not cry out. Ballomar is so impressed that he knocks Wotan over and burns him. From then on the two become fast friends. This is another intense, physical scene between men played with the two principals caught in tight focus: Timonides seething with barely repressed pain while Ballomar applies the torch and scrutinizes his reactions closely. In the intimate agony of this scene, enmity turns into friendship, a friendship that grows out of and against the divisions imposed by the Roman empire. One might compare the extended scene in *Ben-Hur* where Arrius tests out his new crew, keeping a keen eye on Ben-Hur, as the *hortator* takes the rowers gradually up to ramming speed, after which they all collapse limply into a panting, sweating mass. Again, this is the beginning of a relationship between oppressed and oppressor that will lead to Arrius's adoption of Ben-Hur as his son.

From one perspective, the narratives of these friendships might be seen to serve a sexual agenda, finding an acceptable expression, an alibi, for a homoeroticism necessarily (but uncomfortably) implicated in the mainstream male audience's relation to these heroes. But from another perspective, the sexualization of these scenes, their hinting at an impossible love that could not be consummated in its proper mode (at least on the screen), fulfills a narrative purpose, insofar as the very forbiddenness of the love expresses the frustrated yearning of Rome's subjects to transcend the competition and enmity through which they serve its purposes. The narrative uses the mainstream male audience's conflicted relations to homoeroticism for its own agenda. Such scenes, then, dramatize the impact of the cruel demands of the "Roman" world, setting men against or in competition with each other, but the eroticization allows them to express at the same time the participants' frustrated need to transcend this imposed enmity.

Society and Competition

There are two contrasted spectacles of manhood in the toga movie: the armor-clad legions tramping in invulnerable synchrony across the screen and the single, semi-naked man raised on a cross to die or displayed in an *ecce homo*. The former reaches its apogee in the *testudo* that, in the 1963 *Cleopatra*, emerges from the palace to destroy the enemy's siege weapons, an impenetrable column of shields moving relentlessly through the besiegers under the satisfied eye of Caesar (cf. Theweleit 1989.153–59 on "The Troop as Totality-Machine"). The latter appears in several movies, but it also has its secular variants: Ben-Hur in the galleys, clad in a loincloth, and picked out by the stern eye of Arrius; Spartacus standing in front of his fellow trainees in the gladiatorial school while Marcellus paints on his naked torso the target areas, and so on. On the one hand, the anonymous mass and, on the other, the vulnerable hero—both have their attractions and disadvantages. Everyone wants to be noticed, of course, but not if it means being exposed. Nobody wants to be swallowed up in the mass, but it is not always an advantage to be singled out: the only legionary who speaks up from the ranks is flogged at the orders of *Quo Vadis*'s Marcus Vinicius, and Ben-Hur similarly comes under the lash of Quintus Arrius when he draws the latter's attention among the galley slaves.

Although, for the most part, they are cast as the enemy, as a spectacle, the legions provide a reassuring image of the invulnerable male body to compensate for the exposed, vulnerable body of the oppressed hero. Again, the dualistic structure of the toga movie should not be seen simply as an "us and them" antagonism, it is also a structure of complementarity. But if, along one axis, the invulnerable "body" of the legion is contrasted with the vulnerable body that is singled out, along another axis, the society of the legion is contrasted with the society of the gladiatorial school. The gladiatorial school is a group of *individuals*, with different specialties, armor, and weapons, but the individuality of these gladiators is inseparably involved in the murderous competitiveness that is forced on them. The fascination of these modern movies with the Roman gladiatorial school is explained by the fact that it provides a hellish vision of the technologized, competitive society: every skill is individually isolated and practiced with the help of some contraption, every comrade in suffering is a potential threat to your life.[31] When Spartacus, newly arrived at the school, tries to make friends with Draba, the latter responds to his advances with the warning that they may meet in the arena, so it is not advisable for them to know too much about each other. As it turns out, it is the refusal of Draba to kill the defeated Spartacus when performing for Crassus and his entourage and his assault on the spectators that spark the revolt in the gladiatorial barracks.[32] At the end of the movie, when the revolt has failed, this scene is recalled; the rebels have been crucified and only Spartacus and Antoninus remain, saved for the next day when they will be forced to fight to the death. But Crassus, frustrated in his attempt to woo Spartacus's wife Varinia, angrily decides to have them fight there and then before him. The winner will be crucified. He will test this famous slave brotherhood. So the two friends find themselves caught in a double bind: if they love each other they will have to provide Crassus with the spectacle he desires, and the more they love each other the better they will fight. On the other hand, for Crassus, the better the two friends fight the more their brotherhood is confirmed. Spartacus wins, of course, and he kills Antoninus, holding him in his arms, with a sword thrust. As Antoninus dies he says, "I love you, Spartacus, as I loved my father." Spartacus replies, "I love you Antoninus, like the son I shall never see, now go to sleep." This scene makes explicit the connection between the fact that Rome sets men against each other and the quasi-erotic fusion of violence and tenderness that characterizes relations between men in this context.

A similar mixture of violence and tenderness features in *Barabbas*, where the initial relationship between the skeptical Barabbas and the Christian Rachela, who is stoned early in the movie, is replaced by that between Barabbas (a rough-edged Anthony Quinn) and his fellow slave, the Christian Sahak (a delicate Vittorio Gassman). They work together in the mines and in the fields, but eventually find their way to Rome as gladiators. On arrival at the training camp, Barabbas tells his friend that this is a world he can understand, but Sahak refuses to fight and declares himself a Christian; his fellow gladiators are compelled to execute him, Saint Sebastian style, using spears instead of arrows. When they lose their nerve and miss their aim, the sadistic trainer Torvald (Jack Palance) finishes him off. Barabbas rescues the body of the dead Sahak, cradling it as in a *Pietà*, and brings it to the Christians in the catacombs.

A Problem of Fathers

Speaking of the broad range of film genres that feature men in conflict, Ina Rae Hark (1993.152) says: "Males played by movie stars become spectacularized, these narratives assert, only because the rightful exercise of masculine power has been perverted by unmanly tyrants . . . Thus, the usurpers often display characteristics not marked as signifiers of masculinity in the codes of male film performance at the time. They may, for instance, be effete, overweight, short, foreign-accented, or disabled." One thinks here of the infantile, effete Neros of Laughton (*Sign*) and Ustinov (*Quo Vadis*); of the aging and feeble Tiberius of *Ben-Hur*, of the shrill, spindly Caligula of *The Robe* and *Demetrius*, of Christopher Plummer's giggly Commodus in *Fall*. In the toga movie, there is an ongoing problem with male authority that expresses itself clearly in the sphere of fatherhood, real or symbolic. It is part of the difficulty of the Roman world the men must negotiate that fathers (and father figures) are absent, cruel, or otherwise problematic. Spartacus was born, we are told in the opening voice-over, to a slave mother, "increasing his master's wealth." We are not told anything about his father, but are probably to assume that he was the owner who sold him into slavery in the mines, where he "lived out his youth and young manhood." In these movies, the stern Roman *paterfamilias*, capable of executing his sons for reasons of state, is merged with God the Father, who handed over his Son to mortality and crucifixion. The image of Michelangelo's *Creation* that presides over the beginning of *Ben-Hur* is, of course, an image of fatherhood, but one that applies to the movie's narrative in a paradoxical way. In the languid Adam, we may see the exhausted Ben-Hur, brutalized by Roman justice. But it is Jesus the son who lifts up his suffering coeval, bringing Ben-Hur water when he collapses on his way to the galleys, while the Roman Arrius, who will become his adoptive father, lashes him and pushes him to his limits at the oars on their first encounter. True, Arrius gives him the opportunity to escape when he unshackles him before the battle, but, as a result, it is Ben-Hur who rescues Arrius and not vice versa. In this "Tale of the Christ" (Lew Wallace's subtitle), it is appropriate to remember that Jesus' own father gave up his son to be crucified. Ironically, *The Fall of the Roman Empire*, one of the non-Christian movies, is the only one to allude to Jesus' accusation that his father has forsaken him (Matthew 27:46). When Marcus Aurelius lies dead, having passed over Commodus and appointed Livius to succeed him, Commodus asks his father why he denied him. Earlier, the Stoic Marcus said of Commodus, "I, too, love Commodus, but that is just a feeling, a personal feeling." As it turns out, Commodus is really the son of a gladiator, his friend, sparring partner, and constant companion (Anthony Quayle); when Commodus discovers his parentage, and his father tries to embrace him, as his official father had not, Commodus stabs him.

In the world of the toga movie, Rome is a stern father under whose eye "brothers" are set against each other but thereby brought together in a bond that expresses itself as an impossible and paradoxical love. Messala, seeking to solicit Ben-Hur's help in controlling the province of Judaea, tells him that the emperor is watching them. Messala's rise in the Roman world, he promises, will benefit his friend; he then asks for the names of Jewish dissidents. But the watching eye of the emperor will set the friends against each other when Ben-Hur refuses to cooperate. At one point, Messala remarks wryly that the emperor loves his recalcitrant province. When Ben-Hur replies that this love is not reciprocated, Messala asks facetiously, "Is there anything sadder than unrequited love?" It is the eye of the imperial father that turns the relationship between the two friends into one of unrequited love.

In the 1932 *Sign*, the stern Christian elders are killed off well before the end of the movie, and the male voice of fire-and-brimstone Christianity is silenced by the maternal Mercia, who takes over the leadership of the Christians when the moment of truth arrives. But there is no equivalent maternal authority in the movies of the fifties and early sixties, nor are there any father figures as unproblematic as the kindly but courageous Peter and Aulus Plautius of *Quo Vadis* after that movie. In some ways, the heroes of the later toga movies inhabit the same world as the tormented youths played by James Dean, who clearly have a problem with fathers. But Rome is not a family, and these men are anything but alienated. Rome is the name for the unrequited desire for an authority that would restore the public world to these anachronistic men.

The postwar years were a time of crisis for American masculinity. Returning from the all-male world of a successfully waged, heroic war, the soldier settling into civilian life had to negotiate his own domestication as well as a new understanding of gender relations in the wake of women's entry into the workplace on the home front. Family life was taking on new forms in the mushrooming suburbs, and the workplace itself was changing as the white-collar revolution brought new forms of alienation, so memorably described by C. Wright Mills (1953.xvi–xvii):

The salaried employee does not make anything, although he may handle much that he greatly desires but cannot have . . . In his work he often clashes with customer and superior, and must always be the standardized loser: he must smile and be personable, standing behind the counter or waiting in the outer office. In many strata of white collar employment, such traits as courtesy, helpfulness and kindness, once intimate, are now part of the impersonal means of livelihood. Self-alienation is thus an accompaniment of his alienated labor.

The struggle in these movies to accommodate traditional masculine roles to a changing world reflects this self-alienation.

By the end of the period covered by these movies, a new generation that had not lived through the Depression or the war was making itself felt. What would the sons make of the world their fathers had bequeathed them? Both *Cleopatra* (1963) and *The Fall of the Roman Empire* (1964) seem to pose this question through their bipartite structure in which the first part is dominated by great men (Julius Caesar, Marcus Aurelius) whose sons, real or symbolic (Mark Antony, Livius, Commodus), must struggle to live up to their example in the second part. The appropriately named *The Fall of the Roman Empire* was the last of the Hollywood toga epics before *Gladiator:* for the new generation, the world-historical struggles of Christianity and Rome were no longer viable dress with which to clothe their concerns. For that, it took a very different kind of movie, one that was actually inspired by a Roman literary work, *Fellini Satyricon* (1970).

Notes

1. *Quo Vadis* and *Spartacus* provide the best examples of this kind of opening.

2. Vance 1989.1–67 focuses on nineteenth-century American attitudes to Rome, and Douglas Williams 1997 gives an overview that continues through the twentieth century.

3. During the war, Paramount redistributed the 1932 *The Sign of the Cross* with a new prologue in which parallels were drawn between Nero and Hitler (Wyke 1994.19–20).

4. Mayer 1994.12 makes the same point about the toga dramas at the end of the nineteenth century.

5. In *The Sign of the Cross*, DeMille makes a joke of the analogy between Romans attending gladiatorial games and contemporary Americans going out to the movies.

6. Wood 1975.173: "The ancient world of epics was a huge, multi-faceted metaphor for Hollywood itself, because . . . these movies are always *about* the cre-

ation of such a world in a movie, about Hollywood's capacity to duplicate old splendors." For a more generous analysis of this aspect of the epic movie, see the interesting remarks on the phenomenology of history in the Hollywood epic in Sobchack 1990.27–40.

7. Reproduced in Liversidge and Edwards 1996.62, 55.

8. See Martin Winkler 1995.140, who quotes the director Mann as saying that he didn't want to make another movie giving the impression that the Christian movement was the only thing the Roman empire cared about. Winkler also remarks (144) on the unorthodoxy of the movie's opening, with its wintry landscape dominated by a forest and a border fortress. It is not until the movie is into its second quarter that we see the eternal city and the Italian sun.

9. Douglas Williams 1997.606–07 cites speeches of Roosevelt, Truman, and Kennedy that seem to be echoed in this speech.

10. Douglas Williams 1997.390 cites comparisons between early Christians and Communists in the press of the fifties.

11. Babington and Evans 1993.192–93 have a good analysis of Petronius along these lines.

12. As the opening voice-over of *Quo Vadis* makes clear: "The individual is at the mercy of the state . . . There is no escape from the whip and the sword. That any power on earth can shake the foundations of this pyramid of power and corruption, human misery and slavery, seems inconceivable."

13. Not even in the movie that takes us to the latest point in the history of Rome, the Attila biopic *Sign of the Pagan*. But, by now, the empire is Christian (which is what saves it).

14. Martin Winkler 1995.140 points out that Timonides is seen wearing a Chi-Rho pendant toward the end of the movie, a subtle reminder of the marginal presence of Christianity in the late second century.

15. This scene is modeled on the accession of Didius Julianus after the murder of Pertinax in 193 as recounted by Gibbon 1946.1.83.

16. "The cart is the equivalent of the buckboard in westerns, which, in turn, was equivalent to the family station wagon" (Biskind 1983.257).

17. Biskind 1983.250–78 is a good discussion of "coming home" in movies of the fifties.

18. Vance 1989.26 has some interesting remarks on the history of the conventional ascendancy of Christian or "feminine" over Roman or "masculine" values in historical romances.

19. In Wilson Barrett's hugely popular stage play of 1895, on which the movie is based, the scene of Stephan's torture, and particularly his scream, was a great theatrical coup. Tardy theatergoers would anxiously ask the ushers, "Has he screamed yet?" (Mayer 1994.148).

20. *The Last Days of Pompeii* (1935) features a father who has earned wealth and status as a gladiator and *lanista*, but whose son rejects his father's brutal ways and hides escaped Christians—with one of whom he is in love. The father, dis-

appointed in his son's lack of martial spirit, finally sees the wisdom of his son's ways, but only on the point of death.

21. The motif goes back to Victorian toga literature: Shaw has a delicious parody of the "turn the other cheek" scene in *Androcles and the Lion* (well done in the movie).

22. For examples of Victorian bath scenes, see the paintings in Liversidge and Edwards 1996.147, 153, 169, 170. It is true that Claudette Colbert (Poppaea in *The Sign of the Cross*) and Elizabeth Taylor (*Cleopatra*) have titillating bath scenes, but the movies in which they feature fall at the extreme ends of the period I am studying.

23. The phrase "unquiet pleasure" comes from an article on the films of Anthony Mann (which include *The Fall of the Roman Empire* and the opening sequences of *Spartacus*) by Paul Willeman in which he notes that Mann obviates any potential homosexual voyeurism by repressing the eroticism of the male look at the male beneath sadism and violence. Steve Neale discusses this article in Cohan and Hark 1993.13–14.

24. There is a reproduction of this scene in Hark 1993.158. Hark 1993. 169–70 has an interesting note on the analogy between gladiators and actors, in which she quotes Douglas as saying, "I was probably the only man in Hollywood who's had to strip to get a part."

25. A more relevant ancient parallel for this theme would be the remarkable passage (1096–1101) in the Christian Prudentius's *Contra Orationem Symmachi* describing the reactions of the Vestal Virgins to gladiatorial combat. It concludes (the translation is my own):

> Consurgit ad ictus
> et, quotiens victor ferrum iugulo inserit, illa
> delicias ait esse suas, pectusque iacentis
> virgo modesta iubet converso pollice rumpi,
> ne lateat pars ulla animae vitalibus imis,
> altius inpresso dum palpitat ense secutor.

> She rises to the blow, and whenever the victor plunges his sword in the neck, she says he is her darling, and the modest maiden bids him puncture the breast of the fallen, her thumb turned down, so that no portion of life remain deep in the entrails while the gladiator quivers as the sword is driven deeper.

For a Victorian version, see *"Habet!"* the painting of Simeon Solomon (1865) showing a box of aristocratic women watching the death of a gladiator, reproduced and discussed in Liversidge and Edwards 1996.128–30. The painting is probably inspired by chapter 20 of J. G. Whyte-Melville's novel *The Gladiators* (1863), whose seventh chapter is titled *"Habet!"* American examples from William Ware's *Zenobia* and Grace Greenwood's travelogue are discussed by Vance 1989.23, 52.

26. See Hunt 1993.72–73. Hunt distinguishes (75) between "legitimate" and "illegitimate" looks at the male body, and goes on to make the point that *Spartacus, Ben-Hur,* and *The Fall of the Roman Empire* parallel a "legitimate" emotional relation between men with both an "illegitimate" male relationship and a "legitimate" male/female one.

27. Gore Vidal's account can be found in the book that inspired the movie, Russo 1987.76.

28. Groucho Marx was reputed to have said, apropos *Samson and Delilah,* "I never see films where the man's tits are bigger than the woman's." Babington and Evans 1993, who quote this remark, close their book with an excellent section on Victor Mature in which they discuss the complexities of the spectacle of Mature's manhood and of the audience's identifications.

29. In *Demetrius and the Gladiators,* the sequel to *The Robe,* there is a scene that mirrors this, where Demetrius, who now has lost his faith and plunged into an affair with Messalina, is confronted by Peter, his erstwhile friend and mentor. Demetrius rails in disillusionment against Peter and Christianity, just as he had railed against Gallio and Rome in the previous movie, but, in the end, he returns to the fold and leaves Messalina for Peter.

30. As Martin Winkler 1995.139 points out, the method of Marcus's murder (an apple poisoned on one side and shared with the emperor) is the method by which Marcus is rumored to have murdered Lucius Verus in the *Historia Augusta.*

31. There are scenes in a gladiatorial school in *Spartacus, Barabbas,* and *Demetrius and the Gladiators,* and a hilarious parody of these scenes in *A Funny Thing Happened on the Way to the Forum* (1966). Babington and Evans 1993.219 refer to the gladiatorial school as "that terrifying microcosm of an ultimately competitive society." Hark 1993.169 is more specific: "*Spartacus* stops just short of overtly comparing the gladiatorial school to a film studio and the spectacularized combatants to actors." It is interesting to compare the gladiatorial school in *Spartacus* to the rather similar phenomenon of the military boot camp, the setting of the first half of Stanley Kubrick's *Full Metal Jacket* of 1987. Kubrick took over the direction of *Spartacus* from Anthony Mann when most of the scenes at the gladiatorial school had either already been shot or already prepared by Mann.

32. The relationship between Draba and Spartacus is modeled on the similar relationship between Demetrius and the Nubian king in *Demetrius and the Gladiators.* In the earlier movie, the Nubian, who is to fight the novice and pacifist Demetrius, advises Demetrius to put on a good show in the hopes that a satisfied audience will spare both of their lives. But the audience senses that, in the words of Caligula, "These gladiators are too fond of each other," and they are forced to fight in earnest. In 1954, it is the white Demetrius who wins and persuades the emperor to spare his black competitor's life.

2

The Roman Empire in American Cinema after 1945

Martin M. Winkler

The importance of the Roman republic for the United States Constitution and for the country's formative years is a matter of general knowledge. By contrast, the popular American perception of Rome as an empire differs considerably from the idealized image of the republic. We may adduce two general reasons for this, one historical, the other religious. The first lies in the fact that, with Julius Caesar, Rome had become a monarchy, a form of government which frequently leads to tyranny, as historians from Tacitus to Gibbon have shown—to mention only the two most widely read historians of ancient Rome. Given the United States' successful emancipation from the British empire, such a view is not surprising. It also fits in with the second reason, one prevalent not only in the United States. This is the part the Romans played in the condemnation and death of Jesus. Since Pontius Pilate, the local administrator of imperial Roman government, allowed the crucifixion to take place and his soldiers carried it out, Romans are "bad guys" in the fiction and popular culture of Christian societies almost by necessity.

Military power and excessive luxury have been regarded as the two major factors contributing to Rome's fall since Montesquieu published his "Considerations on the Causes of the Greatness of the Romans and Their Decline" in 1734. His perspective echoes that of the ancient Romans themselves, primarily that of Sallust. The moralizing historian, who was to influence Tacitus's negative perspective on the imperial system, attributes Rome's decline to luxury and the hunger for power (*luxuria* and *lubido dominandi*). Late republican and especially imperial Rome has thus come to be an almost archetypal—as well as stereotypical—society characterized by might and vice. The empire's might is embodied in the megalomaniacal tyranny of its rulers (what Germans used to call *Caesarenwahn*), in its military force, and in the exploitation of slaves, while luxury, lurid sex, gladiatorial games, and the persecution of Christians are all seen as proof of Rome's moral decline and foreshadow its fall.[1] That much of this perspective is unhistorical hardly needs emphasizing.[2]

In the United States, the negative view of imperial Rome has received its widest dissemination in the cinema, with the honorable exception of one of Hollywood's last grand-scale Roman epics, *The Fall of the Roman Empire* (1964). What makes these films worthy of our attention, even when they contain predictable plotlines, anachronisms, and any number of historical inaccuracies, is their modern overtones. References to contemporary or recent events which underlie American films set in ancient Rome indicate that the cinema has played a more important part in the reception of Rome in the twentieth century than viewers—or, for that matter, scholars—have generally realized (cf. Winkler 1995.137–38, Wyke 1997b.1–33). For this reason, the films deserve serious consideration. They reveal, on the one hand, the continuing presence of classical antiquity in modern American culture and, on the other, one of the most influential ways in which both modern history and a popular medium can together color the perception of the past. The visual media have, after all, become many people's primary sources for their "knowledge" of the past.

The following pages trace one important aspect of the popular reception of imperial Rome in American films made after World War II: Rome as an analogue of fascist Germany. In this, I do not mean to deny that post-1945 films also reflect Communism, the Cold War, or McCarthyism. (Some of my comments point to these aspects or may remind readers of them.) Since the silent era, Hollywood has seen the Roman empire as an ancient parallel to modern military or totalitarian empires in general. But after the experiences of World War II, the portrayal of ancient Rome in the films of the 1950s and early 1960s bears closer and more specific resemblances to Hitler's Germany than to Mussolini's Italy or the Soviet Union.

Military Tyranny and Religious Persecution

The fundamental theme of American films set in imperial Rome is that of power inevitably leading to corruption. The standard image of the Roman empire presents a military dictatorship which ruthlessly exterminates all resistance to its dominance and enslaves the conquered.

There is little if any trace of the idealism with which Virgil had his Anchises, the father of Aeneas who was destined to found the Roman race, extol Roman statecraft, urging the Romans to rule over other nations but to subdue only the haughty and to spare the defeated (*Aeneid* 6.851–53). The words of the Roman general Marcus Crassus to the Greek slave Antoninus in *Spartacus* (1960) reveal the extent and oppressive nature of the power which Rome exerts over the world: "There, boy, is Rome—there is the might, majesty, the terror of Rome. There is the power that bestrides the known world like a colossus. No man can withstand Rome, no nation can withstand her—how much less a boy? . . . There's only one way to deal with Rome, Antoninus: you must serve her, you must abase yourself before her, you must grovel at her feet, you must—love her. Isn't that so, Antoninus?" The paradoxical juxtaposition of the words "must" and "love" conveys the impossibility of resistance to or escape from Rome's limitless power. That a Roman army is marching out of the city during this scene visually reinforces the meaning of Crassus's speech. His words receive added poignancy by being addressed not merely to a slave but also to someone whom the master wants to seduce. To puritan America, Crassus's bisexuality, as expressed in the film's "oysters and snails" scene immediately preceding this one, is a particularly strong indication of moral corruption resulting from unrestrained power. With its deliberate echo of Shakespeare, the film's Crassus comes close to resembling Julius Caesar, Rome's most famous—or infamous—strongman, whom Cassius had described to Brutus in these well-known words: "He doth bestride the narrow world / Like a Colossus" (*Julius Caesar* 1.2.133–34).

A visual parallel to this verbal description of Rome as a power-driven military empire occurs as late as 1965, at the end of the era of Hollywood's gigantic epics. Early in *The Greatest Story Ever Told*, a film about the life and death of Christ, writer-director George Stevens emphasizes the oppression of the Jews before Jesus begins his messianic work among the people of Judaea. Our first glimpse of the Romans reinforces the somber mood at this point in the film, for Stevens shows us the alliance of two evil powers. We watch King Herod Antipas dictate a message to the Roman governor ("Inform him that the eagle of Rome has been torn down and desecrated by a Jerusalem mob") and hear the noise of that offscreen mob. The sounds from the crowd then begin to be drowned out on the soundtrack by the heavy tread of boots, and the close-up of Herod's face on the screen dissolves to an image of the Roman army marching straight toward the viewer and passing a dead body on a cross by the roadside without paying the slightest attention to it. Stevens holds the sound of the soldiers' march while shots of burning ruins, billowing black smoke, and the aftermath of a slaughter are superimposed on the image of the Roman army, which then enters Jerusalem. With utter economy, and in no more than a few seconds of screen time, Stevens leads us from King Herod's palace directly to the Romans, emphasizing the speed, efficiency, and ruthlessness of their response to the mob's rising. "Let these men be an example to all who challenge the peace of Rome," the Roman commander proclaims, with irony intended in the word "peace." The realistic-looking Roman uniforms in this film, which consist largely of leather and whose predominant color is a subdued brown, reveal the seriousness with which Stevens approaches his subject. He avoids any trace of the colorful outfits, resplendent with gleaming metal, feathered helmets, and bright red cloaks, which most of Hollywood's Roman films show us. Telling in its very brevity and accomplished technique, this scene is a striking moment in this long film and an exemplary distillation of the tradition of Hollywood's portrayal of imperial Roman might.

Throughout American film history, with the obvious exception of comedy, such is the standard way in which audiences have come to see the Roman empire. The moral aspect inherent in the theme of militarism and imperialism, even if presented on the simplistic level of "good guys versus bad guys," provides viewers with immediately understandable drama, involves them emotionally, and is therefore more important to filmmakers than historical accuracy. If the Roman empire is a symbol of oppression, its capital is inevitably the center of the evil and corruption which is symptomatic of the arrogance of luxury and power.[3] In the 1959 version of *Ben-Hur*, the hero says to Pontius Pilate after the death of Messala, his boyhood friend who had become his implacable enemy after his return from Rome and his earlier campaigns with the Roman army, "The deed was not Messala's. I knew him well, before the cruelty of Rome spread in his blood. Rome destroyed Messala." His words summarize the general American view of imperial Rome and are an aural equivalent to Stevens's visual presentation described above.

The struggles of the protagonists in Hollywood's Roman films against their oppressors develop in purely American terms. Their fights become quests for political independence and spiritual freedom or both; as such they are analogous to actual American history and to Americans' perception of themselves as champions of liberty. Hence Hollywood regularly superimposes modern ideas and ideals, such as democracy and "the holy cause of freedom," as the Declaration of Independence had called it, on its historical narratives. When Emperor Tiberius in *The Robe* (1953) characterizes "man's desire to be free" as "the greatest madness of them all," he only proves himself to be thoroughly un-American. Liberty, often taking the form of a rather simple-minded patriotism, makes the pursuit of happiness possible and is the chief virtue extolled in Hollywood's historical films, not only the Roman ones. The films of Cecil B. DeMille are perhaps the best illustration of this. And American audiences can be counted on to identify emotionally with the meek and the persecuted and to root for the underdogs in their fight for liberation.

More than on a political-historical level, American films address the topic of evil Rome on the level of religion, most prominently in the conflict between paganism on the one hand and either Judaism or Christianity on the other. In Hollywood's version of history, Rome has acquired political power through militarism and imperialism and now upholds it by the same means. Unavoidably, this leads to clashes between the secular and the spiritual and to the struggle of the new against the old. The films focus on religious incompatibilities, which modern audiences readily grasp, in order to illustrate ethnic, cultural, and moral differences. Such conflicts, although set in the distant past, appear in thinly disguised contemporary terms.[4] Ironically, and anachronistically, since the United States has traditionally considered itself one nation under God—that is to say, under the Christian god—the subject of Christianity and its struggle against paganism may even appear in a film set before the birth of Christ. The modern overtones in the prologue to *Spartacus* are immediately apparent:

> In the last century before the birth of the new faith called Christianity, which was destined to overthrow the pagan tyranny of Rome and bring about a new society, the Roman republic stood at the very center of the civilized world. "Of all things fairest," sang the poet, "first among cities and home of the gods is golden Rome." Yet even at the zenith of her pride and power, the republic lay fatally stricken with the disease called human slavery. The age of the dictator was at hand, waiting in the shadows for the event to bring it forth.

Here the symptom for the disease of proud and powerful Rome is slavery rather than what ancient and modern Christians have considered its false or idolatrous religion, but the reference to Christianity enables the filmmakers to present a Christ-like Spartacus and to assign to his pagan foes the morally wrong side. As usual, Roman religion is shown to be in opposition to Christianity and, for that reason, is unequivocally associated with tyranny. The prologue concludes with a reference to Spartacus "dreaming the death of slavery, two thousand years before it finally would die," a clear allusion to Abraham Lincoln's Emancipation Proclamation of 1863. What Spartacus could not accomplish, Americans finally did. The prologue implies that America, Christian and free, represents the culmination of history, at least as far as the Western Hemisphere is concerned. The protagonist even acts in accordance with the most ringing restatement of the American commitment to freedom, made by President Kennedy in his inaugural address the year following the film's release, expressing the spirit of the times: "We shall pay any price, bear any burden, meet any hardship, support any friend, oppose any foe to assure the survival and the success of liberty." While these words are intended to address the Cold War politics of the day, they are also a summation of the American ideal—life, liberty, and the pursuit of happiness—across time and space. We may compare the words with which Alex North, the film's composer, described his approach to its subject: "I decided . . . to conjure up the atmosphere of pre-Christian Rome . . . in terms of my own contemporary, modern style—simply because the theme of *Spartacus*, the struggle for freedom and human dignity, is every bit as relevant in today's world as it was then" (Karlin 1994.294).

Quo Vadis and Fascism

The parallels to modern history in the image of imperial Rome become most pronounced in films made after World War II. In this war, the United States, now expanded into a world empire, fought no less than three aggressive and imperialist empires more or less simultaneously: Germany, Italy, and Japan, and some Hollywood films set in the Roman empire reflect an awareness of the ideology of the two twentieth-century empires which trace their roots back to the Romans. In this way, the standard image of Rome's evil empire becomes much more pointed. In particular, the Roman empire can now be identified with a specific modern one: Nazi Germany. Hollywood's first grand postwar Roman spectacle, MGM's *Quo Vadis* (1951), which began production five years after the end of World War II in Europe, is the best example of this.

In *Quo Vadis*, religious and political conflicts are intended to illustrate the moral decline of Rome which foreshadows the eventual fall of its empire, an analogy to the recent fate of fascist Germany. Throughout the film, we can observe such analogies both visually and verbally. Its hero, the Roman commander Marcus Vinicius, will eventually renounce his immoral pagan ways and embrace Christianity. This is an obligatory learning process, set in motion by his love for a Christian maiden as chaste and devout as she is attractive. As long as he is an unregenerate pagan, however, his militarist language points directly to the fascist rhetoric with which American audiences had become familiar during the war: "Just as long as there's money to pay the army, Rome will stand forever. That I'm sure of." And: "Conquest . . . It's the only method of uniting and civilizing the world under one power—you have to spill a little blood to do it." Nothing like these words appears in Henryk Sienkiewicz's 1896 novel, on which the film was based. After World War II, Hollywood presents the "civilizing" mission of Rome as that of a master race imposing its rule and its ideology on other nations by force of arms. "A man must be a soldier," Vinicius will say later in the film.

Fascist totalitarianism is, in fact, the very starting point of *Quo Vadis*. It opens with shots of the Roman army returning victorious, while a narrator explains to the audience that "with this [military] power inevitably comes corruption." He then describes the totalitarian system: "No man is sure of his life. The individual is at the mercy of the state. Murder replaces justice. Rulers of conquered nations surrender their helpless subjects to bondage . . . there is no escape from the whip and the sword." Images of prisoners of war, pulling wagons loaded with booty and either being whipped on by Roman soldiers or collapsing and being trampled into the dust, accompany these words. Within two years, audiences could hear a similar sentiment from Marcellus Gallio, the hero of *The Robe*, a figure comparable to Vinicius in his development. Early on he says: "Worlds are built on force, not charity. Power is all that counts." The film closes with his indictment before Caligula of a Rome pursuing "the course of aggression and slavery that have brought agony and terror and despair to the world."

American war propaganda associated this brand of totalitarian militarism with Nazi Germany. Words to similar effect had appeared in some of the *Why We Fight* series of propaganda films, which Hollywood, in cooperation with the Office of War Information's Department of Motion Pictures, produced in 1942 and 1943, largely from enemy footage. They were required viewing for all American soldiers, intended to enhance their historical and political education and their fighting morale. Director Frank Capra was the general supervisor of these films.[5] Part Three of the series, *Divide and Conquer* (1943), quotes Adolf Hitler in English translation: "There will be a class of subject alien races; we need not hesitate to call them slaves." Earlier in the film, a title card had displayed this text: "The Nazi bid to smash the world into slavery was on."

The modern conquered nations who, we are informed, surrendered their subjects to Nazi bondage include Czechoslovakia, Poland, Holland, Belgium, and France. Later on, narrator Walter Huston sums up the reaction of the people of Paris to their occupiers' rule in these words: "When the people of Paris come to the streets again, it is to hear [via loudspeakers] the voice of dictators, telling them what they must do, how they must live, what they must say, what they must think, telling them how to be slaves." The use of the term *slaves*, which recurs frequently in the *Why We Fight* series, is revealing. *Prelude to War* (1942), the first film in the series, quotes Vice President Henry Wallace saying on May 8, 1942: "This is a fight between a free world and a slave world." Such a fight is standard procedure for the plots of Hollywood's Roman films. Of all the foreign slaveholding societies in history, ancient Rome is the one with which Americans have generally been most familiar, and the rhetorical terminology of slavery in *Why We Fight* fits both the political situation the country was facing and the popular view of ancient Rome, not least at a time when a fascist dictator was attempting to restore the Roman empire.

The first grand sequence in *Quo Vadis* recreates Vinicius's triumphal procession through the Forum before Nero and his court. This sequence contains obvious analogies to modern fascism, which reinforce the film's theme visually. It is worth remembering that the novel contains no such scene. Its hero is not a commander but, more realistically, a military tribune and, as such, neither a victorious conqueror nor eligible to hold a triumph. After the fall of the Roman republic, only an emperor (or an emperor together with an associate, as in the case of Vespasian and Titus in 71 C.E.), could celebrate a triumph, even if he had not been in the field himself.[6] Cinematic triumphs such as those in *Quo Vadis* or *Ben-Hur* are therefore not completely accurate renderings of Roman practice.

The huge mass of people present on the screen is meant to evoke viewers' memories of newsreel and documentary footage of fascist assemblies and parades. It is instructive to juxtapose scenes from *Triumph of the Will*, Leni Riefenstahl's artistic documentary of the Nazi party rally of 1934, or from *Prelude to War* (which contains footage from Riefenstahl's film) with the triumphal sequence in *Quo Vadis*.[7] A theme common to all films mentioned here is the appearance of dictators at a window or balcony above the crowd. The triumphal rally as depicted in *Quo Vadis* is a historical impossibility for Neronian Rome: the Forum was far too built-up to accommodate such an immense mass of people, nor did the city possess any other suitable space in the vicinity of the imperial palaces large enough for the crowd seen on the screen. As *Prelude to War,* with its footage of German, Italian, and Japanese mass rallies, makes clear, fascist assemblies are the obvious inspiration for the triumph in *Quo Vadis.* By contrast, the triumphal sequence in *The Fall of the Roman Empire* shows a different picture of much greater historical accuracy: considerably fewer people are present for Emperor Commodus's procession through the Forum Romanum.

Mobs and Eagles

Two years after *Quo Vadis,* the mob scene in Joseph Mankiewicz's film of Shakespeare's *Julius Caesar* (1953), in which Mark Antony speaks over Caesar's dead body, resembles fascist rallies as well: the crowd yelling in unison, their arms raised. Since Antony is about to "unleash the dogs of war," the scene may even have carried overtones, at least in some viewers' minds, of the infamous moment in February of 1943 when Joseph Goebbels had asked the German people amassed in the Berlin Sportpalast, "Do you want total war?" Mankiewicz's Roman mob is as susceptible to demagoguery as the mob in Nazi Germany.[8] Mass scenes such as those in *Quo Vadis* and *Julius Caesar* visually represent the triumph of the fascist will. But *Quo Vadis* is much more explicit than *Julius Caesar.* In 1951, none of the adults in the audience would have overlooked the implications of Nero's repeated raised-arm salutes to the people and the troops, particularly since they follow the earlier appearance of the *fasces* on either side of his throne and the huge eagle hovering above it. In American cinema, the political significance of the raised-arm salute goes back to the release of *The Last Days of Pompeii* in 1935. The educational guide to this film had asked school children the following two questions, among others: "What form of salute was used by the Romans? In what countries are similar salutes now demanded by the government?" (Wyke 1997b.178). Very likely, some of the students who had been asked these questions later fought in World War II and eventually watched *Quo Vadis* as well. Many of them, in turn, would have seen instances of this salute in the *Why We Fight* series, particularly in *Prelude to War,* which had described the rise of fascism. On the initiative of President Roosevelt, *Prelude to War* was even put into general release to American theaters and reached a wide audience.[9]

Both *fasces* and eagles are prominent symbols of fascist ideology. To the Romans, the eagle was the primary symbol of their power, as the Augustan sardonyx cameo with an eagle holding wreath and palm branch in its claws perhaps illustrates best.[10] This iconography of power has continued until modern times. After 1945, Hollywood loosely, and not always consistently, patterned its Roman eagles on the eagles of fascism, particularly those of Nazi Germany. Their posture, often squat and square-looking, differs enough from that of the American eagle, wings spread wide, to make confusion unlikely.[11] Eagles regularly appear in prominent association with the emperor and his court. In *Quo Vadis*, for instance, when Nero surveys the fire which devastated much of Rome in 64 C.E. and then recites his poetry while playing the lyre, he is wearing a cloak decorated all over with images of eagles holding victory wreaths.[12]

Within three years of the release of *Quo Vadis*, audiences encountered an even more immense eagle and again the *fasces* as throne decorations in *The Robe* and in its sequel, *Demetrius and the Gladiators* (1954); a few years later, a large eagle appeared behind Tiberius's throne in the triumph sequence of *Ben-Hur*.[13] In Mankiewicz's *Julius Caesar*, the very first image, immediately after the MGM lion, is a huge eagle banner, which fills the screen and over which the film's title and credits appear. In its first sequence, we see military officers patrolling the streets of the dictator's Rome with eagles stitched on the back of their cloaks and realize that the director hints at life under dictatorship in terms of modern totalitarianism. Mankiewicz consistently uses eagles in association with Caesar as symbols of his dictatorial power. A servant in Caesar's house has an eagle decoration not on the back but on the front of his tunic because he is facing the camera; obviously the image was important enough to Mankiewicz to make it clearly visible to the audience. Moreover, Caesar's chair is decorated with an eagle rising above its backrest, and when Mark Antony sits down in it after Caesar's assassination and before the scene in which the triumvirate makes up its lists of proscriptions, the viewer begins to realize that the age of terror and bloodshed is not over. The most ingenious example of this symbol in Mankiewicz's film is the eagle-shaped clasp with which Caesar fastens his cloak at his throat before leaving for that fateful senate meeting on the Ides of March.

Nero as Hitler

In her discussion of *Quo Vadis*, Maria Wyke argues that the film presents imperial Rome as a precursor of Mussolini's Rome (Wyke 1997b.142). Mussolini certainly styled himself and his empire on ancient Rome;[14] however, *Quo Vadis* primarily refers its American audience to Hitler's Germany, and the popular perception throughout history of Nero as the Antichrist reinforces this. In the prologue to *Quo Vadis*, this analogy serves as lead-in to the film's plot ("In the reign of the Antichrist known to history as the Emperor Nero ...").[15] For Americans, the rein-carnation of the Antichrist in the first half of the twentieth century was not Mussolini or, for that matter, Emperor Hirohito, but Adolf Hitler, their archenemy in World War II, whose Third Reich had taken its very name from a succession of empires going back to the Holy Roman Empire of the German Nation and thus all the way back to ancient Rome. (As Richard Wagner observed in "Was ist Deutsch?", in their longing for glory Germans can usually dream only of something similar to the restoration of the Roman empire [Lorenz 1938.332].) The ubiquity of Nazis in American mass media long after the war attests to the lasting American fascination with German fascism as the archetype of evil. In the 1950s and 1960s Hollywood turned out large enough numbers of grand-scale World War II films alongside its Roman epics to satisfy any audience's demands for huge spectacles and hissable villains. From this perspective, evil Romans and ice-cold Nazis are kindred cinematic spir-its. And after 1945, the standard exclamation "Hail, Caesar!" in Holly-wood's Roman films, usually accompanied by the raised-arm salute, echoes the familiar German "Heil Hitler!" even in the linguistic simi-larity of both expressions.[16]

In *Quo Vadis*, another major parallel to Nazism may be found in the cult of the emperor. Throughout the film, Nero is regarded as a son of Jupiter, addressed as "Divinity," and treated accordingly; moreover, he believes himself to be a god on earth as well. But this aspect of Neronian culture is unhistorical: Roman emperors, including Nero, did not con-sider themselves to be gods while they were alive and did not receive or encourage divine rites in their honor at Rome. As Edward Gibbon put it in 1776, "the imperious spirit of the first Caesar too easily consented to assume, during his lifetime, a place among the tutelar deities of Rome. The milder temper of his successor declined so dangerous an ambition, which was never afterwards revived, except by the madness of Caligula and Domitian" (Gibbon 1993.1.80; for further discussion see Gibbon 1993.1.79–81). Yet American soldiers learned in 1942 and 1943 from the *Why We Fight* films that divinities were back in earthly power. In *Pre-lude to War*, narrator Huston informs his audience that "to the Japanese people, the emperor is God. Taking advantage of their fanatical worship of the god-emperor, it was no great trick to take away what little free-dom they had ever known." Later Huston summarizes the German per-spective on this over footage of Joseph Goebbels and Julius Streicher ex-pounding their creed: "Our Führer is the intermediary between his people and the throne of God. Everything the Führer utters is religion in the highest sense." Shortly afterwards, a grade-school teacher leads her students in a new song which contains their pledge to obey the Führer, their god, unto death ("Für den Führer bis zum Tod, denn er ist, er ist unser Gott"). In the next installment of the series, *The Nazis Strike*, Huston observes that the Germans' "passion for conquest reached its historical climax when Adolf Hitler enthroned himself as god and the German Führer."[17] Whereas, in prewar cinema, the cult of the emperor had made Roman religion at best a quaint or misguided set of beliefs to Christian America and at worst a sacrilegious antagonist to Christianity, films after 1945 could give this a powerful new political slant.

The fire of Rome as depicted on American screens also points to twentieth-century history. The "modernized production" of DeMille's *The Sign of the Cross*, which was released in 1944, connects a specially added prologue sequence to the old 1932 footage of Rome burning. The prologue explains that "Nero thought he was master of the world. He cared no more for the lives of others than Hitler does." With *Quo Vadis*, studio boss Louis B. Mayer wanted a "DeMille-like religious epic," whereas John Huston, who had originally been set to write and direct the film, aimed for "a modern treatment about Nero and his fanatical determination to eliminate the Christians in much the same manner as his historic counterpart and fellow madman, Adolf Hitler, tried to destroy the Jews two thousand years later."[18] Mayer had Huston replaced as writer and director, and a team of screenwriters was instructed "to eliminate the political parallels and turn the movie into a virtual remake of Cecil B. DeMille's *The Sign of the Cross*" (Higham 1993.389). Nevertheless, it is surprising how much of Huston's perspective is retained in the finished film. A clear example of the Nero-Hitler analogy occurs immediately after the fire-of-Rome sequence. Empress Poppaea coaxes Nero to divert the people's suspicion of his own responsibility for the fire to the Christians. When Nero dictates a proclamation to the Roman people to this effect, his advisor Petronius tries to dissuade him. The dialogue in this scene leaves no doubt that Nero, still in his eagle cloak, is meant to be seen as a precursor of Hitler:

NERO: I hereby proclaim that the guilt of the burning of our beloved city rests with the foul sect which calls itself Christians. They have spread the lie that it was Nero who burned Rome. I will exterminate these criminals in a manner matching the enormity of their crime. Their punishment will be a warning, a spectacle of terror, to all evil men, everywhere and forever, who would harm you or harm Rome or harm your emperor, who loves you.

PETRONIUS: Pause, Nero, before you sign this decree . . . Condemn these Christians, and you make martyrs of them, ensure their immortality. Condemn *them*, and in the eyes of history you'll condemn yourself.

NERO: When I have finished with these Christians, Petronius, history will not be sure that they ever existed.

Unlike almost twenty years earlier, when DeMille's Nero had commanded, "The extermination of Christians must continue," in 1951, the words "exterminate" and "terror" may have struck many in the audience as an unambiguous reference to Nazi atrocities. Nero's last statement quoted above clearly evokes the intention behind the Holocaust.[19] Later in the film, Nero's order after Petronius's suicide ("Burn his books!") may be an echo of Nazi behavior as well. (An instance of Nazis burning books is included in *Prelude to War*.)

The viciousness popularly associated with Nazis finds a dramatic visual expression in the film's depiction of the death of Saint Peter. When Peter says to the centurion come to lead him to crucifixion, "To die as our Lord died is more than I deserve," the centurion snidely answers, "We can change that!" Director Mervyn LeRoy now cuts to an image of Peter on the cross in a manner intended to shock. The camera slowly tilts up from the ground to reveal Peter crucified upside down, with a musical fortissimo on the soundtrack. This is one of the very few moments in almost three hours of screentime, and the most forceful one as well, to draw the viewers' notice to the film's cinematic technique. According to the principles of classic Hollywood filmmaking, audiences are rarely if ever to become conscious of the camera or of the editing; their attention is not to be diverted from the plot. Here the camera's unusual vertical movement departs from this standard to create a strong emotional reaction in the spectator. It is also noteworthy that, in the Christian tradition, Peter himself requests upside-down crucifixion, whereas the film presents this as a particularly choice example of Roman sadism.[20] It is meant to fulfill what Nero, ominously, had said about Peter a little earlier in the film: "Something singular must be done with him."

The Holocaust

A visually more explicit analogy to the Holocaust than Nero's decree in *Quo Vadis* appeared on the screen ten years later at the beginning of Nicholas Ray's film about Jesus, *King of Kings* (1961). Its prologue employs ringing pseudobiblical phrases, which the narrator, Orson Welles, delivers with great solemnity. Some of the images accompanying his words are the most chilling parallel to Holocaust atrocities in all of Hollywood's Roman cinema. Here are the relevant lines of the prologue; I omit an earlier part in which Pompey the Great had invaded and desecrated the temple of Jerusalem:

> Thus, for more than fifty years after Pompey's invasion, the history of Judaea could be read by the light of burning towns. If gold was not the harvest, there was a richness of people to be gathered. The battalions of Caesar Augustus brought in the crop. Like sheep from their own green fields, the Jews went to the slaughter. They went from the stone quarries to build Rome's triumphal arches. But Caesar could find no Jew to press Rome's laws on this fallen land. So Caesar named one Herod the Great, an Arab of the Bedouin tribe, as the new false and maleficent "King of the Jews." But from the dust at Herod's feet, rebellions of Jews rose up, and Herod, in reply, planted evil seeds, from which forests of Roman crosses grew high on Jerusalem's hills. And Herod the Great, passing pleased, bade the forest multiply.

While hearing this, we see on the screen the light of burning towns torched by Romans and images of peaceful Jews being rounded up. With Herod, the Romans' puppet king and collaborator, we watch a long line of Jews walking to their crucifixion; they are carrying the horizontal beams of their crosses up a Jerusalem hill while Roman soldiers whip them along. Another line of people is being herded toward execution as well. The camera then pans left and down from the forest of crosses on the hill to reveal the most haunting images of the whole prologue. A man who has died on one of the crosses is tossed down the hill, where Roman soldiers pick him up by his hands and feet and throw him on a pyre on which a number of corpses are already being burned. This heap of corpses reminds us of similar occurrences in twentieth-century history. Image and text illustrate and complement each other. The pictures of such atrocities resulting from military occupation, and especially the phrase "the Jews went to the slaughter," are meant to evoke memories of the fate of modern European Jews. The stone quarry which had been shown a little earlier in the prologue thus becomes a parallel to a Nazi labor camp. As director Ray remarked in 1975, describing his approach to the film: "If anyone goes in to see this film, at least they will not walk out being anti-Semitic" (Kreidl 1977.190).

Altogether, then, the pagan Romans, running a totalitarian military empire, resemble the Nazis of the filmmakers' recent past, while ancient Jews and Christians take the place of modern Jews. The fact that, in the films' plots, most of the persecuted Christians are Roman citizens reinforces the obvious point that tyranny turns against its own people and causes their destruction. *Quo Vadis* explicitly states this by lifting the report of the Roman biographer Suetonius that Emperor Caligula wanted the Roman people to have only one neck—the more easily to be killed—and attributing it to Nero.[21] When Nero later claims "The world is mine, and mine to end," his words evoke Hitler's megalomania and recklessness in bringing war to the world and leading his own country to the brink of annihilation.

Both Christians and Jews are threatened with extinction, so there is not much difference in filmmakers' portrayals of them as victims of Rome—not surprisingly, since the major ancient Jewish roles, from Jesus to Ben-Hur, tend to be assigned to non-Jewish—and presumably Christian—actors. It is ironic, however, that Jews and Christians should be practically indistinguishable from each other in this way, not least because this circumstance accurately reflects, if wholly accidentally, the first-century C.E. Roman view of both religions. It is also ironic that Christianity, which these films extol, has a long history of anti-Semitism and persecution of Jews. This irony is particularly pronounced in the case of *Quo Vadis* if we consider its Jewish production staff: Louis B. Mayer was head of MGM, Jewish screenwriters rewrote the script after John Huston had been dismissed, Sam Zimbalist produced it, and Mervyn LeRoy directed it.[22] Despite its highly Christian content, and despite the Pope's blessing of the director's copy of the script (LeRoy and Kleiner 1974.174), it is doubtful that Mayer, Zimbalist, LeRoy, or the screenwriters were particularly interested in promoting Christianity for its own sake. A few years later, William Wyler, director of the 1959 *Ben-Hur*, "used to joke that it took a Jew to make a really good movie about Christ" (Herman 1995.400), and the same may be true of films about Christianity in general and about *Quo Vadis* in particular. And most likely nobody involved in making *Quo Vadis* was aware of the irony of filming outside Rome at Cinecittà, the film studios founded in the Mussolini era.

Quo Vadis remains a fascinating comment on its own time. Although the studio's publicity department had modestly noted that "MGM feel privileged to add something of permanent value to the cultural treasure house of mankind" (Halliwell 1995.491), this treasure soon lost much of its attraction to the public, in part because it came a little too early to profit from the widescreen cinematography which, more than anything else, has conveyed epic grandeur since 1953. Twentieth Century Fox deliberately chose *The Robe*, a Romano-biblical subject based on a ten-year-old bestseller, for its first CinemaScope release, although the studio had started filming the widescreen comedy *How to Marry a Millionaire* before production began on *The Robe*.

William Wyler and Anti-fascism

The popular Hollywood image of ancient Rome as evil empire was to receive its most powerful restatement after *Quo Vadis* with the biggest and most famous epic of them all, MGM's remake of its own 1925 *Ben-Hur*. Gore Vidal, who, with British playwright Christopher Fry, was one of the two principal but uncredited screenwriters of the new version of *Ben-Hur*, has characterized the storyline of both novel and film with the acerbic and concise wit characteristic of him: "The plot of *Ben-Hur* is, basically, absurd and any attempt to make sense of it would destroy the story's awful integrity" (Vidal 1976, quoted from Vidal 1993.1176). The accuracy of this verdict will be obvious to any viewer acquainted with Roman history on even the most superficial level. But the novel, purest melodrama, cries out for visual adaptation. Not surprisingly, the three American film versions—the first appeared in 1907—have assured its survival as one of the most popular and influential recreations of the Roman empire, much more so than the book or its nineteenth-century stage adaptations had been able to do. William Wyler, the director of the new *Ben-Hur*, had had no prior experience with ancient epic cinema except for his stint on the 1925 version, where he worked on the chariot-race sequence as one of the film's assistant directors (Herman 1995.71–73, 402). Vidal, who wrote most of the remake roughly up to the climactic race, reports that Wyler prepared himself for his mammoth production by studying earlier Roman films in order to get the right look for his (Vidal 1992.84 and 1995.303). It is a measure of Wyler's accomplished direction that he succeeds in making the "awful integrity" of the plot entirely credible. Rather than merely thrilling to a vast spectacle, audiences become deeply involved in the characters' actions, even to the extent of swallowing all the historical silliness wholesale.

Because of their strong involvement in the fate of Ben-Hur and his family, spectators have tended altogether to miss the contemporary overtones in the film's visuals and in its dialogue. These modern aspects serve to de-emphasize the plot's awfulness and to provide it with much of the sorely needed integrity which enables the creaky story to stand up to the expectations of filmgoers in the late 1950s (and beyond). The film makes the Roman empire comparable to Nazi Germany and turns Messala, the heavy, into a particularly effective cinema villain. Much of the impact of Messala in Wyler's film derives from this new characterization of the story's antagonist.

The chief reason for the modern themes in the film is the presence of Wyler himself, an American immigrant of German-Jewish descent. Wyler, one of whose relatives had been imprisoned in the concentration camp of Dachau for nearly a month (Herman 1995.131–32), took an active part in anti-Nazi efforts. "He was definitely a 'premature anti-Fascist,' as they called him back in the thirties," his wife once said.[23] Even before the United States entered World War II, Wyler had taken a strong anti-Nazi stance in favor of United States involvement and had expressed it in his film *Mrs. Miniver* (1942), which dealt with the German attack on Britain. Winston Churchill called this film "propaganda worth a hundred battleships" (Herman 1995.235). Wyler had made a major change in the film's script in a scene involving a young German pilot shot down over England. In the screenplay from which he was working, this pilot had been a figure without a political or ideological side to him; Wyler's revision turned him into a spokesman for the master race.[24]

The driving force of the plot of *Ben-Hur* is the moment when Judah Ben-Hur and Messala become deadly enemies. The quarrel which erupts between them has to propel the rest of the narrative for about three hours of screen time. For this scene to be able to carry such weight, Vidal slyly introduced a homosexual subtext into the relationship between Messala and Ben-Hur.[25] In addition, Wyler and Vidal updated the characterization of both with visual and verbal overtones of modern history, especially in a number of scenes crucial to the plot. Messala, who cannot understand Ben-Hur's suggestion, "Withdraw your legions," tells Ben-Hur prior to their quarrel about Roman rule in the east: "The emperor is displeased. He wishes Judaea to be made into a more obedient and disciplined province." Here we have standard Nazi talk about order and obedience. Messala continues in the same vein: "The emperor does not approve of your countrymen. There's rebellion in the wind. It will be crushed . . . Be wise, Judah. It's a Roman world; if you want to live in it, you must become part of it . . . It was fate that chose us to civilize the world, and we have . . . Persuade your people that their resistance to Rome is stupid. It's worse than stupid—futile. For it can end in only one way, extinction for your people." The ideology behind such words is clear enough; even Messala's mention of fate points to the Nazis' obsession with Providence as their justification and driving force. In this there is a point of contact with the ancient Roman belief in *providentia* as guide of their destiny and empire. (On this important aspect of Roman history and culture see, e.g., Martin 1982.) It goes without saying that neither such a belief nor modern debates over Roman "imperialism" turn the Romans into exemplars or precursors of twentieth-century fascists.

Shortly after, Messala comes to visit Judah and his mother and sister at their home. He describes his recent experiences in the army, and his listeners, both on screen and in the theater, immediately realize that he has become a brutal militarist. His casual summary of the Roman campaign in Libya reveals his utter lack of compassion: "Then we marched on their capital—barbaric city, but fascinating—or was, till we destroyed it. Now it's nothing but ashes." Messala's clipped speech effectively underscores the Roman army's Nazi-like scorched-earth tactics in which Messala readily participated.

A little later, their quarrel begins when Messala wants Judah to reveal the names of Jews hostile to Roman rule in Judaea: "Who are they? Yes, Judah—who are they?" When Ben-Hur asks in return, "Would I retain your friendship if I became an informer?" the word "informer" not only points to collaboration with the enemy in war, but is probably also a reference to the House Un-American Activities Committee (HUAC), the Hollywood Ten, and McCarthyism.[26] Messala then reveals his obsession with power and his ambition to rise to the top: "The emperor is watching us. At this moment, he watches the east. This is my great opportunity, Judah, and yours, too. If I can bring order into Judaea, I can have any post I want, and you'll rise with me, I promise. And you know where it can end? Rome! Yes, perhaps at the side of Caesar himself—I mean it, I mean it! . . . The emperor is watching us, judging us; all I need do is serve him!" Judah immediately notices the quasi-religious fervor of Messala's words: "You speak of the emperor as if he were God." Messala's answer combines excitement and idealism with the will to power characteristic of Nazism: "He *is* god, the only god. He is power, real power on earth." Here Wyler and Vidal follow the Hollywood tradition of attributing divinity to the emperor, in this case Tiberius, although they wisely do not give this side of their perspective on Roman culture the emphasis it had earlier received in *Quo Vadis* or in *Demetrius and the Gladiators*.

The quarrel between Roman and Jew then reaches its climax with Messala's contemptuous outburst, "In the name of all the gods, Judah, what do the lives of a few Jews mean to you?" This is a question so direct and outspoken that its contemporary meaning points well beyond the context in which it appears. Messala has also referred once more to the order on which dictatorship depends. He will later inform the new governor of Judaea, before the latter's ceremonial entry into Jerusalem, that "Jerusalem's welcome will not be a warm one. But I pledge, my Lord, that it will be a quiet one." We may compare the narrator's comment on the empty streets of Paris at Hitler's entry into the city in *Divide and Conquer:* "No cheering crowds here to welcome in the new order." Messala's words may also have reminded some people in the audience of Reinhard Heydrich, Himmler's "right hand," as he was called, and the driving force behind much of the Nazi terror. As deputy Reichsprotektor, Heydrich had adopted a strategy in Bohemia and Moravia such as Messala describes.[27] In a comparable vein, Messala will later express his belief in terror as a political tool when he coolly informs Ben-Hur that he is sending him to the galleys: "By condemning without hesitation an old friend, I shall be feared."

In the quarrel scene, Messala's repeated mention of the emperor points to the centralized totalitarian system which Rome represents. The callousness in his casual reference to the deaths of a few Jews must have struck home at least to the Jewish part of the film's audience. Ben-Hur's answer ("If I cannot persuade them, that does not mean I would help you *murder* them!") only leads to Messala's next outburst, in which he urges Judah to submit to the closed system of Roman domination: "You are a conquered people. You live on dead dreams, you live on myths of the past . . . There is only one reality in the world today. Look to the west, Judah, don't be a fool—look to Rome!" This is a brief but effective summary of *Realpolitik* calling for survival through collaboration.

A parallel expression of totalitarian "order" was to be seen and heard the following year in *Spartacus*. In the middle of the night and in a darkened senate chamber, Crassus reveals his incipient dictatorship to Gracchus, the old senate leader who represents the traditional virtues and wily politics which had made Rome great. Crassus threatens Gracchus's followers with death "if they falter one instant in loyalty to the new order of affairs." He then continues in language which conflates fascism and McCarthyism:

CRASSUS: The enemies of the state are known. Arrests are in progress; the prisons begin to fill. In every city and province, lists of the disloyal have been compiled. Tomorrow they will learn the cost of their terrible folly, their treason.

GRACCHUS: And where does my name appear on the list of disloyal enemies of the state?

CRASSUS: First.

Crassus then tries to induce Gracchus "to accept destiny and order," as he calls it, and to collaborate with him in return for his life. The figures of Messala and Crassus, as they appeared to American audiences within two years of each other, are strikingly similar in conception.

Messala, Representative of the Master Race

Judah's reply to Messala's encomium of Roman power in Wyler's *Ben-Hur* is the strongest indictment of imperial Rome in post-war Hollywood cinema: "Rome is evil . . . Rome is an affront to God. Rome is strangling my people and my country, the whole world, but not forever. I tell you, the day Rome falls there will be a shout of freedom such as the world has never heard before." The last sentence here quoted was included in the film's theatrical trailer, presumably because it was meant to provide a convenient summary of the plot and to point to the modern significance of the film's theme. A shout of freedom such as this had indeed been heard in May of 1945.

As is to be expected, in the quarrel scene the modern totalitarian overtones lie primarily in the dialogue. Wyler expresses the same perspective in both verbal and visual terms, with emphasis on the latter, when the Romans storm Ben-Hur's house and arrest him and his family after a loose roof tile accidentally strikes the Roman governor. Because of Wyler's consistent re-imagining of the plot in modern terms, this is one of the most accomplished sequences in the whole film. Roman soldiers batter against the entrance to the Hur mansion, and Judah, in the courtyard with his family, instructs the servants to open the gate. Aware of the precariousness of his own situation, he clearly believes that to co-operate with the enraged Romans and to explain the accident makes better sense than to provoke them even more by resisting. It will come as a greater shock to him than to the viewers when appeasement and appeals to reason fall on deaf ears. Judah's order to let the Romans in takes up only a very brief moment, and, in the general excitement, audiences easily miss its importance. It is, in fact, an exact parallel to attempts on the part of modern Jews, faced with threats of Nazi aggression, not to make the situation worse by showing even the slightest resistance: "If we reason with them as with civilized people, they will surely come to their senses. We even opened the door to them of our own accord! This will make them understand that we have nothing to hide and must be innocent." But such thinking does not usually win out over irrationality, either in history or in this film. Judah's willingness to explain and cooperate only brings disaster on himself and his family. A Roman officer pays no heed to his words, but simply commands, "Take him. Take all of them!" without showing the slightest interest in discovering guilt, innocence, or the truth. Roman soldiers now arrest everybody in sight—a clear parallel to indiscriminate Nazi reprisals.

When Messala enters shortly afterwards, his arrival is heralded to soldiers and film audiences alike in modern military fashion: a Roman shouts "Attention!" in such a way that the word's first syllable is barely audible. Messala implacably listens to Judah's explanation. Although Wyler makes it obvious that Messala believes Ben-Hur, the Roman does not save his former friend or listen to the women's entreaties. (He allows only the servants to go.) The posture which Wyler has his Messala strike at this moment is telling: with his hands behind his back, his legs firmly on the ground and slightly apart, he represents the man in total control, a military bully unmoved by emotion and in thrall only to the ideology of dominance. It appears to be an intentional pose patterned on modern examples. After the Hur mansion is deserted, Messala looks around the courtyard as if assessing the situation. Wyler now cuts from a medium close-up of him to a long shot which unmistakably shows that Messala has taken possession of all he surveys. The very silence of the moment reinforces the cruelty of the Romans' behavior.

One other scene in the film is significant for the subject under consideration. Before the climactic chariot race, Sheik Ilderim, the owner of the horses Ben-Hur will drive, visits the Romans in the baths to induce them to bet on the outcome of the race. With flattery and pretended obsequiousness he manipulates them to bet such large sums of money that Messala, at least, will be utterly ruined. Wyler and Vidal (or Fry) inject a particularly revealing moment into this otherwise not much more than functional scene. They emphasize the arrogance of those in power toward the people they both rule and despise in such a way that the parallel to Nazism receives a significant twist. For an appropriate understanding of this moment, we must trace its permutations from the novel through the silent film of 1925 to Wyler's.

In all three, Messala's sense of superiority over non-Romans induces him to bet his entire fortune against Sheik Ilderim. In the novel, Ilderim sends the wily Sanballat, his right-hand man, to raise the stakes. When

Sanballat proposes six-to-one odds, Messala accepts with the reply, "Six to one—the difference between a Roman and a Jew" (Wallace 1959.272). The silent film version preserves this sentence intact, but gives it in an intertitle to Sanballat as a taunt to Messala's national pride before the bet is placed. In Wyler's film, Sheik Ilderim himself visits Messala and his friends and coaxes the Romans to bet at ever higher odds. When the Romans hesitate, Ilderim says to them, "Will no one back the noble tribune against a Jew, a galley slave?" Messala now rises to the bait: "Four to one, Sheik! The difference between a Roman and a Jew." "Or an Arab!" one of Messala's friends immediately adds, looking at Ilderim.

The importance of this brief moment becomes evident not only through the additional words which had not appeared in either novel or silent film but, more importantly, from the way in which Wyler films and edits it. (The difference in the odds may be for the sake of greater verisimilitude, given the huge sums at stake.) In the novel and in the earlier film, the Romans were arrogant lords and masters, but their dominance did not carry overtones of contemporary politics or history as it does in Wyler's version. (The 1925 film had, however, been banned in Italy because Mussolini took exception to a Jew's victory over a Roman; cf. Brownlow 1968.410.) Evidently, Wyler's Romans regard as inferior anybody who does not belong to their own country or race—as movie Romans have done with predictable regularity. But Wyler goes beyond mere restatement of this attitude. That he wants his audience to understand the dialogue just quoted as a reference to the recent past becomes clear immediately afterwards. With rapid cutting, Wyler inserts a close-up of the face of one of Ilderim's attendants who, hearing the Roman's reference to Arabs, reacts to it with an angry look. The moment shows us that the Romans' arrogance and cruelty toward Jews are not due solely to anti-Semitism; rather, it is their conviction that they are a master race which leads them to despise all others. To American audiences of the late 1950s, such an attitude must have evoked the Nazi ideology of Aryan superiority and its successful dissemination among the German people. (As the Petronius of *Quo Vadis* had commented on Nero's attempt to blame the fire on the Christians, "People will believe any lie if it is fantastic enough.") In Wyler's *Ben-Hur,* an additional level of irony lies in the fact that these high-and-mighty Romans are too self-centered to see through the ruse of flattery and submissiveness with which Ilderim thoroughly bamboozles them. The sheik hides his true reaction to the Roman's insult behind a subdued chuckle, primarily so as not to endanger the betting. His revenge, of course, will be that, with the help of his horses and his charioteer, he leaves the great lords and masters of the world flat broke and, in the case of the most arrogant, dead.

Greatness and Tragedy

Before the blood of Christ cleanses the world at the film's grand climax, Wyler recapitulates the theme of power and freedom in a disquisition on Roman statecraft and on government in general, which Pontius Pilate delivers to Ben-Hur. Christopher Fry and Wyler now have Pilate give a more nuanced account of the nature of power than Messala had done in his earlier description of the world dominated by Rome: "Where there is greatness, great government or power, even great feeling or compassion, error also is great. We progress and mature by fault . . . Perfect freedom has no existence." But the filmmakers still turn the scales against Rome, as Pilate's immediately following words reveal: "A grown man knows the world he lives in, and, for the present, the world is Rome . . . There are too many small men of envy and ambition who try to disrupt the government of Rome . . . If you stay here, you'll find yourself a part of this tragedy." Ben-Hur replies: "I'm already part of this tragedy."

This exchange is an effective summary of the moral side of the religious and political conflicts and of the modern themes which the film addresses. Wyler's *Ben-Hur* thus goes well beyond the superficial portrayal of Rome in many American films. But even when their empire represents unadulterated evil, it is a measure of tribute to the Romans that they, rather than any other people, have become such prominent figures in American popular culture that their dramatic function as villains is immediately apparent. Wyler and Vidal's Messala says to Ben-Hur early in the film: "Roman law, architecture, literature are the glory of the human race." This statement is true enough, as Vidal, who wrote it, knew well, but audiences learn none of this from *Ben-Hur* or from most American films or popular fiction.

The only American film set in the age of imperial Rome to do justice to the greatness of Roman history and culture is *The Fall of the Roman Empire*. Rather than setting up ancient Rome as the enemy of Christianity and as the antithesis of all that is good and decent in mankind, director Anthony Mann portrays Roman history on its own terms.[28] Significantly, the triumphal sequence in this film shows us the overwhelming beauty of the Eternal City and demonstrates that the raised-arm salute need not look fascist if fascism is not the issue. The contrast with the triumph in

Quo Vadis could not be stronger. Evidently, by the mid-1960s, Hollywood's equation of imperial Rome with Nazi Germany had run its course.

Notes

1. For an overview of such stereotypes in nineteenth- and early twentieth-century British and American popular culture ("toga plays" and silent films) see Mayer 1994.1–22. The contrast between pagan Romans and Jews or Christians (or both) in popular melodrama may be observed in the intellectual tradition of the nineteenth century as well; cf. Matthew Arnold's "Hebraism and Hellenism" and "Porro Unum Est Necessarium," originally chapters 4 and 5 of *Culture and Anarchy* (1869). Arnold had prepared an edition of his works for the American market in 1883. On his dichotomy see Warren D. Anderson 1971.176–79, 203–04, 268–70 (notes). The present paper was first published in slightly different form in the *Classical Journal* 93 (1998) 167–96.

2. On the tolerant nature of much of Roman society in the early empire see, e.g., Gibbon 1993.1.34–39; on Roman religion, which was polytheistic and, as such, the opposite of exclusive Judaism and Christianity, see Gibbon's famous chapters 15 and 16 (Gibbon 1993.1.487–567, 2.3–80), put into context and defended by Momigliano 1963.2–4. As non-Christian Roman sources reveal, to most Romans the life and death of Jesus were insignificant events. For a recent overview of Roman attitudes toward Christians see Wilken 1984, with additional references.

3. On the historical implications of this see de Romilly 1977.42–62 ("*Hybris* in Politics").

4. Cf. Hirsch 1978.29, 73, adducing Edmund Wilson's review of Lloyd C. Douglas's 1942 novel *The Robe* ("'You Can't Do This to Me!' Shrilled Celia"; reprinted in Wilson 1950.204–08), on the disadvantages of presenting antiquity in merely one-dimensional modern guise. For the record, the title of Wilson's short essay is a combination of two separate phrases from the novel (Douglas 1942.362) and does not occur in the form quoted.

5. On the production history of the series see Capra's autobiography (1971.359–95). His book is notoriously unreliable (on its origin and nature see McBride 1992.645–53), and his account should be supplemented by that given at McBride 1992.455–82. On the inclusion of non-documentary footage in the *Why We Fight* films see McBride 1992.479–82.

6. This is because the emperor was commander-in-chief of the legions, and he alone held the highest *imperium*, the power and authority of office which was a prerequisite of the *triumphator* (Livy 28.38.4, Valerius Maximus 2.8.5).

7. See Capra 1971.362–68 on Riefenstahl's film as inspiration for his approach to the *Why We Fight* films, but cf. McBride 1992.466–67.

8. Cf. Geist 1978.223–24 on political overtones in *Julius Caesar*. The presence of John Houseman, its producer and a co-founder with Orson Welles of the Mercury Theatre, provides a link to Welles's 1937 modern-dress stage adaptation of the play as a comment on the rise of Hitler and fascism; see Leaming

1985.170–72, with excerpts from Welles's press release, also Callow 1995.324 (Welles on the mob in his production) and Welles and Bogdanovich 1998.339–40. Cf. Callow 1995.325, quoting the production's lighting director on staging and lighting patterns "based on the Nazi rallies at Nuremberg." (Naremore 1989.11 quotes Houseman on the same topic.) Around the time of Mankiewicz's film, Welles was planning a modern-dress film version of the play to be "shot like a newsreel" (Welles, quoted at Leaming 1985.474); cf. Welles and Bogdanovich 1998.301–02.

9. Thus Capra 1971.384, 388–89; contrast McBride 1992.475, 479, Koppes and Black 1987.124–25.

10. Kunsthistorisches Museum, Vienna, Austria; an impressive color illustration at Simon 1986, plate 13. Cf. also, among numerous other representations, the sardonyx cameo showing the apotheosis of Claudius, now in the Bibliothèque Nationale de France.

11. That the American eagle is meant to be different from ancient Roman eagles becomes evident, for instance, from the letter of April 18, 1806, by Benjamin Henry Latrobe to Charles Willson Peale about the huge eagle, with a wing span of fourteen feet, which was intended for the Hall of Representatives in the Washington Capitol. To Latrobe's horror, sculptor Giuseppe Franzoni was going to make "an Italian, or a Roman, or a Greek eagle" rather than "an American bald Eagle," but was prevailed upon to alter his design (quotation from Norton 1977.140–41). In an August 1806 letter to Thomas Jefferson, Latrobe considered the eventual result to be greater than any classical model: "When it is completed there is not in ancient or modern sculpture, an eagle's head, which in dignity, spirit, or drawing is superior to Franzoni's." The eagle was destroyed when the British burned the Capitol in 1814. On Latrobe's design of a statue of Liberty "with an Eagle by her side" see Miller 1966.41–42.

12. In the film—but not in Sienkiewicz's novel—Nero's responsibility for the fire of Rome, for which there is no ancient evidence (as there is none for his "fiddling while Rome burns" [on which see Gwyn 1991.455 note 128]), leads directly to his overthrow, although Nero ruled for another four years. The film also does not inform its viewers that Nero's successor Galba, announced to the people as restorer of justice and freedom, was himself overthrown after no more than six months of rule and that the following year saw civil war and the rapid succession of three more emperors. This silence is, however, necessary to allow for the greatest possible contrast between the defeat of Nero the monster and the victory of the good side. On Nero and the fire of Rome see, e.g., Sordi 1983.29–35, with references to the ancient sources. On Nero as typical tyrant in the history of Western political thought see Gwyn 1991. An additional, and in retrospect rather amusing, example of the American appropriation of Nero as tyrant for political purposes is the following statement of Barry Goldwater in an interview with Gore Vidal: "In fact, I've always been in favor of teaching Communism in schools. Show the kids what we're up against. Naturally I'd want a good course

in American history to balance it. After all, the only way you're going to beat Communism is with a better idea, like Nero and the Christians . . . you know? He couldn't stamp 'em out, because there was that idea they had. Well, that's what we've got to have" (Vidal 1961, quoted from Vidal 1993.834 [ellipsis in original]).

13. This is standard iconography in Hollywood; a prominent earlier example is Nero's throne in DeMille's *The Sign of the Cross* (1932). For *The King of Kings* (1927) DeMille had a bronze eagle 37 feet high built for Pontius Pilate (Higham 1973.166). DeMille was himself once caricatured as an American eagle; illustration at Higham 1973.273. There are altogether hundreds of eagles in Hollywood's Roman films, often placed quite ingeniously in historically rather unlikely surroundings.

14. On fascist Rome and its architecture see, e.g., Kostof 1973, esp. 7–40, and now Quartermaine 1995. Cf. also Bondanella 1987.172–206, 266–69 (references) and Canfora 1980.76–103 ("Cultura classica e fascismo in Italia"). Perhaps the most revealing (as well as ridiculous) piece of grandiose architecture indicating the imperial aspirations of fascist Italy was the huge column, with enemy tanks embedded in it, in the Campo Mussolini. This column was modeled on the *columna rostrata* of C. Duilius in the Forum Romanum, a commemoration of his victory over the Carthaginians at Mylae in 260 B.C.E.

15. On Nero as devil see Gwyn 1991.430, 443, 451–52; on Nero as Antichrist, Gwyn 1991.452–53, McGinn 1994.45–54 and passim, Fuller 1995.28–29, and Wright 1995.16.

16. Although it is a standard ingredient in Roman films and denotes militarism and power, the raised-arm salute does not carry political connotations every time it appears. Of all the variations of this form of greeting to occur in the cinema, doubtless the silliest appears in *Salome* (1953), when King Herod's palace guards salute a contingent of arriving Romans.

17. The following year *The Hitler Gang*, a film about Hitler's rise to power, was to contain a speech with this statement: "We need no God on a distant throne. Adolf Hitler is the Jesus Christ as well as the Holy Ghost of the Fatherland" (quoted from Koppes and Black 1987.300, with the spelling "Adolph"). On the insistence of the Production Code Administration (PCA) these words had to be deleted as blasphemous, although they were an exact quotation. On the PCA see Koppes and Black 1987.13–16.

18. Both quotations from Huston 1980.175. For detailed scholarship on the actual relations between Jews and Romans from the first century B.C.E. see Smallwood 1981.

19. McBride 1992.497: "The Allies had learned of the extermination of the Jews as early as August 1942, and the existence of the death camps was widely known by 1943, when Capra's film *The Nazis Strike* showed a concentration camp and stated that Hitler's plan was to 'exterminate all those he considers "inferior races."'" For Hollywood's awareness of the precarious situation of Jews in Germany see Koppes and Black 1987.27–30 on the 1939 film *Confessions of a Nazi*

Spy, especially their quotations of comments on the film from industry insiders at page 28.

20. For Peter's request to be crucified upside down see Eusebius *History of the Church* 3.1.2. Eusebius claims Origen's *Commentary on Genesis* as his source for the deaths of Saints Peter and Paul under Nero. Cf. Perkins 1994.138–40 and, for the wider context, Cullmann 1962.71–157.

21. Suetonius *Caligula* 30.2. The saying has been given to Nero since at least the early seventeenth century; examples at Gwyn 1991.439–40.

22. On Hollywood as a Jewish "empire" see the standard work by Gabler 1988.

23. Quoted from Herman 1995.338. On Wyler's war service and his war documentaries (*The Memphis Belle, Thunderbolt*) see Herman 1995.242–77.

24. When Louis B. Mayer remonstrated with Wyler about this change, Wyler answered him: "Mr. Mayer, if I had several Germans in the picture, I wouldn't mind having one who was a decent young fellow. But I've only got one German. And if I make this picture, this one German is going to be a typical little Nazi son-of-a-bitch. He's not going to be a friendly little pilot but one of Goering's monsters" (quoted in Herman 1995.232).

25. Vidal 1976 (= 1993.1176) and 1995.303–06. He claims that his inspiration was conversations with Federico Fellini about *La Dolce Vita*, which Fellini was preparing at Cinecittà while *Ben-Hur* was shooting nearby (Vidal 1995.304).

26. On Wyler's political activities and his involvement in the anti-HUAC Committee for the First Amendment see Herman 1995.298–305. On Wyler's membership in the Republican and Democratic Joint Committee of Hollywood for the Preservation of Civil Liberties see Ford 1979.226. John Huston also belonged to both these committees. Wyler was himself an intended target of HUAC (Herman 1995.338). For a concise overview of Hollywood's entanglement with HUAC, the loyalty oath, and the blacklist see McBride 1992.561–80, with several references to Wyler. On the topic in general cf. Navasky 1980. As Ben-Hur tells his mother and sister about Messala after their quarrel: "He wanted to use me to betray our people."

27. Heydrich and the fate of Lidice had become familiar to American audiences in two 1943 films: *Hangmen Also Die* and *Hitler's Madman* (originally to be called *Hitler's Hangman*). The latter was filmed almost completely in the style of a documentary. Both films were directed by expatriate Germans, Fritz Lang and Douglas Sirk. Cf. Koppes and Black 1987.296–97.

28. See my detailed discussion of this film at Winkler 1995. Bondanella 1987.227 considers the dance of Commodus over a floor map of the Roman empire to be a historical allusion to Hitler's dance after the fall of France and a cinematic one to Adenoid Hynkel's dance with the globe in Charles Chaplin's Hitler parody *The Great Dictator* (1940). But the modern overtones in Mann's film express events and situations contemporary with its production. The fact that a close-up of Commodus's feet shows him treading on Italy and not on a conquered country speaks against Bondanella's view as well.

Seeing Red

Spartacus as Domestic Economist

Alison Futrell

The press book heralding the opening of *Spartacus* trumpeted its celebration of the "age-old fight for freedom," a theme judged sufficiently innocuous to be consistently emphasized in all press releases and official communications concerning the 1960 film.[1] The cover of this souvenir "guide," however, is redolent of currents underlying the production of the film (fig. 3.1). On a field of vivid scarlet, the principle characters are represented as a handful of coins; they have thus "become" money, the organizing force of a capitalist system, set against the red of Communist solidarity. This was, in fact, the film that broke the blacklist with its open acknowledgment of Dalton Trumbo, one of the "Hollywood Ten," as screenwriter. The meaning of "freedom" in this context could thus be understood in different ways by different audiences. The character of Spartacus is layered in multiple, sometimes conflicted meanings, but this is hardly a new development. *Spartacus* stands at the end of a long process of projection, in which the historical character and the movement he led have been reworked and reinterpreted in light of contemporary political, social, and economic values.

In the modern era, the story of Spartacus's revolt has been used as a metaphor for resistance to industrial capitalism, with Spartacus himself presented as an early leader of a workers revolution and a martyr to archaic communalism. This metaphor was particularly volatile during the McCarthy years, when a coalition of political and economic interests cooperated in an anti-Communist purge. The terms in which this movement were couched were not, however, baldly political or economic; this effort was represented as the defense of the American Way: the protection of quintessentially American values from forces hostile to them. To

Figure 3.1 Characters as coins. Cover of the souvenir guide to *Spartacus* (1960).

challenge or critique property rights of the individual, organized religion, and other traditional bulwarks of American society, was to take an
"un-American" stance. An early and recurrent focus of the House Un-
American Activities Committee (HUAC) was the film industry because
of the pervasiveness of films and their perceived capacity to set social
standards, to model cultural norms and practices (overview in Ceplair
and Englund 1979.200–06). The spheres of Hollywood's influence,
therefore, were particularly open to suspicion because of the subtlety of
the medium. In December of 1947, the heads of the major studios, catalyzed by fear of economic repercussions, issued the Waldorf Statement,
vowing never to employ any known Communist in the film industry (text
in Klingaman 1996, appendix iii.431). The prevailing climate in Hollywood for the next thirteen years would suppress overt political commentary in films, displacing it into distant contexts and different terms
of discourse.

Under these circumstances, the presentation of the story of Spartacus in the mass media was provocative. The manuscript of Howard Fast's
1951 novel had been rejected by every major publishing house to which

it was submitted, to be finally printed and circulated by the author. In Fast's presentation, the Spartacan rebels explicitly reject the Roman system on economic grounds; Roman proto-capitalism represents the valuation of death over life. The proto-Marxist gladiators aim instead for a new society, one in which all property is held in common and all men are brothers in the tribe of mankind. The economics of film production did not admit Fast's narrative option; questions of personnel and content, as well as the requirements of the medium, demanded a shift in emphasis from the Fast source material. The Kirk Douglas film presents the ideology of Spartacus on a personalized scale; politics is encoded in symbolic interactions between individuals, thus avoiding the potential danger of any verbal articulation of a leftist stance. The escaped slaves construct a series of relationships in which the whole is more important than the individual and the viability of the system is measured not by profit but by the benefit to its parts. This whole is configured as a family; the affective bonds of the traditional, patriarchal family unit, of brother, father and husband, are idealized and replicated in the new polity of the slave army.

In *Spartacus*, the domestic paradigm is given political priority over the public, an inversion that, on the surface, catered to contemporary conservative values of home and family. The domestic emphasis of the film also securely locates it within a long tradition of representations of Spartacus in which his private connections both mirror and disrupt his political message. Since the eighteenth century, popular versions of the story of Spartacus have been inspired by his "age-old fight for freedom," but have typically concentrated on private conflicts and family drama, interpreting his political importance through a personal lens. Spartacus is made over into a budding patriarch, a family man, a character whose primary venue of dramatic action is the domestic household. This domestication of Spartacus shifts and diffuses the revolutionary quality of the story; the political and social disruption threatened by the radical slaves is relatively sanitized, serving primarily as a backdrop for the re-enactment of a non-radical personal conflict, one whose goal is not the leveling of unequal power relations but the establishment of a "natural" man at the head of a "natural" familial and gender hierarchy. Spartacus has thus long served as a homily, at best, for the egalitarian reworking of human society. This chapter offers a careful reading of texts and film, in an effort to reveal the projection of patriarchal values onto the modern character of Spartacus, a projection that distracts the contemporary audience from the unsettling radicalism of the ancient rebel.

An Empire Read? Spartacus's Origins

The revolt of Spartacus (73–71 B.C.E.) was the last and perhaps most memorable of a series of major slave wars in the later Roman republic.[2] Our knowledge of this event is dependent on a limited number of texts from antiquity, mostly written long after the event and from the viewpoint of an educated elite, anticipating an audience of elites. There are no surviving texts that represent the rebel voice. Thus from the outset Spartacus is shaped by authors whose sympathies and purposes are outside the original context, whose perspective places Spartacus within the process of Roman imperialism. We can extract an outline of actions from the ancient narratives; the details and motivations supplied by the ancient authors indicate the ancient meanings attributed to the Spartacan War.

In 73 B.C.E., a band of gladiators broke out of their training school; among the leaders was Spartacus, who, as the historian Appian tells us, was formerly a Thracian soldier whose defection from the Roman auxiliaries led to his confinement as a gladiator (*Civil Wars* 1.9.116). Having defeated the local militia based in Capua, Spartacus and his followers were victorious over the armies of both consuls and the army of Cisalpine Gaul in 72. The rebel gains inspired others to join them, with estimates of greatest support ranging between 60,000 (Eutropius *Digest* 6.7) and 120,000 (Appian *Civil Wars* 1.9.117). With the nullification of the northern Italian army, the way lay clear either to Rome, or over the Alps, toward the homeland of many of the rebels, where they could perhaps disperse beyond Rome's reach. M. Licinius Crassus, praetor in 73, was then granted the command in the Spartacan War (Appian *Civil Wars* 1.9.118 and Plutarch *Crassus* 10.1). Firmly imposing discipline on his six legions, he led his new army against Spartacus, eventually cornering him in Apulia in 71 where he could be cut off from his sources of supply. Spartacus was allegedly killed in the last serious battle, although the carnage was such that his body could not be identified. The last six thousand holdouts were rounded up and crucified along the Appian Way between Capua and Rome.

How did ancient authors explain this series of events, the causes, impulses, and personalities driving the dramatic changes in fortune? What sort of "spin" did the Romans put on the Spartacan War? The moral biographer Plutarch acknowledged that the immediate catalyst was Roman mistreatment, here defined discreetly as the wrongful confinement of the gladiators to their barracks rather than the institution of slavery as a whole. This hint of Roman culpability fades in importance next to the attention the ancient authors focus on the caliber of Rome's opponents. In order to achieve that level of success against mighty Rome, they "must" have been extraordinary gladiators, and the Roman authors define their unusual qualities in accordance with Roman values. The gladiators are credited with a very Romanized sense of shame concerning their debased status; Plutarch suggests that an awareness of propriety led them to seek out the weapons of Roman soldiers, discarding their former armature as "dishonorable and barbaric" (*Crassus* 9.1). Spartacus is characterized as a very impressive figure, not at all "slave-like" or un-Roman in his appearance or his priorities. The historian Sallust acknowledges his spirit, strength, and intelligence (*Histories* 3.91); indeed, Plutarch presents him as a cultivated man, "more like a Greek than a Thracian" (*Crassus* 8.2). Appian praises Spartacus's leadership for its adherence to Roman military tradition, here characterized by an emphasis on military discipline, on training, on utilitarian looting to support the campaign, and on scrupulous distribution of spoils (*Civil Wars* 1.9.117). In this, Spartacus seems to surpass contemporary Roman commanders, which would account, in the eyes of a Roman audience, for the series of victories he achieved.

Spartacus's ultimate failure, as presented by the ancient sources, lay in his inability to sustain his "Roman-ness," to conceive a broader vision and fulfill a wide-ranging purpose. The rebel goals, as they appear in the ancient accounts, are short-term, with immediate perceived benefits. Initially the gladiators wanted simply to escape the real danger of their existence as gladiators. Appian suggests that they fled not only danger but shame, preferring freedom to the ignominy of providing amusement for spectators (*Civil Wars* 1.9.116). The decision to take up arms against Rome was likewise attributed by the historian Florus to the immediate concerns of the rebels, either their desire for vengeance or the realization that their swollen ranks did not allow for easy dispersal into the Italian countryside (*Abridgement* 2.8.3). Plutarch credits Spartacus with an awareness of his limitations, noting that Spartacus realized that the rebels could not possibly outlast the resources of Rome; nevertheless, he could not, in the end, persuade his men to seize the opportunity to escape, because his shortsighted and overconfident army preferred to pillage Italy's rich countryside (*Crassus* 9.5–6). Plutarch suggests that Spartacus planned to rouse another revolt on Sicily and was only foiled by the betrayal of the Cilician transport (*Crassus* 10.3). This purported connection with the other, earlier slave uprisings on Sicily is the best, if not the only, evidence to connect the Spartacan War to some sort of overarching anti-slavery ideology, to some sort of spirit of insurrection running throughout the ancient population of slaves. The plan survives to us, however, as an allegation only, unsupported by any known action on the part of Spartacus. On the whole, the revolt of Spartacus is presented as notably lacking in formality, with an apparent absence of efforts to construct an alternative to the Roman system.

The gladiators, Spartacus especially, are thus represented as *nearly* Roman; in the Roman accounts, they possess the same standard of values as their owners and strive toward even greater similarity: to escape not merely from physical confinement but from their shameful status as gladiators. As quasi-Romans, their initial success against local garrisons becomes more comprehensible to an elite Roman reader. But they are not *really* Romans. They, therefore, could not hold out for long against an empire the ancient authors knew was destined to rule the world and was believed by them to be blessed by the gods with the character and virtue necessary to do so.

Roman accounts of the Spartacan War presented the story in ways that reflected imperial interests, all the more so because the revolt occurred at a volatile moment in Roman history. Added to the critical timing of the Spartacan War was the symbolic value of the gladiators and the political prominence of Crassus. Following hard on the heels of the war between Rome and her Italian allies and the coup spearheaded by Sulla, the Spartacan War once more involved Italy in bloody conflict that endangered Roman hegemony. This was a period of transition for Roman rule, a time when the senate's corporate control of the Roman government was gradually giving way to what would become a more monarchical structure under the Roman emperors. M. Licinius Crassus was an agent of this transformation, and used his success at crushing the uprising to fuel his extraordinary political career. The prominence of gladiators in the rebellion also would have captured the Roman imagination. This was a time when gladiatorial combat was becoming much more popular in Rome. It became highly politicized and identified with the ideology of Roman imperialism because of its close association with the cult of Roman power (Futrell 1997.29–33). The political potential of Roman leaders was evaluated by their ability to manipulate gladiatorial action in spectacles of Roman authority. Paradoxically, the actual performers in those games, the gladiators, were very low on the ladder of social status. Many of them were enslaved prisoners of war, living examples of the effects of Roman expansionism. The symbolic value of the gladiators may have intensified Rome's fear: Appian, Plutarch, and Florus all refer to the heightened terror generated by Spartacus (*Civil Wars* 1.9.118; *Crassus* 9.6, 11.1; *Abridgement* 2.8.11). Even discounting the gladiatorial mystique, as soon as he took up arms, Spartacus would be considered in rebellion against Roman imperial policy, which demanded that such a betrayal of Roman control be crushed with the harshest of measures.

The War of Spartacus was the last really dangerous slave revolt in antiquity, although Romans would be ever vigilant in their concern for security and protection from their slaves (Bradley 1987). At the same time, Rome was the most generous of the ancient empires in the rehabilitation of slaves: manumitted slaves, and there were a number of them, had access to Roman citizenship (Hopkins 1978.133–71). This generosity is relative, however; the freedman was heavily embedded in a web of obligations that imposed a severe penalty on those who tested, or even seemed to test, the Roman hierarchy.

These factors interacted to guarantee that the Spartacan Rebellion would loom threateningly in the Roman memory. The characters involved were freighted with meaning, representing the processes of empire and potentially negative ramifications of those processes. Dramatic changes in the distribution of power contemporary with the revolt associated it with patterns of internal social dissent. The flavor of civil war was compounded by the intimacy of the bonds between slaves and slaveowners, between slaves and citizens in the Roman world.

An Acquired Taste for Red? The Development of the Spartacus Icon

Rome's value as a site of contemporary meaning underwent a shift during the eighteenth century. The iconographic status of Spartacus saw a new upsurge at the time of the Enlightenment, when assumptions about human potential and its reflection in the organization of society and politics were being analyzed and challenged.[3] Although the use of antiquity as a source of paradigms for contemporary issues was hardly new, Enlightenment thinkers and writers selected new images from the ancient past to fit their arguments about the individual's relationship to power (Finley 1980.18–19). Classical figures of resistance, like Brutus, Sertorius, and Spartacus, were overlaid with contemporary social meaning and used to question and critique the achievement of classical civilization and, by implication, the *ancien régime*.[4]

Popular representations of Spartacus endow him with a private side that threatens to overwhelm the public but also nuances and comments on the political ideology attributed to the ancient gladiator. This is clearly demonstrated in Bernard-Joseph Saurin's 1760 dramatic production of *Spartacus*, a major European hit that combined the presentation of an "epic" moment in history with the ideology of freedom in human society.[5] Although Saurin's Spartacus is driven by his passion for natural law and the natural rights of man, he is also "domesticated." The emotional appeal of the story is enhanced by an emphasis on Spartacus's personal life, the private side of the public hero. Indeed, Saurin's version condenses the rebellion of Spartacus into a series of choices between the public and private aspects of Spartacus's character, and his vacillation between domestic security and political leadership provides the chief dramatic tension of the play. Saurin's Spartacus regularly conflates the personal and the political conflict into a single war.[6]

The domestic side entails the apocryphal creation of a mother and a love-interest for Spartacus. The mother is a courageous woman whose constancy and tenderness sustain Spartacus emotionally even as she inspires him with "hatred for tyrants and love of virtue" (Saurin 1821.I sc. ii, p. 81). Captured and tortured by the Romans for her son's sake, Spartacus's mother finally takes her own life specifically to promote her son's cause: he vows vengeance on the dagger flecked with his mother's blood. Spartacus discovers that his beloved, Émilie, is the daughter of the enemy commander, Crassus. As his mother's body provides a catalyst for Spartacus's renewed resolution, Émilie's position as a character broadens the nature of political decision-making for Spartacus.

Spartacus's romantic relationship is treated as incompatible with his political stance. Initially, his unwillingness to kill Émilie, now held captive by the rebels, brings the slave army to the verge of mutiny, which only Spartacus's charisma manages to defuse. Spartacus is then asked to consider an unusual proposition: Crassus offers to make the slaves Roman citizens and Spartacus a senator, and to welcome the rebel leader into his family as his daughter's husband, should the gladiator army give up its opposition to Rome. Spartacus rejects this offer; to become Roman would be disgraceful, shameful, as it would mean the renunciation of "the liberty of the world" for the sake of his individual desire to establish a household (Saurin 1821.IV sc. iii, p. 119).[7] Spartacus thus enunciates the ideological priorities of the slave rebellion. Free status is not the "freedom" for which they fight, nor do they desire the rights and protections of citizens within the Roman system. For Spartacus, to become a senator of Rome would tacitly support a corrupt tyranny and Rome's customary disregard of human rights and decency, which the gladiators characterize as "barbarism."[8] Thus Spartacus rejects the offer of domestic reconciliation and renews his struggle against Rome on behalf, it is implied, of all mankind.

Driven by her love for Spartacus, Émilie makes her way through the final battleground to plead with him to reconsider her father's offer. She points to the beneficial quality of Rome's pacification of warring peoples of the world, who try to oppress one another as they ravage the earth. Émilie even suggests that Spartacus could take his final vengeance on Rome by working from within the system to improve it (Saurin 1821.V sc. v, pp. 124–25).[9] Although Spartacus agonizes over his decision still more, he finally claims that the peoples of the world have placed their trust in him to destroy Rome and ensure their freedom. The failure of the rebel army and Spartacus's capture decide the issue. Rather than suffer the humiliation of Crassus's triumphal parade, Spartacus destroys himself. Émilie here leads the way; although her choice of suicide alongside her lover indicates that she prefers Spartacus to all else, she is the first to take up the dagger. The two die in one another's arms. On the verge of eternity, Spartacus declares himself a free man, one not without glory, who dared to take on mighty Rome. Nevertheless, in Saurin's play, Spartacus's inner turmoil, his calamitous relationship with Émilie, rather than the doomed rebellion, provides the real tragic element. Indeed, Émilie dominates the final act of the play, her agonized efforts to reconcile father with lover earning the audience's sympathy. Once more, it is over the corpse of a woman, blood-spattered dagger in hand, that Spartacus articulates his commitment to freedom. Far more memorable than Spartacus's ideology is the imagery of ruined households, families torn asunder, and the dying lovers, over which political rhetoric washes like the faintest of patinas.

Saurin's play was extremely popular, not just in France but outside it as well, which helped make Spartacus an exemplar for the natural equality of all human beings—in contrast to contemporary examples of absolutist monarchy. The eighteenth century thus makes Spartacus a "contemporary" hero in ancient clothing, battling for the equality of man in the political sphere. Major figures such as Gotthold Ephraim Lessing, one of the great dramatist/philosophers of the later eighteenth century, took up the theme of Spartacus.[10] Citing Lessing as an influence, August Gottlieb Meissner wrote a laudatory biography of Spartacus in 1793 (1800). Both emphasize Spartacus's challenge to the concept of class-based access to political privilege, suggesting that the capacities of the individual, his "spirit," should be the factor that determines "greatness."

The Spartacus motif was also put to specifically anti-slavery usages. The Abbé G. T. F. Raynal, in his multi-volume, anti-colonial, anti-slavery work of 1770, called for a "new Spartacus" to bring down the slave system (1770). The slave rebellion on Martinique appeared to some to be the uprising of the Black Spartacus; Toussaint L'Ouverture too, leader of Haiti's successful slave revolution, was linked with the Spartacus legend (Freeman 1988).

In the nineteenth century, a shift toward configuring identity along national lines overshadows the emphasis on the individual. In this period, we see the projection of Spartacus in popular media configured by nationalism. The Spartacan plan for the return of the gladiators to their European homes is reoriented, and a slave rebellion is transformed into a war to establish the homeland as a sovereign state in the face of Roman imperialist domination. The divergent origins of the gladiators are collapsed, and Spartacus becomes a fighter for national independence.

Franz Grillparzer, one of Austria's most acclaimed writers of the nineteenth century, turned, somewhat abortively, to the Spartacus uprising.[11] At the age of nineteen, he composed *Spartakus*, a one-act play that may have been inspired by his sympathy for the rebellion led by Andreas Hoffer in the Tyrol against Napoleon in 1810 (Stanev 1981.99–100). Grillparzer's Spartacus and his freedom-fighters do not articulate a dedication to the natural rights of man; they are early nationalists, battling Roman imperialist aggression as patriots. The freedom of the individual has been conflated with the right of the community to self-determination. The gladiators long for what is presented as the natural aspirations of a people: a fatherland and comradeship.[12] For this, they are punished by Rome, "a curse-filled land . . . which fattens itself on the blood of the people and builds its greatness on their ruins" (Grillparzer 1892.143). Spartacus is called "the hope of the Fatherland," a savior amid misfortune, who has roused the gladiators to fight for their freedom as a people (Grillparzer 1892.146, 133).

The unfinished play is also overlaid by Romantic elements. Set mostly in an Italian wilderness, it refers often both to the shadowy wilds of nature and to gloomy stretches of interior landscape. In his first scene, for example, Spartacus bursts into a poetic, melancholy reverie: his heart wanders through forest and meadow, over chasm and mountain, overcome by passion for Cornelia, the daughter of Crassus.[13] Spartacus's moody obsession with Cornelia represents a danger to the movement; Crixus, Spartacus's comrade, tries to remind him of his patriotic priorities, his twin resolutions of freedom and hatred for Rome, and his sworn commitment to the liberation of the world, vowed by starlight on a Thracian mountaintop (Grillparzer 1892.146). To no avail, Spartacus foregoes his political goals to make another moonlit visit to Cornelia's rooms, only to be taken captive by her father. The play ends at this point, it lacks a final resolution of both the relationship and the rebellion.[14] It appears, however, that this Spartacus is ultimately dominated more by his sensibility than by his sense of duty to his people; his domestic relationship and his Romantic focus on the interior self both conflict with and ultimately betray his political ideology. Indeed, Grillparzer's Spartacus articulates only the Romantic and romantic impulses within him; although characters refer to his past capacity for activist rhetoric, on stage, he speaks only of nature and Cornelia.

Nationalism also shapes a vigorous American Spartacus; Robert Montgomery Bird's 1831 play, *The Gladiator*, became one of the most popular American plays of the nineteenth century.[15] Produced in a climate of cultural nationalism, the play belongs to a widespread effort to encourage art and literature that express the "spirit of America." Bird created his Spartacus specifically as an entry in the actor Edwin Forrest's annual competition to write a five-act "American" tragedy in which the hero or protagonist was "an original of this country" (Foust 1919.36–37). How Forrest interpreted this latter phrase is revealing: of the nine plays awarded prizes, the majority featured heroes outside the American context. "American-ness" was thus defined not by country of origin, nor by ethnic heritage, nor even by chronology, but rather by the expression of an "American spirit." The perception that Bird's Spartacus was quintessentially American comes through in contemporary reactions to the play: the *New York Standard Review* noted "with pride and satisfaction" its appropriateness "to the genius, to the taste, and to the literary enterprise of the American people."[16]

In an American setting, Rome's imperial power is deployed as a metaphor for British imperialism, while the rebels are analogues for the American colonists who had fought to ensure their political independence from Britain and now were trying to free themselves from cultural domination.[17] Such an identification affects the characterization of Bird's rebels: these are very sassy gladiators. The Romans approve of this impudence, finding in it a clear indication of a fighting spirit; Crassus says he likes this "fearless taunting" (Bird 1919.343). Nevertheless, mere feistiness is insufficient motivation for revolution: the revolt of Bird's gladiators is inspired not by the abstract goal of freedom but by Spartacus's determination to recover and to preserve his family.

Spartacus's domesticity precedes and shapes his political efforts; Spartacus's family is now firmly situated outside the Roman social hierarchy, which lessens the conflict between personal happiness and political goals that we have seen in earlier versions. Spartacus is from the outset distinguished by his attachment to the domestic sphere and defined by his ties to home and family. His first appearance shows him dejected, pining, refusing to take the oath of a gladiator. His priorities are clarified by his first lines: he asks how far it is to his homeland, and whether the Romans have fathers, wives, and children (Bird 1919.314). The reunion with his wife and son and the opportunity to fight for their freedom are the only things that compel Spartacus into the arena; he expresses his willingness to give everything for his wife and child (Bird 1919.319). Spartacus's domesticity now encompasses not only a wife but also a son and even a long-lost brother, Phasarius. Spartacus and Phasarius discover each other in the arena, an event that implicitly suggests the brotherhood of all who suffer under Rome. Together, the brothers rouse the gladiatorial bands to rebel against Roman imperialism and to fight for the liberty of all who are oppressed by Roman subjection. The gladiators seek to create a new union of nations: states united by their common hatred of the Roman overlords and their desire to overthrow the yoke of tyranny (Bird 1919.392). Just as the revolt is catalyzed by a family reunion, so its defeat is predicated upon the destruction of the family bond. The fatal flaw in the revolution is a disagreement among the brothers that divides the troops and weakens the revolution. The death of his family drives Spartacus to despair and defeat; as he lies dying, however, he anticipates the return homeward that death promises. Bird's Spartacan rebellion is thus founded upon notions of "home" that predicate community membership upon the family.

Another turn in the process of projecting meaning upon the story of Spartacus can be seen in the later nineteenth century, when Spartacus was connected with the growing workers movement. The Spartacus uprising was presented as a great social conflict that damaged the economic structure of the Roman world. The nineteenth century saw a number of such risings, accompanied by the development of an economic theory that organized the development of human society around shifts in economic organization. Here too, the ancient past was mined as a source of evidence for the eventual development of modern structures, modern movements.[18] Spartacus's rising visibility as a symbol of resistance to Roman oppression made available a specifically non-elite and non-Christian icon from the ancient past. Not surprisingly, Spartacus became one of the touchstones for socialists.[19] Karl Marx, for example, expressed his particular appreciation for Spartacus in an 1861 letter to Frederick Engels: "Spartacus comes across as the most excellent fellow in the whole history of antiquity, a great general . . . of noble character, a real representative of the proletariat of ancient times" (Marx 1975.41.264–65).[20]

Spartacus was known to labor leaders in the United States as well, notably to Cyrenus Osborne Ward, an activist and pamphleteer of the period after the Civil War.[21] In *The Ancient Lowly* (1888), Ward attempts to correlate all the uprisings of oppressed laborers in western antiquity as demonstrations of the same impulse, viewing them through the lens of socialist theory and evangelical Christianity. Using highly emotive descriptions, Ward's monograph represents the ruling classes of the ancient world as uniformly corrupt and evil. This stance informs his depiction of Spartacus; Ward's Romans, at the gladiatorial games, exhibit their "inhuman passion . . . for beholding atrocities of this ghastly nature while they wallowed in inebriate and lascivious beastliness" (Ward 1888.1.237). In contrast, Ward's ancient rebels are witnesses for truth, with distinctly Christian overtones. Although their rebellions were put down, they "did not lose, but won martyrdom, nobler and happier than their life, to which death was a relief, and by their martyrdom taught a lesson to an inexperienced world" (Ward 1888.1.xii). Ward arranges and codifies his material using labels from the contemporary labor movement, conflating ancient slave rebellions with labor union activity.[22] Spartacus, whom Ward calls "the last emancipator," not only proclaims the freedom of all slaves, he also represents the best hope of the ancient working man for political and social representation: "The humane management of Spartacus . . . might have resulted in a permanent recognition of the honor and merit of human labor."[23]

Perhaps the best-known example of the use of Spartacus as a symbol of Communist uprising is Berlin's Spartakusbund, which mounted a coup in January 1919. This offshoot of the SPD, the German Social Democrat party, was headed by Rosa Luxemburg and Karl Liebknecht, who saw the SPD's support of the German war effort as a betrayal of the internationalism of the workers movement.[24] The Spartakusbund's active efforts to claim control of the German government came during the chaotic struggle for political ascendance in Germany after World War I. Luxemburg described the political left as facing a choice between two poles: good and evil. On the side of evil stood the politics of the right, characterized by Luxemburg in the *Junius Pamphlet* of April 1915 as "the triumph of imperialism and the destruction of all culture and, as in ancient Rome, depopulation, desolation, degeneration, a vast cemetery."[25] Again, Rome is represented as "barbaric" in opposition to a Spartacus identified with the socialist movement, a man who "throws the sword of revolutionary struggle with manly resolution upon the scales . . . to cast off slavery to the ruling classes, to become the lord of his own destiny." During the coup, Karl Liebknecht articulated the meaning of the ancient icon in emotive ideological terms: "Then Spartacus—by which I mean fire and spirit, I mean soul and heart, I mean will and action for the revolution of the proletariat. And Spartacus—by which I mean all need and yearning for happiness, all resolution for battle of the class-conscious proletariat. Then Spartacus, by which I mean socialism and world revolution."[26] The failure of the Spartakusbund and the murder of Liebknecht and Luxemburg added resonance to the value of Spartacus as an icon. Howard Fast strongly identified both with Luxemburg and with her ancient avatar, finding in them a source of strength in the "struggle against oppression and wrong" (Fast 1951, dedication).

Writing Red: Howard Fast and Spartacus

From the publication of his first novel in 1933, Howard Fast (1914–) has been a critically acclaimed and best-selling author in the United States, one whose domestic success was mirrored by record sales overseas. By the time he wrote *Spartacus*, he had already published fourteen major novels as well as a number of short stories, extended articles, and non-fiction books in less than twenty years. Beyond this professional dedication, Fast is notable as well for his public stance. Long an activist in leftist and labor causes, Fast was a vigorous member of the Communist Party of the United States from 1943 to 1957, writing on the staff of *The Daily Worker*, serving as a delegate to a number of world congresses and participating in public protests, always a vocal advocate of working-class issues.[27]

It is generally acknowledged that Fast's creative works reflect his politics, focusing as they do on the "common man," that is, the proletarian, and his resistance to the oppression endemic in a world controlled by the wealth of the bourgeoisie.[28] Fast may have been particularly sensitized to these issues in his works of historical fiction; his choice of the past as a setting for his creative work was criticized by one of his first friends in the Party, who pushed him to find his working-class voice.[29] The novels serve as a platform for Fast's revelation of self, but Fast apparently also believed that a public good was served by his recreations of the historical past: the uncovering of a "truth" that had been suppressed by the dominant (capitalist) authority, a truth whose power may inspire modern action.[30]

Howard Fast's creation of a literary Spartacus is intimately connected to his experience of Communism, both as an active member of the Party and as someone whose convictions had prompted public opprobrium and personal suffering. Fast was convicted of contempt of Congress during the first phase of the House Un-American Activities Committee hearings in 1947.[31] The novel began to germinate while he was imprisoned at Mill Point, West Virginia, in 1950. He approached the novel, therefore, with strong sympathies for the political empowerment of the working class, but these were sympathies that had recently been the cause of personal trauma. As he put it, this was the time when he "began more deeply than ever before to comprehend the full agony and hopelessness of the underclass" (Fast 1990.269).

Inspiration for a new project, in which this newly acute identification with class suffering would be expressed, came from a visit to the prison library. Reading about Germany after World War I, Fast came across new insights concerning Rosa Luxemburg; her work seemed to speak to his current situation, to his willingness to serve time for the preservation of a political conscience. Initially, Fast thought that Luxemburg's life, particularly her leadership in the Spartakusbund, would be excellent material for a new work. This plan was soon discarded, however, and Fast turned his attention instead to the figure of Spartacus, to a projection that had served Luxemburg as inspiration—a fountainhead, perhaps, for Fast's present political sentiments.[32]

Research for the novel took Fast back to an earlier phase of his membership in the Communist Party. A major source for him was C. O. Ward's *The Ancient Lowly*, which he had received as a gift to commemorate his completion of what Fast called "the training school." Shortly after World War II, the Party leadership expressed some concern lest Fast's material success as an author sway him from his ideals. An intensive three-week workshop was recommended to renew his commitment to the brotherhood of man and to reawaken Fast's former identification with "the best type of revolutionary working-class intellectual."[33] Fast's overt linkage between the story of Spartacus and leftist activism was thus reinforced by his selection of material to use as historical background for the novel, material that resonated with his ideological commitment, both in content and in personal context.

The "specter of Communism" hangs over *Spartacus*. Fast's fictive Rome is shaped by popular Marxism, in which the ideology of a primitive workers movement is the spirit of progress relieving the otherwise unrelentingly negative presentation of the Roman past. From the outset, Rome is established as a hostile environment, a superficially elegant society whose innate malevolence can never command admiration or sympathy from the reader. The basis of this hostile system is exploitative labor practices: Rome's economics constitute the "meaning" of Rome. Fast presents the Roman world as a simplified class structure with heavy moral overtones; the "Romans," that is, the proto-bourgeois overlords, are evil, while the working classes, including slaves, free workers, common soldiers, peasants (displaced and otherwise), and the poor, are good. Fast's Rome is overwhelmingly powerful but ultimately doomed to be succeeded by a system more closely approximating that envisioned by the slaves, one in which the labor collective controls production for the whole, all property is held in common, and peace and tranquility reign. Echoing the Communist Manifesto's climactic rallying cry, Fast's Spartacus issues a summons to his new society: "To the slaves of the world: Rise up and cast off your chains!"[34]

Transforming the truism into narrative, Fast leads his reader to Rome along her roads, those much-praised emblems of Roman imperial achievement (MacDonald 1996.87–88). Fast characterizes the roads as arteries of empire, through which the Roman heartbeat pumps blood. Rapidly, however, the reader realizes it is not lifeblood but the dying gush of arterial fluid that washes the roads of Rome (Fast 1951.11–13). Fast's descriptions of such "typical" elements of Roman culture constitute a major portion of his invective against Rome, his effort to reveal the "true" nature of the Roman achievement.[35] The paradigmatic status of Roman civilization is acknowledged and undermined simultaneously. Rome, fountainhead of Western culture, is depicted as an unnatural civilization, whose development of a warped economic structure has likewise warped her at the basic level of human existence. Romans, for example, have a destructive relationship with food; for them, the staff of life becomes the stuff of death.[36] Fast introduces this recurring motif early on, with repeated references to crucified gladiators as "meat" to be used for the production of sausage for export. This literalization of Rome's consumption of human resources serves as a gruesome indictment of Roman taste on a quite graphic level. Fast extends the food-corruption-death association in repeated descriptions of Roman eating habits, especially their snacking on/at gladiatorial bouts and their banquets to celebrate mayhem (Fast 1951.127, 133, 232, 310, 329). In contrast, the slaves husband the simple foodstuffs they are allotted. This stance is embodied particularly by Spartacus, who knows that "all food must be honored": carelessness or dishonoring of food results in death (Fast 1951.74). The maxim is proven by the example of Rome; flagrantly dishonoring food, the Romans are mired in death. Romans have become "bags of death" (Fast 1951.48); they are in love with death; they take delight in death, living on the bones and blood of slaves (Fast 1951.118, 126, 144, 245). The fixation on death is built into the system; Roman hierarchy commands death.

Fast pays scant attention to exploring the development of Rome's imperial system. The most extensive analysis comes from Gracchus, the old, corrupt politician, who explains the "truth" of Rome to Cicero, the ruthless young politician.[37] The analysis, markedly modern in tenor, focuses again on Rome's economy, on the unequal distribution of wealth in a system that acts to perpetuate this inequality and thus deprives Rome's people of their humanity. Gracchus sees an increasing gap between Rome's haves and have-nots. Politicians lie to the people, telling them they are the only free people in the world in order to inspire them to offer up their very lives to protect the property of the wealthy. In "fact," Rome's proletariat is on the dole, as Roman elites bust unions and pay slave wages to imported workers (Fast 1951.294).[38]

The capitalist nature of the Roman system is primarily revealed through an utter devotion to commodification: Romans "[assess] everything in terms of money" (Fast 1951.55). Fast's Romans purchase power, death, and pleasure in dizzying amounts and can themselves be bought as well. Capitalist ventures demonstrate the inherent corruption of the Roman system and reveal the seeds of destruction that flourish in morally-bankrupt economic practices. The consumable industry of gladiatorial combat, a chief representative of economic evil, is presented as a cause of even more deterioration in Roman society. Fast describes how scheming vulgar men gain wealth for political bribery through investment in such ventures, through this pandering to base Roman desires. Another form of lucrative investment is in perfume factories, although Fast points out that the sickening sweetness of manufactured scent fails to mask the stench of rotting Rome (Fast 1951.13, 293). Crassus, the wealthiest man in Rome, owns such a factory in Capua; his profit margin grows ever larger because he is not obliged to feed or shelter his imported workers, who are nothing less than wage slaves. The Roman elites do perceive the potential for a workers revolution in such primitive factories, but only at the subconscious level, which, for them, takes the form of a lingering sense of unease (Fast 1951.295–97).[39]

In stark contrast to the greed and debauchery of the Romans shines the dream of the slave rebels. The "good" of the slaves, addressed in ethical terms, is explicitly housed in the domestic virtues: "Home and family and honor and virtue and all that was good and noble was defended by the slaves and owned by the slaves . . . because their masters had turned over to them all that was sacred" (Fast 1951.179). By depriving their slaves of property rights, the Romans have granted them access to a higher, basic truth: the absence of individual possessions allows men to realize their brotherhood, to realize that they all are part of each other (Fast 1951.334–35).

This dissolution of interpersonal barriers is symbolized by the gladiators' need to communicate with each other, to create a community. Inversely, Roman suppression is made manifest in attempts to restrict interaction among the slaves. By establishing a group discourse, the gladiators establish their own system of social ties (Fast 1951.263–64). Thus the intent to rebel is formed when the gladiators Spartacus, Crixus, and Gannicus call each other "friend," and direct action against their Roman guards is catalyzed by Spartacus's statement: "I want to stand up and speak. I want to open my heart" (Fast 1951.144–45, 151–52).

The slaves seek the disruption of the Roman world to form a new society, modeled on an earlier Golden Age, that avoids the corruption of contemporary Rome (Fast 1951.303). The new world order will be based on quasi-tribal bonds, in which a quasi-familial connection between individuals is perceived as a shared, inborn identity. Just as the social ties constructed by the gladiators are idealized as an outgrowth of their sympathy for one another, so Spartacus's leadership takes on an emotionally charged quality: he is the "father" of the community "in the old tribal way" (Fast 1951.76).

Spartacus, the embodiment of the rebellion, time and again is described as a father to his community and as a patriarch of the movement. He is unlike Roman fathers in the generosity of his fatherhood, and his leadership is linked to his desire to give to others. Spartacus, despite his artless humanity, has thoroughly transcendent personal qualities. He is a legend, touched by the gods, godlike himself, with a destiny written in the stars (Fast 1951.120, 163, 169). Spartacus is the tool of fate, of larger forces at work in the universe (Fast 1951.139). He is timeless, deathless, inseparable from his vision that sees the endless yearning of humanity, stretching back to the time when the first slave was put in chains, stretching forward "for ages unknown and unborn," beginning anew with every generation (Fast 1951.88, 139, 143, 145, 149, 158, 273, 289).

The new tribe of man will replace Roman law with a new, simple law, that expresses the essence of the collective: "What is taken is held in common" (Fast 1951.166–67, 268). Inherent in this law, however, is its exclusion of women, who are placed in the category of property as the sole exception to the rule of commonality. Women are possessed *only* personally and *only* as wives. The male possession of women is meant to represent the rule of morality in the slave society. Not for them the shallow promiscuity of the Romans: sex takes place only within marriage. It is on this basis that Fast characterizes the slave women as the only "real women" in the anti-civilization of Rome; their Roman counterparts surrendered some essential femininity when they took on promiscuity, which, for them, is connected to their indifference to human suffering and is even identified as a necessary consequence of Roman imperial domination (Fast 1951.9, 25, 235–36). Female chastity is thus a basic element of the slaves' creation of the family unit, the original economic structure, as the basis of the new community. Hierarchy is preserved within the family unit, but it is depicted as a natural one, based on natural distinctions of gender.

Accordingly, the narrative role of Spartacus's wife Varinia plays out the domestic ideology of the rebellion: where Spartacus is the father of the movement, Varinia is its mother. The traditional roles of wife and mother make Varinia a passive conduit for Spartacanism, which she passes on to the next generation as the mother of Spartacus's son (Fast 1951.103).[40] Varinia serves as the emblem of an ideology in her interactions with the Roman leaders Gracchus and Crassus, rather than an activist herself. The politician Gracchus falls in love with the idea of Varinia, long before he meets her, because she, as the wife of Spartacus, is a "real" woman (Fast 1951.300–01, 337).[41] Gracchus sees Varinia as the antithesis of Rome, a dichotomy expressed in familial terms. Rome is Gracchus's mother, but she is an unnatural mother, supremely uncaring, a whore whose love is purchased (Fast 1951.318, 347, 353). In contrast, Varinia is no whore but a wife; she is a mother not of death but of life. Varinia's symbolic value places her beyond Gracchus's existence: she represents life and the freedom waiting in humanity's future, while Gracchus, as a doomed Roman, can truly comprehend neither life nor freedom (Fast 1951.347–49). Transformed by this realization, Gracchus, in his "single act of love" helps Varinia to escape and then commits suicide (Fast 1951.345).

Crassus, the leader of the quintessentially evil empire, embodies its destructive, invalid authority. Crassus is a bad father, a patriarch whose household is a sink of jealousy, hatred, and frustration. His own son despises him, and his absent wife would like nothing better than to see his throat cut (Fast 1951.316, 325). Crassus's negative governance of his household is paralleled by his political leadership. Despite his being reared on legends of Roman simplicity and selflessness, Crassus no longer has any real sense of ethics, of justice. He has reoriented his moral center around the maintenance of Rome's system of economic exploitation; justice, for Crassus, is defined primarily by the maintenance of wealth and thus of power (Fast 1951.246–47). His military command against Spartacus is likewise a negation of Roman ethical traditions; no legends will be crafted around Crassus's achievement (Fast 1951.32). Gracchus can intuit the transformative quality of Varinia's love and wants access to that creation of a new self. Crassus, however, sees a loving relationship with Varinia as a chance to "rule the world"; this misappropriation reveals Crassus's perception of love as power.[42] His victory over Spartacus would be incomplete without the creation of a new domestic hierarchy, represented by Varinia's willing surrender or "love" for him. Varinia's passivity, her essentialized status as the wife of Spartacus, here constitutes resistance to Crassus's Rome. She is impervious to emasculated Roman command (Fast 1951.330).[43] Crassus's inability to comprehend the true affective bonds of the family dooms his personal agenda as his political ambitions are stymied by the ultimate failure of Fast's Rome.

Fast's Spartacan rebels explicitly reject the Roman system on economic grounds; they embrace an ideology that foregrounds the family as an ethical paradigm and the domestic economy as the basis of a new society. As we have seen, the relative value of domesticity has undergone a shift in popular projections of the story of Spartacus. Saurin and Grillparzer created an ancient rebel whose personal desires were in conflict with his political aims, whose private longings for domestic bliss presented an obstacle to victory, located as they were in love interests identified as Roman and therefore inherently hostile to Spartacus's goals. Unable or unwilling to choose a private life, these versions of Spartacus fling themselves into their public duty and promptly fail. With Bird's staging of Spartacus, we see a coalescence of the patriarch and the statesman, in which the essential status of the former is fundamental to the creation of the latter. Conversely, the loss of the family fatally undermines the rebellion for Bird's Spartacus. For Howard Fast, the connection between the family and the polity of the rebels is more than seamless: the two are identical. The meaning of the rebellion has shifted. As we have seen,

Spartacus's opposition to Roman authority has been identified with individualism, with nationalism, with socialism. How then are these options handled in the film version of the Spartacan rebellion? What did Spartacus mean in Hollywood?

Seeing Red: *Spartacus* as Film

The dominant creative force behind the movie *Spartacus* was Kirk Douglas, who was head of Bryna Productions, the company responsible for the making of the film. In late 1957, Douglas read Howard Fast's novel and was intrigued by the story, especially because, as he later explained in his autobiography, it seemed to tell a hidden truth that had been suppressed for years by an embarrassed Rome and then by historians (Douglas 1988.303–04). Douglas was also moved by the "grandeur of Rome," by Rome's achievement measured by its capacity to alter such a large territory. For him, the impact of Rome is as visible in its physical ruins as it is in written history. Douglas, however, also saw in these monuments their implied antitheses. Just as the silence of the texts tells us about Roman fear and shame regarding Spartacus, so the monuments of powerful Rome speak of those who suffered under her rule: "Looking at these ruins . . . I wince. I see thousands and thousands of slaves carrying rocks, beaten, starved, crushed, dying. I identify with them" (Douglas 1988.304). *Spartacus* thus represented to Douglas the opportunity to give voice to those who had been silenced, to show the "true" grandeur of resistance to systematic oppression.[44]

The making of *Spartacus* took place against the backdrop of McCarthyism in Hollywood, what Dalton Trumbo called the "time of the toad" (1949). From the time of its incorporation in 1955, Bryna Productions made extensive use of blacklisted screenwriters, a practice that became more and more an open secret in other studios.[45] The Academy of Motion Picture Arts and Sciences was forced to address the issue in February 1957, when an organizational bylaw mandated that any blacklistee be ineligible for an Oscar (Smith 1989.81–82).[46] The conservative effort to maintain the appearance of compliance with the goals of HUAC was a failing one: again in 1957, "Robert Rich," a pseudonym for Dalton Trumbo, won the best screenplay award for *The Brave One*.[47] The furor caused by the award led to greater visibility for Trumbo and to greater public questioning of the red ban as a whole.[48]

In that same year, Bryna Productions began making arrangements for their film version of *Spartacus*.[49] Bryna distinguished itself in its efforts to use *Spartacus* to undermine the restrictions of McCarthyism. As

early as December of 1957, discussions at Bryna centered on the open
use of a blacklisted writer, and by March of 1958, the company had con-
tracted for a professional assessment of potential audience reaction to
Dalton Trumbo as credited screenwriter.[50] In June 1958, Kirk Douglas
met with Vice President Richard Nixon to gauge the Eisenhower administration's reaction to the public use of blacklisted professionals in
Hollywood.[51]

Production, therefore, took place in a volatile atmosphere. Despite
Bryna Productions' apparent commitment to breaking the blacklist, this
was still a very controversial issue, and powerful groups were interested
in maintaining a hard line against leftist participation in film. The American Legion, the most active, kept up pressure on the studios to hold to
the Waldorf Statement. The Legion's resistance to an easing of the
blacklist prompted Bryna to keep a close watch for signs of an imminent
hostile action against *Spartacus*. On the one hand, there were many
highly vocal opponents of Communism threatening to back up HUAC
at the box office; there were also rumors concerning a new round of congressional hearings. On the other hand, the blacklist was being publicly
denounced by a number of public figures, including Harry Truman,
under whose administration the current witch-hunts had begun (*Variety*,
8 April 1959). Universal International was in the hot-seat; the studio
would invest twelve million dollars in *Spartacus*: a production handled by
an independent film company, using a relatively unknown director, a
controversial screenwriter, and a best-selling novel that many considered
a Marxist parable. The situation was risky, to say the least, and sparked
much disagreement over how best to minimize the risk while retaining
the artistic vision.[52]

But what was the artistic vision, the "meaning" of *Spartacus*? This
too was a source of controversy. Kirk Douglas had linked the Spartacan
War to the eventual disruption of evil institutions, specifically Rome and
slavery. Dalton Trumbo, the screenwriter, largely agreed, emphasizing
both the moral quality of Spartacus's leadership and the major impact the
rebellion had on Rome (Trumbo 1991). Director Stanley Kubrick's vision differed: he wanted to explore the "real" intent of Spartacus, by
injecting some ambiguity into the motivation of the gladiators, suggesting internal conflict within the rebellion. Kubrick also felt that ideological discourse simply did not come across effectively in the primarily visual medium of cinema; meaning was transmitted better through actions
than through words, which, he felt, should be kept to a minimum.[53]
Added to the dispute was an unusually active interest on the part of

Figure 3.2 Left-pointing hand from the title sequence of *Spartacus*.

the upper echelon of Universal Studios; its head, Ed Muhl, wanted to maximize the profit-making potential of the film by downplaying "deep ideas" in order to enhance its popular appeal (Cooper 1996). The mix of all these various motivations had a tremendous influence on the production process; complete reconsiderations of the entire presentation were performed with some frequency, culminating in a final energetic bout of re-editing in the summer of 1960 just before release of the film.

The resulting project avoids the overt leftist politicization of Fast's novel by leaving the ideology of the gladiators largely unarticulated. The context of meaningful interaction is configured along domestic lines, as is consistent with the popular tradition of Spartacus. While the film version retains the familial nature of the rebel society, the ideology is dealt with only implicitly. Instead, the community of the Spartacans is emphasized using more subtle means; the rhetoric of appropriate power relations is demonstrated through action, character, and imagery. This process begins with the opening credits, which start off with a hand pointing toward the left, suggesting delicately, at most, a left-of-center orientation for the production to follow (fig. 3.2).[54]

Following the titles, the establishing scene of the narrative is devoid of almost all overt cinematic signs of Rome: we see no columned city, no baths, no banquets. Instead we see a single Roman legionary: the point of his upright spear parallels the jagged peaks of the mountains in the background and the pointed stakes of a palisade that contains a mining camp in Libya. Rome's presence in the world is thus reduced to its basic impact: containment through force. Here slaves are worked to death in a hostile and barren environment, a physical manifestation of the institution of slavery. A voice-over asserts the connection between state and domestic politics by comparing "the age of the dictator" to the dictatorial status of the slaveowner who profits from the fecundity of his female slave, Spartacus's mother. The particular is then aggrandized and universalized: Spartacus's pride and rebelliousness are characterized as the dream of the "death of slavery two thousand years before it finally would die."[55] Implicitly, his actions are no longer limited to his personal grievances, nor even to the Roman social system; rather they belong to the universal struggle for self-determination.

Spartacus begins his community-building efforts in the gladiatorial school or *ludus*, working from the moment of his arrival to establish a network of relations that does not depend on Rome. Active efforts toward this end get underway when first we see the gladiators gathered together in their subterranean barracks, after a sequence of scenes of vigorous, brutal training. Alone for the first time, the slaves engage in quiet conversation as they wash the sweat from their bodies. As in Fast's novel, the self-expression of the gladiators constitutes resistance; in hushed, furtive discussion of their suffering, they share their stories of endurance and controlled hostility to Rome. Through a grate overhead, the Roman trainer Marcellus barks out an order for quiet, an effort to suppress their interaction through enforced silence. The discussion continues quietly, as the slaves try to balance their hatred of Rome and their need to resist Rome's oppressive control with the need for self-protection. They reject overt, reckless opposition because of the risk to the group. Spartacus enters the discussion cautiously, aware of the Romans above; bending down to the gladiator Draba's level, he asks his name, thus engaging in overt community-building, establishing a group identity as a collective of individuals. Draba rejects the overture: "You don't want to know my name. I don't want to know your name." Spartacus persists, attributing a friendly quality to his question, implying that, contrary to the prevailing ideology, slaves can be agents within a social nexus of their own creation. Draba's response is that, "Gladiators don't make friends. If we're ever matched in the arena together, I'll have to kill you." The prevailing system holds that there can be no community of gladiators as long as gladiators are contained within the Roman power structure. Spartacus will defy this containment, both by making friends among his fellow gladiators as well as outside his own collective, and by claiming the capacity to choose life instead of death in the arena.

The slave girl Varinia is the first to help Spartacus create community, to join her individuality to his through the sharing of names. This occurs when a powerful effort to co-opt Spartacus into the Roman system backfires. Batiatus, the owner of the school, has disrupted the usual distribution of women to cooperative gladiators in order to divert one to Spartacus. Varinia joins Spartacus in his barren cell, and the love theme plays as the two hesitantly reach out to one another. As they discover, this intimate setting is also intended as a performance arena: Marcellus and Batiatus watch and try to direct the sexual spectacle through a ventilation grate in the ceiling. Spartacus resists their control, yelling at these spectators to go away, trying to exclude Rome from this relationship. Marcellus and Batiatus refuse in a parody of communalism, telling Spartacus that, "We must learn to share our pleasures." Spartacus lunges at the grate, lashing out at the dehumanizing treatment by asserting, over and over, that despite his confinement to this cage, he is *not* an animal. His resistance seems to awaken the political sense of Varinia; she snaps that she is not an animal either. Spartacus is clearly taken aback by her action; it may not have occurred to him, in the primarily male bastions of mine and *ludus*, that women, too, are participants in the human community. He acknowledges her claim, incorporating it into his worldview by asking her name. "Varinia," she answers, asserting an individual identity that transcends the dehumanizing process of slavery. This assertion is the foundation of the gladiatorial community on which Spartacus's freedom is predicated. Although it begins with a woman, this will be a community constructed primarily as a series of male family relationships: the gladiators become brothers, fathers, sons, and husbands.

Unification of the gladiatorial community is galvanized by the circumstances and consequences of their first combat, the fighting of pairs ordered by Crassus and his self-indulgent Roman friends. In celebration of a marriage, "a mating of eagles," the visitors insist on being presented with, "two pairs to the death. Surely you don't think we came all the way to Capua for . . . gymnastics." Overriding Batiatus's scruples about cost and the negative impact on the school's morale, Claudia and Helena, the Roman women, select "beautiful" and "impertinent" gladiators for their viewing pleasure. The combat between "beautiful" Draba and "impertinent" Spartacus promises the women relief, albeit temporarily, from the monotony of their jaded lives. When Spartacus is disarmed and pinned against the wall, Claudia and Helena turn thumbs down, then urge, "Kill him! Kill him!" increasingly stridently when Draba hesitates. Draba then chooses death, but not for Spartacus. In a doomed attempt to usurp Roman control, Draba turns his weapons against the Roman spectators. Draba's subsequent death brings the gladiators together, a merging demonstrated visually by the next scene. The camera scans down the body of Draba, suspended upside down. In the visual field on either side of the body, two lines of gladiators walk slowly toward the stairs leading down to their quarters, stairs that parallel the inverted body. The movement of the gladiators takes Draba as its focal point; the gladiators are unified in pace and in the direction of their gaze as they head toward the axis of the inverted body. The gladiators meet at Draba's body and join, never again to part.

The actual revolt is instigated by the removal of Varinia. The slave girl had caught the eye of Crassus during the deadly combat and was purchased for his own household. Varinia's departure constitutes the disruption of Spartacus's primary social bond, and Varinia's loss is exacerbated by the more stringent controls on the gladiators introduced after the death of Draba. A renewed suppression of communication further tears at the building blocks of the fledgling gladiatorial community. In contrast to the Fast novel in which a speaking Spartacus signals revolt, forced silence is the film's catalyst for the outbreak, as silent gladiators slaughter their oppressive keepers and take over the school. The primacy of the community is reiterated in the scene showing Spartacus's return to the *ludus* after the outbreak. He returns to the locations of greatest significance, visually relives the moment of unity in the barracks, retracing the coalescence of gladiators around and through Draba, then he returns to his own cell, where he first bonded with Varinia; the soundtrack's love theme plays to clarify the connection for the viewer.

Into his quiet reverie intrude the howls of the as-yet lawless gladiators, and Spartacus responds by organizing the rebels into a movement. Spartacus condemns the current efforts of the rebels to simply invert the hierarchy of power yet leave the system itself fundamentally intact. He asks them, "What are we becoming? Romans? Have we learned nothing?" Calling upon the symbol of Draba as a unifying icon, Spartacus urges the gladiators to hunt bread instead of wine, to seek the staff of life instead of the lassitude of drunkenness. This is one of the few verbal expressions of the gladiator's ideology. Here, as elsewhere, its simplicity and its lack of an explicit statement of goals and values make this a "code" rather than a doctrine, a code that emphasizes the brotherhood of the rebels, in implicit contrast to the Roman hierarchy.[56]

Varinia's role in the community makes clear that this is a "brotherhood," that male relationships are prioritized by the rebels; as in the Fast novel, Varinia does not participate in the revolt on the same level as Spartacus and the gladiators. She fights no battles, nor does she plan attacks or even arrange for supplies. Instead we see her engaged in the actions

Figure 3.3 Varinia's jug from the title sequence of *Spartacus*.

of a wife and mother. She is a tool of sociopolitical development, a receptacle for another's action: this role is emphasized by the repeated presence of her attribute, the jar, which appears in the title sequence, in her arms, and even in her environment: in one scene she stands in a field of buried *pithoi* (fig. 3.3). Varinia is a container of meaning but isolated from the ideological process; her location outside the political contest continues throughout the film.[57] She is a home-front supporter of the rebellion, providing food and comfort, even though the film develops her character as lucid, articulate, literate, more innately intelligent than Spartacus and thus as capable of political perception. Her rebellion is conducted along gendered lines and is peripheral to the battlefield struggle on which the film focuses. Varinia's resistance to Rome is couched (in all senses of the term) as an issue of love—love as loyalty to a man and, indirectly, to what he may represent ideologically.

This is clarified in the reunion scene between Varinia and Spartacus shortly after the rebellion gets underway. The importance of this scene is emphasized by its highly formalized structure: three sets of thrice-repeated statements begin with an assertion of the rights of the individual to self-determination, as, in a laughing sing-song, Spartacus and Varinia take turns reassuring each other that never again can anyone sell them, or give them away, or make them stay with anybody. The chanting pattern is broken by Varinia, who giggles, "Oh, I love you Spartacus." Her mood shifts abruptly to seriousness as she repeats her assertion three times. Spartacus answers her avowal with, "I still can't believe it," an ambiguous declaration that commands further commitment on her part. She obliges, undercutting her previous statements of independence by urging Spartacus, "Forbid me ever to leave you." Spartacus becomes serious and formally assertive; he leans forward and grasps her shoulders

Figure 3.4 Spartacus forbids Varinia to leave him. *Spartacus.*

as he declares, "I do forbid you," a proclamation of authority that he repeats three times (fig. 3.4). Thus, even in an avowedly egalitarian revolution, certain gendered notions of authority prevail; love invites submission and mastery, the "natural" hierarchy of gender relations is preserved. The seal of approval is set on their relationship through the use of a cinematic trope borrowed from the western: the two ride off into the sunset, their joined silhouette moving left across the westering sky. This scene is the first of three that foreground sexual relationships as the means of demonstrating and evaluating social models. The positioning of the Spartacus-Varinia scene in the triad privileges it, making it fulfill a normative function, establishing expectations for the audience.

The following scene between Batiatus and Gracchus, the cynical populist politician, offers a second evaluation of power relationships, domestic and political. Gracchus has offered refuge to Batiatus, who fled the uprising of the gladiators. The two commiserate over a feast, and, in the course of their discussion, we witness their verbal rejection of pair-bonding and their embrace, instead, of narcissistic hedonism based on their mutual ability to exploit female slaves, the exchange of whom, for pleasure and profit, forms the foundation of their friendship. So stark an outlook is softened by an implicit comparison to the narcissism of a child: the bodies of Ustinov and Laughton each display the chubby roundness of a toddler.[58] The two assume childish postures as well, sitting before seemingly oversized food served up by a crew of nurturing, smiling women (fig. 3.5). Gracchus claims to have embraced the Roman value system, paradoxically, by avoiding the foundation of Roman ethics: marriage and the family.[59] He then proceeds to devalue the system in its entirety, claiming a causal link between Roman morality and virtue and "stealing two-thirds of the world from its rightful own-

Figure 3.5 Gracchus and Batiatus commiserate. *Spartacus.*

Figure 3.6 Crassus and Antoninus in the bath. *Spartacus.*

ers," between aristocratic promiscuity and political rapacity and the lip service the Romans pay to marriage and family. In the facile sophistry of a Roman intellectual, Gracchus casts aside such inherently warped behavioral systems, claiming he does so as "the most virtuous man in Rome."

The next scene, the last of the trio, takes place at patrician Crassus's palatial home. A slave, Antoninus, Crassus's new body servant, is active with towel and sponge; the camera parts the veil of the bath as the viewer witnesses an intimate moment for master and slave (fig. 3.6).[60] Crassus quizzes his servant as Antoninus helps him wash, towel dry, and dress. More so even than in the earlier two scenes, here we have social dictates presented in the form of a dialogue; in a series of highly directed yes-no responses, Antoninus participates in the development of a Roman ethical catalog. Clearly immoral are the vices of theft, dishonesty, and impiety. Antoninus is then coached by Crassus to assign morally neutral status to the eating of snails and oysters, here coded references to sex; these are matters of taste, not appetite, and thus their assignation to an ethical category is inappropriate.[61] From this Crassus moves to more overt forms of aggression against his slave. Crassus leads Antoninus to a balcony, commanding him to look at Rome's garrison marching to crush slave resistance, to see, from Crassus's boudoir, "the might, the majesty, the terror of Rome . . . No man can withstand Rome, no nation can withstand her—how much less a boy, hm?" He thus dictates a linkage between himself as domineering partner and Rome's capacity to dominate the world: what Rome is in public, Crassus is in private. Crassus adds to his catalog of ethics a definition of love, as demonstrated daily by the proper response to Rome: to love Rome, "you must serve her, you must abase yourself before her, you must grovel at her feet." As an analogue of Rome, Crassus expects the same treatment, the serving, the abasing, the groveling, in his personal relationships.[62]

This overt demonstration of unequal power relations does not by itself invalidate this part of the triad; controller and controllee are just as clearly marked in the exchange between Spartacus and Varinia. The transgressive nature of the relationship lies in elision of difference, an elision that is a marker of disorder. Crassus does not distinguish between genders in his couplings, he refuses to categorize desire in a system of ethics, and he identifies himself with Rome, which he repeatedly refers to with female pronouns. The permeability of gender roles and the negation of ethical categories are points of inversion when compared to the ideals and practices of the rebel community.

Spartacus also uses the natural landscape to distance the rebels from Roman city dwellers and to elide the imagery of communalism with the quintessentially American symbology of the western. Throughout the film, long shots of western landscape are taken from a raised perspective, a type of cinematic visual that has been characterized as the "master of all I survey" image (Wexman 1993.78–81, Wood 1977). From this point of view, the landscape appears as territory discovered and claimed in the same action. In westerns, the protagonist shares the viewpoint with the camera, thus becoming the proprietor of the vast and empty wilderness; his gaze/ownership gives it meaning and purpose, connecting it to "civilization" understood as the site of the homestead and the home base for the patriarchal family structure. The landscape also offers scope for expansion, the *Lebensraum* necessary for progress. By using this visual language, *Spartacus* extends dominion over territory depicted as an analogue to the American frontier, expressing a perspective that is distanced from the land subject to ownership and control.

Figure 3.7 Burying a baby. *Spartacus.*

At the same time, cinematic technique encourages the viewer to identify the gladiators *with* nature; truly salt of the earth, they live in man's original state. Establishing long shots of landscape that close in to reveal the rebels within make the rebels seem part of nature. This pattern is initiated after the first organizational meeting of the rebels with a long shot of the hills surrounding Vesuvius. In the center of the visual field, the gladiator army swarms over these hills, erupting out of nature. In the rebel camp, the mounted gladiators follow the lines of landscape, a surging flow along the gullies of the outstretched plains. A Copland-esque soundtrack is laid over the image of the gladiators. The connection is also given verbal form. As the gladiators sit around a campfire at day's end, their new volunteer, Antoninus, composes a song conflating the glories of the natural world—sunset, mountains, sea, and meadow—with the gladiators' sense of home and family. As the song has it, "I turn home. Through blue shadow and purple woods. I turn home. I turn to the place that I was born. To the mother who bore me and the father who taught me. Long ago, long ago, long ago."[63] It is thus in connection with the landscape that the rebels reconstruct their original, primal community. The rebel movement builds as the gladiators move through the landscape. Silent vignettes show family groups among the rebels, families dominated by adult males, who carry children, assist the elderly, and are wracked with pain over the burial of an infant, returning its tiny body to the earth/mother who bore them all (fig. 3.7). The growth of the army is thus paralleled by the growth of the family unit; the rebels reach Brundisium swollen in number, swollen like Varinia's pregnant body, and bristling with weaponry.

The gladiators' connection to the earth is reinforced by pairs of posed shots that shift repeatedly between Rome and the rebel camp out-

Figure 3.8 Spartacus's pre-battle speech to the rebels. *Spartacus.*

side Brundisium before the final battle. The massed forces of the gladiator army dissolve into landscape (fig. 3.8). In simple phrases, Spartacus verbalizes the "code" of the gladiatorial community: their essential brotherhood, their shared life experience, and the essential value of labor, all set in opposition to Rome's exploitative system. The imagery reiterates his message: as they listen to Spartacus, the rebels merge with each other, with hill and sea; the use of a soft focus blurring the boundaries between them.

This is intercut with, and thus explicitly contrasted to, the recreation of the Roman regime that surrounds Crassus's pre-battle speech. Amid pure white classical architecture, a prestigious emblem of elitism, Crassus dictates the "New Order" to a regimented assembly of legionaries and, in the background, a gaggle of senators (fig. 3.9). Crassus promises, "the destruction of the slave army [and] the living body of Spartacus for whatever punishment you may deem fit," swearing by his dead ancestors in the temple of their bones. These repeated references to death and destruction are fundamental to Crassus's concept of order, based on the "cleansing" of Rome and the return to tradition that he vows throughout the film. The "people" and nature and life have been purged from Rome by Crassus's "cleansing" suppression of Gracchus; populists are conflated with Spartacans in Crassus's roundups of the "rabble" and his McCarthyesque compilations of "lists of the disloyal."

The visual presentation of the battle's aftermath is configured using these primary themes, presenting the family of rebellious gladiators as a natural community. The overview of the battlefield transposes humans into nature, as the seamless movement of the camera transforms heaped masses of undifferentiated dead into the blue shadows and purple woods of Antoninus's song. Touched by twilight, the slaughtered rebels have

Figure 3.9 Crassus's pre-battle speech to the Romans. *Spartacus.*

Figure 3.10 Rebel dead as part of the natural world. *Spartacus.*

come "home" (fig. 3.10). The surviving gladiators, when asked to betray Spartacus to save their individual lives, respond by affirming their group loyalty. Just as the community began by sharing names and identities, so does the movement triumph over defeat as, one after another, each stands to declare, "I am Spartacus!" The movement has thus come full circle, as now they share a single identity, a single name: Spartacus. The collective identity transcends the individual. The final combat, ordered, like the first, by Crassus, confirms the affective, familial bonds of the Spartacan community. The last surviving rebels, Spartacus and Antoninus, have been saved from crucifixion by Crassus until the gates of Rome. In rage and frustration at their silent resistance to him, he demands a duel to the death as "a test of this myth of slave brotherhood." The combat between Spartacus and Antoninus validates the relationship: this is no "myth" but rather a revealed truth. As Antoninus dies in Spartacus's arms, the two affirm their familial love, the father-son relationship constructed within the community (fig. 3.11). Spartacus's final words claim that the

Figure 3.11 Antoninus and Spartacus as father and son. *Spartacus.*

establishment of this bond, independent of Rome and based on deeper truths beyond Roman understanding, constitutes the real victory of the rebels. Spartacus rejects the death of Antoninus, declaring in a voice made rough by the intensity of his emotion: "He'll come back. He'll come back and he'll be millions." The final scene points to this future freedom as well. Varinia tells a dying Spartacus that his son will know his dream, will know his father, and thus will know a freedom profoundly shaped by the experience of the rebel community. Upon this goal, it is implied, Varinia will focus her entire existence; her love and her life, which began with Spartacus, will die with Spartacus. The film ends on an unsettling note.

Projecting *Spartacus* was a challenge in the highly charged anti-Communist atmosphere of the 1950s. *Spartacus* needed to retain an inspirational quality as a symbol of the eternal human capacity for self-determination, yet it could not blatantly call for the unification of the working class in revolution. By downplaying the explicit political rhetoric of Spartacus's rebellion, his revolution can be viewed as one that is at heart conservative in its ordering of society into traditional family units. And indeed, the strong interest in the private side of the public man has been shared by popular representations of Spartacus since the eighteenth century.[64] *Spartacus* is a complex film, however, and the lack of resolution in the ending distinguishes it from earlier treatments of the story. Destruction of the family had previously been presented as a reflection or even as a cause of the crushing of the rebels' political dreams. But, in the film, Varinia and her son survive, to be escorted to a new home by the newly protective, even fatherly, Batiatus. *Spartacus* presents an ambiguous version of the "age-old fight for freedom," one in which hope and resistance coalesce in the crucifixion of the father and the flight of the son. The grim resolution of the final scene is only partially offset by the verbal references to future freedom. It is an uneasy reconciliation, appropriate perhaps to a film mired in controversy and vicious dispute throughout its production, a film that went on, nevertheless, to be the major box office success for 1960.

Notes

1. Margulies 1960, frontispiece by Howard Fast quoted here, illustrations by Tom Van Sant. On press books and epic film see Sobchack 1990.24–49.

2. Events of the Spartacan War were recorded by a number of ancient authors, including Livy *Summaries* 95–97, Sallust *Histories* 4.20–41, Florus *Abridgement of All the Wars Over 1200 Years* 2.8, Eutropius *Digest* 6.7, Frontinus *Stratagems* 2.5.34, Appian *Civil Wars* 1.9.116–20, Plutarch *Crassus* 8–11, and Diodorus Siculus *Library* 39.21. The secondary bibliography on this subject is quite large. Bradley 1989 offers an overview; see also Vogt 1974. On Roman slavery see Bradley 1994 and Dumont 1987.

3. The two major works on the theme of Spartacus are those of Müller 1905 and Muszkat-Muszkowski 1909, with a shorter piece by Olivova 1980.89–99, who offers insight into Spartacus's influence on the Czech novel. Wyke 1997b.34–72 also presents an intriguing overview of the popular treatment of Spartacus. Extremely useful on the reworking of the theme of classical slave uprisings is Rubinsohn 1993; less so is Stanev 1981.95–101.

4. Diderot and Voltaire are representative of the revised view of Spartacus. The article on slavery in Diderot's *Encyclopedia* refers to "natural law," asserting that all men were born free. Diderot goes on to undermine the achievements of classical civilization as a whole because they were all predicated on this ancient injustice. He draws a connection between the slave wars and Rome's decline, claiming that Rome's own inhumanity to slaves would rebound to shake the empire to its foundations. Spartacus's efforts are thus justified; Diderot characterized Spartacus as a man of courage and skill, facing adversity without flinching, whose army was prepared to sacrifice everything for the sake of freedom. See Diderot 1779–82.12.959–67. Voltaire's emphasis on the meaning of history for all men at all times laid the groundwork for a new focus on the slave rebellions of antiquity, to which he himself gave legitimacy; he articulated the moral worth of the Spartacus uprising in particular, as the most justified, if not the only justified, war in history. See Voltaire 1974.118.389 (letter # D15572).

5. By the end of 1760, Saurin was invited to become a member of the Académie Française, joining the ranks of the *philosophe* dramaturges. Even so, today his work receives little attention. A brief assessment of Saurin can be found in Truchet 1974.2.1405–11; see also Stanev 1981.99–100, Rubinsohn 1993.30–31, Muszkat-Muszkowski 1909.19–24, Olivova 1980.90.

6. An example of this conflation can be found in *Spartacus*, II sc. ii, p. 94:

"Ma mère, les Romains, et ma haine et ma flamme, tout combat à la fois, tout déchire mon coeur" (My mother and the Romans, both my hatred and my passion, every battle at the same time, it all tears at my heart).

7. The linkage between domesticity and universal freedom is made earlier by Spartacus's mother, whose dying words include a request that he avenge his mother by liberating the world (Saurin 1821, I sc. iii, p. 84).

8. Both sides accuse the other of "barbarism"; the label seems to stick more securely to the Romans, as Saurin is careful to emphasize Roman brutality. See, for example, Spartacus's elaboration of the term at III sc. iv, pp. 103–05, V sc. xii, p.133, and Crassus's use of it, V sc. xiii, p. 134.

9. Émilie's argument is lucid and convincing, against which Spartacus sighs and suffers and stubbornly insists on holding the course. Indeed, for all of Spartacus's vaunted heroism and leadership, Émilie is fully his equal in the strength of her convictions and her devotion to father, fatherland, and lover.

10. Only Lessing's notes survive to suggest his intentions for the unfinished work. Lessing's brief comments point to the political focus of the work, as the representation of a last, desperate battle against tyranny by men who were plain and simple and yet, or perhaps because of this, extraordinary human beings, Spartacus pre-eminent among them. Spartacus fights for the equality of all mankind, undermining Roman claims to political achievement through pointed speeches and questions aimed at the relatively inarticulate Roman characters. See Batley 1990. The text of the Spartacus material can be found in Lessing 1970.2.574–77, 788–89. Comments in Olivova 1980.90–92 and Muszkat-Muszkowski 1909. 13–53.

11. For a general non-specialist treatment of Grillparzer's life and work, see Thompson 1981. The text of the play can be found in Grillparzer 1892.11. 127–56. This play is rarely analyzed as part of the Grillparzer corpus or even as part of his "classical" group of works. Part of the reason for this neglect may be *Spartakus*'s incompleteness and the fact that it was not published during its author's lifetime.

12. Grillparzer 1892.155: ". . . was andern Tugend ist, all uns Verbrechen! Vaterlandes, Freundesliebe, die Rom am Römer lohnt mit Ehrensäulen, es wird gestraft am Gladiator. O, wann wird ein Retter kommen unserm Unglück!" (What is to others a virtue is for us a crime! Fatherland, love of friends, that for which Rome rewards Romans with a commemorative monument is a punishable offense for the gladiator. Oh, when will a savior come for our misfortune!).

13. Like Saurin's Émilie, Grillparzer's Cornelia is an apocryphal love interest. The wandering poet is seen best in Grillparzer 1892.139.

14. Olivova 1980.95 notes that, ten years later, Grillparzer did go back to the theme of Roman history, but he concentrated then on Crassus, the man who crushed the slave uprising.

15. *The Gladiator* set new records for production; by 1854, it had been performed over one thousand times by the noted actor Edwin Forrest alone. The

role of Spartacus became Forrest's signature piece. See Bird 1919, commentary by Foust, pp. 28–49, text of play, pp. 297–440. See also Dahl 1963.56–61 on *The Gladiator*. Bird is today perhaps best remembered for his later novel, *Nick of the Woods* (1837), a major effort in the construction of the frontier/expansion *topos* within American literature.

16. Comments on the first performance of September 26, 1831. Quoted in Foust 1919.42. Bird himself likewise described an "American" feeling in the packed house at the Philadelphia opening of the play on October 24, what with the American performers, American author, and American play. See Harris 1959 passim.

17. Spartacus's humble origins may likewise have struck a chord as an ancient analogue to Andrew Jackson, then president of the United States, whose public image played upon his frontier background and upon his rise to leadership from rustic obscurity. See McConachie 1992.97–104. Maria Wyke 1997b.56–60 points to *The Gladiator*'s meaning for contemporary class conflict: the tension between public personae, like Forrest and Jackson, identified with a working or frontier non-elite, and the established, moneyed class.

18. See, importantly, Bücher 1874.114–15, who suggests that Roman slave wars were evidence for social movements in antiquity, perhaps aiming at some form of socialism.

19. Industrial oppression is likewise read into the so-called toga plays of this period in which the long-suffering, persecuted Christians, as members of a class, are encoded as victims of bourgeois exploitation. See Mayer 1994.10–11, 13.

20. Marx's enthusiasm, originally generated by reading Appian for relaxation, still lingered with him four years later when filling out a list of likes and dislikes for his daughters Jenny and Laura in which he says his personal heroes are Spartacus and Johannes Keppler. See "Confession" of 1 April 1875, Marx 1975.42.567–78.

21. See comments of Rubinsohn 1993.57–58.

22. Ward 1888.2.90 claims these are "more dignified" labels for what is, really, the same thing. In the case of Spartacus, Ward interprets legislation against *collegia* of 58 B.C.E. as the last in a long line of union-busting efforts on the part of the Romans. His treatment of the Spartacus rebellion is in 1.235–94, with specific attention to the labor/*collegia* identification on pp. 243–45, 252.

23. Spartacus is portrayed as an emancipator, complete with proclamation, in Ward 1888.1.257, 264, 291. Spartacus is presented as the leader of some sort of labor coalition on p. 279.

24. The classic Luxemburg biography is Nettl 1966. Her favored status as a martyred female socialist activist has produced numerous brief, popular summaries of her life, including Abraham 1989. For Liebknecht see Trotnow 1980.

25. *Die Krise der Sozialdemokratie*, a.k.a. the *Junius Pamphlet*, can be found in Luxemburg 1974.4.62. The *Junius Pamphlet* has repeated references throughout to imperialism as barbarism.

26. From "Trotz Alledem!" an article that originally appeared in *Die Rote Fahne*, the paper of the Spartakusbund, collected in Liebknecht 1968.9.678–79.

27. Fast resigned from the Communist Party in 1957 in a very public fashion, giving numerous interviews and writing a number of papers explaining his dissatisfaction with the Party. The lengthiest of these was published in book form as *The Naked God: The Writer and the Communist Party* (1957). The territory was explored again more recently in his autobiography (Fast 1990), in which he traces his career and personal life as intimately connected to his politics. Skepticism over Fast's motivations in 1957 and the role played by self-interest therein is expressed by Meyer 1958. Murolo 1984.22–31, esp. 23, also points to the advantages accrued by Fast's public "rehabilitation" following his public departure from Communism. The caliber of the leftist sympathies in his pre-1957 work comes under scrutiny in Wald 1992.

28. Daniel Traister 1995.530 notes that "it would be . . . difficult to overestimate the effect of such [leftist political] commitments upon his work as a writer of imaginative fictions." See also MacDonald 1996.2–3, 6. This is acknowledged by Fast 1950, when he draws connections between his own public and artistic stance. Fast's articulation of political theory in fiction would draw fire from the left, however, due to its relative lack of sophistication and its clear subordination to plotline.

29. Fast 1990.65. The friend in question was Sarah Kunitz. This is noted as a "watershed event" by MacDonald 1996.12.

30. He claims this in various essays about his work as well, including Fast 1944.7–9, where he refers to stories of "great and splendid forgotten men" being "traduced and falsified" by "scoundrels." The theme of suppression and revisionism in history recurs in his novels; for examples in *Spartacus* see 1951.9, 150, 333.

31. At issue was Fast's participation in channeling funds for leftist groups in Spain resisting Franco.

32. Fast 1990.275–76. Fast claims he decided not to write on Luxemburg because the Holocaust was too recent; presumably Germany's earlier silencing of Luxemburg, who was born to a Jewish family in Poland, might prove too sensitive a focus for popular historical fiction. See below, however, for Fast's dichotomized treatment of women in *Spartacus*.

33. This goal is specified by the inscription on the flyleaf of Fast's own copy of *The Ancient Lowly*, written by Hy Gordon, one of the workshop leaders. See Fast 1990.276; the training school is described on pp. 136–38.

34. Fast 1951.215, 284. Fast does put a certain amount of economic theorizing into the mouths of his characters, but the thrust of the didactic value of the work is Fast's connection of Roman symbols, characters, and landscape with politico-economic evil. Nevertheless, the work was perceived as Marxist "polemics" in Melville Heath's review of the novel in the *New York Times*, 3 February 1952.22.

35. Fast 1951.250 lists the escalating "benefits" of Roman "civilization": crucifixion, the plantation system, gladiatorial combat, contempt for human life, and the hunger to derive profit from the blood and sweat of the underclass.

36. They also have "bad sex," which is, perhaps, a more obvious symbol of Roman decadence. Caius, a young elite male (non-historical) character, is one of the chief practitioners of Roman corruption in this regard; interestingly, his corruption comes in paired loci of disruption, either food-and-sex (1951.40, 47) or sex-and-death (1951.5, 96–98).

37. Fast 1951.304–06. Cicero is arguably the most irredeemably negative character in the novel, a treatment that may be anchored in Ward's assessment of Cicero as "the most terrible enemy of the working classes" (Ward 1888.1.244).

38. Although Gracchus does refer to the nobility, wisdom, and greatness of the senate, it is in a passage laden with irony: Fast 1951.187.

39. The Capuan perfume factory episode provides one of the clearest connections between Fast's novel and Ward 1888.1.252. Indeed, Ward claims that the presence of such factories is prime evidence for his reconstruction of the existence of ancient trade unions and concomitant Roman union-busting. His reasoning is as follows: there was a huge demand for perfume, ergo the industry in Capua must have been huge, to supply it. There must therefore have been large numbers of laborers, who must have organized into groups or *collegia* specifically to improve their working conditions, leading to the known historical event of Roman legislation against *collegia* by the *senatusconsultum* of 64 B.C.E., for which see Cicero *Against Piso* 8.

40. Varinia is always referred to as Spartacus's "wife"; see Fast 1951.109, 163, 336. "Motherhood" is her "beauty," a constant quality expressed by Varinia as an ethical stance: 1951.350, 361.

41. The nature of the attraction is never clarified directly, but it is associated with Gracchus's recognition that here is a "real" woman, a woman who is not less than a human being, unlike the corrupted women of Rome.

42. Indeed, Fast repeatedly conflates Crassus's desire for Varinia with his desire for domination; see, for example, 1951.333 and 346, where Varinia appears as a prefiguration of Cleopatra.

43. The affinity between sexual conquest and imperial control plays a relatively small role in the politics of Fast's *Spartacus*. Beyond Crassus's desire for Varinia, it crops up only once, during Cicero's "conquest" of Helena. Midway through his physical possession of her, Cicero suddenly perceives himself as the embodiment of Roman territorial acquisition and the humbling of Spartacus. The metaphor is immediately undermined when the external viewpoint of the narrator intrudes to particularize the feeling as, on the one hand, Cicero's hatred and cruelty, and, on the other, Helena's fear and self-loathing. The episode thus becomes an example of Roman corruption in the distortion of human intimacy.

44. Douglas was also committed to the "love story" of Spartacus: the connection between the rebel gladiator and Varinia. Tony Curtis claimed this focus

on romance was a major cause of disagreement during the filming of *Spartacus* and a key element in the dismissal of Anthony Mann as director. While the love story as a major plotline is typical in Hollywood cinema, one should not disregard the strong transformative quality of Varinia's love in the Fast novel. For dominance of the love story in Hollywood cinema, see Wexman 1993.3–16 and Bordwell, Staiger, and Thompson 1985.5, 16–17; both affirm that some 85% of classical Hollywood films present a heterosexual romantic relationship as the chief plot line.

45. Sam Norton, at the time the consulting lawyer for Bryna, advised that this practice made good economic sense in that Bryna could thus gain access to known talent at a discount. Apparently Bryna took him at his word; personnel records document that in March of 1959, *only* blacklistees were employed as screenwriters by Bryna. See Smith 1989.84.

46. The Academy's effort had been galvanized by the concern that *Friendly Persuasion* might win a screenplay Oscar for blacklistee Michael Wilson; this despite the fact that Wilson had written his draft of the screenplay in 1946, before the issuance of the Waldorf Statement banning the employment of Communists by the major studios.

47. The relative obscurity of *The Brave One* has led some to suggest that knowledge of Trumbo's involvement was in fact key to the decision of the voting members of the Academy and that the award was intended to be a statement of support for blacklistees, opening the door to the removal of any constraints on their employment in Hollywood. See Smith 1989.83.

48. Trumbo, as early as April 3, 1957 (following the Academy Awards presentation on March 27), was called upon by *Variety* for comment. On May 4, an article by Trumbo appeared in *The Nation* discussing the permeability of the ban and the creation of a black market for blacklisted talent in Hollywood.

49. Another Spartacus movie based on the Arthur Koestler novel, *The Gladiators*, starring Anthony Quinn and Yul Brynner, was underway at United Artists at the same time. Spurred by the spirit of competition, Douglas and his group sped up their production process and successfully wooed a trio of acclaimed British actors (Olivier, Ustinov, and Laughton) to commit to the Bryna film, with the result that the UA project was abandoned. See Douglas 1988.304–13. Interestingly, the UA project also involved blacklistees in its formative stages: the script was to be written by Abe Polonsky, who had perhaps the strongest background in labor activism and the Communist Party of all the initial victims of the Waldorf Statement. See Ceplair and Englund 1979.191–92.

50. Documentation of Bryna's activism comes primarily from Dalton Trumbo. Note especially a letter from him, dated March 30, 1958, on how Bryna Productions was developing ways of crediting Trumbo openly for his work as screenwriter, a development taking place with the full knowledge of Lew Wasserman, head of MCA. This letter refers as well to Bryna's use of a public relations firm to explore public reaction to this. See Manfull 1970.414–17.

51. A letter of Trumbo to Edward Lewis, dated May 31, 1958, acknowledges his preparation of supplementary information for Douglas to use at this meeting: see Manfull 1970.424–25. This whole process goes unacknowledged by Douglas in his autobiography. Instead, he presents *Spartacus*'s breaking of the blacklist as a spontaneous action, motivated chiefly by his own revulsion at Stanley Kubrick's egomaniacal eagerness to take credit for Trumbo's creative efforts. In disgust, Douglas issued a studio pass to Trumbo, legitimizing his presence on the set of *Spartacus*. The breaking of the blacklist in this reconstruction thus becomes an act of personal integrity. Douglas, perhaps disingenuously, disclaims any notion of the significance of his decision, let alone any idea of heroism at the time. See Douglas 1988.322–24.

52. Duncan Cooper emphasizes the cautious attitude of UA studio personnel concerning the political content of the film, alleging that they were particularly motivated to remove scenes of military success by the slave army, in order to keep "this film's explosive historical content . . . within the confines of the implicitly established . . . limits of acceptable political discourse" (Cooper 1996).

53. In this he may have been in basic agreement with Douglas, who rejected Howard Fast's original script because of its "talking heads" sort of style, its emphasis on speech-making at the expense of drama. See Douglas 1988.307. Trumbo profoundly disagreed with Kubrick's approach in this case, suspecting him of inciting disagreement on the set in order to impose his vision and thus decrease the ideological content of the film. Entering this fray were the different visions of the major actors, particularly Ustinov, who rewrote all of his scenes with Charles Laughton. The result was to emphasize an often inappropriate comedic element and detract from the overall narrative. Peter Ustinov 1977.301–02 claims he was ordered by "management" to soothe Laughton's sulks and competitiveness toward Olivier by doing these rewrites. There is a critique of Ustinov in Trumbo 1991.33. Olivier, who was initially interested in playing the title character, perceived Spartacus as a man with a divine aura, as a patriarch/father figure among the slaves, based on his reading of the novel. Douglas says this interpretation of the character was completely different from his own; Douglas thought Spartacus was transformed by the rebellion, starting out as an illiterate animal, then reacting against his circumstances, and finally beginning to shape his own circumstances to conform with a self-generated ideology. This capacity to drive and to affect others Douglas saw as key to Spartacus as a leader (1988.310).

54. One could see this approach as characteristic of the epic film as a genre, in which signal events of the human past are explained through the actions of individuals, especially the romantic actions. See Babington and Evans 1993.12. Title credits for *Spartacus* were designed by Saul Bass.

55. The prologue was composed and inserted in post-production as part of the controversial, late re-editing.

56. Analogous to the code given laconic expression by heroes in western

genre films; see Wright 1974. Zaniello 1996.226–27 finds here and elsewhere in the film the representation of an idealized labor union.

57. The deliberate isolation of Varinia was planned in preproduction: the original casting in the part of Sabina Bethmann, a German actress, was meant to distinguish her by accent from all other characters, to set her apart as an anomaly. See Douglas 1988.314. For the trope of good women and their jars see Babington and Evans 1993.188–89.

58. Both actors had previously played the role of the quintessential ancient narcissist: the emperor Nero. Laughton was Nero in *The Sign of the Cross* (1932) and Ustinov won a Golden Globe (and was nominated for an Oscar) for his Nero in *Quo Vadis* (1951). For Nero as a cultural icon see Elsner and Masters 1994.

59. It may be that the infantilism in imagery is reflected by Gracchus's ethico-political stance, his rejection of adult responsibilities in favor of a childish egocentrism.

60. This is the notorious snails-and-oysters scene, cut in the very last re-editing immediately prior to release and restored in 1990. The charged content of the scene was an open secret in film circles even prior to its restoration, providing food for commentary by Russo 1987.119–22, Hark 1993.166–67, Babington and Evans 1993.190, and Elley 1984.111. For Douglas's pre-restoration commentary see 1988.319–322, in which he characterizes this as a "gentle, ironic inquisition" and "just another way Romans abused the slaves." Kubrick essentially agrees: in crafting the restoration of the film in 1990, he describes the scene as a parody of Socratic dialogue. See the text of a fax from Kubrick, quoted by Robert Harris in Cooper and Crowdus 1991.28–29.

61. Are theft, dishonesty, and impiety, then, matters of appetite? Antoninus clearly recognizes the manipulation of semantic meanings by Crassus, with his cautious, "It could be argued so, master."

62. Douglas acknowledges that when Crassus is talking about Roman power, "he is speaking of himself" (1988.322). The scene ends with another triplet; Crassus requests confirmation of these truths from his slave, but his three repetitions of "Antoninus?" are left unanswered.

63. More or less explicit references to the Song of Antoninus, as a sort of anthem for the movement, are made by Varinia in her bath scene and in the final assessment of the rebellion by Spartacus and Antoninus outside the gates of Rome, where Spartacus says that the rebels' victory was located in their capacity to "storm the mountains, shouting . . . [to] sing along the plains."

64. By foregrounding the family as a fundamental unit of the gladiatorial collective, the makers of *Spartacus* participated in the prevalent presentation of the family in Hollywood as antithetical to Communism. See discussion of *My Son John* in Whitfield 1991.136–40.

I, Claudius

Projection and Imperial Soap Opera

Sandra R. Joshel

Based on Robert Graves's best-selling novels about dirty work in ancient Rome, the Mobil-funded PBS series lavishly depicts the orgiastic society of the all-powerful Claudians, the family whose business was ruling the world.—*Masterpiece Theatre Promotional Material*

The material wealth portrayed is hard for the British actor to understand because we're a poor country now. Of course there are great differences, but America is the only place you could relate ancient Rome to.—*Brian Blessed (Augustus)*, New York Post, *4 November 1977*

Through the 1960s, Hollywood films like *Quo Vadis, Spartacus, Ben-Hur*, and *Cleopatra* nourished popular sensibilities about ancient Roman corruption and decadence (Wyke 1997b). As Peter Bondanella observes, imperial Rome offered opportunities for spectacular lessons on the "perils of overreaching power" and for cinematic exploitation of an "ever present prurient interest in Roman decadence and in corruption produced by supreme power and unbridled sensuality" (1987.210). It might be more correct to say that Hollywood shaped American prurience from 1925 through 1978. In the Rome of the emperors, directors found and produced extremes of imperial dimensions: political power, material life, and sexuality. Hollywood films offered a recurrent vision of Roman history: ancient Romans were tyrants or lived under them, consumed lavishly, and indulged in excessive and often deviant sexual activities (Winkler, Fitzgerald, and Futrell in this volume).

In the last twenty years, however, the more widely viewed experience of the Roman empire has come from television: the BBC production *I, Claudius*, a thirteen-part serial based on Robert Graves's novels, *I, Claudius* and *Claudius the God*, originally broadcast in the United States on PBS in 1977–78.[1] As an offering of Mobil Masterpiece Theatre, *I, Claudius* had the aura of an elite cultural event, a status furthered by its British theatrical style. Yet *TV Guide*, reaching a popular audience, urged viewers potentially "intimidated by the prospect of keeping all those emperors straight" not to miss the program: "One episode should get you sufficiently hooked that you will look out for the series's eventual rerun" (MacKenzie 1977).[2]

The serial's producers and reviewers in the print media assured every viewer of a picture of "dirty work in ancient Rome"—what *TV Guide* called "the palace intrigues, power struggles, murders, and debaucheries that were common in Rome's ruling class" ("Close Up," 6 November 1977). Above all, ads and reviews sounded the long-familiar note of the "fall of Rome": "the political and personal intrigue, corruption, and lust that toppled the glory of vainglorious Rome will unfold on Masterpiece Theatre" (Brown 1977, Promotional Material, hereafter PM).

Television, however, altered the cinematic spectacle of Roman imperial power and corruption. In film, the spectacle is externalized, fully staged in elaborate, often monumental, sets, peopled by vast crowds, and accompanied by special effects. On television in *I, Claudius*, the family becomes the spectacle. The advertised topic of the series, "the family whose business was ruling the world," promises to reveal the workings of empire through a domestic drama: the "dirty work" of ancient Rome is done by its ruling family. The limits of budget and of the television screen turn the Hollywood signifiers of imperial Rome (armies on the march, gladiatorial games, fantastical debauches) into what are largely a series of gestures, most of which translate the spectacular into familial scenes or contain it within domestic space.[3] So, for example, scenes at the gladiatorial games focus exclusively on the imperial family in their box relishing the violent struggle of imaginary gladiators to the roar of a Roman mob whose presence is suggested by sound effects. Any fully realized spectacles take place in the enclosed space of palace rooms or gardens: a sex party attended by an emperor's daughter, a drunken celebration put on by an imperial wife, or a brothel set up in the palace by the emperor himself. For the rest, the television audience watches some acts of violent murder and, most often, characters conversing, exchanging confidences, and making speeches. The spectacle of *I, Claudius* consists primarily of sex and talk—with a dose of dastardly deaths.

Television's translation and containment of cinema's Roman spectacle belong to a larger process of domestication. To domesticate an element of nature is to convert it from a natural state and adapt it to human use. The domesticated object is brought under human control: domestication is taming. With fire, for example, domestication involves bringing something from the outside into the home. As a part of the household's everyday life, it becomes familiar. Losing control of what is brought in, however, poses the danger that the foreign object will destroy the household from within. Fire, confined to the hearth, can be used for cooking and heating, but if it is left untended or mishandled, it can destroy the house and injure its inhabitants. Playing with these notions of adaptation, taming, and bringing the outside inside, I argue that television domesticates both Graves's novels and empire itself so as to project empire and its disintegration onto the family. Women, often regarded as both intimate family members and "outsiders," have a key role to play in a narrative of familial and imperial disorder (cf. Parker 1998.154–55). This representation of empire arrived at a moment of imperial crisis in the United States. Contemporary politics colluded with a medium that mixes past and present, fiction and fact, to create the conditions for a disturbing allegorical reading of *I, Claudius* that makes family a metonymy for empire. Domestication offered American television viewers many pleasures, but it also brought them dangerously close to their own social and imperial troubles. But even as the Romans were perceived as familiar, counter responses allowed audiences in the United States to distance themselves from the "bad" empire of imperial Rome.

On the ground laid by film, mass cultural forms like the soap opera and the pretensions of high culture associated with Masterpiece Theatre work together and constitute this reading formation of *I, Claudius*. PBS's promotional material and reviews in the print media exemplify aspects of this reading formation, for they themselves respond to the program even as they guide its audience. Although the figure of Claudius and the picture of empire are central concerns, neither the real Claudius, emperor from 41 to 54 C.E., nor his depiction in the ancient Roman sources receive detailed analysis here. Claudius and Rome are examined as sites of projection of the present onto the past, of one empire onto another, and of empire onto family. At issue are Graves's particular readings of the Roman sources through the dissolution of the British empire and then television's reading of Graves and the reception of this televisual Rome

in the United States at a moment of social and imperial crisis. I begin
with a brief discussion of Graves's novels in the context of post–World
War I Britain, to highlight the process of projection that produces the
raw material for a televisual Rome and to indicate those elements adapted
and those abandoned by television.

History and Projection: From Popular Novel to Television

Graves's novels, *I, Claudius* and *Claudius the God* (first published
in May and November 1934), recount the reigns of the first four emperors of Rome. Narrated by the emperor Claudius, the story purports to
be a "confidential history" inspired by the sibyl who predicts that
Claudius's voice will be heard 1900 years or so in the future. Although
working from ancient Roman sources that depict the emperor as a pedant
and a fool, ignorant of the activities of his wives and freedmen or manipulated by them, Graves turns Claudius into a learned man, a reform-
ing emperor, and, above all, an individual of deep moral conviction, devoted to his "friends, to Rome, and to the truth" (Graves 1989b.190).[4]
His account of the lethal convolutions of power within the imperial
household illustrates the difficulties of taking action for a good man like
Claudius, since good men, including his grandfather, father, and brother,
are destroyed. In a corrupt world, Graves's Claudius wavers between resigned cynicism and impossible idealism. Before his accession to the
throne, he stutters and limps, playing the fool to survive. Yet he believes
in the end of the principate (the rule of an emperor) and the restoration
of the republic (the rule of the senate and the people). Thus, when
Claudius becomes emperor, he strives to rule well, but plans to resign
and restore republican government.

Claudius's republicanism is a futile dream in what is depicted as the
tyranny of the principate.[5] Claudius himself realizes that, as a good
prince, he has "dull[ed] the blade of tyranny." He must whet it again to
make Romans yearn for the republic. Nero, the son of his fourth wife
Agrippinilla, is to be his instrument, for it has been prophesied that Nero
will become a bloody tyrant (Graves 1989c.474, 489). Rome is a "stagnant pool," and Claudius will play "old King Log" by allowing his wife
and freedmen to dominate him and to engineer Nero's succession to the
throne: "I shall float inertly in the stagnant pool. Let all the poisons that
lurk in the mud hatch out" (Graves 1989c.475). For Graves, Claudius's
actions constitute "a deliberate resolution, and a cynical one" (Letter to
Tom and Julie Matthews, 10 February 1935 in O'Prey 1982.243), but
they are not without idealistic hope. He plans to hide his own son Bri-

tannicus among the northern Britons until Nero's death, when he will return to save Rome by restoring the republic (Graves 1989c.505).

In Graves's narrative, women thrive in the "stagnant pool," sexually and politically. Following an association typical of ancient Roman moral discourse, Graves makes the unchastity of women like Claudius's wives Messalina and Agrippinilla, his sister Livilla, and Augustus's daughter Julia symptomatic of imperial Rome. Even Livia, wife of the first emperor Augustus, who believes the "republic was always humbug," associates chastity with the republic and unchastity with the empire: "One can no more reintroduce republican government at this stage than one can reimpose primitive feelings of chastity on modern wives and husbands" (1989b.17, 340).[6] In the stagnant pool of Roman monarchy, women like Livia gain political power: "Augustus ruled the world, but Livia ruled Augustus," Claudius explains (1989b.21). For Graves, female power depends on male weakness: Livia uses Augustus's sexual impotence with her "as a weapon for subjecting his will to hers" (1989b.21), and Messalina, Claudius's third wife, "played very cleverly and very cruelly on [Claudius's] blind love for her" (1989c.209). By destroying innocent men and women who stand in the way of their plans, imperial women contribute to the tyranny of the principate. So special is their contribution that Claudius avers "it takes a woman to run an empire like this" (1989c.485).

Although his narrative recounts a violent family history of murderous (step)mothers, scheming wives, sexually voracious women, trusting husbands, and hapless but good men, Graves devotes a relatively small number of pages to unchaste and manipulative wives. In fact, although Graves notes cases of female sexual misbehavior, he stages no scenes of sexual excess. In an uneven mix, Graves's account of every reign extends far beyond domestic machinations to political events at Rome, provincial affairs, and external wars. Moreover, through the voice of Claudius, Graves displays and comments on his own classical education. Both novels, especially the second, include long discourses on Roman historiography, religion, and literature (1989b.114ff.; 1989c.84–85, 117ff., 354ff., 384–86), and ethnographies of Rome's enemies and subjects (1989b.164–65, 245–49, 261–62; 1989c.158, 204, 252–70, 333–34). Some of the staples of British imperial education come in for rough treatment, especially the ancient Roman heroes of Livy's history who were held up to British boys as models of courage, patriotism, and sacrifice. Graves's Claudius doubts the veracity of the "heroic legends of ancient Rome related by the historian Livy" and questions Livy's famous preface in which the historian looks to "ancient virtue" as a relief from the immorality of the present (1989b.118, 122; 1989c.84–85).[7]

Although Graves takes a cynical view of Livy's noble, duty-bound, self-sacrificing Roman heroes, he seems unable to give up the ideal. Having debunked Roman versions of such heroes in Livy, Graves projects their purity onto the ancient Britons, his own putative ancestors. Graves's ethnographic imagination turns the Britons into Homeric heroes, descended from "a tall, sandy-haired, big-limbed, boastful, excitable but noble race, gifted in all the arts" (1989c.253). Of all Rome's imperial subjects, the Britons will make the best true Romans: "The islanders, who are racially akin to us," notes Graves's Augustus, "will become far better Romans than we shall ever succeed in making of the Germans, who, in spite of their apparent docility and willingness to learn our arts, I find more alien-minded even than the Moors or the Jews" (1989c.258).[8] Indeed, in the mind of Claudius, who added Britain to the Roman empire, the Britons, especially the northern Britons, uphold the ancient Roman virtues abandoned by imperial Romans. Such men become a resource for empire or, rather, the morally correct heirs to empire.

Graves's novels inscribe a particular version of Roman history at a moment of crisis for the British empire that included the loss of Ireland in 1922–23, the growth of the Indian Congress Party in the 1920s and 1930s, and the total failure of the expected recovery of the imperial economy during the Depression. Especially important for Graves, the effects of World War I called into question the *mentalité* of discipline, hierarchy, and privilege that underlay the British imperial order. Men like Graves, Siegfried Sassoon, and Wilfred Owen saw the continuance of the war as "merely a sacrifice of the idealistic younger generation to the stupidity and self-protective alarm of the elder" (Graves 1989a.245). In *Good-bye to All That* (1929), Graves himself records the violence, brutality, and waste experienced by men in the trenches, their perception of the inanity of old-school officers, and their alienation from those on the Home Front who spoke of upholding "the honour and traditions not only of our Empire but of the whole civilized world." For Graves, such sentiments were a "foreign language . . . [a] newspaper language" (1989a.228–29). The attempt to transfer "the values of the public-school tradition—courage, self-sacrifice, honour, duty, playing the game . . . to the battlefield" failed (Hynes 1982.18). In the "'chaos of values' mood of the twenties" and the perception of the thirties that "all the comforting pre-war concepts" were gone, English poets struggled with the problem of heroism (Hynes 1982.66, 70, 78). For poets sensitive to the economic crisis of the thirties, the problem was intensified by a vision of a world "subject to one natural law of dissolution": the "theme of entropy, the old life running down" marks the landscape of the poetry of the thirties (Hynes 1982.53).

Graves's Claudius novels translate British visions of dissolution, the "chaos of values," and the problem of right action to ancient Rome. Relying on a nineteenth-century vision of imperial Rome as the corrupt root of Western civilization, Graves's "stagnant pool" constitutes an image of "bad empire": decadence, corruption, and, in general, an exercise of power oppressive to good men, to which his noble Britons are an external alternative. A tradition that goes back to the seventeenth century allowed men of Graves's class to identify themselves with the peoples of ancient Britain. In effect, the ruling class of a twentieth-century empire could experience itself as the colonized by evoking a fantasy of the corruption of their own, albeit ancient, imperial rulers. Yet Graves also felt invested in a Claudius struggling to do good in the corrupt world at the center of empire.

Graves imagines that Claudius confronted a moral landscape similar to his own: "He lived in an age in which every moral safeguard of a religious or patriotic or social sort had gone West—things were just disintegrating. He realized this and found it impossible to reintegrate them" (Seymour-Smith 1995.254–55, quoting Graves). Graves's assertion answers the criticism of the twentieth-century imperial adventurer T. E. Lawrence. Disturbed by Graves's choice of Claudius as hero, Lawrence found the tone of the first novel "sickening." He chastised Graves because, unlike the great Romans worthy of emulation by English public school boys, Claudius was not "even . . . a heroic 'minority' character resisting bravely: Claudius is no Brutus" (quoted in Seymour-Smith 1995.254–55). One of the tough, courageous heroes of Livy's history, Brutus founded the Roman republic; devoted to the state, he ordered the execution of his treacherous sons to maintain it. Graves, who counted himself among those sacrificed sons, was hardly likely to find an affinity with Livy's Brutus. Moreover, pure and noble heroes like Graves's ancient barbarian ancestors appeared extraneous to a world in disintegration. The man who wavered between resigned cynicism and impossible idealism seemed more relevant than Brutus or the Britons. Graves, who had catalogued his own postwar "disabilities" in *Good-bye to All That*, discovered "some strange confluent feeling" with Claudius (Graves 1989a.288, Kersnowski 1989.100).[9] Claudius's avocation as a writer, if not heroic, at least allowed him space for right action: "The best he could do was to be a historian and keep a historian's faith. The more he tried, as Emperor, to interfere with the process of disintegration, the madder things got" (quoted in Seymour-Smith 1995.254).

Although those who translated the novels to the screen and stage and their reviewers ignored Graves's take on Roman history, they regarded Graves's depiction of Claudius as a true portrait of the Roman ruler: the good man among immoral wolves, a republican emperor disillusioned in his hopes to restore the republic.[10] At the same time, Claudius became a screen for the projection of their own present.[11] John Mortimer, whose play based on the novels opened in London on July 11, 1972, admits that his *I, Claudius* is "a kind of English view of Roman history" ("Talking about *I, Claudius*," p. 20). Like Graves, Tony Richardson, the director of Mortimer's play, finds the Romans familiar: "Incredible people—pagans, of course, with entirely different surface values to ours, yet basically they're the same" ("Talking about *I, Claudius*," p. 19). Jack Pullman, who adapted Graves's novels for television, and Herbert Wise, the director of *I, Claudius*, also self-consciously nurtured this sort of familiarity. According to Wise, "We decided, as a basic thing, long before we started filming, that we were going to make it both modern and not modern. The colloquialisms Jack Pullman wrote into the script are deliberate. They are there to make you feel that although this thing happened two thousand-odd years ago, it could in fact happen today" (PM). This affinity was effected by turning Graves's novels into a domestic drama that could be read through the conventions of modern soap opera, a process I explore below.[12] For the moment, an outline of the television narrative will indicate its preoccupation with the imperial family, the near disappearance of politics, commentary on classical culture, and ethnography, and the absence of even Graves's inchoate criticism of imperialism (for example, 1989b.163).

After an introduction by Alistair Cooke, the host of Masterpiece Theatre, and the credits, viewers enter the setting of the story's narration—an old Claudius writing a history of his family, inspired by a prophecy of the sibyl. The first five episodes on the reign of Augustus, Rome's first emperor, focus on his potential successors and his wife Livia's elimination of all rivals to her son Tiberius, Augustus's stepson. Episodes 6–8 on Tiberius's reign begin with the death of the emperor's nephew Germanicus and the trial of his supposed murderers and continue with the plots of Sejanus, prefect of the praetorian guard, and his mistress Livilla, wife of Tiberius's son Castor. The treason trials of senators become mere background to Sejanus's destruction of Germanicus's wife Agrippina and their sons, his affair with Livilla, and their plot to get rid of Tiberius himself. Episodes 9 and 10 dramatize the emperor Caligula's incestuous relations with his sister Drusilla, his insane delusions of divinity, and his assassination. Claudius's reign returns to the machinations of wives. Two episodes (11 and 12) chart the adulteries of Messalina, Claudius's third wife. As in the novel, her betrayal, paralleled by the attempted revolt of Claudius's friend Herod, leaves Claudius believing his benevolence has "reconciled Rome and the world to monarchy." He decides to "let all the poisons that lurk in the mud hatch out" by marrying his niece Agrippinilla and allowing her son to succeed him in the hope of destroying the monarchy. From over Claudius's dead body, the last episode (13) flashes back to Agrippinilla's plots and her murder of Claudius.

Before a closer consideration of this imperial family drama, it is useful to look at the contemporary conditions that made for a powerful and popular response to this offering of a PBS program usually associated with high culture. Although *I, Claudius* was produced and first broadcast in Britain, my concern is with its reception in the United States, another imperial society in crisis. The next section outlines the political, social, and economic dimensions of this crisis and examines television as a formative system of representation. By discussing the nature of a televisual medium that shapes the news of the present and the fiction of a distant past, I hope to lay the ground for what I call "imperiality" at the levels of narrative, reception, and medium.

The American Crisis, Television, and Empire

I, Claudius's familial narrative of empire in which good men are endangered by scheming women pursuing their desires, political and sexual, arrived in the United States amid a crisis of American empire and society that put women and family in the spotlight. The failure of the United States' military intervention in Vietnam and, especially, the fall of Saigon in the spring of 1975 displayed the limits of American power abroad and signified a larger failure of imperial pretensions and policies rarely publicly acknowledged as imperial. The economic recessions of the early and mid-1970s meant inflation and severe unemployment and brought widespread fears of economic instability. Revelations of criminal and unethical practices in the executive branch, intelligence agencies, and private sector produced general distrust in government and business. The Watergate cover-up that resulted in the resignation of President Richard Nixon in August 1974 was only one of a procession of scandals:

the publication of the Pentagon Papers in the *New York Times* in June 1971; the indictment of Vice President Spiro Agnew for receiving bribes from Maryland contractors and his resignation in October 1973; the congressional investigations of the FBI and CIA in 1975; and disclosures of corporate misdeeds, as, for example, in the cases of ITT and Lockheed. The social movements of the sixties continued and even expanded in the early seventies. The civil rights movement, black militancy, the student movement against the war, feminism, and the counterculture changed perceptions of race, family, and sexuality and challenged traditional social, economic, and religious values. In the seventies, feminism, in particular, became especially visible on the screen of national politics in the U.S. Supreme Court's legalization of abortion in 1973 and Congress's approval of the Equal Rights Amendment.

For some, the 1970s appeared to be the culmination of a dramatic coming apart of American power abroad, American society at home, and a masculine maintenance of power.[13] American military and economic hegemony in the wake of World War II led to the assumption of imperial responsibility in the Truman Doctrine "to intervene wherever 'freedom' was threatened" (Hodgson 1978.31–33). Faith in American capitalism accompanied the perceived need for American strength abroad. In the ideology of free enterprise, capitalism would produce more than enough to conquer poverty and the divisions of class; science and technology would make life better in the kitchen and on the battlefield. Military intervention, treaties, and corporate investment secured "free" markets and American economic interests, turning some countries into virtual client states. In Cold War ideology, American strength abroad and the success of capitalism were necessary bulwarks against the threat of the Soviet Union.

Cynthia Enloe points out the degree to which success in international relations and finance is figured in terms of masculinity. In effect, the maintenance of power in the entwined ideologies of capitalism and the Cold War involve gendered expectations (1990.12–13): "When it's a patriarchal world that is 'dangerous,' masculine men and feminine women are expected to react in opposite but complementary ways. A 'real man' will become the protector in such a world. He will suppress his own fears, brace himself, and step forward to defend the weak, women and children. In the same 'dangerous world,' women will turn gratefully and expectantly to their fathers and husbands, real or surrogate. If a woman is a mother, then she will think first of her children, protecting them not in a manly way, but as a self-sacrificing mother." Implicitly, empire abroad depends on the patriarchal family at home—a perception that informs the rhetoric of Nixonian conservatives and the New Right.

The audience of *I, Claudius* was inundated with the right's contention that, in the sixties and seventies, this Cold War order was undone at home by women, children, and blacks, resulting in an emasculation that could only aid the "evil" empire of the Soviets. In the early seventies, Nixon's strategists made protestors the enemy within who attacked traditional American values at home and threatened American success abroad. In the 1972 election, Nixon successfully cast George McGovern "as the candidate of the three A's—abortion, acid, and amnesty for draft resisters," thus associating women's increased control over reproduction with drugs, rebellious students, and American military failure (Ryan and Kellner 1990.39). The New Right, which emerged as a powerful force in national politics in the late seventies, fastened on the Equal Rights Amendment and the legalization of abortion as the accomplishments of a feminism that they blamed for the recession, social disorder, and, above all, the decline of American power abroad. Paul Weyrich, creator of the Heritage Foundation, informs the readers of *Conservative Digest* that feminists are a new kind of political radical who assault the American capitalist order by attacking the family and emasculating the father/husband: "There are people who want a different political order, who are not necessarily Marxists. Symbolized by the women's liberation movement, they believe that the future of their political power lies in the restructuring of the traditional family, and particularly in the downgrading of the male or father role in the traditional family" (quoted in Faludi 1992.232). For the Moral Majority's Reverend Jerry Falwell, the fate of the nation lies in the fate of this endangered "traditional family": "Need I say it is time that moral Americans became informed and involved in helping to preserve family values in our nation? . . . We cannot wait. The twilight of our nation could well be at hand" (quoted in Faludi 1992.234). The New Right offered a "politics of return": return to the traditional patriarchal family in which children and wife were under the control of its male head; return to traditional religious and moral values that eliminated abortion, homosexuality, and promiscuity; return to a free market economy without government regulation and social welfare programs; and a return to American imperial hegemony (Ryan and Kellner 1990.11).

Television, the medium of representation of the Roman empire in *I, Claudius*, was instrumental in shaping knowledge and experience of an American crisis of empire. Since the early sixties, television has been "the principle storyteller" in the United States (Kozloff 1992.67); through it, most Americans receive their information about the national and international scene (Hodgson 1978.140–41). A change in network policy in the early 1960s emphasized national news, cultivating, in Godfrey Hodgson's words, a "sense of personal involvement, in every American family, with 'how we're doing'" (1978.143). Television nationalized the American consciousness, forging what Benedict Anderson has called an "imagined community" "in a way which is more extensive and intimate than the newspaper . . . [Anderson's] exemplary medium" (Anderson 1991, Croft 1995.114, Hodgson 1978.140ff.). In these terms, televised news in the 1960s and 1970s provided a visceral experience that we, the "imagined community," were not doing so well.

Television brought the war in Vietnam and the war at home into American homes. Until early 1969, infantry actions, bombings, and napalm raids in a land an ocean away crossed American television screens every evening. The protests and demands of blacks, students, and women, followed by those of Chicanos and Indians, appeared in two- or three-minute segments. According to Byron Shafer and Richard Larson, "the development of the evening news as a social institution . . . made social disorganization a realistic threat to the comfortably-off, middle-class urbanites, to suburbanites, to rural residents—to all those . . . who have seldom faced robbery, muggings, protest marches, chanting, blockbusting, black-power salutes, or perhaps even hostile questions about their values" (quoted in Hodgson 1978.151). The broadcast of the Senate's Watergate hearings to a large, fascinated audience carried the details of corruption in Washington and the president's avidity for power into living rooms in Iowa, Montana, and California.

Within this televisual experience of contemporary crisis, the very nature of the medium conditioned the reading of ancient empire in *I, Claudius*. Television operates, argues Raymond Williams, as "flow." Unlike films and literary texts, television programs are not a series of discrete, isolated texts; rather one program blends into another (Williams 1975.86–96, Dienst 1994.3–35, Allen 1992b, White 1992). The boundaries of television diegesis are permeable: the worlds of soap operas bleed into those of sitcoms and dramas; these fictions bleed into the realities represented on the news; and the worlds of fiction and fact bleed into the worlds constructed in commercials (Feuer 1986.104–05, Kozloff 1992). This flow supports what Stephen Heath and Gillian Skirrow call a "perpetual present" (1977.54). The "continuous scanning of whatever is in front of the camera by an electronic beam" produces a sense of "immediacy": an illusion that we receive unmediated images of events as they occur creates "a permanently alive view on the world" (Heath and Skirrow 1977.54). According to Jane Feuer, these "notions of liveness" carry over from live broadcasts to taped programs, from the news to fictions: "It hardly matters what content is communicated by the television, so long as the communicating situation created by this sense of presentness is maintained" (Feuer 1983.19, Flitterman-Lewis 1992.219). "Liveness" is conflated with the "real," and the reality of televisual sights and sounds is shored up by the quotidian nature of television reception as "an entirely ordinary experience" (Feuer 1983.15).

Television viewing is "a profoundly domestic phenomenon" and a "family affair." The apparatus itself is a "domestic appliance," located among furniture, photographs, pictures, and other household objects in living rooms, kitchens, and bedrooms (Ellis 1982.113, Joyrich 1991–92.28, Allen 1992b.12). As Robert Allen observes, "television's penetration into the private spaces of our lives, its unnoticed connection with the rituals and routines of daily life, inevitably make television viewing a part of our relations with other people with whom we share those private spaces" (1992c.134). Unlike the film spectator, who watches a large, lit screen in the darkness of the theater, isolated in his or her seat, the television spectator is a "fully socialized family member," who watches a small screen in a familiar space among family and friends (Feuer 1986.103; on spectatorship, Flitterman-Lewis 1992).

Televisual flow and the permeable boundaries of television diegesis drew ancient Rome into a continuous present, mixing an historical fiction of the Roman empire with the contemporary news of the American empire. According to the director, Herbert Wise, "*I, Claudius* is about today. It's about the marketplace" and "the workings of a city today." He sees little "substantive difference between the malpractice in government revealed in today's headlines and the corrupt practices in ancient Rome" (PM). Reviewers in the print media agreed, drawing what the *Christian Science Monitor* calls "shocking parallels" to "the atmosphere of post-Watergate America" (Unger 1977). Watergate and political corruption in general, the sexual revolution, the Mafia, and the debate on sex and violence in the media became touchstones for understanding Rome on television: even more than simple points of comparison, sensibilities about these contemporary phenomena bled into visions of ancient empire (and vice versa).[14]

The flow of fiction into the news, of past into present, was facilitated by the perception that Masterpiece Theatre's Rome had the same facticity as the news. As noted above, Hollywood spectacles laid the ground for the popular idea that "orgies, incest, and murder were par for the Roman course" (Gardella 1977). This vision is so much a matter of common sense, it hardly requires comment: "Needless to say, Roman history in this period is splattered with scandalous behavior" (O'Connor 1977). However, television's ideology of "liveness" and its conflation of "liveness" with the "real" turn televisual Rome into a "real" ancient Rome. Even as they acknowledge the serial as a version of Graves's novels or attribute his depiction of Rome to his reliance on Suetonius (the Roman biographer of emperors), reviewers like Les Brown of the *New York Times* insist that the program's "sex and violence belong to the historical fabric" (1977).[15] While the review in the *Christian Science Monitor* attempts to distinguish fact from fiction by observing that Rome's decline "took more than two hundred additional years," the slippage from fact to fiction becomes irresistible: "It was an erotic and violent period . . . it was a vile and violent time" (Unger 1977). Thus, the association of lust and corruption with the disintegration of empire becomes fact: the "lust for power and flesh . . . prevailed during the reigns [of these emperors and] set the stage for the fall of the Roman Empire" (Brown 1977).

The domesticity of television and the familial nature of television spectatorship set the cultural production of *I, Claudius* in a mirroring relation with its reception. In *I, Claudius*, interiors predominate: palace, senate house, rooms in private houses, tents in army camps. The few scenes that take place out-of-doors are shot in fairly tight focus; most convey a sense of space that barely includes a front door or patio. Crowds are kept to a minimum, and, generally, family members occupy the frame. Television viewers spend most of their thirteen hours in Rome within the imperial palace: on television, the territory of the Roman empire becomes a series of domestic spaces. The televisual fiction of empire, seen on a household appliance located in the twentieth-century home, then, was both received and set within the home. Moreover, this imperial drama is launched from a space that mirrors the space in which viewers receive that drama: Masterpiece Theatre opens in a drawing room with the camera panning across pictures from other Masterpiece Theatre offerings that appear to be a collection of family photographs. Families occupy these isomorphic places of production and reception: familial relations define the audience on one side of the screen and the fictional characters on the other side. "To be perversely literal-minded," notes Jane Feuer, "the television screen *does* reflect the body of the family, if we turn the images off" (Feuer 1986.103). Tuned into PBS at 9:00 P.M. on Sunday nights from November 1977 through January 1978, "the body of the family" observed those advertised as its Roman ancestors or alter egos.

The imperial home and family of *I, Claudius* presented in Alistair Cooke's drawing room exist in a stream of television families. The drama of ancient family relations is watched by the late twentieth-century family (or familial subject) at a moment when it is bombarded by the rhetoric of endangered "family values" on the news. The serial on an ancient Roman family also flows into other televisual fictions. Naming a few of these contemporary programs, *Time*'s review of *I, Claudius*, begins with the declaration, "This is television's year of the family" (Clarke 1977).[16] Jill Betz Bloom, a clinical psychologist and faculty member at the Massachusetts School of Professional Psychology, testifies to the flow of family programs and the degree to which one plugs into another. Asked about the experience of watching *I, Claudius* in 1977–78, she laughed and commented that "when I was a kid at home, my family watched *Bonanza* at 9:00 P.M. on Sunday nights. When I grew up and became an intellectual, we [her own family] watched *Upstairs, Downstairs* and *I, Claudius* instead. Isn't Sunday night traditionally family viewing night?"[17]

What distinguishes *I, Claudius* as a family drama is a particularly symbiotic relation between family, empire, and the medium of their representation. On *Bonanza*, the imperial relations that underlie the Cartwrights' possession of their huge ranch, the Ponderosa, surface in the appearance of an occasional Indian and in the family's patronizing relations with their Chinese cook Hop Sing. In televisual Rome, the expansion, domination, and exploitation constitutive of empire are registered by the brief appearance of exotic objects,[18] non-Roman bodies, and the talk exchanged by family members within the palace, the family home. Symptomatic of this domestication of imperial relations is the use made of a map of the Roman empire in a close-up shot at the beginning of the second episode (a similar map was printed in the *New York Times* as part of a program guide): the cartographic representation of empire becomes a household item—the board of a dice game, "Empire," played by the emperor Augustus and his two young grandsons. The conquered and the colonized themselves show up briefly or decoratively at the margins of familial scenes. The opening of the serial is a paradigm for the place of colonized bodies in a televisual Roman empire. Claudius's introductory remarks fade into the story he tells whose first image is a gyrating black female pelvis. Scantily clad black women doing a pseudo-African dance perform for imperial diners, while Augustus looks on excitedly: "Excellent," he says, ordering an official to feed them well, "no scraps or leftovers."[19] Black and exotic bodies, however, *are* "scraps" or "leftovers" in the representation of a dinner party celebrating Actium, the battle that secured Augustus sole control of the empire; they exist only as background to the central drama of the scene: a generational tension between a young, disrespectful Marcellus, Augustus's nephew and current favorite in the succession, and a mature, disgruntled Agrippa, Augustus's friend and the general who won the battle.

More often, provincial affairs, conquests, and colonized peoples become objects of verbal exchange, appearing only in the reports of officials and the conversations of members of the imperial family.[20] The words that represent Rome's subjects emphasize the superiority of Romans and describe the use value of non-Romans and their willingness to be ruled. When Augustus lectures his grandson Postumus on the work and responsibility that have "gone into making this little place master of the world," he asks rhetorically, "Did you ever think how fortunate we are not to be born in a wattle hut on the banks of the Rhine or a grubby tent in Syria?"[21] In a dialogue between Augustus's young grandsons and the general Drusus on conquering Britain, Drusus explains that the conquest of the island is not worth it: "There is nothing of value there; the people make very poor slaves."

Such exchanges not only naturalize imperial relations of exploitation and domination, they also double the exploitation by reducing the conquered and colonized to the material out of which family members and their relations are characterized. The conquered and colonized are present in the narrative in order to portray the family or to enhance its dramas. When Augustus's daughter Julia complains about immigrants pouring into the city of Rome or chatters about buying good-looking slaves, the bare mention of immigrants and slaves serves only to depict Julia as frivolous and lustful. Augustus's remarks on empire, cited above, occur during a conversation with Postumus, overheard by Livia, in which Augustus reveals that he wants Postumus to succeed him. The tête-à-tête on empire exists as a secret discovered, motivating the next segment of the narrative: Livia's plot to secure the disgrace of Postumus who would take the place she intends for her son Tiberius.

The knowledge and experience of an ancient Roman empire *in the televisual narrative* is isomorphic with its viewers' knowledge and experience of a present-day American empire *in the place of the narrative's reception* (cf. Berland 1992). In the narrative, verbal exchanges about empire recur among family members in the domestic space of the palace; in the place of reception, televisual images and sounds of the United States' imperial efforts abroad play before families or familial subjects in their own homes, "castles" in the postwar American ideal of the homeowner as *the landed consumer* (Ewen and Ewen 1982.235). In *I, Claudius*, a soldier's graphic description of savage German barbarians destroying three Roman legions makes present to the emperor and his family the defeat of Rome's imperial ambitions at a border of empire; on network television, two years before the reception of this scene, footage of the chaos in Saigon and the hasty evacuation of the United States embassy brought home, and into the American home, the first defeat of American forces since World War II and the loss of a client state.

Like the televisual representation of Roman imperialism that reduces non-Romans and imperial relations to family affairs, the practices of television news in the United States represent other nations and peoples in "domestic" terms. Oversimplification, the personalization of events, and the commercial appeal of emotionality and a good story result in "the technique of mirror imaging or explaining foreign events in terms of situations familiar to Americans" (Schwoch, White, and Reilly 1992.51).[22] Other people become like us or not like us, and therefore friends or foes, good or bad: "The ethnocentric view of the American news media is fundamentally dualistic, resting on a series of mythic polarities which oppose the pure 'we' to the evil 'they.'"[23] Similar or different, those outside the United States, like non-Romans in *I, Claudius*, can be seen only in terms relevant to the familial viewer of both Masterpiece Theatre and the news.

This isomorphism of the televisual narrative of ancient empire and the televisual experience of present-day empire recurs in a representational regime that might well be labeled imperial. Richard Dienst warns against sharp distinctions between television's cultural form and its technology, between its content and its means (1994.12–25). The development of wire- and wave-based communications technologies from the 1890s through the 1940s accompanied the end of European expansion based on human exploration, conquest, and settlement. In the United States, they accompanied the limit of continental expansion and the end of manifest destiny in the 1890s and the rise of "mechanical expansion through technology and information" (Schwoch, White, and Reilly 1992.110). As James Schwoch, Mimi White, and Susan Reilly observe, communications technologies including television "became surrogates for the industrialized nations, reaffirming their empires but also reconstructing them in economic and cultural manifestations, helping to confirm the proprietary rights the industrialized world believed it held over

the poorer regions of the world" (1992.110). In line with the development of televisual technology, televisual representation is "global": from
the beginning, "televisuality was immediately imagined as an all-en-
compassing putting-into-view of the world" (Dienst 1994.4). Thus,
Dienst argues: "Television's first imaginary horizon is the utopia of un-
interrupted free trade, already transnational, a realization of specifically
metropolitan, imperialist geopolitical ambitions. The 'worlding' image
of television, with its ideals of total flow and tendential completion of the
network, bears the unmistakable stamp of post–World War I Anglo-
American corporate optimism and liberal universalism. Like an archaic
legacy, this ur-image persists through subsequent developments"
(1994.5–6). Not only is the world collected in one space, the screen, one
system of representation dominates all others. "Worlding" is predicated
on a set of rules that govern the format of television's images and mes-
sages. These rules elide veracity and verisimilitude. To take the image
as true, we must be convinced of its verisimilitude: the "light on the
screen" must be recognized "as a transmitted image"—live, present, and
"real." Producers and receivers of the image operate as if this is the sole
regime of representation; implicitly, they must assume that "the world
can be assembled under a single rule and process" (Dienst 1994.6).

I, Claudius, then, engages what might be called "imperiality" at three
levels: the narrative, the reception of viewers, and the medium of representation. First, the narrative tells a story of empire. In the production
of that narrative, imperial expansion, domination, and exploitation are
made present in objects and bodies within the family home and in the
talk exchanged among family members. Second, this narrative and its domestication of empire is received by subjects who, like the imperial family
of the televisual world, grasp contemporary imperial successes and failures through images and conversation in their living rooms. Third, the
medium of television, which gathers the world into one space and depends on a single, universalizing regimen of truth, translates imperialism into the practice of representation itself. These levels of "imperiality" shape a perception of empire and imperial society as undone from
within. Since all viewers ever see of the empire is its ruling family, and
since empire is narratively contained within the family in the form of objects, marginalized subject people, and talk, the family stands in for the
empire it rules. The imperial family becomes a metonymy for Rome, and
Rome means empire. The tag line for the series, set out in Masterpiece
Theatre's promotional material and used by reviewers, certainly privileged the trope: "The family whose business was ruling the world"

("Every Cough and Orgy," Yanni 1977, Unger 1977). The relegation of "business" to the relative clause well represents the domestication of empire, but it is also a move familiar to audiences of another type of continuing serial within the flow of television programs, the soap opera.

The Imperial Soap Opera: Domestication, Disintegration, and Untamed Women

By the time of the first broadcast of *I, Claudius*, the generic rules of daytime soap opera were familiar even to viewers who had never seen a soap. The popular, prime-time *Dallas* and *Dynasty* appeared a few years later, but, in 1977, the prime-time serials *Soap* and *Mary Hartman, Mary Hartman* circulated the conventions of soap opera by parodying them. Moreover, the 1970s saw the growing popularity of daytime serials and programming shifts that laid the ground for a "general movement on American television toward the continuing serial form" typical of soap opera (Feuer 1986.111). The predominance of interior sets in *I, Claudius* and the show's editing and camera work, especially the centrality of the close-up that "privileges facial signs of performance," approximate the visual world of the soap opera. The show's intricate complement of characters, its emphasis on the domestic, and the complex, dense web of personal relations in a serial narrative that attenuates events signal the narrative world of the soap opera. The similarities were not lost on reviewers like Gerald Clarke in *Time* who called *I, Claudius* "a high-gloss soap opera."[24] I argue that the often disparaged, pre-eminently popular-culture soap opera offers a paradigm for reading this offering of the culturally elite Masterpiece Theatre, and begin a close examination of tele-visual Rome with a brief discussion of the key aspects of soap opera that shape a reading of *I, Claudius*.

Soap opera features a complex community of characters whose central structure is the family: the identity of individuals depends primarily on their relations to and within a particular family (Mumford 1995.107, Allen 1992c.108–09). The dramas and traumas of these characters repeat themselves endlessly: the details of particular events vary, but the events themselves are similar; the specific identities of victims and perpetrators change, but they occupy the same familial roles. Repetition results from a tendency to "displace audience interest from the syntagmatic axis to the paradigmatic axis—that is from the flow of events per se to the revelation and development" of the characters and their interrelations (Kozloff 1992.75). David Jacobs, co-creator of *Knots Landing*, explains that "the story is just a clothesline to hang the relationships on. It's not about

the story—or plot—but the . . . relationships between characters"
(quoted in Flitterman-Lewis 1992.232).

Although soap characters are entangled economically and politically,
their relations in the public worlds of business and politics are subordinated to their personal relations (Mumford 1995.40–41). As Charlotte
Brunsdon observes, "The action of soap-opera is not restricted to familial or quasi-familial institutions but, as it were, *colonises* the public masculine sphere, representing it from the point of view of the personal"
(1981.34). The representation of space mirrors these relations of personal
and political. The soap opera is "a world of interiors" (Allen 1985.65), but,
as Laura Stempel Mumford shows, "traditionally private spaces like the
home are refigured as public turf through communal living and working
arrangements," while "experiences that viewers might understand as private—declarations of love, the exchange of secrets, discussions of intimate family problems—are in turn refigured as public by being set in
public locations" (1995.57). The "mutability" of private and public "emphasizes just how permeable the barrier is between the aspects of life
considered private and those that are made public" (Mumford 1995.56).

These operations of the soap belong to a larger pattern of televisual
content. Jane Feuer points out that television in general trains its audience to perceive the external, public world in terms of the interior, private world of the family. Although "the dominant binary opposition . . .
of inside the family/outside the family" informs both the episodic series like the sitcom and the continuing serial like the soap opera, sitcom
and soap opera "differ in their narrative strategies" (Feuer 1986.105–06).
These strategies express the "impossible dilemma" of thinking "outside
the family" in terms of "inside the family" (Feuer 1986.106). In the sit-
com, outside forces threaten the family and are expelled on a weekly
basis; in the soap opera, these forces are internalized and threaten the
"internal disintegration of the . . . family" (Feuer 1986.112–13).

Disintegration has much to do with what David Buckingham calls
"trash": sexual misdeeds, deceptions, betrayals. Trash is especially a matter of talk and information; it involves the acquisition and revelation of
"the dirty little secrets of characters' lives" and results in frequent viola-
tions of privacy (Buckingham 1987). The emphasis on talk over action,
characteristic of soap in general, enriches the paradigmatic axis (Allen
1992c.112, Allen 1995b.20, Mumford 1995.43, 58). Who knows what and
who tells whom position characters in the soap opera diegesis, establishing their relative power. Indeed, one of the most common demonstrations of villainy, and an important part of the villain's power, is the

acquisition of "dirt about another character" and the threat to reveal it (Buckingham 1987).

Soap operas offer up a series of women-gone-bad and villainesses who produce and disseminate "trash," thus playing important roles in the disintegration of the family that expresses the tensions between public and private in the world of soap opera. Sexually active women out of male control pose a constant threat to the patriarchal order of the family. Perhaps more disturbing to that order are the women who wield financial or political power; almost invariably coded as villainesses, such women derive their money, property, business interests, and political power through marriage or its termination in divorce or widowhood.[25] In the 1980s, Alexis (Joan Collins), the villainess of the prime-time soap opera *Dynasty*, provided an "excessive orgy" of transgressions of "socially accepted femininity": aristocratic status, sexual aggression, autonomy, and authoritarian behavior. Alexis, who indulged in both the execution of power and the possession of wealth, has been characterized as "a narcissistic personality, out for pleasure and power just to confirm her own grandiosity." Yet narratively, her "private and public 'war' against the familial patriarch" provided "the serial's main source of conflict" and structured the "framework into which all other conflicts [were] inscribed" (Kreutzner and Seiter 1995.247–49).

When Masterpiece Theatre advertised its new series as "the inside story of the corrupt royal family whose lust for power brought about the fall of Rome" or the "inside story of dirty work in ancient Rome," the producers implicitly associated this Masterpiece Theatre production with the soap opera that notoriously deals in "trash" and "dirty secrets" (PM).[26] The emphasis on "inside" evokes a soap opera–like figuring of the social in terms of the coming apart of the familial. Not accidentally, "inside" describes the predominant space in which the narrative's events unfold—the family home. Lastly, "inside" refers to the narrational structure of the programs. Claudius, a member of the family, tells the family's story from a point of view inside spatially as well as relationally; the audience watches him write the story in the interior rooms of the palace: his bedroom, private study, and even toilet.

Together, Claudius as narrator and Alistair Cooke as host of Masterpiece Theatre shape a reading formation of an imperial soap opera. The narrative set-up of *I, Claudius* follows that of Graves's novels with two important exceptions. First, where, in the novels, Claudius's narrational voice is ever present, on television, viewers begin and return only periodically to the space of writing, visually and aurally. In addition, the audience frequently sees the story enacted and, at the same time, hears in voice-over Claudius's editorial comments on the events and characters. Second, Alistair Cooke extends Claudius's judgments when he introduces and closes each episode.[27] Claudius and Cooke provide intersubjective connections between television viewers and the characters in the narrative. In Stuart Hall's terms, narrator and host articulate the audience and the fiction (1996.141):

> In England, the term has a nice double meaning because "articulate" means to utter, to speak forth, to be articulate . . . But we also speak of an "articulated" lorry (truck): a lorry where the front (cab) and back (trailer) can, but need not necessarily, be connected to one another. The two parts are connected to each other, but through a specific linkage that can be broken. An articulation is thus the form of the connection that can make a unity of two different elements, under certain conditions . . . The "unity" which matters is a linkage between that articulated discourse and the social forces with which it can, under certain historical conditions, but need not necessarily, be connected. Thus, a theory of articulation is both a way of understanding how ideological elements come, under certain conditions, to cohere together within a discourse and a way of asking how they do or do not become articulated at specific conjunctures to certain political subjects.

Graves's decent, truth-seeking Claudius becomes a tour guide to "the corrupt royal family" and the "dirty work in ancient Rome": he speaks to us and interprets the story and characters. At the very opening of the series, Claudius defines us as the recipients of the story. His history, he says in voice-over, is "not for fools in Rome but for them out there—them in remote posterity." He looks into the camera, addressing us directly: "You will find it—it will all be in here, I promise you." When he comes to the terrible events of Caligula's reign, he renews his promise, commanding our belief, "I said I'd tell everything and I shall. I shall hide nothing, nothing! And if what comes next may seem incredible, believe it, believe it." Claudius has authority because he knows the results of the events that only gradually unfold for the television audience. Like the narrator of the radio soap opera, his "very description of a particular character . . . position[s] him or her on a normative hierarchy."[28] His interventions carry weight because he is a touchstone of decency, an historian concerned to tell the truth, and an intelligent man disguised as a fool to survive in the dangerous familial world he describes.

Like Claudius, Alistair Cooke looks directly at the television audience, bidding us "good evening." He shares his greater knowledge, fills in the story, and reminds us of what we have seen, soliciting our agreement in a particular interpretation. What *TV Guide* calls his "silvery presence" invites our trust. Sharing his point of view, viewers are constructed as knowing and cultured: "And as in every Masterpiece Theatre series, there is the warming company of Cooke, our amiable host, who reminds us by his obvious joy in his work that it's fun to be civilized" (MacKenzie 1977). The power of his articulation is registered by the statements of reviewers who repeat his judgments, often verbatim.[29] Seated between the audience and Claudius, between the viewers' world and the televisual "classic" they are about to see, Cooke mediates "reality" and imagination, history and fiction, the present of the broadcast and the ancient Rome of the narrative.[30] As "the news anchor, in his or her 'ceremonial role,' secur[es] our belief in the news and our sense of its authenticity," Cooke helps "to verify the referent from television's sounds and images" (Kozloff 1992.38). The direct address of Cooke, like that of the news anchor or the character in a commercial, helps "to break down any barriers between the fictional diegesis, the advertising diegesis, and the diegesis of the viewing family" (Feuer 1986.105). Breaking the boundaries between the world of the fiction and the world of the watching family, he draws the audience into imperial Rome and imperial Rome into the politics of the 1970s described above.

If we believe Claudius and Cooke, we can occupy a satisfying position as viewing subjects: cultured, knowledgeable, and unlike those "fools in Rome." Accepting our designated position as narratees, we participate in the domestication of Graves's narrative effected by television and, with it, the domestication of empire. The following discussion of *I, Claudius* as an imperial soap opera notes where, in Hall's terms, the "articulated discourse" of Claudius and Cooke is linked to the "social forces" of the serial's "historical conditions."

Family becomes the central structure of a complex community of characters, as in soap opera, through television's particular reworking of Graves. In the process, to rewrite Charlotte Brunsdon's observations on soap opera, *I, Claudius* colonizes an empire, "representing it from the point of view of the personal" (see above, p. 138). Beyond simplifying some of Graves's complex plots, the television serial boils Graves's story down to its domestic bare bones, focusing almost exclusively on the relations and struggles among the members of the imperial family. As noted above, the world outside the family is dragged into the family in the form of exotic objects, conquered bodies, and talk exchanged among family members. The operation of the television narrative to make imperial relations mere background to domestic intrigues is relentless in its representation of Claudius's reign. In *Claudius the God*, Graves details Claudius's official acts, imperial administration, and wars at the borders of empire, especially the conquest of Britain; only the last 67 pages of the 507-page novel focus exclusively on the machinations of Claudius's wives. The television series generally reduces his reign to the stories of his wives, especially Messalina, whose adulteries and plots occupy two of the three episodes devoted to his rule. The public activities of the televisual Claudius consist primarily of remarks that he is working too hard and several scenes in which he consults his advisors about building a harbor at Ostia. Viewers only hear about Claudius's conquest of Britain from a conversation between his officials, but they see his wife's sexual adventures in Claudius's absence: Messalina in bed with the actor Mnester and her elaborate sex contest with the prostitute Scylla.

The difference here between television and literary text is symptomatic of the reshaping of the imperial story. Television retains only the familial aspects of Graves's story and then enlarges them by dramatizing what Graves only mentions. In *Claudius the God*, Messalina's contest with the prostitute takes up a single paragraph, a minor addendum to Messalina's affair with the noble Gaius Silius (1989c.452); on television, the single paragraph becomes two fully visualized scenes. Similarly, where Graves comments briefly on Caligula's incestuous relations with his sister Drusilla and his responsibility in her death (1989b.389, 402), television makes Caligula's incest with Drusilla the focus of episode 9. By concluding the episode with a scene in which Caligula murders his sister by cutting her open to devour their child, the television narrative dramatizes not only the emperor's insanity but an "abortion" of family life.[31]

The representation of space shores up the domestication of empire: where Graves takes his readers to different parts of the empire, Masterpiece Theatre's Rome, like the soap opera, is "a world of interiors" (Allen 1985.65). The secrets, manipulations, and lies that compose so much of the plot take us into the most private spaces of the palace, the bedrooms of members of the imperial family. This is "the family whose business is ruling the world," so even when the camera retreats into bedrooms for adultery or the plotting of a relative's demise, such private "affairs" affect the public affairs of state. Soap opera's permeable barrier between private and public space is paradigmatic for televisual Rome where the palace, the predominant site of the narrative, is both a family home and the seat of government. By translating the conflation of public and private into sexual terms, television's mad Caligula and decadent Messalina demonstrate imperial corruption on a domestic scale: Caligula turns the palace into a brothel; Messalina makes her bedroom the site of a public sex contest.

The spectacles of Caligula and Messalina exemplify how Masterpiece Theatre presents a domesticated empire—how, in Jane Feuer's terms, it expresses the "impossible dilemma" of thinking "outside the family" in terms of "inside the family" (1986.106). The inchoate politics of Graves's novels and any critique of empire disappear; in their place are family dysfunction and corruption. In the dissolved boundary between inside and outside, the imperial family and, therefore, the world disintegrate from within—a phenomenon for which viewers are prepared by television in general and soap opera in particular. Medium, however, abets politics: the dire warnings of the New Right that made the endangered patriarchal family tantamount to or even responsible for civic disorder and national loss facilitated a reading of familial dysfunction as broader social disintegration.

In *I, Claudius*, as in soap opera, family disintegration is repetitive, not cumulative. The narrative makes no progress: it opens in the midst of a dinner party that features a scheming wife (Livia), who will eventually poison her husband (Augustus), and it closes at a dinner party at which a scheming wife (Agrippinilla) poisons her husband (Claudius).[32] The characters have changed but not their familial roles nor the nature of events. Repetition produces what one reviewer calls "the monotony of unrelenting evil" (Gardella 1977). During Augustus's reign, family struggles result in the death or exile of six nephews, sons-in-law, and grandsons, one daughter, and the murder of the patriarch himself. In Tiberius's reign, viewers watch the death agonies of a father murdered with the aid of his son and the destruction of his wife and other sons—save the patricide who commits incest with his sisters. The emperor's daughter-in-law commits adultery, poisons her husband, and tries to do the same to her daughter when it appears the girl will marry her mother's lover. As emperor and head of the family, the incestuous Caligula murders his cousin, his sister, and her child and turns the family home into a brothel. During Claudius's reign as emperor and family patriarch, his sexually voracious wife indulges her desires, manipulates and betrays her doting husband, and is eventually beheaded. Claudius's next wife poisons him, and, having committed incest with her brother, she will, the story suggests, seduce her infantile, petulant son.

Family dysfunction spells the corruption of Rome, but it is unclear whether family members are its cause or its symptom. Characters like Antonia, Claudius's mother, have it both ways. On the one hand, aberrant individuals turn Rome into "a sewer . . . fit only for rats to live in," Antonia tells the ex-wife of Sejanus, prefect of the praetorian guard, who has come to ask for her help in wresting her children from their father and his mistress, Antonia's daughter. "Honor, service, duty mean nothing anymore," Antonia says. "Your kids are everything to you. And what of Rome? Everything you are you owe to Rome. But you've destroyed it, all of you, with your greedy ambition and your petty selfishness." On the other hand, having watched the murder of her son and grandsons and the degeneracy of her daughter, Antonia sees the murderous, incestuous Caligula, emperor and head of the imperial family, as merely the symptom of a diseased Rome: "Rome is sick, sick to its heart; he's just the rash that's come out."

The serial strikes a contemporary chord among American viewers when it associates imperial corruption with men's failure to perform within the family or with their loss of patriarchal control. The often-voiced behavioral platitudes of Augustus, the first emperor and family patriarch, base "good" empire on family unity: "We are family and we all work together for the greater good of Rome." He insists that family members put "duties and responsibilities" above "private desires." In his view, the "work and dedication needed to maintain" Rome's mastery of the world necessitate, indeed depend upon, proper performance of one's familial role. Thus, in televisual Rome, evil emperors, like Tiberius and Caligula, are bad sons, husbands, and fathers; good emperors, like Augustus and Claudius, are good sons, husbands, and fathers. Yet a fine performance in his family role is not enough for an emperor: he must control the family if he is to control the empire. At a moment of frustration after a fight between his daughter and her husband, Augustus makes the point more truly than he imagines: "I'm supposed to rule an empire, and I can't even rule my own family." Ultimately, he does not control his family because he does not control his wife Livia and remains ignorant of the plots through which she secretly controls events.

Although evil emperors and their henchmen (Tiberius, Sejanus, and Caligula) create havoc, such male agents are outnumbered by scheming, corrupt, or lustful women who, in pursuit of their private desires, produce disintegration and deal in "dirt."[33] The domestication of empire augments the narrative role of women, whose traditional place is in the home. It seems to augment, too, a misogyny that sees women in general as "other" and wives in particular as "outsiders brought in" (Parker 1998.154–55). In *I, Claudius*, it appears that women, especially wives, although domesticated, are not tamed. The televisual treatment of Graves's women and the visual medium itself make the female members of the family more sexual and/or duplicitous. Where Graves (1989b.73, 78) mentions Julia's sexual excesses, television displays a Julia, who otherwise gossips, drinks, and stuffs herself with food, in the center of a sexual orgy of entangled bodies. Where Graves's Livia is guilty only of giving Julia Spanish Fly to induce uncontrollable sexual desire, television's Livia devises a complex plot to promote Julia's adulteries and secure her exile which offers viewers duplicity elaborated in five separate scenes.[34] The interplay of image and sound track, too, often adds a sadistic touch to female sexual desire and duplicity. Graves describes Livilla as "so much in love with [Sejanus] that he could count on her to betray [her husband] Castor" (1989b.295). Television treats its viewers to a scene in which Livilla drugs Castor into sleep and then has sex with Sejanus, who excites her with a vivid sexual fantasy: he will lock her in a room without clothes and watch his guards have intercourse with her. Later, Graves's bare notice that Livilla poisoned Castor becomes, on television, a death scene that puts viewers in the position of the male victim. We look at a close-up of Castor's ill face as he opens dying eyes; from his point of view, we see Livilla and Sejanus together looking down on him (us). Sejanus strokes her breast, she covers his hand, and the image fades. Castor closes his eyes and the screen fades to black.

Where women like Livilla produce dirt, Livia, more than any other character, traffics in it. Livia knows not only her own secrets but everyone else's: "Do you think I, who know everything that happens in Rome, don't know what happens under my own roof?" she asks rhetorically when a granddaughter believes one of her affairs is a secret. Livia's traffic in dirt presents particular difficulties and, if the reviews are testimony, pleasures for viewers. Close-ups of her deadpan face are pervasive in the seven episodes in which she appears as a major character. That face is difficult to read: Thrasyllus, the astrologer, comments to Tiberius, "Your mother is not the most scrutable of women. One may read her letters, but never her face." However, television viewers are aided, as the characters are not, by Claudius's narrational interventions. In one of the earliest close-ups of Livia, Claudius's voice-over identifies her as "my grandmother, Livia, her mind always turning, always scheming," and thereafter viewers expect such close-ups to signify Livia's calculations.

Claudius's comments and the camera enable the television audience to read Livia's patently figurative words as literally true and her literal statements as figuratively true. When Livia offers to nurse an ill Marcellus (only in order to poison him), a close-up of her impassive face answers his grateful comment, "It's very good of you" with the bold truth, "No, no, my dear, goodness has nothing to do with it." While the "hip" viewer will recognize Mae West's double entendre, every viewer can read her meaning because, only a short time before, Claudius's narrational voice had told us, "Now my grandmother's mind turned more and more toward the removal of Marcellus." At the end of the second episode, Augustus, looking at his grandsons, sighs that they are "our one hope." Livia embraces the two boys whom she will order killed: "Oh, they are promising all right, aren't you, my little beauties? Still you have a long way to go, a long, long way. We must take good care of them, Augustus, and we shall. The very best care." Since we have seen Livia eliminate Marcellus as a rival to her son, we doubt the literal truth of her words, and a close-up of her hand gripping the boys' shoulders strengthens our suspicions. Figuratively, however, she will indeed take good care of them— to make sure they are good and dead. Our suspicions about her words and trust in the image of those grasping hands give Augustus's closing words a nasty, if unintended, irony: "Ah, that's how it should be. Stay like that a moment. What a picture you make. It expresses the true spirit of the Roman family." Literally, the image of a grandmother with her arms around her grandsons expresses Augustus's frequently expressed platitudes about family unity. Figuratively, a grandmother holding in her clutches the grandsons she will murder reflects the Roman family we have seen and will see in every episode.

The *Village Voice* does no more than any American television viewer when it talks about Livia as a "shrew . . . [a] truly malignant force, pacing the palace like a soap-opera villainess looking for happy marriages to wreck" (Wolcott 1977). Not surprisingly, for viewers of the 1991 rebroadcast of *I, Claudius*, Livia becomes a Roman version of *Dynasty's* Alexis: "The most vicious, venomous vixen this side of Joan Collins . . . so casual in her murderous ways, so silkily insinuating about it all . . . Such a beautiful, brittle, pure-bred bitch!" (Krupnick 1991). Indeed, like Alexis's "private and public 'war' against the familial patriarch," Livia's machinations "constitute . . . the serial's main source of conflict and provide a structural framework into which all other conflicts are inscribed" (Kreutzner and Seiter 1995.247–49).[35] Again, the televisual medium and contemporary politics work together. The audience can read Livia, Julia, Livilla, Plancina, Aelia, Drusilla, Messalina, and Agrippinilla through soap opera's villainesses and women-gone-bad; at the same time, television's Roman imperial women evoke the dangers of feminists who, in the imagination of the New Right, threaten home and nation. Under these conditions, viewers might observe that the imperialism depicted in *I, Claudius* is not pure but an imperialism brought on by uppity women. The demise of the Roman patriarch, the advocate of "family values" as the basis of good empire, is a dramatic illustration.

When Augustus finally discovers his wife's machinations and acts to thwart them, she poisons him. As he dies, Livia lists his mistakes and her corrections. In extreme close-up, viewers watch both his death and his dawning horror, as she bespeaks her control in an I-know-better-than-you tone: "You should have listened to me more; you should have. You know that, don't you. I've been right more often than not and because I am a woman, you pushed me into the background. Oh yes, yes, you did. And all I have ever wanted was for you and for Rome; nothing I ever did was for myself, nothing, only for you and for Rome, as a Claudian should. Oh yes, my dear, I'm a Claudian. I think you were apt to forget that at times, but I never did, no, never, no." We have observed the blindness of Augustus and experienced our own greater knowledge because we have been privy to Livia's private space where the plots were hatched and the secrets revealed. Up to this point, our access has allowed us to enjoy her one-liners, even as we watched the hapless state of her victims. Here, her tone, certainty, and self-satisfaction before a helpless, motionless Augustus make her cruel and him pathetic. It is in this sadistic light that she explains her actions by citing a pseudo-feminist complaint that Augustus pushed her into the background only because of her sex, although she had "been right more often than not." Livia makes clear the danger she represents, a danger her husband was "apt to forget": as a Claudian, she is not a member of his family but an indigestible alien who acts on her own independent judgment of what needs to be done even if it includes the removal of her husband.

The scene is a dramatic instance of a larger pattern of male victims and female perpetrators that associates republican men with good empire and royal women with bad empire. The pattern, brought home to an American audience by the articulations of Claudius and Cooke, relies on an obfuscation of history and political terminology, especially around the meanings of "republic" and "republican," familiar terms in American political discourse whose ancient Roman signification is quite different. In the United States, "republic" popularly denotes a (our) democratic form of government. The Roman republic, however, was fundamentally undemocratic: an elite ruled Rome, Italy, and an empire through its domination of the most powerful political institutions, the senate and the magistracies. While "republican" in modern political rhetoric might refer to an advocate of democracy, to a popular audience in the 1970s, it could signal the political party of Nixon, Reagan, and family values. Roman republicans were not advocates of an egalitarian order but of the privileges of their own class. Television's handling of political terminology, however, domesticates politics and facilitates an association between Roman republicans, modern advocates of democracy, and, perhaps, members of the party who urged a return to family values to counter national loss.

In the family narrative of empire, the good men who are the chief victims of female agency are not only good fathers, loving husbands, and loyal brothers, they (Augustus, Drusus, Postumus, Germanicus, and Claudius himself) are also advocates of the republic. The meaning of Roman republicanism in the television narrative is vague: a twentieth-century audience gathers only that "republic" signifies the rule of a senate (whose form and function are limited to men in togas assembled in a hall), and an antipathy to the principate, an imperial state ruled by a single man. In these terms, the credentials of Augustus, the first emperor and founder of the principate, would seem to contradict his assertion to Claudius that, at heart, he is a republican and that he never intended to rule so long—"Things just didn't work out." The discourse of family abets the vagueness of political terminology to cover over this nonsense. An earlier exchange with Claudius's father Drusus occludes political considerations by explaining civil war in familial terms. Augustus blames the war that gave him sole control of the Roman world and made him emperor on the husbandly failures of Antony, his rival and brother-in-law: "If he'd been a proper husband to my sister, things would have been very different." Augustus longs to be a private citizen again; ruling an empire, he tells Drusus, is a heavy burden, one he would have given up long ago if it had not been for his wife Livia.

Alistair Cooke has defined in advance the way the audience should read Augustus: a man without ambitions of absolute power, who cared only for the good of Rome. Before the first episode, Cooke explains: "Augustus . . . was now the ruler of the known world. He proclaimed himself emperor, but he promised, like a good republican, to rule with the advice and consent of the senate. All he wanted to do now was to fix the borders of the provinces, build public works, and settle agreeably into middle age." After the fourth episode in which Livia plots the fall of Postumus, Augustus's grandson and intended heir, and Augustus dismisses Postumus's account of Livia's crimes, Cooke steps in to tell viewers about the "historical Augustus": "He was once called the most enlightened statesman of the ancient world. He wrote a constitution which, through the channel of Roman law, passed first to Britain and then to America, as a model, an outline of our own constitution . . . most of all he reconciled the old nobility and the new republicans and merchants and middle classes to a system of government that was fundamentally republican and had an emperor as a figurehead. You might say he was the first constitutional monarch." Cooke's historical facts are largely fictions: Augustus's system is only a model for modern Britain and the United States by the greatest stretch of the imagination; it was "fundamentally" monarchical, not republican; and the emperor was a military autocrat, not a "constitutional monarch."

Yet viewers unacquainted with Roman history will be guided by Cooke. His authoritative assertions prepare them to read the forces that assault the "model . . . of our own constitution." Drusus defines these forces: in a letter to his brother Tiberius, he connects "corruption and petty place-seeking in Rome" with Augustus's "supreme power," yet, he claims, Augustus could be persuaded or compelled to resign "but for the stubbornness of our mother, Livia, who derives such satisfaction from the exercise of supreme power through him." Ensuing episodes instance the "corruption and petty place-seeking" under emperors, good and bad, who are manipulated by corrupt agents. We expect this, as Claudius's narrational voice informs us that "all power corrupts." The destructive force most on display throughout thirteen episodes stems from female agents, especially but not exclusively Livia, who, as in Graves, is an articulate enemy of republicans. In the first episode, the narrating Claudius observes that the republic was "the last thing my grandmother wanted." Livia disdains republicanism as an "infantile disorder": the senate from which she is excluded because she is a woman and Claudius because he is a fool, "is full of nothing but old women and fools."

When Livia justifies her plots, she claims to have acted only for the good of Rome. Cooke and Claudius give viewers ground to doubt this altruistic assertion or to see it as the confusion of her private desires with the public good. Cooke, who keeps count of Livia's murders, categorically states what the viewer should understand after the first episode: "You will have gathered that Livia's one aim in life is to have her son Tiberius succeed Augustus." In his role as narrator, Claudius calls her a "wicked woman" three times, thus defining the murders and manipulations she claims serve Rome. Livia's ends require the destruction of good men and leave Rome in the hands of two tyrants: the morose Tiberius and the mad Caligula, both of them sexually deviant and violent. Ultimately, deviance, violence, and madness are the result of Livia's murder of "the most enlightened statesman of the ancient world" and "the first constitutional monarch." As we watch him die of her poison, we watch the female destruction of the "model . . . of our own constitution."[36]

"Us" and "Not Us"

The visual style and narrative devices of soap opera through which Graves's novels are domesticated privilege a reading that makes family a metonymy for empire. Domestication is pleasurable but also troublesome when metonymy facilitates allegory: perceiving in the narrative of ancient Roman familial and imperial corruption what the *New York Times* calls the "intended parallels to our times" (Brown 1977). On the one hand, televisual Rome, where female sexual activities, plots, and manipulations make a mockery of the "family values" of Augustus, destroy republican men, and ruin a good imperialist like Claudius, might serve as an instructive warning, but, on the other hand, this Rome perhaps comes too close to "home." The pleasures and dangers of imperial domestication produce a multivalent response that turns ancient Romans into "us" and "not us."

The televisual domestication of empire makes the historically remote and geographically vast world of the Roman empire seem both real and familiar—or rather, it becomes real to the degree to which it appears familiar. The "down-to-earth and colloquial" speech of the serial's characters, a deliberate and celebrated element of Jack Pullman's script, nurtured a perception that the Romans "were real people, just like you and me" (Kelly 1977, Unger 1977; also Clarke 1977, Yanni 1977, "A Touch of Murder"). In the producers' advertised logic of familiarity, "we're not in Rome, but we're still doing as Romans did" because our desires and our actions are the same: "The desires and the way people behaved then are exactly the way they behave today," claims the director Herbert Wise (PM). Ultimately, familiarity is attributed to an unchanging human nature: "Styles and customs change," but "human nature, twentieth-century edition, is pretty much the same as it was better than two thousand years ago," and that explains for Wise why Masterpiece Theatre's Romans "should not seem total strangers to viewers" (PM).

Perceptions of familiarity bring in their wake the danger of similarity. According to Wise, the arena of action has shifted in the contemporary world, and the ability to act openly is restricted: ancient Romans were "a bit more overt, because it was more fashionable and the power was absolute"; modern businessmen "don't go out and kill each other with the same gay abandon, but they'd like to. Or they kill each other in business" (PM). However, "it ["business, politics, the dirty tricks"] is all there" (PM). When producers and reviewers discussed the Rome of *I, Claudius* in terms of the current American crisis of empire, they confirmed, in Wise's words, that "the lust, chicanery and wheeling and dealing . . . are still with us today" (PM). Whether Masterpiece Theatre's Roman rulers create their corrupt world or are only the symptom of their world's corruption, their similarity to us endows us with a parallel conundrum of corruption: do the scandalous practices of the presidency, intelligence agencies, and corporations mean that our leaders corrupt the world? Or are these leaders only the symptom of our corrupt world— "the rash that's come out," to borrow Antonia's description of the emperor Caligula? In the latter case, they are the leaders we deserve. If our similarity to corrupt Romans is the result of universal human nature, then nothing and no one, including ourselves, is sacred, pure, or heroic, and the allegory of empire leaves us with unappealing behavioral alternatives. Like Livia or Caligula, we can thrive in the "stagnant pool," indulging wholeheartedly in "dirty tricks," violence, or decadence. Or, like Claudius, we can play the fool to survive, holding onto an impossible dream of a better world that, in the end, gives way to cynicism.

Visual fulfillment of Claudius's promise that he "shall hide nothing! nothing!" allows the audience to see it all, but this pleasure, too, has its dangers. Television's domestication of empire, especially through the adaptation of soap opera conventions, offers viewers an "inside" view of all the action, even the most covert, in an historically and socially distant world. This process seems egalitarian in comparison to both history and the theater: "The significance of this series is that it completely democratizes the amazing characters, who often speak directly to their audience with the kind of intimacy not possible in classical proscenium theater," notes one of the reviewers who see the program as a soap: "That is, perhaps, the key to *I, Claudius*'s success—it is not done as classical theater, but as television drama" (Yanni 1977). Ordinary people who watch the program are neither so low on the social hierarchy nor so deprived as to be excluded from what could be represented as the exalted realm of those who rule an empire. Quite the reverse, according to Katie Kelly of the *New York Post*—we viewers see Rome's imperial family as just "a simple, albeit royal, Roman family," behaving the way any family behaves: "Ceasar [*sic*] in an old straw hat pottering about the garden, someone else complaining about the traffic noise and everyone discussing family affairs" (1977). Seeing it all from the "inside" has its special thrills when

events turn down and dirty in this "juicy" soap.[37] Television puts its audience in intimate contact with "an extraordinary potpourri of villainy,
corruption, and degradation . . . In other words, thirteen weeks of old-
fashioned, new-fangled electronic decadence" (Unger 1977).

Yet the pleasure of viewing dirt dirties the viewer. The permeable
boundaries between the worlds of televisual fictions, news, and commercials and the world of the viewing family mix viewer and viewed.[38]
If one world bleeds into another, Roman "villainy, corruption, and degradation," much of it wrought by imperial women, bleed into the American home, which, the New Right warns, faces the moral perversions of
feminists, the "enemies of every decent society" (Faludi 1992.232). Quite
literally, of course, "electronic decadence" on the screen is, physically, in
the home. Like contemporaneous arguments about televisual content
and "family values," a controversy about the show's scenes of sex and violence reflected a concern with what was brought into the home.[39] Joan
Sullivan, executive producer at Boston's WGBH-TV and responsible for
Masterpiece Theatre, cut particularly explicit sexual and violent moments from the BBC production, acting on what she called "a sense of
responsibility to a mass audience." For Sullivan, the issue was not merely
what would be "disturbing to people in some parts of the country" but
"extensive permissiveness" (Brown 1977). Implicitly, the danger lies in a
cannibalistic consumption of images: you become what you see, as you
become what you eat.

The dangers of domestication are countered by distancing mechan-
isms in the process of reception: history, humor, and the venue of Masterpiece Theatre itself shape a reading formation that decadent Romans
are "not us." Assertions of the serial's historical accuracy set the Roman
family and empire in a world apart, and reviewers perceive excesses in
televisual Romans that separate "us" from "them." In effect, they assert
that we are bad, but not as bad as those Romans. Politically, the "intrigue,
ambition, and corruption . . . of the Roman empire . . . makes Watergate
look like child's play" (Gardella 1977), and personally, the sexual behavior of Romans "would leave many of our 'liberated' notions looking somewhat prissy" (O'Connor 1977). The historicity of televisual Roman excess
ensures the truth of the distinction between the "U.S." and ancient Rome.

Horror at the Romans meshes with a self-satisfied appreciation of
the serial's humor to widen the gap between "us" and "them": "The
machinations of these emperors are often terrifying, but the episodes are
full of funny moments," *TV Guide* assures its readers (MacKenzie 1977).
Across a wide spectrum of the press, reviewers demonstrate their grasp

of the irony, wit, and black humor of the characters' speeches, soliciting the appreciation of viewers—or at least those that want to feel "in on it." All in all, the serial gives its viewers "campy irreverence" and "tongue-in-cheek, high-camp dialogue" (Unger 1977).[40] A confident, often smug, sense that one gets the joke sets the knowing viewer at a distance from the characters. The keys to the jokes, like the superior knowledge gleaned from Claudius and Cooke, allow viewers to feel that they know more than any agent in the story, even the nearly omniscient Livia. Reviewers turn horror at Livia into humor, and their almost patronizing appreciation of Sian Phillips's performance lessens the sting of any allegorical associations with the feminism of the present. Claudius tells us that Livia is a "wicked woman," Cooke that she is "a lady of unsleeping malevolence." However, through the knowing eyes of the *New York Times* reviewer, Livia's malevolence becomes "gorgeous" (O'Connor 1977). *Time* reduces Livia to "the wicked witch of the Tiber," who, as viewers will remember from the annual television broadcast of *The Wizard of Oz*, is dissolved into muck by a bucket of water (Clarke 1977).

Appreciation of the serial's humor, and Phillips's performance in particular, should be associated with the way in which Masterpiece Theatre shapes a reading of *I, Claudius*. Perhaps more powerfully than perceptions of historicity and humor, this venue disrupts allegorical identification with the soap opera–like imperial family of *I, Claudius*. It constructs these Romans as "not us" by making them British. Masterpiece Theatre sets the Roman soap opera and imperial narrative amid other imperial stories in which empire is firmly identified as British: "A British import encrusted with the glory of Rome," Harriet Van Horne of the *New York Post* observes (1977b). The stills from other Masterpiece Theatre programs that decorate Alistair Cooke's drawing room like family photographs situate the Roman imperial family alongside the British royal family as well as other families living through the British imperial order and its crises. For Masterpiece Theatre's twentieth anniversary, these photographs came to life in a flow of scenes from twenty years of programming the British empire: *Upstairs, Downstairs; The Flame Trees of Thika; On Approval; I, Claudius; All for Love; A Dedicated Man; Elizabeth R.; The Jewel in the Crown; The Tale of Beatrix Potter; The Six Wives of Henry VIII.*

Masterpiece Theatre, a program of "classics" and "quality" television, associates "classics" and "quality" with the former colonial rulers of the United States. The perceived advantage of British productions in this sort of programming raises the specter of cultural imperialism, when, in fact, Masterpiece Theatre is one of the few successes of British television in a world televisual market dominated by American producers.[41] With few exceptions, reviewers praise the ensemble work of the cast, rave about individual actors, and cite their awards and accomplishments.[42] Such reviews, even negative ones, identify the characters as British. Harriet Van Horne, who calls *I, Claudius* a "masterpiece of a bore," complains, "this is the kind of drama in which everybody speaks the clenched-teeth stage-English that goes sailing past the American ear as another damned furrin' tongue" (1977a; cf. Kitman 1991). Arthur Unger in the *Christian Science Monitor* relishes the "scenery-chewing performances right out of the Monty Python Royal Academy of Overacting" (1977.26). Addressing a large and varied television audience, *TV Guide* informs viewers they will see "a display of English acting at its keenest honing" (MacKenzie 1977).[43]

Acting style, theatrical gesture, and the accents of the main characters solidify the place of *I, Claudius* in Masterpiece Theatre's stream of British imperial tales. For an audience in the United States, moreover, these features conflate the rulers of the Roman empire with those of the British empire and evoke the colonial history of the United States and Britain. Reflecting the perceptions of its audience, *TV Guide* could not make this conflation clearer: "Forty years of movie spectacles have taught us that the ancient Romans spoke with British accents (lower-class Romans spoke Cockney . . .)" (MacKenzie 1977). Through the Britishness of the actors and of Masterpiece Theatre itself, American viewers could understand Rome through a fantastical association with their own colonial past. The audience of a modern American empire could experience itself as the colonized, implicitly attributing the corruption of the family and state wrought by women and mad tyrants to the colonizer and, at the same time, masking its own imperial pretensions and policies at a moment of imperial crisis.[44] Yet for the actor who played Rome's first emperor, Britain, the colonizer of the past, is only "a poor country now . . . America is the only place you could relate ancient Rome to" (quoted in Weingrad 1977).

Notes

I am grateful for the help of many friends and colleagues. My special thanks to Andrew Herman for lessons in television and contemporary theory; to James A. Klein for the benefit of his considerable knowledge of British and American history; to Carlin Barton for her insightful comments and criticisms; and to Sheila Murnaghan, Margaret Malamud, and Martha Malamud for their many suggestions, both big and small.

1. The novels were adapted for television by Jack Pullman for a co-production of BBC-2 and London Films in 1976. Produced by Martin Lisemore and directed by Herbert Wise, *I, Claudius* starred British actors from the stage and television: Derek Jacobi (Claudius), Brian Blessed (Augustus), Sian Phillips (Livia), and John Hurt (Caligula). Acquired by Joan Sullivan of Boston's WGBH-TV for PBS's Masterpiece Theatre, the serial aired on Sunday nights from November 6, 1977, to January 29, 1978. It was rebroadcast on PBS in 1986 and 1991. On the acquisition of syndication rights in the United States, see note 2.

2. PBS, which received on average a 3% share of the prime-time television audience, was seen as programming for "high income, high status, high education types who've been bored by commercial TV too often to watch it any more" (Von Hoffman 1977); cf. Brennan 1987. In a program guide published in the *New York Times* and paid for by Mobil, information on Robert Graves shores up the program's status as a "classic" by calling Graves "one of the major poets of the twentieth century" and noting his "distinguished contributions as an essayist, scholar, historian, librettist, and lecturer"; a page entitled "The Cast" simulates a theater program. On its popular appeal, see Yanni 1977 and Kitman 1991. Better testimony to its popular appeal than its selection as the series PBS viewers most wanted to see again for Masterpiece Theatre's twentieth anniversary was the acquisition of American syndication rights in 1980 by Metromedia Producers Corp., whose most remunerative properties included *The Merv Griffin Show*. MPC's stations could then run *I, Claudius* on Saturday or Sunday as a "weekly primetime miniseries" ("MPC Buys").

3. The serial was shot entirely in the studio on a budget of approximately two million dollars.

4. In Roman literary sources, Claudius generally evokes hostility and disgust: see Levick 1990 and Joshel 1997. Graves acknowledges a debt to Arnaldo Momigliano, who generally eschews the ancient picture of Claudius as an uxorious fool and argues for a "centralizing" Claudius, an emperor with a "desire for reform" inspired by his "minute and loving familiarity with history" (Graves 1989c.viii, Momigliano 1934.18, 39–73). For Graves, Claudius is a victim of "the bad press he was given by contemporary historians" who "had obviously got Claudius wrong" (quoted in Kersnowski 1989.100).

I use the names Graves assigns to historical figures: so, for example, Agrippinilla for Agrippina the Younger, mother of Nero, and Castor for Drusus, son of Tiberius.

5. For example, in a catalogue of rulers in an oracle, each emperor is said "to enslave the State" (Graves 1989b.11–12).

6. Graves puts the diatribe against women and unchastity of ancient Roman male authors into the mouths of ex-slaves, female servants of Claudius's mother (1989b.94–95). Sexual laxity gives Livia a tool: Graves imagines that the women of Rome confess their adulteries and incest to Livia's friend Urgulania, and, as

"penance," they are instructed to kill those men Livia wants to get rid of (1989b.108–09, 341).

7. Also, for example, a denunciation of Cato the Censor makes that famous embodiment of ancient virtue nothing more than an avaricious imperialist and a cruel slaveholder (1989b.6off.). Seneca, famous as a Stoic and statesman, appears as a base flatterer and hypocrite (1989c.192–93, 341).

8. Implicitly and explicitly, Graves associates Rome's ancient enemies and subjects with Britain's contemporary enemies and subjects: here he lines up the enemy "other" of World War I, the colonized "other," and the internal "other." Not surprisingly, while the Britons are good barbarians, Graves's Germans are "the most insolent and boastful nation in the world when things go well with them, but once they are defeated they are the most cowardly and abject" (1989b.249; also 1989c.158). Yet the ancient Germans can also be assimilated to non-Europeans, like the "Ama-Zulu warriors, with whom the Germans of Claudius's day had culturally much in common" (1989b.x).

9. "I identify myself with him as much as with any historical character I know about" (quoted in Seymour-Smith 1995.255). The novels have also been read as "an objective correlative for [Graves's] situation" and as *romans à clef* (Seymour-Smith 1995.231, 232–37 and Seymour 1995.212–17). Biographies of Graves make Claudius's weaknesses Graves's own and make Livia and Messalina versions of his lover, Laura Riding.

10. Attempts include: Alexander Korda's never-finished film of *I, Claudius*, directed by Josef von Sternberg, starring Charles Laughton as Claudius and Merle Oberon as Messalina (1937); *The Epic That Never Was*, a BBC television program on the film (1965); unfulfilled plans for a film with Alec Guinness (1956–57); and John Mortimer's play, *I, Claudius* (1972). Tony Richardson, director of Mortimer's play, exemplifies the adoption of Graves's Claudius as a "fairly decent man in the middle who is just trying to survive" ("Talking about *I, Claudius*," 19).

11. Perhaps the best example of the projection of contemporary politics is Charles Laughton's understanding of Claudius. Those involved in Korda's film report Laughton's difficulty with his role. He "couldn't find the man" until he had transferred Britain's royal trauma to ancient Rome: one day Laughton arrived on the set and announced, "he'd found the man—Edward VIII." Thereafter he would listen to Edward's abdication speech every day before filming (*The Epic That Never Was*).

12. Turning Graves's works into a domestic drama had already been imagined by Alec Guinness, who wanted to star in a film of the novels. In a letter to Will Price in June 1956, Graves explains that Guinness "doesn't want to do anything on a great and glorious scale . . . he wants to make this a real stay-at-home treat for himself . . . He feels just the same about Claudius—doesn't want any *Ben-Hur* or *Quo Vadis* stuff, just the domestic Palace drama" (quoted in Seymour-Smith 1995.460).

13. Speaking to a Business Council meeting in Hot Springs, Virginia, William Simon, secretary of the treasury under Presidents Richard Nixon and Gerald Ford, summarized this moment of crisis in the fall of 1976 as it was perceived by a member of the American corporate elite: "Vietnam, Watergate, student unrest, shifting moral codes, the worst economic recession in a generation, and a number of other jarring cultural shocks have combined to create a new climate of questions and doubt . . . It all adds up to a general malaise, a society-wide crisis of institutional confidence" (quoted in Zinn 1984.257).

14. PM, "Boston Worried," Brown 1977, Gardella 1977, Krupnick 1991, "MPC Buys," Unger 1977, Weingrad 1977, Wolcott 1977.

15. The assertion that the program's sex and violence are simply historical facts helps Brown distinguish *I, Claudius* from *Soap*, a prime-time parody on ABC whose sexual content created controversy. He can then dismiss *Soap* as a program in search of shock value and higher Nielsen ratings (see note 39). Television viewers are assured by Alistair Cooke, whom Brown cites as an authority: "I think I ought to say at the start that some people are going to be more shocked by this series than by most of the dramas we've shown on 'Masterpiece Theatre.' But Robert Graves did not make it more cruel or more gamy than the manuscript of Suetonius from which he worked . . . Violence is not shown for titillation."

16. To the review's notice of *The Best of Families, Mulligan Stew*, and *Eight Is Enough*, we can add *All in the Family, Little House on the Prairie, Soap, Family, The Jeffersons*, to name a few prime-time programs. *I, Claudius* arrived one year after *Roots*, an immensely popular television serial on the African-American family, and accompanied the first television broadcast of *The Godfather*, which *TV Guide* called "a sympathetic family portrait . . . and a corrupt version of the American dream" ("Close Up," 12 November 1977). NBC aired part one of *The Godfather* at the end of the same week that saw the broadcast of the first episode of *I, Claudius*; part two appeared opposite (and in competition with) the second episode of *I, Claudius*.

17. Private communication.

18. Egypt, for example, is the source of a pornographic scroll. On receiving a vase imported from India, Livia remarks, "It's a pity we never got that far; so many fine things we could have picked up cheap."

19. In addition, black slaves wait on Julia and Antonia and silent gladiators are scolded by Livia. A half-clothed belly dancer from Antioch dances at a dinner party attended by Claudius and Agrippilla. German guards appear as thugs with a limited vocabulary. The noble British chieftain Caractacus briefly addresses the senate in accented English. The doctor Musa and the poisoner Martina, ignoble characters typed as Semitic and sneaky, have brief but destructive roles in the plots of the imperial family and speak English with distinctly Middle-Eastern inflections. The urbane, sophisticated Herod, who makes witty, deprecating remarks about his own people, the Jews, instances the mimicry discussed by Homi Bhabha (1984) and Jenny Sharpe (1989).

20. Reports of a formal nature include: an exchange between Livia and Augustus on the situations in Germany and Parthia; a soldier's report on the Germans and Varus's loss of three legions; a conversation between two of Claudius's officials on his conquest of Britain; a governor's report and letters on Herod's activities in the eastern provinces.

21. When Augustus comments on the cleverness of the Greeks, Marcellus asks rhetorically, "If they are so clever, why are they a province of ours?" Criticizing the spoiled behavior of the boy Caligula, who wants to sleep with his sister, his grandmother Antonia blames his stay in the eastern provinces: "Syria is no place to bring up a Roman child."

22. For representational practices of television news, see also Gans 1979 and Bourdieu 1998.

23. Myles Breen and Farrell Corcoran 1982, cited in Schwoch, White, and Reilly 1992.58. For examples, see Schwoch, White, and Reilly 1992.54.

24. For the conventions of soap opera, see Allen 1985.6–95, Allen 1995a, Mumford 1995.14–46. It should also be noted that, in the 1970s, a number of soap operas expanded from thirty to sixty minutes (*The Guiding Light* during the first week of *I, Claudius*). Other reviews that discuss *I, Claudius* in terms of soap opera: "A Touch of Murder," Brown 1977, Wolcott 1977, Yanni 1977, Mannes 1991.

25. On soap opera's women-gone-bad and villainesses, see Modleski 1982, Geraghty 1991, Nochimson 1993, Kreutzner and Seiter 1995.247–49.

26. The notion of "dirt," too, runs through reviewers' descriptions of *I, Claudius*, although some, like Nicholas Von Hoffman of the *San Francisco Examiner*, are at pains to distinguish this PBS serial as finer than "any of the dull dramatizations of trash fiction on commercial TV" (Von Hoffman 1977; cf. Brown 1977).

27. The narrational functions of Claudius and Cooke are enclosed within Masterpiece Theatre's "visual and musical signature" (cf. Allen 1985.155). Each episode begins with the icon of a turning red leather book embossed in gold with the words "Masterpiece Theatre" and "Introduced by Alistair Cooke." Then the boldface words MOBIL CORPORATION appear on the screen, while a disembodied, cultured voice intones: "Masterpiece Theatre is made possible by a grant from Mobil Corporation."

28. Allen 1985.158. Claudius and Cooke share some of the qualities of the host-narrator of the radio soap; for Claudius as both the host-narrator and the central character who periodically addresses the audience directly, see Allen 1985.154–75.

29. For example, Brown 1977 (see note 15) and Gardella 1977.

30. As an "Americanized Englishman," Cooke bridges the imagined gap between the British production of a literary "classic" and the American audience of a popular medium; cf. Brennan 1987.

31. Caligula, clothed as Zeus, fears Drusilla will give birth to a god greater

than himself. Although the more vivid portions were cut from the BBC production and then "rearranged" by Joan Sullivan, the excised elements were widely reported in the press so as to enable viewers to read the horrific scene. This familial expansion of Graves has deleterious effects on the portrayal of Drusilla. Pullman wanted viewers to have "pity for that silly girl . . . who knew [Caligula] was mad and played up to him without realizing until the end what he was going to do to her" (Brown 1977). He underestimates her silliness and sycophancy. Earlier, in a temple before statues of Jupiter and Juno, she enacts her assigned role as goddess with enthusiasm. In the scene before the "abortion," she wanders around drugged, calling "Zeusy, my husband," comes on to her uncle Claudius, and feels no shame at her pregnancy, seeing it as her hedge against Caligula.

32. Beside the opening and closing scenes, nine other dinners feature family struggles or reports of corruption: in episodes 2, 4, 6 (two), 7 (three), 11, and 13. Not surprisingly, in the very last scene, when the sibyl informs Claudius that Nero, his adopted son, will kill Britannicus, who is Claudius's natural son; that Nero's mother will kill Claudius's official Narcissus; and that Nero will kill his mother, Claudius responds: "Sounds depressingly familiar."

33. Repetitively, we watch female characters engage in illicit sex and manipulate men through lies and dissimulation. Even the good women are problematic. Agrippina, wife of Germanicus, is moral and chaste, but her outspoken, high-handed behavior secures neither her own nor her sons' safety; she indulges a young Caligula whom viewers clearly see as spoiled and dangerous. Antonia is a Roman with a finely tuned sense of duty, a woman of strict morality, and a devoted wife, but she is a cold-hearted mother to Claudius, whom she treats with disdain even up to the moment of her suicide. The chief male villains are effeminate or associated with women. As a boy, Caligula has a delicate, feminine appearance. John Hurt's performance gives the adult Caligula's speech and gestures what Wolcott (1978) calls "faggoty-fey inflection"; in one scene, he performs a ballet in drag. In addition, Caligula's dry, cynical lines, like Livia's, play with the literal and figurative meanings of words. Sejanus, who first appears as Livia's henchman, also has her oily way of speaking, and his behavior in a scene in which he orders around a senator in episode 7 approximates Livia's in a scene in episode 2. Tiberius is under Livia's control for the first five episodes.

34. Other elaborations have a similar effect on the characterization of imperial women. Where Graves briefly mentions Marcellus's death and describes Augustus's death in two pages, later noting Livia's hand in both (1989b.37, 183–85), the series elaborates the men's suffering and Livia's agency. Graves's short descriptions of Livilla's role in Postumus's exile, her obsession with Sejanus, and the poisoning of her husband are augmented and take up more time and space in the narrative.

35. No single character or actor attracted more comment than Livia played by Sian Phillips, and when a review is accompanied by a still, the photograph usually features or, at least, includes her. The promotional material identifies her as

"the breathtakingly beautiful, murdering mother of Rome—a female Machiavelli who is Medea and all the Borgias rolled into one." The program guide published in the *New York Times* and paid for by Mobil explains that: "Although Augustus had conquered every foe, he was unable to deny the will of Livia." For reviewers, the "power-hungry Livia" plans "death as coolly as most women would take a trip to the supermarket" (Yanni 1977); she is "a patrician by birth and by vicious instinct" and a "student of exotic poisons and destructive gossip" (O'Connor 1977). She is associated with the snake that crawls across the opening credits: "A Medici of the old school who orchestrates the nasty business with all the morality of the slithering snake featured over the opening titles" ("A Touch of Murder," Wolcott 1978; cf. Livia as spider, Yanni 1977 and Wolcott 1977). Livia's omniscience is such that an article in the *New York Post* on the cuts made by Joan Sullivan inadvertently has Livia knowing what comes after her death. The caption between two stills, one of the emperor Caligula (misidentified as Derek Jacobi) and one of Livia staring over a cup of wine reads: "We'll never get to see what Emperor Caligula . . . does to his wife and sister, but Livia . . . looks as though she already knows" ("Boston Worried"). Livia dies in episode 7, and the murder of Drusilla referred to here occurs in episode 9. Throughout, it is clear that reviewers found enormous pleasure in the character and in Phillips's performance: Clarke 1977, Gardella 1977, MacKenzie 1977, O'Connor 1977, Yanni 1977, Wolcott 1977, Krupnick 1991.

36. Reviewers who adopt Cooke's vision sympathize with Augustus: a "kindly, understanding emperor who only wants to enjoy his middle years and keep harmony in his family. He is a civilizing influence, uncomfortable with power and, if he had his way, would probably prefer to see Rome as a republic" (Gardella 1977). See also PM, Clarke 1977, MacKenzie 1977, O'Connor 1977.

37. "Juicy," used explicitly by Yanni 1977, is implied by other reviewers who unanimously relish the pleasures of viewing the dirt. In fact, viewers in the United States did not "see it all" because of the cuts made for the PBS broadcast. By filling in the missing details, however, reviewers allowed viewers to imagine them: see notes 31 and 35.

38. Nicholas Von Hoffman of the *San Francisco Examiner* provides a colorful illustration of bleeding diegesis: "Readers of Suetonius will tell you that next to the Emperor Caligula, Charlie Manson looks like the amiable fat monk in the Xerox commercials" (1977).

39. See also Unger 1977, "MPC Buys," and "Boston Worried." The furor over televisual content was focused in particular on ABC's *Soap*, according to the *New York Times*, "a sex-orientated comedy series that got religious groups and some network affiliates in a lather over its preoccupation with adultery, sexual promiscuity, impotency, and transvestitism" (Brown 1977).

40. The show is "sardonic fun," "a honey of a funny show" ("A Touch of Murder"), a "high and subtle domestic comedy" (MacKenzie 1977), and a "fun-filled Roman holiday" (Yanni 1977); it has "an enthralling and frequently hilari-

ous collection of schemers" (MacKenzie 1977); "political intrigues, murderous, ambitious, and consuming passions . . . add up to fascinating spectacle and perhaps, with fitting perversity, great fun" (O'Connor 1977).

41. Classics and quality: O'Connor 1977, Clarke 1977, Von Hoffman 1977. On the success of Masterpiece Theatre in the American television market, see Allen 1995b.16 and Brennan 1987. On the effect of such British serials on American commercial television see Hagedorn 1995.38.

42. In addition to the reviews cited below, see "Every Cough and Orgy," O'Connor 1977, Yanni 1977, Unger 1977. PM instructed reviewers by including phrases from British reviews and notices of the actors' other accomplishments, roles, and prizes.

43. Wolcott 1977 observes: "When a Roman general, with a noticeable English accent, confides in Augustus, 'You know, I don't get on with my wife,' the viewer may feel he's watching Evelyn Waugh's *Decline and Fall*, not Gibbon's."

44. The show's perceived excess of sexual explicitness is viewed as British, thus projecting televisual decadence onto former colonial rulers: "The series stirred no significant protest in that country, but racy programming has always gone down more easily on British television than it has here" (Brown 1977). Brennan 1987 argues that, contrary to the apparent conflict between Britain and the United States as colonizer and colonized, "Masterpiece Theatre is a cultural colonization in the heart of the empire, an attempt to fuse together the apparently incompatible national myths of England and the United States in order to strengthen imperial attitudes in an era of European and North American decline" (374). The commercialization of public television and, especially, the role of Mobil are part of the process: "The object, of course, is not always to sell a dirty little commodity. It is just as important to set the tone within which many commodities can be sold efficiently. An empire is a feel-good community" (Brennan 1987.376).

5

"Infamy! Infamy! They've All Got It in for Me!"

Carry On Cleo and the British Camp Comedies of Ancient Rome

Nicholas J. Cull

By late 1964, ancient Rome was overly familiar territory for British cinema audiences. Hollywood's cycle of postwar epics had ground to a climax with Twentieth Century Fox's *Cleopatra*. Then came a shaft of light. It is night at the Temple of Vesta. Julius Caesar enters with a detachment of soldiers. To his horror, his bodyguard draws his sword: "I'm sorry Sir, but for the good of Rome you must die!" Caesar protests: "But you're my personal bodyguard and champion gladiator. I don't want to die. I may not be a very good live emperor, but I'll be a worse one dead." Then, charging towards the camera, the emperor bursts into histrionics: "Treachery . . . Infamy! Infamy! They've all got it in for me!" Later, in her palace beside the Nile, Cleopatra looks winsomely at Mark Antony. "I have a poisonous asp," she lisps. Mark Antony glances at her behind, "I wouldn't say that," he says. Cleopatra produces a small snake from a casket: "One bite from this is enough." Mark Antony takes it, bites off its head, and, in a broad cockney accent, declares: "You're right . . . one bite's enough for anyone. It's shockin.'" (fig. 5.1). The film was *Carry On Cleo*, a relentless demolition of the classical film epic. It was part of a subgenre of British comedy that included locally inflected productions of the Broadway show *A Funny Thing Happened on the Way to the Forum*, British collaboration in the 1966 film version of that musical, the wildly successful TV sit-com *Up Pompeii!*, a spin-off movie of the same title, and numerous television sketches.

This subgenre tells us little about Rome but much about Britain in the 1960s, its cultural needs and obsessions. This is essentially a tale of three empires. First is the imagined historical Roman empire, a zone of license in which the imagination could run riot. The second is the newly

Figure 5.1 Cleopatra (Amanda Barrie) shows Mark Antony (Sid James) her poisonous asp in *Carry On Cleo* (1964).

declined British empire and the associated question of Britain's future. The loss of empire was still too raw to be addressed directly, but it could be discussed tangentially through the story of the rise, transient glory, and fall of Rome. Classical Rome was a singularly appropriate location for such discussion; classics sat at the heart of the British public school education that, for over a century, had built the men who supposedly built the British empire. Classics also underpinned the class system at home. Knowledge of Latin and Greek was a passport to higher things, and ignorance of them was a bar. Rome remained a cultural icon for those who, like the mandarins of the BBC, sought to preserve high culture in the face of the rising tide of game shows and television westerns. The third empire was the source of those westerns and game-show formats: the American empire. The United States was potent and omnipresent in the minds of the British audiences of the 1960s. Britain experienced both Hollywood's cultural power, which outshone its domestic film industry, and the political power of Washington, D.C., which recast Britain as a supporting player in America's geopolitical drama. Here was an empire that not only dominated like a new Rome, but cited the classics in its political rhetoric and epic film culture alike.

Reactions to these three empires—the imagined Rome, the newly absent British, and the newly dominant American—interweave throughout the writing, performance, and reception of these comedies. Their interrelationship is complex and shifting. In the course of *Carry On Cleo*, a single Roman character like Julius Caesar is used to ridicule contemporary British conservative politicians, then the conventions of Hollywood cinema or British gender relations. One moment he is "in" on the joke, using colloquial British expressions, and the next he is in the position of America: an outsider, a powerful "other" looking in on a world he does not know and presiding over the subjugation of Britain.

The British tradition of camp comedy lies at the core of this subgenre. The films were not only camp in the sense that they showcased the talents of comic actors like Kenneth Williams, Charles Hawtrey, or Frankie Howerd, who projected overtly camp personae, they were also camp at a fundamental level. The camp aesthetic has long served as a gay cultural response to heterosexual hegemony. Like African-American blues, camp has been an aesthetic of self-expression and, hence, self-defense. In the world of camp (from the French verb *se camper*, 'to posture or flaunt'), the signs of sexual identity are repeated with a twist, exaggerated until they are revealed not as facets of nature but as the constructs of culture. Received identity is revealed to be artificial and transformed into a mask of performance. A space for existence is created behind that mask and a means of expression is established through the medium of the performance. When one has acknowledged that all life is theater, one can both enjoy the performance and, perhaps, begin to change the script.[1]

Camp comedy is deeply rooted in British culture. Twentieth-century British camp displays traces of the overstated inflections of the foppish man-about-town, the Regency dandy; the play with gender identity familiar from Christmas pantomimes in which men and women exchange roles; the exaggerations and twists of Gilbert and Sullivan's world of "topsy turvy"; and, of course, the dazzling contribution of the writer whose life and work took camp to a new level, Oscar Wilde. Apparently removed from its twentieth-century origins in homosexual culture, the camp aesthetic has informed innumerable standup comedians and can be seen at the heart of maybe the two most enduring icons of British humor: the *Carry On* films and the *Monty Python* television programs and associated films. Despite some shared targets (including the Roman epic), *Carry On* and *Python* share different roots, albeit in all-male institutions. *Carry On* grew from the music hall humor recycled during the war to entertain the troops. Several *Carry On* regulars including Kenneth Williams cut their teeth in ENSA (the British equivalent of the USO), and the scripts were studded with the slang of the enlisted men and the middle-class junior officers swept up in wartime conscription. *Carry On* humor remained raw and proudly unsophisticated. *Monty Python* was, in contrast, the humor of the public school or Oxbridge college revue; at once more knowing and cynical, while also stealing a little class from the highbrow matter it selected as its target.

Whatever its origin, camp offered the perfect means to explore some of the tensions and dilemmas of the 1960s, not least in the areas of both personal and national identity. The Roman comedies turned on a collision between the attitudes and manners of the present and the stereotypical images of the past. As both Roman and contemporary behaviors were repeated in camp mode, they were rendered absurd: all three empires, Roman, British, and American, were subverted. Such comedy made the cultural straightjacket of sixties Britain bearable and opened the door for alternative ways of imagining the past and of imagining one's class, national, and sexual identity in the present.

Talbot Rothwell and the *Carry On* Series

Although the Roman subgenre chimed with a variety of audiences and performers, it is inseparable from the work of a single writer: Talbot Rothwell, author of *Carry On Cleo* (and nineteen other films in the *Carry On* series) and creator of *Up Pompeii!* "Tolly" Rothwell was born in Kent in 1916 and educated at Brighton College of Art in the heyday of the saucy seaside postcard and "end of the pier" humor that so influenced his later work. After working as a clerk for the Brighton town council, he enlisted in the Palestine Police in 1938 and acquired personal experience of an empire at work. On the outbreak of war in 1939, he joined the Royal Air Force as a pilot officer, only to be shot down the following year over Norway. Rothwell spent the rest of the war in a succession of German prisoner of war camps. His prisons included Stalag Luft III, which was destined to become familiar to the postwar British public as the setting for such films as *The Wooden Horse* and *The Great Escape*. Rothwell first ventured into show business while a prisoner. He was responsible for co-writing and staging noisy revues to maintain morale and distract the German guards (who were invited to the show) from any escape bids. Rothwell's postwar scripts never seemed quite free of the wartime necessity of having all the characters played by men; his women remained female impersonations. Yet the wartime origins of his comedy now seem oddly appropriate. Rothwell's work began as and remained in two senses camp escapism.[2]

After the war, Rothwell devoted himself to writing comedy first for such radio variety artists as Arthur Askey and the Crazy Gang, then for the stage, and eventually for the British cinema. In 1963, he completed his first *Carry On* script. He was a late addition to the *Carry On* team. The series began in 1958 with an unexpectedly successful army comedy, *Carry On Sergeant*. Producer Peter Rogers, director Gerald Thomas, and writer Norman Hudis built on their success with a series of follow-up films tackling work-related comic situations: a hospital (*Carry On Nurse*, 1959), a school (*Carry On Teacher*, 1959), the police (*Carry On Constable*, 1959), an employment agency (*Carry On Regardless*, 1961), and a cruise liner (*Carry On Cruising*, 1962).

The *Carry On* films rested on a strong ensemble company of regular performers who swiftly became identified with particular English types. Kenneth Connor was the frustrated little man; Charles Hawtrey, the effeminate weakling; Kenneth Williams, a campy man of letters; Hattie Jacques, the stern matron; Joan Sims, the strident wife; and Sid James, the lovable cockney rogue with an eye for girls and a rasping laugh. The plots were slight but the jokes quick and as cheeky as the censor allowed. It was a winning formula. To the amazement of the British press, who from an early stage regarded the *Carry On* films as an English institution, even American audiences enjoyed the films. American enthusiasm for *Carry On Nurse* allowed the writer Norman Hudis to seek his fortune in Hollywood, where he launched the *Man from U.N.C.L.E.* series. With Hudis seeking fresh pasture, Talbot Rothwell stepped into the breach. A new sensibility came with him.[3]

With Rothwell at the typewriter, Rogers and Thomas refocused the *Carry On* films on the satire of film genres and the roles assigned to Britain by its own film industry (as it alternated between lush historical drama and gritty contemporary realism), but, above all, on Hollywood. The *Carry On* gang "sent up" kitchen sink realism in *Carry On Cabby;* the spy thriller in *Carry On Spying;* and the swashbuckling naval tradition of Horatio Hornblower in *Carry On Jack*. Rothwell's idea for *Carry On Jack* (the only *Carry On* not conceived by Rogers himself) was a major departure for the series. He liberated the stock characters from the present and relocated them in historical genre situations. The original title was to be *Carry On Up the Armada*, but the censor objected to this as a coded reference to sodomy. Rothwell also freed the films from the sentimentality that had underpinned Hudis's work. As Peter Rogers recalled, Rothwell had been writing comedy for so long that, "He just couldn't write sentiment even if he had wanted to" (Interview: Peter Rogers, 21 July 1998). With three successes under their belts, the new team was well equipped to take aim at their next target: the Hollywood Roman epic.⁴ Rogers got the idea while drinking in the bar at Pinewood Studios during the making of *Cleopatra*. He bet the studio manager that he could make an entire film about Cleopatra in the time that it took the Twentieth Century Fox team to build a single set. He won his bet with *Carry On Cleo* (Interview: Peter Rogers, 21 July 1998).

The epic was more than just another genre. By 1963, when Rothwell began work on his script, the epic symbolized the worst excesses of the Hollywood system. The genre was characterized by conspicuous consumption on and off the screen: the films could not be made without armies of extras, vast sets, and acres of silk for costumes. It was a genre that attempted to bring moral certainties to the Cold War world, with American heroes perpetually bringing Christianity and/or liberty to a Rome in which British character actors ruled hordes of Italian extras. The plots seemed to question the institutions of empire and the material values of Rome, yet the *mise en scène* affirmed these values with every chariot race and mass naval battle. Each frame proclaimed: "Only Hollywood can produce such a lavish spectacle" and proclaimed it at ramming speed. Skimpy, suggestive costumes and plots loaded with concubines, courtesans, and slave boys turned epics into an ideal realm for exploring sexual license and desire, yet epics were usually framed by religion. Hence any challenge to the genre carried the extra frisson of stepping into the forbidden territory of joking about God. To don a breastplate with humorous intent was to play with the world of illustrated Victorian bibles and the associated codes of social and sexual conservatism, and to open the subversive subject of the classical era when these codes and the faith that went with them were new and contested.

To question the epic was also to question not only America's world and values but Britain's place in that world. The British who had once boasted of a *pax Britannica* now accepted the *pax Americana*. The Americans were increasingly comfortable with the role. References to the Roman empire abounded in the political culture of the time. John F. Kennedy made frequent classical allusions. He cited Greek philosophers when asked to define happiness, and he told his audience in Berlin in June 1962 that the modern equivalent of the proud Roman "boast": *civis romanus sum* (I am a Roman citizen) was *Ich bin ein Berliner*. In the wake of the Suez debacle, the British Prime Minister Harold Macmillan had enthusiastically peddled a formulation that first occurred to him in 1943, that the British must learn to be the Greeks to the American Rome: "The power has passed from us to Rome's equivalent, the United States of

America, and we can at most aspire to civilise and occasionally influence them." It was fitting that Macmillan was to be evoked twice in the *Carry On* version of the Roman empire.[5] *Carry On* producer Peter Rogers had a less charitable view of the United States. As he recalled in an interview in 1998, "I never went there and never wanted to" (Interview: Peter Rogers, 21 July 1998).

Carry On Cleo: The Plot

Carry On Cleo told the story of a British slave caught up in the struggle for power in ancient Rome. Caesar (Kenneth Williams) returns home from the wars to his jealous wife Calpurnia (Joan Sims) and a rebellious senate. His father-in-law Seneca (Charles Hawtrey) predicts an assassination. Meanwhile, Mark Antony (Sid James) is persuaded by Cleopatra (Amanda Barrie) to attempt Caesar's overthrow. Into this maelstrom comes the sexually inadequate British maker of square wheels, the slave Hengist Pod (Kenneth Connor). When Hengist is mistakenly believed to have saved Caesar's life—the real hero is his fellow Briton Horsa (Jim Dale)—he becomes the emperor's bodyguard. Caesar goes to Egypt to cement an alliance with Cleopatra, but learns in a vision of a new attempt on his life. He and Hengist change places. After drinking an Egyptian love philter, Hengist foils the plot by leaping on Cleopatra so heavily that her bed collapses on Mark Antony, who is concealed beneath waiting to kill Caesar. Pod kicks Mark Antony in the groin, kills Cleopatra's bodyguard, and escapes with the love potion. He and Horsa return to Britain where, as the film ends, Hengist is seen at the center of a vast family, with his nagging wife Senna (Sheila Hancock) now satisfied and his manhood restored. Caesar returns to Rome, but is assassinated in the senate, while for Mark Antony and Cleopatra, we are told, "Life was just one Saturday night."

Camping the Epic

The chief target of *Carry On Cleo* was, needless to say, *Cleopatra,* directed by Joseph L. Mankiewicz and starring Elizabeth Taylor and Richard Burton, which had premiered in London in July 1963.[6] *Carry On Cleo* not only owed its genesis to Rogers's experience of the excesses at Pinewood, but also used many of the same costumes as the Twentieth Century Fox film, rented from the Bermans costume agency. Sid James wears Richard Burton's armor throughout, with the addition of a neck scarf to hoist up the breastplate on his lighter frame. Elements from the elaborate sets built at Pinewood Studios for that film also resurfaced, along with scenery inherited from the West End play *Caligula*, although such recycling was common in the film industry. There was one overlap in the cast. As the restorers of the Twentieth Century Fox *Cleopatra* have noted, footage cut from that film included the appearance of Francis de Wolff as the Egyptian general Achilles. De Wolff appears in *Carry On Cleo* as the galley commander Agrippa, wearing exactly the same costume he wore as Achilles.[7] More than this, *Cleo* parodied entire scenes, the most obvious being Cleopatra's prolonged baths in asses' milk. The *Carry On* team used skimmed milk to shoot the scene and were alarmed when it went bad after a few hours under the studio lights.[8] In both films, Cleopatra is smuggled into Caesar's presence rolled up in a carpet, although purists will note that the original source of this story, the ancient writer Plutarch, specifies a "bed sack."[9] In *Carry On Cleo*, the scene is played twice, once when Caesar sees it in a vision and once "for real." On the first occasion, Cleopatra rolls out elegantly like Liz Taylor. She is asked how she did it so well and explains, "practice." On the second, Hengist, in Caesar's palace, opens the rug too quickly, spinning her across the room to knock over a table.

Twentieth Century Fox objected to *Carry On Cleo* only when they saw the poster for the film (fig. 5.2). It was a deliberate parody of the artwork for their own film; hence, they felt, it threatened their advertising campaign for the general release of *Cleopatra* scheduled for the middle of 1965. They sued for infringement of copyright in what the press dubbed "the battle of the two Cleos." The Conservative politician Quentin Hogg, who returned to the bar to defend the *Carry On* gang, pointed out that the film was supposed to be a parody and that Twentieth Century Fox had been unable to show any material damage. The *Carry On* team resolved the case by withdrawing their poster.[10]

The Burton and Taylor *Cleopatra* may have provided the immediate occasion for *Carry On Cleo*, but its wider targets included Hollywood epic film in general and even, in the *mise en scène*, the historical paintings of artists like Sir Lawrence Alma-Tadema, whose visions of classical marble vistas adorned with fur, fruit, and scantily clad handmaidens so titillated the Victorian male.[11] The slave-saves-life plot device and rowing scenes echo *Ben-Hur*. Moreover, *Carry On Cleo* borrowed numerous establishing shots for its Egyptian scenes from the only British contribution to the epic genre: the wildly expensive *Caesar and Cleopatra* (1945). The footage is well integrated into the film; the diegetic drumbeat of Caesar's legions as they enter Alexandria is perfectly matched to *Cleo*'s mock-epic score.

Figure 5.2 Taking it too far: the parody of the *Cleopatra* (1963) poster that Twentieth Century Fox sued to ban. Note the bespectacled face of Charles Hawtrey in the bottom right.

The film jokes about Hollywood's claim to represent historical reality. *Cleo* opens with a title parodying a standard filmic disclaimer: "Whilst the characters and events in this story are based on actual characters and events, certain liberties have been taken with Cleopatra." Rothwell also introduces numerous anachronisms into his version of 50 B.C.E. The Britons are discovered by the Romans living in caves, rather like the *Flintstones*.[12] Hengist tells Horsa (the names are Saxon and hence 1,000 years too early) that his mother-in-law has been eaten by a Brontosaurus (150 million years too late). *Carry On* regular Charles Hawtrey wears his trademark spectacles throughout. Devotees of the Twentieth Century Fox film and readers of Plutarch would also have noticed that the action is compressed: Julius Caesar and Mark Antony court Cleopatra simultaneously rather than at opposite ends of the fourth decade B.C.E. The whole bundle is tied together by a "voice of God" narrator: a booming unseen voice who sets the scene and provides links with a pastiche of the epic style. Such voices were common in historical films of the era, as with Cecil B. DeMille's *The Ten Commandments* (1956) or Orson Welles's prologue to *The Vikings* (1958). Here, the producer recruited the respected wartime British newsreel commentator E. V. H. Emmett for the part, suggesting fun at the expense of both Hollywood and Gaumont British News.

Camping "Culture" / Camping Class

Beside its transatlantic target, much of Rothwell's humor was directed at the cultural underpinnings of the British class system: the hallowed institutions of "great" literature and the school classics lesson. Initiation into such things was central to the educational rites of passage that perpetuated the British ruling classes. From the mid-1920s, the associated values of conservatism had found expression in the newest British sacred cow: the public service broadcasting ethic of the BBC, which emphasized not what the public wanted, but what was educational and improving. Rome and Shakespeare both figured in this approach. In 1959, those British television viewers who had yet to succumb to the charms of commercial television had been treated to a nine-part BBC adaptation of Shakespeare's three Roman histories under the title: *Spread the Eagle*.[13] Rothwell drew on these plays, and especially on *Julius Caesar*. Four times in *Cleo* Kenneth Williams's Caesar begins a speech, "Friends, Romans . . . ," only to be interrupted with the prompt of "countrymen" from a companion. He whines indignantly, "I know," before continuing. Rothwell also throws in lines from other Shakespeare plays. When stabbed in the chest in a vision, Caesar delivers a line from *Macbeth*: "Is this a dagger that I see before me? It is!" He also parodies Shakespearean histrionics, as when Caesar rails against fate: "Oh dark invidious muse that blights my life, come show your fearful haggish face," at which point Charles Hawtrey pops his face around the door and says "hello." Billing the screenplay as "from an original idea by William Shakespeare" not only raised a laugh, but doubtless also helped to remind the lawyers at Twentieth Century Fox that *Cleo* was dealing with material in the public domain.[14] There was one nod to the broader treatment of Rome in English literature. The narrator notes that Cleopatra was described by Macaulay (the Victorian poet, historian, and parliamentarian) as "the lay of ancient Rome."

Rothwell was able to assume that a passing knowledge of Latin was part of the cultural literacy of his audience. He jokes with the Latin language in much the same way as the established British satires of school-room history and classics classes, *1066 and All That* and the subversive pupil's eye view, *How to Be Topp* (Sellar and Yateman 1930, Williams and Searle 1954). The audience is not especially stretched by the jokes, and certainly no one would be alienated from the film by their presence. The jokes include translating British commonplace phrases into Latin; hence the army marches to the command of *sinister, dexter, sinister, dexter,* and, after first making love to Cleopatra, Mark Antony exclaims: *Puer, oh puer, oh puer!* which the narrator translates as "Boy, oh Boy, oh Boy!" Roth-well also extracts humor from mistranslating Latin epigrams. When swooning after a brush with death in the Temple of Vesta, Caesar de-clares: "*Veni, vidi, vici* . . . I came, I saw, I conked out!" Similarly, the British slave girl Gloria (Julie Stevens) is clearly so named just to allow Caesar to turn to her and describe his queasiness at sea as, "Just a little *sic transit* Gloria . . ." This is a pun on the quotation from the fifteenth-century theologian Thomas A. Kempis, familiar from innumerable graveyard inscriptions: *sic transit gloria mundi,* thus the glory of the world passes away (Thomas A. Kempis, *Imitatio Christi,* ch. 3, vi).

   Carry On Cleo also has much fun at the expense of received notions of history. The "great man" theories of historical orthodoxy are neces-sarily subverted when the great men are shown to be foolish. But more than this, *Cleo* plays with the notion that history itself is performance, that historical characters are themselves actors caught in a greater drama and condemned to act out roles predetermined for them. One scene cut after the first draft of *Carry On Cleo* played explicitly with the idea of a tyrannical historical script that the characters were forced to fulfill. Cae-sar was not merely obliged to die on the Ides of March as his father-in-law had predicted but to die in the manner of the received historical ac-count. Hence, after the first blow is struck, Mark Antony checks that the date is correct. Then the action is interrupted until Brutus arrives. The assembled company agree that Brutus "should" stab Caesar; unfortu-nately, Brutus has forgotten his dagger. He borrows one from Caesar. Seneca then suggests that the dying Caesar move to the statue of Pom-pey under which he is "supposed" to die. Caesar is told that the statue has been taken away for cleaning. He expires saying, "Oh, I can see this is going to be one of those days."[15] The death of Caesar in the final ver-sion is played without this level of reflexivity. Caesar is merely prompted yet again during his dying attempt to deliver a "Friends, Romans, Coun-trymen" oration, and dies saying, "Oh, what's the use."

   Although the final film resists joking about history as a tyrannical written text, it does play with the causal connection between events in the past and culture in the present. Chance events in the fictional drama are used to "explain" things in the present. In the opening scene of *Carry On Cleo*, Horsa takes one of Hengist's square wheels and reuses it to create and name the window frame. Later, while demonstrating his swordsmanship to Mark Antony, Hengist accidentally chops the arms off the Venus de Milo. "Oh forget it!" Mark Antony quips, "Nobody will ever notice the difference."[16] Such moments subvert the grand narratives of cause and effect favored by both traditional British history and Hollywood film and suggest an alternative model of random or chaotic influences on the present.

Camping Sixties Britain

Many of the jokes in *Carry On Cleo* give a camp spin not only to representations of the Roman past but also to the British present. The two come together perfectly at the moment in which the puny and bespectacled Charles Hawtrey sings in his bath: "Where ever I wander, there's no place like Rome." By repeating archetypically British "home" behavior and vocabulary in an ancient Roman setting, both the past and present are rendered absurd. Sometimes the humor is derived from imagining how Romans from sunny Italy might have experienced the rain-soaked British Isles. We meet Mark Antony in a torrent of British rain that fills his helmet the moment he removes it from his head. Julius Caesar is first seen miserable from a British head cold in his tent with his feet in a bowl of hot water. In a comic reversal of the British holiday-maker's experience of Mediterranean hygiene, here it is Mediterraneans who complain that British water "makes very irregular soldiers of us all." In a similar vein, the first draft of the script included a scene in which Caesar looks at a map of Britain and comments that it looks like a foot kicking a ball, reversing the standard foreign perception of the map of Italy.[17] Sometimes the ancient and modern converge. Some Roman characters use contemporary British colloquialisms or a hybrid of Latin and Cockney, as when Mark Antony exclaims, "Blimus!" Mark Antony and the Egyptian soothsayer both use cockney rhyming slang: "loaf" (loaf of bread) for "head" and "butcher's" (butcher's hook) for "look."[18] Yet in other scenes, the Romans puzzle to understand British colloquialisms and practices. Caesar suspects that both the expression "tea up!" that causes Britons to leave the battlefield and the term "crumpet" (a twentieth-century British colloquialism for a woman) refer to local deities. The situation switches when an Egyptian soothsayer (Jon Pertwee) calls,

Figure 5.3 "There will be two…" Caesar (Kenneth Williams) inadvertently delivers a modern-day British obscene gesture, unrecognized by his ancient British bodyguard Hengist Pod (Kenneth Connor). *Carry On Cleo* (1964).

"Isis! Sweet Isis!" and Hengist Pod compulsively completes the sentence, "They're lovely," as though selling ice cream at an English seaside resort. When Caesar is trying to explain with sign language that "there will be two" at a meeting with Cleopatra, he inadvertently delivers an obscene gesture (fig. 5.3). There is no diegetic recognition of this, but a whistle effect on the soundtrack emphasizes the moment for the audience.

References to British life in the 1960s abound. The slave market in ancient Rome is called Marcus et Spencius and uses the same green and gold color scheme as the high-street store Marks and Spencer. As a champion gladiator, Hengist is subject to a Beatlemania-style mobbing. Caesar confesses that he failed his "ex-one plus" (the "eleven plus" exam was at that time the chief exam for determining which British children went to the academically geared grammar schools). Caesar describes his military campaigns as "business trips" and arrives at the gate of Cleopatra's palace like a door-to-door salesman. His line, "My name is Julius Caesar, I represent the Roman empire," is met with the stock brush-off for a salesman: "No thanks, not today." A vision summoned in the flames by the Egyptian soothsayer is discussed as though it were a program on

a temperamental television set. But perhaps the most interesting collision of past and present comes during Julius Caesar's speech to the senate. As Caesar enters, Brutus is predicting the decline and fall of Rome.
Caesar then delivers a speech that includes a sustained impersonation
of Winston Churchill and a final slogan borrowed from Harold Macmillan: "You've never had it so good." Caesar dies while trying to "sell the
senate on his idea of the Wind of Change," borrowing Macmillan's
famous metaphor for the end of the British empire in Africa. Hence,
modern Britain is associated both with Rome in its decline and with the
position that ancient Britain held in the eyes of the Roman empire: a nation of savages to be enslaved.

Finally, as with all the *Carry On* films, the audience never loses touch
with the established qualities of the *Carry On* actors. The audience knows
that they are looking at Sid James pretending to be Mark Antony, that
it is Charles Hawtrey in the tunic, and so forth. There are even in-jokes
relating to other projects outside the *Carry On* cycle. Sid James and Kenneth Connor had starred together in a 1961 comedy called *What a Carve
Up* (Pat Jackson, director), which is exactly the line delivered by Sid
James/Mark Antony when he first surveys the damage that Kenneth
Connor/Hengist has apparently done to the imperial guard.

Camping British Masculinity

A Roman setting was particularly well suited for the safe exploration of the twists and turns of British gender and sexual identity issues
in the 1960s. The world of togas and tunics seemed naturally suggestive;
in a straight-laced Britain in which people still found it difficult to discuss issues of sex and sexuality openly, Rome offered an ideal stage on
which to act out fantasies of license. The words *orgy*, *lesbian*, and *sodomy*
all evoked biblical and classical practices; the sexual nature of the art un-
covered at Pompeii had confirmed such links. More than this, for a nation that had just lost its empire, it made sense to parody men of power
and turn to a comic setting uniquely well suited to evoke fears related
to the loss of male power: decline, fall, and castration.

Jokes about male identity are at the core of all British camp comedy.
Carry On Cleo was no exception. All gender roles become performance
in *Cleo*. The most effeminate actors in the piece, Charles Hawtrey and
Kenneth Williams, play the patriarch Seneca and Julius Caesar respectively. Both are supposed to be compulsive womanizers. Yet the flu-
ridden Caesar introduces himself by staring into the camera and re-
marking, "Ooooh, I do feel queer."[19] Mark Antony may be represented

as a successful soldier, but even he is easily manipulated by Cleopatra. Hengist is impotent and ineffectual for most of the film. When disguised as the emperor, he stumbles while rehearsing for his meeting with Cleopatra and says, "I'm a great queen." When he tries to project manliness as a champion gladiator, he resorts to a display of chest puffing and swaggering. All manliness is turned into a performance barely concealing effeminacy, weakness, and cowardice underneath.

The mask-like quality of identity is emphasized by the way in which the assigned male roles are twisted and challenged by the action of the plot. Hengist has occasion to pretend to be a Vestal Virgin/eunuch, a warrior, and the emperor himself before he returns home a man. The subversive message of the film is not blunted by its conventional hero, the hunter Horsa (Jim Dale). Although Horsa repeatedly saves Hengist and defies the Romans to their faces, he, too, is performing a role. Dale's overemphasized movements—kicking up his legs when running or flailing his arms—make it clear that he is only playing a part. The representation of women is also directed to the same purpose of camping masculinity. Women are represented as nags (Calpurnia and Hengist's wife, Senna Pod), as dim, attractive manipulators (Cleopatra), or as faithful but powerless (the slave girl Gloria). Despite the opening scene of British men dragging their wives around by the hair, marriage is shown as an area of female power and male impotence.

The concept of castration is never far from the surface in *Carry On Cleo* or the Roman camp comedy subgenre as a whole: the chief vehicles being jokes about eunuchs. In *Cleo* (echoing 1960s Britain again), we learn that the eunuchs have gone on strike: "They're protesting about loss of assets." When hiding in the Temple of Vesta, Horsa says, "If anyone asks, say we're eunuchs." Hengist replies, "Oh yes. What have we got to lose?" In Cleopatra's palace, their reaction to meeting Sosages (Tom Clegg), a bodyguard whose tongue has been cut out, is, "It could have been worse." Impotence is represented visually in a sequence in which Sosages bends Hengist's sword into a useless knot. Although *Carry On Cleo* and subsequent examples of the subgenre all include gratuitous, scantily clad handmaidens, courtesans, and assorted nubile slave girls, they remain out of reach. Male characters seldom attain sexual gratification. Arguably, although such images reinscribe the female as an object, the male on the screen and the male viewer are positioned as eunuchs, forever looking and denied consummation.

The final issue readily discussed through comedies set in Rome was perhaps the most potent: slavery. Britain had long defined itself in terms of liberty. Since 1740, Britons had sung: "Rule Britannia, Britannia rule the waves, Britons never, never, never shall be slaves" (Colley 1992.11). In ancient Rome, they were and always would be slaves. In *Carry On Cleo*, they are, moreover, discussed as consumer durables of declining quality. The slave trader Spencius (Warren Mitchell) says, "Can't use this British stuff, they don't make it like they used to." The male British captives in the film are transformed into sexual objects for the Roman woman who can bid the most at auction. It was both a reversal of the British treatment of the subjects of their own empire and a metaphor for the new reality of living in America's world. The British male is now a colonized and feminized "other" on sale beside Africans. Hengist goes so far as to compare their predicament to the female experience of impregnation when he points out that the prospect of being "knocked down" at auction is not so bad: "It's better than being knocked up."

The positioning of the audience in all this identity play is complex. As Margaret Anderson has noted, the use of such extreme camp characters opens questions of identity to humor, in part, by distancing the audience from the issue on the screen. The presumed straight male viewer can laugh at the effeminate Hawtrey, Williams, and Connor at some points and feel safe behind his dissimilarity from them, while identifying with them at other moments (Anderson 1998.37–47). The film ends with the restoration of the gender status quo. Horsa wins back Gloria and Hengist is able to satisfy Senna. Yet so much has been called into question in the process that the reassurance can be only superficial.

Carry On and Nation Building

Carry On Cleo was not a meditation on British imperial decline or the crisis in British masculinity, rather it provided a space in which such things could be joked about and made safe. More than this, by its very nature, this sort of comedy created a newly imagined national community that transcended class divisions, a community based on a presumed shared ability to recognize the jokes. It was as though Rothwell were still writing for the inmates of Stalag Luft III, enjoying a laugh at something the foreign guards could never understand. The key to this community was use of the English language. Puns are thrown around with breathtaking speed. Mark Antony tells Cleo to "get Caesar alone." She replies, "Oh that's what he's come for, money." Seneca tells Mark Antony that Arabs are "intense lovers," he replies, "Of course, they do everything in tents!" There are many sexual double entendres, as when Cleo says to Caesar, "I've seen your bust," and he quips back, "I wish I could say the same!"[20] Double entendre is used to convey the background to Hengist's marriage. When Caesar says, "You are impregnable, aren't you?" he replies, "No Sir, it's just that Senna didn't want any kids just now." Frequently, the puns point to the lavatory. When Horsa is stamped with the initials of his new slave mistress "W. C.," Hengist remarks that they are "making a convenience of you!" There is even a passing reference to Cleopatra's chamber pot. According to his obituary in the London *Times*, Rothwell claimed that "to succeed the British humorist should stay as close to the toilet as possible without actually sitting on it" (2 March 1981).

By the time of *Carry On Cleo*, the *Carry On* films were regularly hailed as a British institution. One Sunday morning while shooting the film, Kenneth Williams awoke to find an article "In Praise of Carrying On" in the *Observer* newspaper, a bastion of educated liberal thought. Williams wrote in his diary: "This is very odd . . . They've even started to justify the bad scripts now and talk about the classlessness of them. What hog wash! You can only call a mess a mess!" (Davis [ed.] 1993.239, entry for 9 August 1964). Still, it was a mess that the British public of all classes and regions relished. *Carry On Cleo* was a massive hit in Britain. The London distributor reported that only the big budget *Zulu* matched it at the box office in the previous twelve months. The film also did excellent business in Australia, which had its own interest in escaping from the burden of British and American cultural imperialism.[21]

Following *Cleo*, the *Carry On*-ers spent the rest of the decade in a prolonged assault on British and American film genres including western, horror, and, in perhaps the best film of all, the British Raj epic *Carry On . . . Up the Khyber* (1968). In the 1970s, they reverted to cheaper (in both senses) contemporary material.[22] But there was still plenty of mileage left in ancient Rome as a source for humor. In January 1965, the BBC's science fiction series *Doctor Who* visited Nero's Rome using the sets from *Carry On Cleo* for a light-hearted, four-part adventure that included two characters being sold into slavery before the Doctor could save the day and inadvertently prompt Nero to burn Rome to the ground.[23] More significantly, as the *Carry On* team worked on *Cleo*, British audiences flocked to see the London run of the Stephen Sondheim musical, *A Funny Thing Happened on the Way to the Forum*.

A Funny Thing Happened on the Way to the Forum

Despite its share of jokes about eunuchs, *Forum* was considerably more sophisticated than *Cleo*. Here was a heady cocktail of genuine

Roman comic characters and situations culled from the works of Plautus, the winning music and lyrics of Sondheim, and the frenetic pace of the New York Jewish comic tradition, splendidly mounted by the writers of the "book," Burt Shevelove and Larry Gelbart, and hammered home by its Broadway star, Zero Mostel. Much of the humor came from the juxtaposition of Brooklyn and Rome; *Forum* joked both with the nature of ancient Rome and the role of Jews in American society. When Mostel sang of his longing to be free, it was implicitly an appeal for both ethnic and (given his background as a victim of McCarthyism) political tolerance.[24]

In Britain, the implicit cultural meaning of *Forum* changed. Mostel's role passed to the greatest British standup comedian of the age, Frankie Howerd. Here again was the spectacle of British actors playing the roles of both slaves and masters, with the added dimension of Howerd as an essentially camp figure conniving for love and freedom. It was inspired casting, suggested, according to Howerd, by Sir John Gielgud. The entire production had a *Carry On* flavor, more especially as Howerd's costar and fellow slave was *Carry On* regular Kenneth Connor. Jon Pertwee (the Egyptian soothsayer from *Cleo*) appeared as the procurer Lycus. Cast against type as the patrician Senex was "Monsewer" Eddie Gray, a founding member of the Crazy Gang. The show ran at London's Strand Theatre from October 1963 to July 1965 to rave reviews and packed houses. It then began a national tour. Connor took over as director, casting Charles Hawtrey in his part. Audiences across the country lapped it up.[25]

In 1965, United Artists began filming an adaptation of *A Funny Thing Happened on the Way to the Forum*. Despite its American producer, Melvin Frank, and British-based American director, Richard Lester, the film was in essence an Anglo-American coproduction, or to be more precise, a triangular meeting of the comic sensibilities of Rome, Brooklyn, and Brighton. The British screenwriter Michael Pertwee (brother of Jon Pertwee) and Melvin Frank collaborated on the script; Zero Mostel, Phil Silvers, Jack Gilford, and Buster Keaton starred, but the rest of the cast were British character actors, including Michael Hordern, Michael Crawford, and, in a critically acclaimed cameo as a golf-style gladiator trainer, Roy Kinnear. Other British talents on show included the brilliant young cinematographer Nicolas Roeg and the designer Tony Walton (who had also designed the West End production). Working with the art director Syd Cain, Walton constructed a realistically dirty set of Roman streets in the hills above Madrid. For his part, Lester made no secret of his ambition to make a statement with the film. He pledged to disrupt the niceties of mainstream Hollywood and expose the underlying nastiness of both classical Rome and slavery.[26]

The film had much to engage the audience: manic performances, glorious production values, and such magnificent set-piece scenes as a "sit-down orgy for forty." The script bristled with sight gags and winning one-liners, as when Mostel is handed a bottle of wine and asks, "Was one a good year?" The camp dimension to the comedy shone through in over-the-top gender performances and cross-dressing, including a sequence in which a soldier falls in love with the singularly unconvincing dancing girl, Phil Silvers. Unfortunately, the film was not widely admired. In the United States, *Time* mourned the loss of the complexity of the Broadway show, arguing that Lester had "about the same effect on this picture as a Dachshund puppy might have on a game of chess" (28 October 1966). In Britain, Penelope Houston of the *Spectator* noted the "line of knockabout, so at odds with the visual sophistication that it is as though *Carry On* had joined forces with *Vogue*" (10 February 1967). Most London critics considered Lester's style too relentless. They devoted much of their space to describing the refurbished cinema in which the film had opened and mourning the recent death of Buster Keaton.[27] Hollis Alpert of the New York *Saturday Review* alone entered into the spirit of the piece noting that: "The comic corruption of all levels of Roman society is a welcome corrective to those noble Romans who have infested movies for generations" (15 October 1966). Yet such responses missed the story at the core of *Forum*. Here was the underside of the Roman empire, revealed using elements marginalized by the mainstream of the American cultural empire: British character actors; Jewish-American vaudevillians; a blacklisted liberal, Mostel; and the old comic genius abandoned by the march of film technology, Buster Keaton, all brought to the screen by the too-innovative-for-Hollywood director, Lester.

Up Pompeii!

Although the critics doubted Lester, the BBC's Head of Comedy Michael Mills suspected that there might be some more mileage in Frankie Howerd's stage performance. Inspiration struck during an actual visit to the ruins of Pompeii. Mills recalled the stage production of *Forum* and quipped to his travelling companion: "I expect to see Frankie Howerd come loping round the corner." The idea of a Roman vehicle for Howerd took immediate root, and Rothwell seemed the ideal man to write it. Mills decided to go back to the source of *Forum* and therefore commissioned a single "thirty minute script to be written in the style of Plautus for our Comedy Playhouse series." His invocation of Plautus showed that even BBC comedy still traded in the highbrow. Rothwell changed this. He thumbed through Mills's Penguin translation of Plautus, tossed it aside, and started from scratch. He created the world of Lurcio, mischievous slave in the house of the senator Ludicrus Sextus and his wife Ammonia. The pilot script—crammed with wicked double entendres—pushed the boundaries of British television humor and proved that the BBC was capable of winning the ratings war.[28]

While Frankie Howerd worried whether the BBC could get away with the vulgarity of *Up Pompeii!*, the BBC was rather more concerned about being sued by the writers of *A Funny Thing Happened on the Way to the Forum*. The BBC Copyright Department breathed easier on learning that Rothwell had seen neither the play nor film. Rothwell noted that "his idea for our programme" was "sparked off by the script which he wrote for the film *Carry On Cleo*" and that Howerd was Michael Mills's choice of star and not his. He told the Copyright Department "in confidence" that he had "devised the programme with Kenneth Williams in mind."[29] To ward off any trouble, the pilot script and prepublicity stressed the joint *Carry On*/Plautine origins of *Up Pompeii!* The title (a pun uniting a sporting cheer with the concept of sexual penetration) reflected recent *Carry On* films, and the script shamelessly recycled material from *Cleo*. The BBC's own *Radio Times* described the pilot as "a sort of *Carry On Up the Forum* . . . based, very loosely indeed, on the works of Plautus." Plautus himself appeared reading from a scroll, interrupting the action as an authority on Pompeiian life rather like the unseen narrator of *Cleo*.[30]

Up Pompeii! used the Plautine device (seen in the film adaptation of *Forum* and familiar from British music hall) of allowing Howerd to speak directly to the audience. Typically, an entire episode of the eventual series would take the form of interruptions of Howerd's attempt to deliver a prologue to the audience. As the action unfolded, Howerd would make comic asides to the camera, as when, in the pilot, Ludicrus (Max Adrian) remarks that his daughter Erotica (Georgina Moon) is "delightfully chaste." Lurcio turns to the audience and mutters: "Yes, and so easily caught up with." The script revolved around Howerd. The program was billed as "Frankie Howerd in *Up Pompeii!*" Beyond this, many of the jokes turned on Howerd's camp persona. In the pilot episode, he introduces himself with a play on the word *homo*: "They made me the major-domo of the household. I said *domo*. Well, I don't want any misunderstanding this early on."[31]

The plot of the pilot was familiar stuff. A cargo of beautiful British slave girls arrives, and the young master, Nausius (Kerry Gardner), prevails on Lurcio to obtain one for him. Yet *Up Pompeii!* engaged the notion of decadence far more explicitly than *Carry On Cleo*. In *Cleo*, a "decline and fall" was merely predicted by Brutus, and only Caesar was doomed by the soothsayers. *Up Pompeii!*, however, played with the idea of a society fated to perish because of its "swinging 60s" immorality. In the pilot, Howerd's prologue is interrupted by the arrival of the elderly prophetess Cassandra saying a sooth of doom: "Hear my words, oh wicked citizens of Pompeii . . . Oh! I see a great fall. Your proud city will vanish in the sands of time!" After shooing her off, Lurcio turns to the camera and explains: "Shocking things go on here. You wouldn't believe it! Licentiousness! Libertinage! Orgies!" After looking around cautiously, he adds a reference to contemporary Britain: "Even bingo. Oh yes."[32] The episode included ominous rumblings from the volcano. The idea of a parallel between Britain and Pompeii was not new. It had fascinated the Victorians who saw evidence of the lost city in lavishly illustrated books of Pompeiana. Their enthusiasm for the subject turned Edward Bulwer-Lytton's novel of 1834, *The Last Days of Pompeii*, into the century's bestseller.

Despite Howerd's worries, the pilot of *Up Pompeii!* was a success. The BBC promptly commissioned seven further episodes, which aired in the spring of 1970. Here Rothwell had room to explore rather more of the classical world than had been possible in *Cleo*. The theme of slavery predominated. This and the setting in a doomed city gave a tinge of sadness to the otherwise manic proceedings. Episodes still featured Plautus (now played by Willie Rushton) and prophecies of doom first from Cassandra and then from a regular soothsayer called Senna (Jeanne Mockford). Lurcio successively was mistaken for Caesar, murdered the wrong senator, visited Roman Britain, and struggled to avoid the Spartacus rebellion.[33] Puns and innuendo abounded. The self-appointed guardian of British morality Mary Whitehouse was outraged, but most viewers adored it. Even before the BBC had transmitted all these episodes, they commissioned a second series of six more. Rothwell's old collaborator Sid Colin joined him as coauthor.[34] The second series built on the reputation of the first. Situations included Lurcio's search for a new Vestal Virgin and a scrape with the Roman equivalent of James Bond. The BBC's audience research department reported that the second episode, transmitted on September 21, 1970, captured an estimated 24.2 percent of the viewing public (against 15% for the rival ITV). The researchers cited a typical re-action: "I never thought I would see the day when I would find a script that is pure corn and a show of such unabashed vulgarity, funny—but I must admit I laugh myself sick watching *Up Pompeii!* It's an absolute riot." They noted the general view that: "Only Frankie Howerd could 'get away' with the sort of blatant vulgarity and *double-entendre* indulged in here. Thanks to his frank and 'curiously innocent' approach, even the bawdiest jokes were rendered entirely inoffensive."[35]

Howerd was now permanently linked to toga humor. The material even entered into his regular variety performances. A 1973 edition of the *Frankie Howerd Show* included a sketch by Rothwell based around Antony and Cleopatra. Similar material also featured in the work of other comedians of the era. In the summer of 1971, Morcambe and Wise per-suaded Glenda Jackson (fresh from playing the "Siren of the Nile" in the West End) to appear in a Cleopatra parody. The sketch became a favorite in repeats and compilation programs for years to come.[36]

A film version *Up Pompeii!* followed hard on Howerd's TV success, appearing in the spring of 1971. The script came entirely from the new co-author, Sid Colin. Rothwell's absence showed. The strongest element in the film was probably its opening song with rhymes like "there's no decorum in the forum." The rest left too little to the imagination. There was an argument for showing a low budget eruption of Vesuvius, but the bare bottoms of bathing Roman senators added little to proceedings. The film earned an "AA" (age 15 and over) censorship certificate for its trouble. The kindest critic, Christopher Hudson of the *Spectator*, wrote: "Frankie Howerd . . . lumbers after *double-entendres* like a crazy lepi-dopterist and savours them with such huge relish that you can't help laughing." Reviewers judged the best joke to be the moment when How-erd, in blackface as a Nubian eunuch, remarks to the camera: "Only two things might give me away." [37] Even so, Lurcio had become a British in-stitution, living on in repeat broadcasts of the original fourteen pro-grams. He returned to the screen in fine form in a Rothwell-scripted Bank Holiday Monday special at Easter 1975, running rings round a pair of apothecaries called Castor and Pollux. Needless to say, Howerd milked much merriment from the proximity of the latter's name to the British colloquial term for both testicles and an untruth, "bollocks." [38]

The Last Laugh

As the critical response to the movie version of *Up Pompeii!* had suggested, by the early 1970s, Roman camp was approaching the limits of its life. Much of the *Carry On* style depended on both innocence and repression. As Andy Medhurst has observed: "After Barbara Windsor's brassiere had at last burst (in *Carry On Camping*, 1969), where was the humour in teasing about the possibility of such an occurrence?" (1986.184) The jokes rested on the need for the language of sex, and of homosexuality especially, to be coded. The *Carry On*s resorted to ever more explicit humor to try and maintain their audience. They failed, and the films withered in the mid-1970s. With the relaxing of censorship, it became possible to discuss the issues dealt with implicitly in the camp Rome of the 1960s head-on. The homoerotic subtext of the epic no longer had to be veiled in innuendo, as Derek Jarman demonstrated in his explicit treatment of ancient homosexuality in *Sebastiane* (1976).

Part of the attraction of jokes about ancient Rome had always been their proximity to the forbidden subject of the Bible. In 1979, Britain's Monty Python team broke the taboo of joking directly about the Bible with their *Life of Brian*. It recycled many of the same approaches as *Cleo*, including the past/present collisions, jokes about Latin classes, and numerous puns based on Roman names. The religious dimension also figured in the Roman sequence of Mel Brooks's *History of the World Part One*.[39] It even became possible to represent the brutality of ancient Rome, as a hapless British cast demonstrated in *Caligula*, the notorious 1979 excursion through the realms of incest and mutilation that made cinematic restraint seem attractive by contrast.

The 1980s brought a revival of interest in Rome. The extremes of the classical period seemed appropriate for the polarized politics of the era. While Ronald Reagan spoke of an "evil empire," witty opponents of Margaret Thatcher dubbed her "Attila the Hen" and a "bargain basement–Boadicea."[40] In 1980, the National Theatre drew explicit parallels between the 1980s and 54 B.C.E. in Howard Brenton's controversial allegory of British imperialism and policy in Northern Ireland, *The Romans in Britain*. The play included full male nudity and depicted the rape of a young Druid by a Roman soldier. The director Michael Bogdanov was taken to court by the old enemy of *Up Pompeii!*, Mary Whitehouse. Although unable to cite laws for censorship, Mrs. Whitehouse used 1956 anti-gay prostitution legislation and sued Bogdanov for having "procured" male actors to commit "an act of gross indecency" on stage. The case collapsed, but the Conservative Greater London Council had already cut the theater's grant in punishment.[41]

Roman camp comedy remained in demand, but now it had an added nostalgia value, reminding audiences of more innocent times. In August

1986, Frankie Howerd revived *Forum* at the Chichester Festival. The *Daily Telegraph* dubbed the production *"Carry On Up the Tiber."* That same year, the BBC included *Up Pompeii!* in a special season to mark fifty years of television. Howerd reprised his role as Lurcio in 1991 in a final Bank Holiday special again entitled *Further Up Pompeii!* for ITV.[42] From 1989 to 1992, Channel Four broadcast two series of a new Romano-British sit-com in the Rothwellian mode: *Chelmsford 123.*[43] *Carry On Cleo*, *Up Pompeii!*, and *A Funny Thing Happened on the Way to the Forum*, which had always been staples of British TV film schedules, now appeared on videocassette, with *Cleo* being one of only three *Carry On* films issued in the United States. But the years also saw the death of Rothwell in 1981 and Kenneth Williams in 1988. Howerd himself died in 1992 on the same day as fellow British comedian Benny Hill.

With the American empire of the high Cold War now as historically remote as the British empire, it appears that the camp view of Rome has prevailed. When the Hollywood epics are viewed today, it is increasingly because they, too, have value in a camp aesthetic that finds it amusing to see Tony Curtis in a tunic or Charlton Heston chained to an oar. Hollywood still seeks its epic "fix," but generally looks for it in outer space rather than classical Rome. Sometimes entire sequences are recycled; the pod race in George Lucas's *Star Wars Episode I: The Phantom Menace* (1999) was an extended homage to the chariot race in *Ben-Hur*. In Britain, the ancient world has remained the happy hunting ground of public service broadcasting, most notably in the multi-episode extravaganzas *The Caesars* (Granada 1968), *I, Claudius* (BBC 1976), *The Cleopatras* (BBC 1983), and perennial Shakespeare adaptations.[44] Yet for a generation of Britons who grew up with *Carry On Cleo* and *Up Pompeii!*, it remains impossible to see a toga without thinking of Frankie Howerd or to listen to a seasoned Shakespearean deliver the "Friends, Romans, Countrymen . . ." funeral oration from *Julius Caesar*, without hearing the indignant tones of Kenneth Williams cutting in: "I know!"

Notes

The author has benefited from conversations with Karen Ford, Clive Kennedy, Phillip Lindley, Ann Miller, Gregory Murphy, Vince Newey, Jay Prosser, and the creator of the *Carry On* series, Peter Rogers. A version of this piece was presented as a plenary paper at the eighteenth conference of the International Association for Media and History at Leeds University in July 1999.

1. For an introduction to camp see Core 1984, esp. 115. Indispensable discussions may be found in Bubuscio 1980.40–58 and Sontag 1961.275–92. Camp

is as rooted in the historical experience of the gay community as blues is in the development of the African-American community. One must question Sontag's contention that "if homosexuals hadn't invented Camp someone else would have done," but she concedes that camp, like the blues, is paralleled by the cultural practices of other communities and can be performed by others. This is particularly true with camp, where some things performed "straight" can be recognized as camp by others. The "straight" style of one era can be camp for a later generation. The *Carry On* films discussed in this chapter have become increasingly camp with time. For a discussion of the role of the camp character in the *Carry Ons* see Margaret Anderson 1998.

2. In 1974, Rothwell told Ian Christie: "I see the [*Carry On*] series as an extension of the real music hall that young people today have never seen." He paid particular tribute to the archetypal "end of the pier" comedian Max Miller (Ian Christie, "Oh What a Lovely *Carry On*," *Daily Express*, 12 July 1974). For further details of Rothwell's career, married life, and war service see obituaries in the *Times* and *Daily Telegraph*, both 2 March 1981. Ross 1996.37–48 notes that the "Infamy, Infamy" line in *Cleo* was originally written by Denis Norden and Frank Muir for their *Take It From Here* radio show.

3. Interview: Peter Rogers, 21 July 1998 (by telephone). The essential introduction to the *Carry On* series is Ross 1996. The contribution of Rogers to Hibbin and Hibbin 1988 gives that book considerable interest. On American audiences see Michael Wade: "Astonishing thing about these so-English *Carry On* epics . . . they're a wow in America," *Sun*, 10 December 1964.

4. The Americanness of the genre was strengthened by the fact that classical subjects were avoided by British filmmakers of the sound era. Gabriel Pascal (dir.), *Caesar and Cleopatra* (Rank 1945), and the time-travel comedy *Fiddlers Three*, Harry Watt (dir.) (Ealing 1944), are the only examples cited in Harper 1994. There was a heritage of humor at the expense of Rome on stage as in Bernard Shaw's *Androcles and the Lion*, but even this was produced for the screen by Gabriel Pascal in 1952 with an American cast.

5. Macmillan's "Britons as Greeks" concept is eloquently deconstructed in Hitchens 1990.22–37.

6. Joseph L. Mankiewicz (dir.), *Cleopatra* (Twentieth Century Fox/Walter Wanger 1963). Wanger and Hyams 1963.

7. Interview: Richard Green and Geoff Sharpe, 9 July 1998. Green and Sharpe point out that since the exterior Pinewood *Cleopatra* sets were demolished before the production relocated to Rome, all borrowings were smaller interior items. Peter Rogers agrees, and points out that any art director worth his or her salt would reuse whatever the studio had in store. The most frequently recycled set at Pinewood was the so-called Irish Village which appears in *Carry On . . . Up the Khyber* (Interview: Peter Rogers, 21 July 1998). On the *Caligula* sets see Ross 1996.51, also British Film Institute (BFI) London, Gerald Thomas Collection: *Carry On Cleo*, Information Folder 38.

8. BFI, London, Gerald Thomas Collection: *Carry On Cleo*, Information Folder 41.

9. See Plutarch's *Caesar* 49.1–2, Perin (trans.) 1918.559. Plutarch might have preferred Sid James to Richard Burton as an interpretation of Mark Antony. He notes: "The Alexandrians took delight in his coarse wit," Perin (trans.) 1920.203.

10. See the *Evening Standard*, 15 January 1965; the *Times*, Law Reports, 16 January 1965 and 21 January 1965; the "Battle of the Two Cleos" headline is from the *Daily Express*, 21 January 1965. The first draft of the script of *Carry On Cleo* was illustrated by a hand-drawn Sphinx with Elizabeth Taylor's head pasted on and a bone between its paws. BFI, London, Gerald Thomas Collection: *Carry On Cleo*.

11. On Alma-Tadema see Swanson 1977. The first draft for the screenplay of *Cleo* included scenes set in the gladiatorial arena, scenes familiar from such films as *Spartacus* and *Demetrius and the Gladiators*. A poster advertising a combat between Pod and the Egyptian Sosages also promised: "Ten supporting contests all to the death, also see forty people get thrown to the lions! Six slaves pulled apart by wild horses (for one performance only)." The camera was to cut to a lone protester campaigning for the abolition of blood sports. BFI, London, Gerald Thomas Collection: *Carry On Cleo*, first draft, 84.

12. Made in 1960, but first seen in Britain on ITV (the commercial television station) in 1961.

13. Vahimagi 1996.83, 119. Previous major classical productions had included the BBC's 1959 World Theatre production of *Julius Caesar* with Eric Porter. This era was characterized by a major loss of BBC ratings to the independent channels. The BBC argued that it was maintaining cultural standards and was rewarded with a second TV channel: BBC 2 in 1963. See Negrine 1998 and Briggs 1995.

14. Such a suit had been threatened by the producers of James Bond over *Carry On Spying*; see Ross 1996.44.

15. BFI, London, Gerald Thomas Collection: *Carry On Cleo*, first draft, 97.

16. This joke is applied to the nose falling off the Sphinx in the French comic book *Asterix et Cleopatra*: Goscinny and Uderzo 1965.21–22, the "Whole New World" sequence in John Musker et al. (dir.), *Aladdin* (Buena Vista/Disney 1992), and a chariot scene in Brenda Chapman and Steve Hickner (dir.), *The Prince of Egypt* (Dreamworks 1998).

17. BFI, London, Gerald Thomas Collection: *Carry On Cleo*, first draft.

18. One early joke turns on Caesar knowing that Bristol is a slang term for female breasts (this is a rhyming slang play on the football team Bristol City and the word "titty").

19. Ross 1996.48 notes that the British censor required the filmmakers to redub a line in which Caesar tells his wife that the countries he has conquered don't have women and are "very backward people" to "very bashful people" to avoid an allusion to homosexual intercourse.

20. There is also much wordplay around the word *cock* as a colloquial term for penis. Caesar negotiates his liaison with Cleopatra at "cock crow," and Hengist's hometown is Coccium in Cornoveii (the real Roman name for the northern industrial town of Wigan). The name Senna Pod is a pun on a well-known herbal laxative.

21. Gerald Thomas Collection: *Carry On Cleo*, D. J. Goodlatter (Associated British Cinemas Ltd.) to Peter Rogers, 3 February 1965, and Philip Jacobs (Overseas Manager, Anglo-Amalgamated) to Peter Rogers, 25 January 1966. Rogers notes that he never received the Australian revenue. Interview: Peter Rogers, 21 July 1998.

22. The genre comedies were *Carry On Cowboy*, 1965, *Carry On Screaming!* 1966, and versions of *The Scarlet Pimpernel* (*Carry On . . . Don't Lose Your Head*, 1966), *Beau Geste* (*Carry On . . . Follow That Camel*, 1967), and *Doctor Kildare* (*Carry On Doctor*, 1967), which featured a character called Doctor Kilmore. Later parodies included *Carry On Henry* (1970, on Henry VIII), *Carry On Dick* (1974, on Dick Turpin), and TV special parodies of *Upstairs Downstairs*, *A Christmas Carol*, *Sherlock Holmes*, and other British classics. The film *Carry On . . . Up the Jungle* (1969) played with the safari movie. All of the other films until 1992 were contemporary romps in cheeky postcard mode.

23. *The Romans* (transmitted 16 January to 6 February 1965), now available from BBC video. For background see Tulloch and Alvarado 1983.

24. The London production program (Theatre Museum, Covent Garden, London) included a biographical note on Plautus as "the basis for all low comedy." The Jewish origins of *Forum* were noted by John Russell Taylor in his film review: London *Times*, 2 February 1967. For Mostel and McCarthyism see *Films Illustrated* 6.65, January 1977.189. See also the chapter by Margaret Malamud in this volume.

25. Theatre Museum: *Forum* program; Howerd 1976.197–232. Coincidentally, Gielgud had suffered for his sexuality in Britain at the same time that Mostel and his comrades were under fire for their politics. See Jivani 1997.104–05. For a review of the opening of *Forum* see *Punch*, 9 October 1963.539 and the ad in the *Evening Standard*, 10 October 1963. See also Ross 1996.49.

26. See Margaret Hixson's *Forum* review in the *Sunday Telegraph*, 5 February 1967. Pertwee appeared in the film of *Forum* in a cameo, but the role of the braggart soldier was taken, as in the West End, by the Sadler's Wells bass Leon Greene.

27. BFI London, micro-jacket: *A Funny Thing Happened on the Way to the Forum*.

28. The origins are described in Took 1992 and Hill 1992.159 and documented in BBC Written Archives Centre, Caversham (hereafter BBC WAC), copyright file, Talbot Rothwell, pt. 1, esp. BBC Copyright Dept. to Kavanagh Productions, 8 October 1969, and BBC Copyright Dept. to Mills, 4 June 1969.

29. BBC WAC, Copyright Dept. to Mills, 4 June 1969. There was no men-

tion of either the Edward Bulwer-Lytton novel or the multiple film versions of *The Last Days of Pompeii* at any point in this discussion of inspirations.

30. BBC WAC, script: *Up Pompeii!* (transmitted 17 September 1969). Familiar jokes included a character called Bilius, a busty slave girl from Bristol, and "a sage who knows his onions." A routine in which Senator Ludicrus begins a speech: "Friends, Romans, and Countrymen lend me your feet" is interrupted by Lurcio who suggests altering the line to "ears," only to be told that the speech continues, "help me to stamp out the curse of slavery." For early images of Pompeii see Gell 1824 and Bulwer-Lytton 1834.

31. BBC WAC, script: *Up Pompeii!* (transmitted 17 September 1969).

32. BBC WAC, script: *Up Pompeii!* (transmitted 17 September 1969).

33. BBC WAC, scripts and file T12/1.285/1. Series I was produced by David Croft and ran for seven weeks from 30 March 1970. Episode 1 (transmitted 30 March 1970) had Cassandra predicting: "The very ground will tremble! And all will perish in the holocaust." Lurcio responds: "And that is the end of the weather forecast." In a coincidental link to the previous examples of the Roman camp genre, the warm-up man for the studio recordings of *Up Pompeii!* was Bill Pertwee, brother of both the screenwriter of *Forum*, Michael, and the actor Jon Pertwee from *Cleo* and both the stage and (in a cameo) screen versions of *Forum*.

34. Series II, produced by Sydney Lotterby, ran for six weeks from 14 September 1970.

35. BBC WAC, file T12/1.422.1: *Up Pompeii!* series II, BBC Audience Research Report, 26 November 1970.

36. BBC WAC, Talbot Rothwell copyright file, 1970–74, re: payment of £365 for sketch for the *Frankie Howerd Show*, agreed 24 January 1973. Similar humor had surfaced in a much repeated Antony and Cleopatra sketch featuring Glenda Jackson on the *Morcambe and Wise Show* first transmitted 3 June 1971.

37. See Bob Kellett (dir.), *Up Pompeii!* (EMI/Associated London Films 1971). For reviews: BFI, London, micro-jacket: *Up Pompeii!*; esp. John Russell Taylor, *Times*, 19 March 1971, and Christopher Hudson, *The Spectator*, 27 March 1971. The film did well enough at the box office for Sid Colin to co-write two non-Roman follow-up films. Bob Kellett (dir.), *Up the Chastity Belt* (EMI/Associated London Films 1971), featured Howerd as Sir Lurkalot in the Middle Ages, and Bob Kellett (dir.), *Up the Front* (EMI/Associated London Films 1972), found Howerd in World War I, with enemy plans tattooed on his backside. All were produced by Ned Sherrin.

38. *Further Up Pompeii!*, transmitted 30 March 1975, (prod.) David Croft. For reviews and script see BBC WAC: *Up Pompeii!* microfiche. At the same time as this production, the BBC was screening a multi-episode docu-drama on the abolitionist movement: *The Fight Against Slavery*. Rothwell declined the invitation to write a third series for *Up Pompeii!*, and the format was relocated to the ancient east for *Whoops Baghdad* (BBC 1, 1973). See Took 1992.128.

39. See also the essays by Maria Wyke and William Fitzgerald in this vol-

ume. Terry Jones (dir.), *Monty Python's Life of Brian* (Handmade Films 1979); Mel Brooks (dir.), *History of the World Part One* (Brooksfilms 1981). In 1988, the *Carry On* gang themselves announced a parody comeback project—a parody of the *Dallas* mega-soap genre entitled *Carry On Texas*. The idea evaporated when Lorimar productions threatened to sue. The last film, *Carry On Columbus*, appeared in 1992. See Ross 1996.172ff.

40. The Thatcher quotes are from the Liberal MP Clement Freud (October 1979) and Labour MP Denis Healey (November 1982), collected in Pepper 1985.

41. Theatre Museum, Covent Garden: *Romans in Britain* reviews and trial files. The show opened in October 1980. For a full description of the scene (Act 1, Scene 3) see the *Times*, 30 July 1981. In March 1983, the Attorney General stopped proceedings, which had become something of a show in their own right. See Hall 1993.

42. *Daily Telegraph*, 14 August 1986; Howerd 1976; and Took 1992.131. On repeats see BBC WAC, file T12/1.422.1: *Up Pompeii!*—the last reshowing of the series followed the ITV special in 1991.

43. *Chelmsford 123* (Hat Trick productions), season one, transmitted 1989, season two, transmitted 1992. The funniest ongoing treatments of the Roman world in English were the Anthea Hockridge and Derek Bell translations of the French Goscinny/Uderzo comic strip *Asterix* (first published in the French newspapers in 1959 and, in book form, in the UK in 1969). Asterix managed to get through some thirty volumes and numerous animated films with enough puns to put Rothwell to shame—and without a single eunuch joke.

44. Both *The Caesars* and *The Cleopatras* were written by Philip Mackie. The latter was a notorious flop with both viewers and critics. Other Roman productions included BBC 2's *Review: Martial's Rome* (transmitted 16 May 1970), a dramatized reading by John Roanne of Peter Porter's translation of Martial's poetry.

Brooklyn-on-the-Tiber

Roman Comedy on Broadway and in Film

Margaret Malamud

Jewish humor retains even today a preoccupation with cultural assimilation. In a joke that circulates on the internet with the title "Hebonics," that assimilation is represented literally as a process of translation: not from one language to another, but from one culture to another.[1]

Sample Usage Comparisons:

Standard English Phrase	Hebonics Phrase
"He walks slow"	"Like a fly in the ointment he walks"
"You're sexy"	(unknown concept)
"Sorry, I do not know the time"	"What do I look like, a clock?"
"I hope things turn out for the best"	"You should BE so lucky"
"Anything can happen"	"It's never so bad it can't get worse"

Jewish-American humor flourished in the earlier part of the twentieth century in the Borscht Belt:

A century ago the celebrated Borscht Belt began in Sullivan and Ulster counties in the Catskill Mountains of upstate New York. Thousands of Jews, hungry for the mountain air, good food, and the American way of leisure came to the Catskills for vacation, and by the 1950s, more than a million people inhabited the summer world of bungalow colonies, summer camps, and small hotels. "These institutions shaped American Jewish culture, enabling Jews to become more American while at the same time introducing the American public to immigrant Jewish culture," said Phil Brown, professor of sociology. Today, the Borscht Belt has shrunk to include only a handful of major resorts in the two-county Catskills area. The once teeming roads of the Borscht Belt are largely barren, with most hotels and bungalow colonies burned, decayed, or destroyed. "Some people got bored with the old ways," said Brown. "It was too much for people who were becoming more American."[2]

Entertainment, especially comedy, was one of the big draws of the Borscht Belt, a collection of resorts where Jews could both take a vacation from the all-pervasive embrace of American culture in a community of their own and, at the same time, try out their newly found American values and social practices. The comedy produced by the Borscht Belt comedians reflected the tensions and conflicts, both inner and social, generated by the difficult process of assimilation. But precisely because America is still a nation of immigrants, the humor of the Borscht Belt proved to have a durability that was not shared by the crumbling bungalows of the Catskills resorts in which it flourished. The plays of the Roman playwright Plautus, themselves "translations" or rewritings of Greek comedies, became the inspiration for an icon of Jewish-American humor: *A Funny Thing Happened on the Way to the Forum* was how Jewish-American humor met the classics. It appeared first in 1962 as a smash Broadway hit by the American Jewish comic writers Larry Gelbart and Burt Shevelove and then, in 1966, as a film, directed by Richard Lester.[3] Zero Mostel, the quintessential Jewish-American comic actor, starred in both the stage and the screen versions.

On the Way to Broadway

A Funny Thing Happened on the Way to the Forum is a fascinating fusion of Roman comic convention and American comic invention: Plautus meets the Borscht Belt. Larry Gelbart and Burt Shevelove wrote the book; the lyrics and music were by Stephen Sondheim. The musical was directed by George Abbot and starred Zero Mostel, Phil Silvers, Jack Gilford, and Michael Crawford.[4] Like Plautus, who assimilated what was for him high culture, Greek New Comedy, and adapted it for popular Roman tastes, Gelbart and Shevelove took what was for them high culture, the "classics," and made Roman comedy popular by translating Plautine humor into vaudevillian and burlesque humor, the Roman slave into a Jewish comic, and Rome into Brooklyn. The idea of adapting Plautus for Broadway had been Burt Shevelove's desire since his student days at Yale, where he had studied drama and written his first play based on the works of Plautus. As head of Yale's student dramatic society, he put on a production of Aristophanes' *Frogs*, which was performed in the Yale swimming pool. Later he and Stephen Sondheim collaborated on a stage production of *Frogs*. Shevelove went on to direct comedy routines for television shows starring comedians Jack Benny and Art Carney, and he won Emmy Awards for directing *The Red Buttons Show*, *The Judy Garland Show*, and *The Jack Paar Show*, but his interest in adapting classical comedy for the modern theater never left him. In 1957, he got in touch with comedy writer Larry Gelbart with the idea of writing a musical comedy based on the works of Plautus.

Larry Gelbart's background and education were rather different from those of the Yale-educated Shevelove. The son of Latvian immigrants, he spoke only Yiddish until he was four. At fifteen, his family moved from New York to Los Angeles, where his father became a barber for some Hollywood studios, numbering among his personal clients the producer David Selznick and the comedian Danny Thomas who, having heard some of the teenager's jokes, gave him a start writing for the radio show *Maxwell House Coffee Time*. At seventeen, Gelbart joined the staff of *Duffy's Tavern*, an NBC radio comedy show. He never went to college, and called *Duffy's* his higher education. In 1955, he joined Carl Reiner, Neil Simon, Mel Tolkin, and Mel Brooks, writing comedy for the legendary Sid Caesar's *Caesar's Hour*, an experience he has described as "going to work every day of the week inside a Marx Brothers movie" (Gelbart 1998.20).

Gelbart and Shevelove invited the young New York composer and songwriter Stephen Sondheim, another son of East European Jewish immigrants, to write the music and lyrics for their comedy. He, too, read Plautus in translation and saw him as the originator of the situation comedy, the first to domesticate comedy (Secrest 1998.152). He liked the idea of making a musical based on Plautus and agreed to collaborate. George Abbott was hired to direct the play. No stranger to Roman comedies, Abbott had collaborated with Rodgers and Hart in a 1938 Broadway production of *The Boys from Syracuse* (revived in 1963) that drew heavily on Shakespeare's *Comedy of Errors*, much of it borrowed from Plautus's *The Brothers Menaechmi*.

In 1957, Gelbart, Shevelove, and Sondheim set about adapting Plautus for Broadway, consciously conflating the Roman comic tradition with the wit and urbanity associated with the American comic tradition, particularly vaudeville, burlesque, and the Broadway musical comedy. According to Gelbart, "Our goal was to construct a show based on Plautus, who, borrowing from the Greeks . . . taught amphitheater audiences up and down the original Caesar's circuit to laugh for the first time at character and situation instead of those old staples they found so amusing, bloodshed and tragedy" (Gelbart 1998.207). Gelbart and Shevelove wanted to fill what they called a "vulgarity vacuum" on Broadway, to move away from the pretty musicals of Rodgers and Hammerstein and Lerner and Loewe back to the vaudeville-burlesque-slapstick tradition on stage and in early film farces. They admired the zany slapstick humor of 1920s musicals and farces like the Marx Brothers' *The Cocoanuts*. "Writers now think a punch line is something you wait in for a drink," Gelbart complained (1998.207). Plautus's bawdy, witty, earthy humor seemed a perfect antidote to sticky sweet musicals like *Oklahoma, The King and I, South Pacific*, and *The Sound of Music*.

Gelbart loved Plautus's plays. For him, Plautus was a comic master who created many of the comic conventions that he and other comics used in their work: stand-up monologues, puns, malapropisms, tongue twisters, double entendre, insults, disguise, slapstick, mistaken identity, mime, wit, and witlessness. He claimed that if his undergraduate education was at *Duffy's Tavern*, his postgraduate work was Plautus: "The Roman playwright Plautus was really my plotting teacher and I read his plays over and over in adapting them for *Funny Thing*, dissecting his masterful construction and his manipulation of the characters" (1998.42, 208–09).

Gelbart described the five-year process of adapting Plautus in this way: "We began the task of digging around in the surviving plays . . . and began to take extracts from his works . . . cribbing a character here, a relationship there, creating a connective dramatic and musical tissue to bond our work to his by fashioning a cat's cradle of a plot" (1998.207). Indeed, a cat's cradle well describes the plot of *Funny Thing*, a densely woven pastiche of narrative strands, stock characters, and comic ploys and devices taken from Plautus's plays, especially *Casina, Pseudolus*, and *Miles Gloriosus*. According to Gelbart, "We used Plautus's cunning slave, braggart-warrior, hen-pecking shrewish wife and cringing husband, moonstruck young man, the lass with unused body and brain, doddering old geezer barely able to see or to hear, cross-dressing, and female impersonation" (1998.209). Like the trickster-slave of Plautus's plays, Pseudolus is the source of the comic action on stage and the ironic commentator on events as he engages in dialogue with the audience. Like Plautus's slaves, he is at once a member of the cast and of the audience.

The star of the play, the clever and self-promoting slave Pseudolus (Zero Mostel), introduces himself and the main characters of the comedy in Sondheim's brilliant opening number, "Comedy Tonight." The song sets the tone of the play and prepares the audience for the comic

chaos about to unfold on stage. Comedy not tragedy, levity not seriousness will follow: "Nothing with gods / Nothing with fate / Weighty affairs will just have to wait." The characters are not divinities or members
of the elite but "philanderers and panderers," the scoundrels and rogues
who inhabit the back streets of Rome. Tony Walton's sets presented spectators with the three houses of the principle characters, located on a
somewhat seedy street in a rather run-down Roman neighborhood.

The plot centers on the tricks of Pseudolus to forward the love affair of his young master, Hero, with Philia, a young virgin living in the
brothel next door. Hero is being thwarted by a pimp, Lycus, who runs
the brothel. Hero's parents, the master Senex and the mistress Domina,
go off to visit Domina's mother, leaving their chief slave, Hysterium, in
charge of the household. Pseudolus agrees to help Hero get Philia, who
has been sold to the soldier Miles Gloriosus, in exchange for his freedom. Various complications ensue: Senex returns early, Philia mistakes
him for Miles Gloriosus, and soon Miles Gloriosus himself arrives de-
manding his bride. Confusion and mistaken identities reach a climax
when Hysterium impersonates Philia to cover up an earlier scheme in
which the soldier had been told she had died of the plague. In the end,
Philia and Miles turn out to be the long-lost children of Erronius, the
doddering old man next door. Hero and Philia are united, and Pseudolus gets his freedom.

It need hardly be said that nearly all of the action, the characters, and
the comic devices are lifted from Plautus. In the *Pseudolus*, a young man,
madly in love with a courtesan, lacks the money to purchase her. When
a soldier buys the girl instead and leaves her with a pimp, the young
man's cunning slave contrives to deceive the pimp and get the girl, who
turns out to be free. In the *Casina*, on which *Funny Thing* draws most
heavily, we find conniving slaves, father-son rivalry for a maidservant,
Casina, and a wedding where a male slave dresses up as Casina and tricks
the father, who thinks he is marrying her.[5] In the end, the young man
marries Casina, who is recognized as a citizen. Finally, *Funny Thing*'s out-
rageously vain and pompous soldier, convinced of his strength and irresistible beauty, is, of course, modeled on the soldier in *Miles Gloriosus*.

Broadway's Rome

Although Plautus's works provided the basic ingredients and
narrative structure of the play, Gelbart and Shevelove shaped the material for American audiences. Perhaps the key difference between the
Roman material and the American comedy is the emphasis placed on

Pseudolus's desire for liberty. Erich Segal has pointed out that, in the Roman plays, a slave may be elevated above his master by his wit and cleverness, and a reversal of norms and the inversion of normal relationships and status do occur, but liberty is neither sought nor granted (Segal 1987.104, 165–66). At the end of Plautus's play *Pseudolus*, for example, Pseudolus gets drunk; he is not set free. As Segal put it, the Plautine slave "would rather take liberty than receive it" (1987.166). In *Funny Thing*, however, Pseudolus wants more than anything to be free, and it is this desire that fuels his frenetic comic maneuverings. In Pseudolus's song "Free," he voices American, not Roman sentiments: "Be you anything from king to baker of cakes / You're a vegetable unless you're free / It's a little word but oh, the difference it makes / It's the necessary essence of democracy / It's the thing that every slave should have the right to be." When these words are sung by the Jewish Zero Mostel, who was blacklisted during the McCarthy era, and by a black woman, Whoopi Goldberg, who played Pseudolus in the recent revival, they have an added ironic resonance. The ethnic/racial identity of the performer extends and sharpens the meaning of freedom: rather than a general American value, it takes on a particular edge for those who, at different times, have been dispossessed, marginalized, and/or the object of American racism.

Equally absent from the Roman plays is the prominent attention *Funny Thing* gives to the display of female sexuality. *Funny Thing* gets a lot of bawdy comic mileage out of the courtesans next door. The primary sources of *Funny Thing*'s images of Roman sexual license and debauchery lie in Hollywood's cinematic depictions of the decadence that was Rome and in the new loosening of restraints on the pursuit of sexual pleasure that characterized the late 1950s and 1960s. Pseudolus and Hero's visit to the brothel provides the occasion for the display of male sexual fantasies when the courtesans perform erotic dances for the prospective customers: Tintinabula does an oriental dance dressed in a belly-dancer outfit; Panacea wears a bikini made of grapes and dances to striptease music; the Geminae (twins) pander to the fantasy of possessing two women at once; Vibrata is a wild animal of a woman who wears skins and dances to jungle music; and Gymnasia is a dominatrix, a statuesque woman in thigh-high boots who cracks a whip and spanks Pseudolus. Rome has often been the site of projected sexual fantasies and desires, and these displays reflect this tradition and the particular tastes of the "swinging" early 1960s rather than ancient Roman sexual attitudes and desires.[6]

Funny Thing's brothel scene seems indebted to Hollywood and to *Playboy*. Hollywood epics set in Roman antiquity typically feature spectacles of Roman excess and debauchery. In the 1960s, these images of Roman license and promiscuousness are given a positive spin, and there is little desire to censor or condemn them; instead, they are made to signify sexual freedom and the pleasures of uninhibited sex. In a lengthy 1965 article entitled "Sex and the Cinema," *Playboy* featured stills of scenes censored from Hollywood films, including a number of excised stills from films set in Roman antiquity. The motto carved in Latin above the door of Hugh Hefner's Playboy Mansion in Chicago proclaimed: si non oscillas, noli tintinnare (If you don't swing, don't ring!), seemingly promising a perpetual Roman orgy inside (Wolfe 1968.4). The scantily clad, voluptuous courtesans resemble fantasy pinups in *Playboy*, ready to participate in one of cinema's Roman orgies.

Plautus and Borscht Belt Humor

Gelbart and Shevelove translate Plautus's "funny things": his dazzling wordplay, puns, double entendres, alliteration, and neologisms, and his colloquial, earthy, and slangy language by drawing on the idioms of American Jewish humor and the vaudeville tradition.[7] This racy humor and wit characterized East Coast Jewish comedians like Eddie Cantor, the fast-talking, pun- and slapstick-filled routines of the Marx Brothers, the vaudevillian-burlesque style of Milton Berle, and the comic antics of Sid Caesar's *Caesar's Hour*, where Gelbart had worked. In the heyday of vaudeville, a typical program had "something for everyone": a variety of acts that drew on opera, drama, dance, pantomime, farce, and burlesque. Its humor often came from spoofs of the serious arts: Fanny Brice, for example, frequently performed a dance satire called the "Dying Swan" and burlesques of the Martha Graham style of modern dance. There were parodies of Shakespeare, especially scenes from *Antony and Cleopatra*, burlesques of toga drama (a spoof of *Quo Vadis* called *Quo Vass iss?*), and plenty of pantomime, slapstick, juggling, and acrobatics. With the coming of movies, live vaudeville waned as vaudevillians like Charlie Chaplin, Eddie Cantor, and the Marx Brothers flocked to Hollywood to film their acts. Live comedy, however, continued in New York City and in the resorts in the Catskills, and radio and, later, television, especially programs like *The Milton Berle Show*, absorbed the talents of many and helped keep the vaudeville-burlesque tradition alive.

Funny Thing's dependence on vaudevillian verbal wit and its physicality of performance is inscribed in the author's preface to the script:

"This is a scenario for vaudevillians. There are many details omitted from the script. They are part of any comedian's bag of tricks. The double take, the mad walk, the sighs, the smirks, the stammerings. All these and more are intended to be supplied by the actor and, hopefully, the reader" (Preface to Gelbart and Shevelove 1985). Zero Mostel and Phil Silvers possessed in abundance the qualities critic Robert Lytell defined as characteristic of the best vaudeville performers: "Human horsepower, size, energy, zingo . . . These people have a fire in their belly which makes you sit up and listen whether you want to or not . . . They seize you and do pretty nearly everything they want with you and, while it is going on, you sit with your mouth open and laugh and laugh again" (Jenkins 1992.37). Zero Mostel played the slave in the guise of a popular Jewish entertainer: outspoken, insolent, full of tricks and guile, coarse jokes, leers and winks, wordplay and alliteration (as Pseudolus says of Miles Gloriosus, "He raped Thrace thrice?"). Others involved in the original production had worked in vaudeville, and this training aided and shaped their performances. Phil Silvers was initially hesitant about taking the role of the pimp Lycus because he thought he might be in over his head in a classical Roman comedy. But Gelbart assured him that "he could use more of himself, more of his professional experience in our piece than he could ever imagine; that, despite the show's classic setting, it was grounded in the very traditions of vaudeville and burlesque that had so shaped and sharpened his skills" (1998.210). Silvers's performance was appreciated in just these terms; a reviewer for NBC noted that: "Mr. Silvers sounds as if he arrived in Rome via Flatbush (Avenue) but that's part of his charm."[8]

"In its original incarnation, *Funny Thing* was written for a troupe of ex-vaudevillians—to whom shtick was second nature" (*Boston Phoenix*, 7 July, 1981).[9] This "shtick" was heavily influenced by a New York Jewish-American humor and sensibility and was fed by visits to the Jewish resorts in the Catskill mountains, where live comedy flourished.[10] The majority of the comics who performed in the Catskills had grown up in Manhattan, Brooklyn, or the Bronx, and their shtick, delivered in the nasal cadences of New York Jewish speech, had debuted on the New York vaudeville circuit and in Coney Island saloons. Many young comics went on from the Catskills to radio and television fame and, through these media, their particular brand of humor reached the nation at large. Gelbart noted that most of the writers on Sid Caesar's *Caesar's Hour* were "second generation American Borscht Belt people" and all were "white and Jewish" (1998.23–24).[11] A number of Shevelove and Gelbart's comic heroes and some of the original cast of *Funny Thing* had earned their comic stripes in the Catskills, including Sid Caesar, Milton Berle, Zero Mostel, and Phil Silvers.[12]

The Catskills are located about 250 miles northwest of New York City or, as New Yorkers liked to put it, "just 90 minutes from Broadway" (leading one to wonder how fast they were driving), and they were *the* vacation spot for millions of American Jews from New York City, especially from the boroughs of Brooklyn and the Bronx.[13] In the heyday of the Catskills, from the 1940s through the 1960s, stand-up comedy and theater were a major part of the entertainment; and the Catskills served as a kind of a training camp for aspiring Jewish comics and actors. Like many of the performers, most of the clientele were second-generation East European Jewish immigrants, and the Catskills quickly became known as the Borscht Circuit or the Borscht Belt.

The veteran Catskills performer Jack Eagle defines Catskills humor as "Jewish humor that has been going on in Jewish life since its inception. It's often black. The only way Jews have been able to survive all these years is by thinking, by living by their wits. When you're at the bottom, you live by your wits. We're used to the indignity of failure. We're used to rejection" (Frommer and Frommer 1991.187). It draws on a particular view of life, one in which disaster is expected, and can be summed up in the saying, "The Cossacks are always coming." It is filled with pathos, irony, self-mockery, sarcasm, and earthy vulgarity. This shtetl humor was transposed and transformed in the Catskills where it was performed in front of an audience of assimilated Jews.

According to Steve Rossi, another Catskills veteran comic: "I see the Catskills as basically vaudeville. It's Jewish-oriented comedy that has become more Gentile-oriented" (Frommer and Frommer 1991.187). Here the career of Sol Zim is instructive. Zim, a Dean Martin look-alike, appeared as both a cantor and a pop singer in the Catskills in the late 1950s and early 1960s. The ease with which he combined his religious and secular careers signals how far the assimilation of Jews into American society had come since the days of the famous 1927 film *The Jazz Singer*. That film, the first "talkie" (sound film), starred Al Jolson, who played the son of an immigrant East European cantor in New York City. The film explored the problems of identity and assimilation that troubled first generation immigrants. The plot is centered around the struggle between the son's desire to assimilate and become a jazz singer and his loyalty to his ethnic background and his father's insistence that he become a cantor. By the 1950s, that dilemma was largely resolved or at least muted; as Sol Zim put it: "I am the Jazz Singer with a twist: I started out as a cantor and became a pop singer and managed to combine both" (Frommer and Frommer 1991.118).[14] Vacations in the Catskills marked successful assimilation into middle-class American life, and Jewish assimilation and enjoyment of America as the horn of plenty were what the visitors to the Catskills celebrated, even as they retreated from the gentile world to their own colony. Jewish comics whose shtick focused on alienation bombed. Catskills audiences walked out on Woody Allen's neurotic intellectual angst, Jerry Lewis's moronic, high-strung adolescent male persona, and Lenny Bruce's searing honesty and lacerating wit. According to Eagle, "Lenny Bruce spoke the truth, but he was 'too true,' if you can say such a thing, for the Mountains—too hip, too outrageous, ahead of his time" (Frommer and Frommer 1991.187). Instead, one of the most popular daytime entertainments at Grossinger's was Simon Sez, a game in which participants must obey the instructions of Simon and all do exactly as he "sez." The game might be read as a metaphor for assimilation: participants who successfully copy Simon's actions and obey his commands are rewarded, and those who fail to conform and obey the leader are weeded out.

Gelbart and Shevelove's adaptation of Plautus's Roman comedies deliberately avoided critiquing either Roman or American society. When Stephen Sondheim composed lyrics that did contain satirical material, Shevelove vetoed them, saying he wanted *Funny Thing* to be strictly a domestic farce and not a commentary: he told Sondheim that there should be no political or satirical edge to the songs.

A Jewish-American Rome

Gelbart and Shevelove's adaptation of Roman comedy for Broadway is part of a long tradition in American theater of transforming the arts associated with high culture into popular culture. Rodgers and Hart's 1938 *The Boys from Syracuse*, an adaptation of Shakespeare's *Comedy of Errors* (itself based on Plautus), and Cole Porter's 1947 *Kiss Me, Kate*, loosely based on *The Taming of the Shrew*, are two Broadway musical prototypes for *Funny Thing*. Gelbart and Shevelove's additions to and shaping of Plautus offered comic relief from the standard images of Rome and Romans in American culture and redefined Rome in their own image. Like Plautus, who thumbed his nose at the conventions of Greek New Comedy, part of the "high" culture of his day, Gelbart and Shevelove punctured the well-known image of a monumental city inhabited by toga-clad, sober, patriotic, and sturdy citizens of a virtuous republic. Nor is their Rome the decadent, corrupt city of tyrants and mad emperors, an image that has regularly cropped up in political rhetoric as an admonition and in popular Hollywood films where it has been exploited for its sensationalist value.

Like Plautus's Rome, the Rome of *Funny Thing* is inhabited by low-level tricksters, rogues, and panderers, not patricians and senators; its focus is a household in a not-so-fashionable quarter of Rome like the Subura, rather than a palace on the Palatine Hill. In American terms, this is Flatbush Avenue rather than Park Avenue. Reviewers noted with pleasure the musical's "Jewish-American humor" and called its stars "Catskills comics" and its Rome a "Brooklyn-on-the-Tiber."[15] In their adaptation of Plautus for the stage, Gelbart and Shevelove translated what had become "high culture," the classics in general and Roman comedy in particular, into a popular American cultural idiom: the urban Jewish humor of New York. For them, this cultural idiom *was* America and, accordingly (and fittingly), they drew on the vibrant and innovative popular arts that flourished in New York for their translation of Plautus for American theater audiences.

"Why is it," Gelbart asked, "that the (American) West is supposed to say America to people? To me, Milton Berle, with his eastern cheekiness . . . is as American as a stage Mom and apple pie." Berle's long career spanned vaudeville, radio, and television, and vaudeville and burlesque routines remained staples of his acts throughout his career. Describing Berle's comic style and performance, Gelbart commented: "Now *that* is America, not John Wayne and the West." For comics like him, Berle was "a comic George Washington." Berle's style was kinetic, electric, slapstick, and according to Gelbart, his gags were timeless—the same as those "that must have caused Nero to giggle" (1998.64, 66).[16] Hard as it may be to imagine *Funny Thing* without Zero Mostel, Gelbart and Shevelove had first offered Milton Berle the role of Pseudolus. When Berle declined, they put the vital, bawdy, Jewish-American comic Zero Mostel in a toga and let him loose on stage.

The Cinematic Forum

Richard Lester's cinematic interpretation and manipulation of the original Broadway production adds another fascinating layer to the transmission and translation process. While Shevelove and Gelbart deliberately avoided political or social commentary in their musical comedy, the film director Richard Lester (known for *A Hard Day's Night* and

Help!), who was hired to direct the film version of the comedy, had a different agenda. Lester aimed for more than filming a stage farce; he claimed his vision had "nothing to do with all those Broadway Jewish jokes." He wanted his film comedy to expose the seamy underside of Rome and highlight its social and economic injustices, *and* he wanted to parody Hollywood film genres, particularly the historical epic and its images of ancient Rome (Cameron and Shivas 1969.19).

However, the producer Melvin Frank, one of the powerful Jewish moguls of the Hollywood film industry, wanted a film of the Broadway production, a bawdy farce. Lester complained about his lack of control and freedom as a director; he was used to complete artistic control of his films, but Frank was a product of the old Hollywood studio system where producers had final artistic control and authority over films. It was not a happy relationship. Frank hated Lester's attempts to inject some of the harshness of Roman society into the film, and he locked up in a vault some of the footage Lester had shot so that the director could not get at it (Sinyard 1985.39–47). Yet, by rewriting and adding to the screenplay, particularly the scenes involving Hero, planning the musical numbers, and working closely with cinematographer Nicolas Roeg, Lester was able to convey some of his vision of Rome and his critique of Hollywood films. Faced with the demands of producer Melvin Frank for a Broadway farce and having been handed a completed script, Lester tried to control the final product by developing his own fast-paced editorial style, adding to the script where he could, and inserting shots that subverted the surface meaning of the musical numbers.

The original Broadway farce depended on a vaudeville style and pace that belonged to the live theater; in coming up with a cinematic style, Lester turned back to the traditions of early cinema farce, especially the films of Buster Keaton, one of his childhood idols, who played Erronius in the film. Drawing on classic cinema farce, Lester used a number of sight gags: a man in the market painting zebra stripes on a donkey; a pigeon, dispatched by Hero with a message for Philia inscribed on a wax tablet, is unable to carry the weight and falls to the ground; a horse sits stolidly in a steam bath because Hero needs mare's sweat for an aphrodisiac he is concocting. Yet Lester combined these sight gags with a fast-paced rhythm through editing to achieve his own comic style that one reviewer called "cinemafarce" (Roddick 1980.593).

Lester and Roeg also added their own comic dimensions to scenes from the original play, such as the scenes where Hero and Philia sing "I'm Lovely" to each other. Lester filmed Hero and the blonde Philia singing to each other as they happily trip through misty fields and soft-focus green woods in a series of mock-romantic dissolves punctuated by farcical collisions with trees in a kind of pastiche of a television commercial. The lyrics of "I'm Lovely" are solipsistic, and the genre of love song is made ridiculous by its setting and performance. This satire of romantic love is itself satirized when Pseudolus and Hysterium, in obvious and ridiculous drag, reprise the scene.

According to Lester, one of his main interests was to expose the injustices of life in ancient Rome. He became fascinated with the "sordid" aspects of ancient Roman society and urbanism, and wanted to portray the squalor beneath the splendid surface of Rome, especially the utter disregard for the slave's life and its humiliations (*British Film Institute Monthly Film Bulletin* 1967.34–41). Lester tried to convey this visually with shots of slaves being bought, sold, or beaten. A scene in which Pseudolus asks passersby for assistance and is then kicked and beaten by each integrates a display of brutality into the comedy. In a parody of a set piece of a Busby Berkeley musical, Zero Mostel, Jack Gilford, Michael Hordern, and Phil Silvers dance in a toga kickline on top of an aqueduct and then cakewalk through the house singing "Everybody Ought to Have a Maid." Yet Lester inserts shots of slaves toiling away at their menial, degrading jobs as the main characters sing and dance. Thus, he establishes a contradiction between the sentiments of the song and the visual image on the screen. By making the image convey the reality of the life of a maid, Lester disrupts the message of the song (Sinyard 1985.42).

Lester and production designer Tony Walton read Jerome Carcopino's *Daily Life in Ancient Rome* instead of Plautus. Whatever its historical quality, Carcopino's book attempted to describe "real" life in Rome, the gritty texture of daily life in the ancient metropolis. Lester wanted to undermine Hollywood's Rome of gleaming marble palaces, magnificent monuments, and lavish spectacles. Carcopino helped Lester and Walton create what they hoped was an "authentic" Roman urban landscape: a decaying, rather squalid, and smelly back street in Rome. The magnificently gaudy and tacky decor of the Roman houses was carefully planned. The house of Lycus, the seller of courtesans, was painted in "awful purple," and hideous cherubs and urns clutter the rooms where the eunuchs massage the girls. According to Lester, "We tried as hard as we could to create bad taste—bad Roman taste of the first century A.D. It's about the back streets, the suburbia of Rome, and it has a very nouveau riche quality" (*New York Times*, 7 November 1965).

In his attempt to create an "anti-epic," Lester added a number of scenes that are not part of the original Broadway production, but rather serve to parody the cinematic spectacles of 1950s Hollywood epics set in ancient Rome: chariot races, orgies, bath scenes, and gladiatorial combats. These films, produced during the Cold War, reflect that era's concerns and anxieties. On the narrative level, Romans signify the tyrannical oppressor, figured in the films as modern totalitarianism, and Christians, Jews, and slaves are us (Wyke 1997b; Fitzgerald, Futrell, and Winkler in this volume). In most of these epics, Judaeo-Christian values triumph over oppressive Romans (and, correspondingly, Nazis, fascists, and Communists). *Funny Thing* comically subverts these heavily moralizing Roman epics, especially *Quo Vadis, Ben-Hur*, and *Spartacus*, by parodying the spectacles that were mandatory in Hollywood's representations of the grandeur and decadence of ancient Rome.

The entrance of the soldier Miles Gloriosus, for example, mocks the Roman triumphs familiar to audiences who had seen *Quo Vadis* or other epics. Instead of triumphal pomp and circumstance, an off-key fanfare announces Miles's arrival, and the soldiers are pelted with garbage as they march behind their leader, tripping over their drums. Full of self-importance, Miles demands his bride in the song "Bring Me My Bride"; he is in a hurry for "there are lands to conquer, cities to loot, and people to degrade." He is fabulously vain ("I am my ideal"), and when he arrives at Lycus's house to fetch his bride, he orders "a sit-down orgy for forty" and pompously dictates his Caesar-like memoirs as a comic revel goes on around him. Ken Thorne's orchestral arrangements contribute to the undermining of the historical epic: his mock fanfares and orgy music parody the epic methods of *Spartacus*'s composer Alex North (Sinyard 1985.43).

Lester also stages a send-up of a chariot race, alluding to cinema's most famous chariot race in *Ben-Hur*. Lester dressed Miles and his soldiers in black, like the evil Messala in *Ben-Hur* and, as in *Ben-Hur*, there are close-up shots of the spokes and wheels of the chariots rubbing together and becoming entangled. Finally, Lester parodies gladiatorial training and combat in a scene where a bored professional gladiatorial trainer instructs gladiators on how to improve their strokes by using the heads of slaves as if they were golf balls. Lester's target is the famous scene in *Spartacus* where Spartacus (Kirk Douglas) and other slaves train as gladiators at a school in Roman Capua. Lester follows this parody of gladiatorial training with a parodic combat: Pseudolus (Zero Mostel) enters the arena with a net and trident, but must be saved by one of the courtesans, who successfully aims a trident at Pseudolus's opponent, mocking the gladiatorial matches found in nearly every Roman epic film.

In his satire of the Hollywood epic and its representations of the Roman world, Lester was likely influenced by British comedy, especially the *Carry On* films popular in England since the late 1950s, a series which parodied a variety of film genres. *Carry On Spying* satirized the spythriller; *Carry On Cowboy*, the western; *Carry On . . . Up the Khyber*, the British Raj epic. *Carry On Cleo*, released in 1964, took aim at the Hollywood Roman epic in general and Joseph Mankiewicz's recently released *Cleopatra* in particular. Lester had moved to London in the mid-1960s, and his film was really an Anglo-American co-production, a triangular meeting of the comic sensibilities of Rome, Brooklyn, and Brighton (Cull). British screenwriter Michael Pertwee collaborated with producer Melvin Frank on the script, a number of the cast were British character actors, cinematography was by Nicolas Roeg, and artistic design was by Tony Walton. The manic, zany quality of the British *Carry On* satires of film genres seems to have worked its way into Lester's film. Like *Carry On Cleo*, many of the jokes in Lester's film come from a parodic representation of a past and distant empire (Rome) *and* from a parody of Hollywood's appropriation of that empire to inscribe modern imperial myths.

Lester's film offered American audiences comic relief from the popular images of Rome and Romans in American culture. Most Americans have a double image of Rome: the "good" Rome, the Roman republic, and the "bad" Rome, the Roman empire. The film, like the original Broadway musical comedy, punctures the image of the "noble Romans" of the republic, those togaed figures of fortitude, self-denial, and patriotism that used to crop up with great regularity in civics lessons, political discourse, and the arts. Critic Hollis Alpert noted with pleasure that "the comic corruption on all levels of Roman society is a welcome corrective to those noble Romans who have infested movies for generations" (*Saturday Review*, 15 October 1966). And according to *Variety*, "One of *Funny Thing*'s great services is that it satirizes a 'film-myth' culture, the Romans, too long burdened under the homogenized and idealized unreality of laundered togas and gleaming columns" (27 September 1966). Lester's film also deflates the myth of the grandeur and decadence of imperial Rome, a myth the Hollywood film industry helped to disseminate in American culture. This is not the corrupt Rome of mad emperors like Nero, and Romans are not the decadent oppressors of Christians and slaves. Instead of Hollywood spectacles of armies on the march, monumental, white marble palaces, depraved imperial elites, and bread and circuses, Lester's Romans have dirty togas; the columns and friezes of his

Roman houses are chipped; and his Roman streets are full of rotting vegetables, toiling proles, and worn-out slaves.

In his adaptation of Gelbart and Shevelove's adaptation of Plautus,
Lester utilized a variety of cinematic techniques and comic references including classic farce, British satire, the historical epic, and musical comedy. *Funny Thing*'s pastiche of references provides a commentary on
American film culture and a comic critique of ancient Rome. It is ironic,
however, given Lester's twin goals, that he realized them by utilizing the
imperial resources of Hollywood, including its established economy of
production, using sets built for other epics. Lester explained that his film
was made in Spain, in part, because the props of Anthony Mann's *The
Fall of the Roman Empire* were still there and because of the familiarity
of the Spaniards with what Hollywood wanted: "The stagehands know
not to put forks on a table. The horses are trained. There's a general familiarity with these types of films" (*New York Times*, 7 November 1965).

To create Carcopino's real Rome, Lester recycled some of Hollywood's sets and exploited an already established economic relationship
between Spanish peasants and Hollywood directors: "I became very interested in the sordid quality of Rome and started reading Carcopino and
examining life and behavior in Rome from a historical point of view and
so built the set, filled it with vegetables and fruit, and left them to rot for
two weeks so that all the flies and wasps got into it. I brought peasants
down from the hills and little villages in the center of Spain and made
them live in the sets. We gave them each a particular job, sharpening
knives, making pottery . . . We just left them to do a specific job for the
whole film. I liked all that and was getting involved in it" (Sinyard
1985.40). Lester attempted to undermine Hollywood's representations of
Rome and its distortions of history by creating a more authentic, "sordid"
Rome, but he did not escape Hollywood's influence: he depended on the
economic power of Hollywood to command resources and labor.

When *Funny Thing* premiered in 1966, United Artists staged a promotional chariot race. The starting gate was at Caesars Palace, Las
Vegas, and the finish line was at the Fine Arts Theater in Los Angeles,
where the film opened. Caesars Palace's designers relied heavily on
Hollywood's representations of Roman decadence and excess in erecting
a temple dedicated to indulgence and excess in the deserts of Nevada
(Malamud and McGuire in this volume), and it was therefore fitting that
the two epicenters of popular images of the Roman world collaborate
in promoting a film about Rome. In what must have seemed a final irony
to Lester, Hollywood's promotional stunt for his adaptation of a Rome

imagined by second-generation Jewish immigrants, an adaptation Lester hoped would critique celluloid visions of antiquity, was held at a faux Roman pleasure palace where patrons could star in their own Hollywood-inspired Roman fantasy.

Notes

This article is an expanded version of talks given at a University of New Mexico conference, *Roman Holiday: Classical Comedy/Contemporary Commentary*, held in Albuquerque, October 19–24, 1998, and at the Pacific Rim Latin Seminar, *Roma Theatrum Mundi*, held in Rome, June 29–July 3, 1999. Thanks to the participants at both conferences for comments and suggestions, especially Charles Mercier and Dorothy Chanksy. Special thanks to Sandra Joshel and Martha Malamud for their close readings and suggestions.

1. "Hebonics," Haruth Website Design & Publishing Company, webmaster@haruth.com. Thanks to Martha Malamud for drawing to my attention this Website and the following item.

2. "Catskills Institute," distributed November 29, 1995, by the Brown University News Bureau.

3. The Broadway production was an enormous success: it opened on May 8, 1962, at the Alvin Theater in New York and ran for nearly 1,000 performances. It has been successfully revived a number of times since then, most recently in 1996. It isn't necessary to go to New York to see *Funny Thing;* it has been a perennial favorite in off-Broadway productions and has been performed all over the country from high schools in Omaha to summer stock theater in New England.

4. The musical comedy won a number of Tony Awards: Shevelove and Gelbart won for the book, George Abbott for directing, and Zero Mostel for best actor. It was revived in 1972 and starred Phil Silvers and again in 1996 with Nathan Lane, then Whoopi Goldberg, and finally David Grier playing the role of Pseudolus. Phil Silvers and Nathan Lane received Tony Awards for their performances.

5. *Funny Thing* draws most heavily on Plautus's *Casina*, so much so that Richard Beacham's translation of the latter is entitled *Casina: A Funny Thing Happened on the Way to the Wedding*.

6. How did the different sociopolitical climate of 1996 or the casting of Whoopi Goldberg affect the brothel scene? Very little. The courtesans remained scantily clad, and they continued to perform sexually suggestive dances; no lip service was paid to political correctness. One female reviewer asked the six women who played them if they felt sexually exploited. For their answers see O'Haire 1996.3. When Whoopi Goldberg played Pseudolus she did not ogle the courtesans; instead she acted as a kind of "personal shopper" for Hero, and she developed a slight crush on Miles Gloriosus rather than on one of the women.

7. For Plautus's linguistic originality see Erich Segal's introduction to his translation of Plautus (Segal 1996).

8. Flatbush refers to Flatbush Avenue in Brooklyn. The quotation is from Betty Rollin, NBC TV, Clippings File, Billy Rose Theater Collection, New York Public Library, no date.

9. The reviewer points out that the problem with revivals of *Funny Thing* is that actors now lack "these low-comic reflexes. The adroitness with gag lines, the precise timing, and the ease that were the lifeblood of American vaudeville abilities . . . are rapidly fading and they are hard to learn from scratch."

10. For the Jewish comic tradition, I have found Sarah Blacher Cohen's 1983 book helpful.

11. When asked why Sid Caesar's writers were all young and Jewish, Gelbart replied: "Probably because all our parents were old and Jewish" (Gelbart 1998.24).

12. Other comics who were well received in the Catskills include Eddie Cantor, Red Buttons, Danny Kaye, Red Skelton, Don Rickles, and Neil Simon, who said about his stint there: "In two seasons there I did eight original musical comedies, sixteen shows. After that, Broadway was a piece of cake, Hollywood was a rocking chair" (Frommer and Frommer 1991.72).

13. I have found Frommer and Frommer's oral history of the Catskills an invaluable source (1991).

14. Zim may have accommodated himself to American culture and enjoyed the best of both worlds, old and new, but a certain ambivalence surely remained a part of the Jewish-American experience. Jews may have assimilated much of American culture, but they were not yet socially integrated. Jews were not welcome in many places, including country clubs and resorts, and it is hard not to see a paradox in a celebration of assimilation in a Jewish resort colony.

15. For examples, see the reviews in the *Saturday Review* 45, 26 May 1962.22 and in the *New Republic* 146, 28 May 1962.28–30.

16. Berle was also "the king of drag": female impersonation was a staple in his acts and on his show. Gelbart has used female impersonation in much of his work—something he first started with *Funny Thing*, continued in the *M*A*S*H* television series for which he was a co-writer, and then featured as the central comic device in his screenplay for the movie *Tootsie*.

7   Serial Romans

Martha Malamud

Classics concerns whole cultures and the whole range of our responses to
those cultures. And so it concerns what is salacious, sordid, or funny, no less
than what is informative or improving.—*Mary Beard and John Henderson
(1995.105)*

"Next, I think I will do something contemporary, nasty, bitter, and steamy,"
McCullough said . . . , "Yes, something steamy, after the Romans."—*Colleen
McCullough in a 1990 interview (quoted in Mehren 1990)*

There has been an upsurge of interest in the last few years in classics and contemporary culture. John Henderson and Mary Beard's *Classics: A Very Short Introduction* (1995) makes the point that classics is as
much about our responses to and constructions of ancient cultures as it
is about a body of knowledge restricted by strict linguistic, geographic,
or chronological limits. In the past, the focus of study has tended to be
upon the classical tradition in high culture: the influence of Roman
thought on America's founding fathers, classical allusion in Joyce or
Eliot, and so on. The classical world was, de facto, the possession of the
elite; what trickled down to the masses was not worth much thought.
Now though, we are willing to pursue the classical tradition even into
the belly of the beast—mass culture. From Caesars Palace to bodybuilding, from the relative refinement of *I, Claudius* to the shrieks and
swordplay of *Xena Warrior Princess*, classics is alive and well in the popular imagination. There is a growing body of analysis of classics in popular culture, ranging from studies of museum collections to classical
poses in male bodybuilding, to the architecture of Caesars Palace, and
the significance of the domestication of the theme of empire in the BBC

television production of *I, Claudius* (Beard 1993, Wyke 1997a, Malamud 1998, Joshel in this volume).

In this chapter, I want to take a look at a publishing phenomenon whose roots are planted firmly in classical soil—or perhaps I should say dirt: Colleen McCullough's best-selling *Masters of Rome* series, which traces the intricate and often lurid tale of the collapse of the Roman republic, beginning with Marius and Sulla and extending, we are told, at least through the affair between Julius Caesar and Cleopatra. There are five books in the series so far: *The First Man in Rome, The Grass Crown, Fortune's Favorites, Caesar's Women,* and *Caesar: Let the Dice Fly.*[1]

McCullough's Rome is painted on a broad canvas: the total number of pages in the series to date is well over three thousand, and each volume includes an introduction, an annotated glossary providing substantial historical background, and illustrations of the major characters drawn by the author herself. In this chapter's brief format, it is impossible to do justice to the scope of the undertaking; what follows is an attempt to isolate some ideological features of McCullough's Rome (the emphasis on family and her treatment of women and homosexuals), and then to discuss both the way the series is marketed as a product for mass-market consumption and how McCullough's own life story, which reads like the plot of a women's romance novel, has become a part of the series' marketing strategy.

Family Values

They giggle uncontrollably. They fall into terrible screaming rages. They turn red and stamp their feet. They call each other by childish nicknames like Piggle-Wiggle (better known to historians as Quintus Caecilius Metellus Numidicus) and Piglet (Quintus Caecilius Metellus Pius). They kill without remorse. These are the Romans of the late republic as seen through the eyes of Colleen McCullough, whose imagined Rome epitomizes the banality of evil. McCullough traces the history of Rome from the Social Wars that ravaged the Italian peninsula, through the bloody proscriptions of Sulla, into the tumultuous period of the late republic when aristocratic strongmen with independent armies struggled for control of Rome. Her books concentrate upon the leading men of each stage of the collapse of the republic: Marius, Sulla, Pompey, and Julius Caesar. Blending sadistic cruelty with relentless didacticism and voluminous research, her novels are epic in scope but narrated in a style that frequently recalls the nursery, as this scene, taken from *Fortune's Favorites*, demonstrates. Here the young Julius Caesar meets King

Nicomedes of Bithynia; while waiting to be admitted to the king's presence, Caesar hears (McCullough 1994.375):

> the sound of raised voices coming from beyond a half-opened door . . . a male voice, high and lisping, and a female voice, deep and booming.
>
> "Jump!" said the woman. "Upsy-daisy!"
>
> "Rubbish!" said the man. "You degrade it!"
>
> "Oozly-woozly-soozly!" said the woman, and produced a huge whinny of laughter.
>
> "Go away!" said the man.
>
> "Diddums!" from the woman, laughing again . . . The scene . . . was fascinating. It involved a very old man, a big woman perhaps ten years younger, and an elderly, roly-poly dog . . .

Such lapses into nursery talk are aligned with McCullough's tendency to portray her heroes and heroines as infantilized egoists: the Inner Child is never buried very far beneath the surface of these would-be world leaders. Here, for example, Pompey, a successful young general, confronts Sulla, who, as dictator, has refused to allow him a triumph. The dialogue is a "triumph" of statesmanship (McCullough 1994.290):

> "I *want* a triumph!" said Pompey loudly, and stamped his foot.
>
> "And I say you can't have one!" said Sulla, equally loudly.
>
> Pompey's broad, temper-reddened face grew beetling, the thin lips drew back to reveal small white teeth. "You would do well to remember, Lucius Cornelius Sulla, that more people worship the rising than the setting sun!"
>
> For no reason that any of the enthralled listeners could determine, Sulla burst out laughing . . . "Oh, very well!" he gasped when he could speak at all. "Have your triumph!" And then, still shaken by fresh guffaws, he said, "Don't just stand there, Magnus, you great booby! Help me pick up my toga!"

Magnus, the "great booby" of this scene and, later, the sentimentally fond husband of Caesar's daughter Julia, comes across in the series as having the mentality of a foolish adolescent, although the historical Pompey enjoyed a phenomenal career based, in the words of Ronald Syme, on "illegality and treachery" (1939.28). At the age of twenty-three, he had raised a private army to come to the support of Sulla, and his campaigns in Sicily and Africa were notoriously brutal, earning him the title of *adulescentulus carnifex*, the "boy butcher." This is typical of McCullough's technique. Despite the incredible wealth of historical detail in these novels, each of which comes with an annotated glossary of terms and names averaging one hundred pages in length, history is reduced to a satisfying simplicity. It is the result of the actions of strong-willed men who are, like Pompey, nothing more than overgrown children, motivated by powerful but basic impulses of rage and desire. Character is destiny and greatness is inherent and subject to objective verification: it is inextricably linked with Luck or Fortune. The Great Man *knows* he is great. An irrational but indomitable instinct informs him of his destiny; omens confirm it. Moments of epiphany, when the Great Man realizes his luck, form a leitmotif in the series.

Here, to take one example, is Gaius Marius at age forty-seven, a provincial upstart with no clients, feeling his greatness despite the bleakness of his prospects and his lack of aristocratic connections: "And still his unwelcome guest, the feeling, refused to go away; in fact, of late it had greatly increased in strength. As if the moment approached. The moment in which he, Gaius Marius, would become the First Man in Rome. Every particle of common sense in him—and there were many—screamed that his feeling was a traitor, a trap which would betray him and lead to ignominy and death. Yet he went on experiencing it, the ineradicable feeling that he would become the First Man in Rome" (McCullough 1990.25). That "ineradicable feeling" foreshadows greatness, but the true guarantor of luck in the series is a blood-tie: connection to the Julius Caesar clan, which—poor but purely patrician, as blue-blooded and blond-haired as a family can be—is in these novels Fortune's conduit. Marriage to a Julia enables Marius to make his mark on the senate; marriage to her younger sister (a character invented by McCullough) enables Sulla to break with his scandalous past and assume the senate seat to which he is entitled by his pure patrician pedigree. Great as the destinies of Marius and Sulla prove to be, however, only a man with Julian blood in his veins—not simply marriage connections to the Julian *gens*—will attain the pinnacle of Fortune. This man is McCullough's impossibly perfect hero, Julius Caesar, who conveniently spells out the overriding importance of family in this passage from *Caesar's Women*. Here Caesar breaks the news to his vicious mistress Servilia that he is ending the engagement between her son Brutus and Caesar's daughter Julia (McCullough 1996.581–82):

> "Do you mean you'd sacrifice *my* son to feather your own political nest, Caesar?" she asked, teeth bared.

"Yes. Just as you'd sacrifice my daughter to serve your ends, Servilia. We produce children to inherit the fame and enhancement we bring the family, and the price our children pay is to be there to serve our needs and the needs of our families . . . the family is perpetual. We and our children are but a small part of it. Romans create their own Gods, Servilia, and all the truly Roman Gods are Gods of the Family."

And, in McCullough's world, family boils down to blood—not terribly surprising in a novelist whose reputation and fortune were made by the family saga *The Thorn Birds*. Despite the fact that the Romans themselves took a broader view of family and regularly adopted heirs in order to preserve the family name and property, in McCullough's Rome, bloodlines count as much as they do in the eugenically engineered world of thoroughbred racing. Like the family values espoused by Patrick Buchanan and other conservatives, this series projects a fantasy based on racial and genetic superiority. It portrays as entirely natural a social hierarchy in which Romans are superior to other races, aristocrats are superior to plebeians (and, of course, to slaves), and men are superior to women. McCullough's essential conservatism is a key element in her popularity. It is no surprise to find that one of her enthusiastic fans is also an ardent proponent of conservatism, essentialism, and family values: former Speaker of the House Newt Gingrich.[2] In 1996, Gingrich shared a power breakfast in Washington with McCullough, who was in town on a promotional tour; after breakfast they announced their agreement to collaborate on a non-fiction book about the educational value of historical fiction.[3]

Sucking, Devouring, Wriggling, Wet

Indicative of the overwhelming importance of the perpetuation of aristocratic bloodlines in McCullough's conception of Roman society is the double status of women, who are at once vital links in the chain of inheritance while generally portrayed as worthless, inconvenient chattel. Indeed, so important is the existence of family connections in this series that McCullough, for all her claims to authenticity and meticulous research, is led to create a non-historical character to cement the bond between Sulla and the Julian line. This is the unfortunate Julilla, who exists to enable Sulla to achieve his destiny, thus fulfilling her own role as a vital link in the chain of inheritance, but who also epitomizes the negative qualities McCullough associates with women.[4] In this passage, a far from happily married Sulla gloomily contemplates the excessive nature of his disappointing wife, a marriage he was drawn into for the sake of producing an heir with Julian blood: "I ought never to have married her, he thought. I got carried away by a vision of my future son seen through the medium of her eyes—for that was all she did, serve as a vessel to pass a vision through on his way from Fortune to Fortune's chosen one . . . I don't mind excess—but not an excess I'm the object of. Only excess I'm the perpetrator of, thank you!" (McCullough 1990.466).

There is a strong satirical element to McCullough's portrayal of women: their excesses are described with excessive relish. Plenty of bodily fluids are splashed about, and, in the few cases where the female characters are not clearly weaker than their men, imagery aligns them with the monstrous or the unnatural. In Julilla's case, her initial dazzling beauty quickly fades as her overwhelming love for Sulla leads her first to an eating disorder, portrayed in contemptuous detail, and then to alcoholism. Uncontrolled drinking and anorexia are physical manifestations of her excessive sexual appetites, which McCullough portrays as disgusting: "And all this she threw over Sulla like a pall woven from the most clinging and tentacular cobwebs . . . before he could look at her or collect himself to feel anything, she had glued her mouth to his like a leech on an arm, sucking, devouring, wriggling, wet, all blood and blackness. Her hands were groping after his genitals, she made noises of the most lascivious pleasure, then she actually began to wind her legs around him" (McCullough 1996.347). Julilla's passion is associated with a host of disgusting notions here: death (the pall), slime, spiders, tentacles, entrapment, and perhaps even cannibalism or vampirism in the description of her leechlike kisses. The reader shares Sulla's revulsion; a couple of hundred pages later, Julilla finally puts both out of their misery by committing suicide.

It is significant that the most sympathetic female character in the novels to date is Aurelia, the vessel chosen by Fortune to bear Julius Caesar.[5] Stunningly beautiful, endowed by her creator with large violet eyes and golden hair, she distinguishes herself from all the other female characters less by her beauty than by her pragmatism: she is a natural businesswoman. Ignoring the wishes of her husband, she takes over the administration of a large tenement building in the low-rent Subura district (an area between the Esquiline, Viminal, and Quirinal hills that was notorious for prostitution, among other seedy activities), and runs it profitably on her own. Unlike most of the other women in the saga, Aurelia is far more devoted to her business than to her husband. Indeed, her marriage reverses the usual pattern of gender relations in the series: she is the dominant partner, making all the business decisions, while he is notable only for providing the Julian blood necessary for engendering the future dictator. Far from exhibiting the leaky emotionalism of the other female characters, she is consistently perceived by other characters as cold, hard, controlled, and untouched by passion. She is the exception that proves the rule, the woman with the mind of a man, whose virtues reveal the weaknesses and failings of ordinary women.

There is room for all sorts of women in a series this long: beautiful, strong, and good women; pretty, silly, and weak women; and the Cruella DeVille model: seductive, sexually voracious, and evil. In the latter category, we find one of McCullough's empowered female characters, the monstrous Servilia, sister of Cato and mother of Brutus, a woman even more repulsive than the tentacular Julilla. Sly, brutal, and dogged as a child in the earlier novels, she comes into her own in *Caesar's Women* as Caesar's long-term mistress, a woman whom he dislikes personally but whose sexual prowess he admires greatly. As McCullough describes her, she is some sort of grotesque animal, as we can see in the following two scenes. In the first, Servilia attacks her unbearable brother Cato (McCullough 1996.347):

> Servilia moved with the speed of a striking snake, straight for Cato . . . Between them she went with both hands up, fingers crooked into claws, took Cato's face in their embrace, and dug her nails into his flesh until they sank like grapples. Had he not instinctively screwed his eyes shut, she would have blinded him, but her talons raked him from brow to jawline on right side and on left side, gouged down to muscle and then kept on going along his neck and into his shoulders.
>
> Even a warrior like Cato retreated, thin howls of terrible pain dying away as his opening eyes took in the sight of . . . a Servilia whose lips were peeled back from her teeth and whose eyes blazed murder. Then under the distended gaze of her son, her husband, and her half-brother, she lifted her dripping fingers to her mouth and luxuriously sucked Cato's flesh from them.

As is the case with Julilla, Servilia is characterized by a cluster of disgusting images that associate the female with death, entrapment, animals, and cannibalism. She moves like a snake, has talons like a bird of prey, and (reminiscent of but exceeding Julilla's leech-like kissing) sucks human flesh from her fingers.

In another scene, Servilia's animal characteristics mark her as an archetypal female monster, a Harpy. Harpies, half women and half bird, are, like the Sirens and the Furies, hybrid female monsters in Greek and Roman myth. According to Virgil, there is no worse monster (*Aeneid* 3.214–18):

tristius haud illis monstrum, nec saevior ulla
pestis et ira deum Stygiis sese extulit undis.
virginei volucrum vultus, foedissima ventris
proluvies uncaeque manus et pallida semper
ora fame.

No grimmer monster than these, no more savage plague or rage of the gods
ever raised itself from the waters of Hell. They are birds with the faces of
maidens, a foul discharge issues from their bellies, their hands are claws,
their faces always wan with hunger.[6]

Their name in Greek means "Snatchers," and though they were originally probably personifications of the storm winds, they came to be particularly associated with the pollution of food. In Apollonius's *Argonautica*
2.178f., they are sent by Zeus to snatch away the food of Phineus, the
king of Bithynia, and to pollute what remained; they were driven off,
however, by Calais and Zetes, stalwart young heroes from the Argonaut
expedition. Like the Harpies, who are at least temporarily tamed by a virile hero, Servilia, too, can be domesticated, at least for a time: "She got
out of the chair and began to remove her clothing. Suddenly Caesar
wanted her badly, but not to cradle her or treat her tenderly. One didn't
tame a harpy by kindness. A harpy was a grotesque one took on the floor
with teeth in her neck and her claws locked behind her back, then took
again and again. Rough usage always did tame her; she became soft and
slightly kittenish" (McCullough 1994.189). A striking snake, a bird of
prey, a Harpy, and finally, after being tamed by the masterful Caesar, a
soft kitten, Servilia is defined throughout by her animality. Still, terrifying as she may be, she can be managed by a man who knows how to
handle a woman. It is consistent with McCullough's deployment of bes-
tial images to describe women that Servilia's most notable physical characteristic, which Caesar finds irresistible, is a line of fine, black, fur-like
hair that runs from the nape of her neck all the way down her spine.[7]

Unmanly Men

In another echo of the rhetorical pose of the Roman satirist,
McCullough provides titillating entertainment for her readers with her
detailed portraits of homosexual males. Homosexuality is a recurrent
feature in these novels, and it is clear that McCullough has either not
read or else not been convinced by recent scholarship on ancient sexuality.[8] In contrast to ancient Roman males, McCullough's Romans make
no distinction between active and passive sexual roles: any homosexual

act is condemned and is furthermore an index of interior weakness or vice. Performative acts reveal essential truths about one's nature; gender is emphatically not constituted, but innate.[9] The overt homosexual appears as a grotesque caricature, described in terms that would not be out of place in the Roman satirists Persius and Juvenal, both of whom include scornful portraits of homosexuals in their satire collections.[10] As in the Roman satirists, dress, body type, posture, and makeup are the markers that distinguish the homosexual from McCullough's vision of the normative Roman heterosexual male. Here, for example, is an Egyptian ruler seen through the eyes of Sulla: "From the moment he set eyes on Ptolemy Alexander the Younger, Sulla had understood why Egypt had preferred to be ruled by old Lathyrus the Chickpea. Ptolemy Alexander the Younger was womanish to the extreme of dressing like an incarnation of Isis in floating draperies knotted and twisted in the fashion of the Hellenized goddess of Egypt, with a golden crown upon his wig of golden curls, and an elaborate painting of his face. He minced, he ogled, he simpered, he fluttered; and yet, thought Sulla shrewdly, beneath all that effeminate façade lay something steely" (McCullough 1994.189). McCullough here insistently uses feminizing language to describe Ptolemy: he is "womanish," an "incarnation of Isis," dressed like a goddess, his face an "effeminate façade." The verbs *(minced, ogled, simpered, fluttered)* used of his womanish gestures and demeanor all convey not merely feminine behavior but also disgust. Juvenal's description of the deviant male worshipers of the goddess Cybele shares similar characteristics, including concern over makeup and emphasis on feminine fabrics:

> You'll see one initiate busy with eye-brow pencil, kohl
> And mascara, eyelids aflutter; a second sips his wine
> From a big glass phallus, his long luxuriant curls
> Caught up in a golden hair-net. He'll be wearing fancy checks
> With a sky-blue motif, or smooth green gabardine,
> And he and his slave will both swear by women's oaths.
> Here's another clutching a mirror, just like that fag of an Emperor
> Otho, who peeked at himself to see how his armour looked
> Before riding into battle.[11]

Sulla is an interesting focalizer for this passage, since he is portrayed in the series as a man torn by the conflict between his desire to exhibit the outward signs of Roman respectability to further his drive for absolute power and his abiding love for the Greek actor Metrobius. His double

status, First Man in public, homosexual lover in private, enables him to
see through the façade to the steel beneath.

Another eastern potentate, Nicomedes the Third of Bithynia (the
very old man playing with a dog we glimpsed above), is described in
terms that highlight the artificial and the camp in his costume; an added
frisson is the contrast drawn between his willowy frame, flimsy garments,
and made-up face, and his white hair, which he keeps unadorned in a
simple masculine cut. He thus appears as both male and female, youthful and aged, another potentially dangerous hybrid representing a threat
to unadorned Roman masculinity: "Tall and thin and willowy, he wore
a floor-length robe of Tyrian purple embroidered with gold and sewn
with pearls, and flimsy pearl-studded golden sandals which revealed that
he gilded his toenails. Though he wore his own hair—cut fairly short and
whitish-grey in color—he had caked his face with an elaborate maquil-
lage of snow-white cream and powder, carefully drawn in soot-black
brows and lashes, artificially pinkened his cheeks, and heavily carmined
his puckered old mouth" (McCullough 1994.375). Here, for example, is
Julius Caesar who appears immediately after the description of Nicomedes quoted above: "The King of Bithynia goggled. There before him
stood a young Roman, clad for the road in a plain leather cuirass and kilt.
He was very tall and wide-shouldered, but the rest of him looked more
slender . . . 'Well, *hello*,' said the King, sitting upright in a hurry, his pose
one of bridling seductiveness. 'Oh, stop that,' said Caesar" (McCullough
1994.375). Caesar is everything Nicomedes is not: associated with the
outdoors ("clad for the road" as opposed to Nicomedes, who wears flimsy
sandals more appropriate for the boudoir), robust ("tall and wide-shouldered" as opposed to the "tall and thin and willowy" Nicomedes), and
dressed in simple leather rather than the potentate's purple and pearls.
Under the guise of authentically recreating Roman views of sexuality,
McCullough is able to indulge in an Orientalist discourse that projects
effeminacy, artificiality, and excessive luxury onto easterners like Nicomedes and Ptolemy, while Romans are portrayed as masculine, unadorned,
and moderate (at least the Romans who haven't fully declined yet; the deviant, monstrous, but consistently amusing Sulla is an exception).

In these novels, homosexuality is not a behavior, a choice, a set of
sexual practices, or a social construction (though it is signaled by posture
and costume): it is part of one's essence. The attempt to conceal and suppress a homosexual nature and the attempt to overcome untrue allegations of homosexuality are both important motivating factors in the novels: the bizarre and excessive behavior of Sulla, for example, is motivated,

at least in part, by his ruthless suppression of his "true nature." His genuine love for the Greek actor Metrobius is sacrificed to his ambition. In
contrast, faced with allegations in the historical record that Julius Caesar frequently indulged in homosexual acts, McCullough creates an elaborate subplot that explains away these charges as fabrications and clears
Caesar of any slur against his manhood, for in this value system that clas-
sifies homosexual behavior of any sort as weak, deviant, effeminate, and
foreign, a homosexual Caesar is unthinkable.

Think like a Roman

While classicists might argue that her portrayal of Roman culture, like her portrayal of ancient sexuality, is sometimes far off-base, Mc-
Cullough presents her project as a true recreation of Roman experience.
She stresses that the books' historical accuracy is based on painstaking
research. "The thing that I object to in many historical novels," she said,
"is that the characters think in the present." By contrast, McCullough
asserts, her characters "think like Romans." This is possible, she explained, "because when I was writing, I *was* a Roman."[12] "Research never
stops," she said blithely in another interview (Tarr 1991), and, from the
author's notes to the novels, we learn that she hired a multilingual research assistant to travel around the world collecting materials for her;
amassed a personal library she describes as "the best private library on
republican Rome . . . anywhere in the world" (Johnson 1993), including
180 volumes of the Loeb Classical Library; and consulted with classical
scholars from universities around the world.

In other words, McCullough promises her readers a certain *authenticity of experience:* the reader is given an opportunity not just to read a
novel set in Rome but to "be a Roman" by immersing herself in the author's total knowledge of the Roman world. Another example of Mc-
Cullough's desire to achieve authenticity is her decision to include her
own charcoal drawings of the major figures in the books. In *The First
Man in Rome,* she explains her didactic intent: "I am so tired of people
thinking that Cleopatra looked like Elizabeth Taylor, Mark Antony like
Richard Burton, and so forth, that I decided to supply my readers with
genuine Republican Roman faces. Where possible, these are authenti-
cated likenesses; where no such identification has been made, I have chosen an anonymous Republican Roman head of the right age and type and
given it a historical name" (McCullough 1994.784). While McCullough
engaged in considerable research in her search for real republican Roman
faces for her illustrations, she is happy to alter Roman originals in order

to convey an authentic experience, so, for example, she "youthened" her portrait of Pompey, and used the same portrait as a model for both Aurelia, Julius Caesar's mother, and Julia, his daughter, in order to create an impression of family resemblance among her characters.

This technique of enforcing total immersion on her readers does not always endear her to her critics. Some love it, like this reviewer for the *Atlanta Journal and Constitution*, whose enthusiasm may be partially explained by her admission in her byline that she grew up in a household of Latin scholars: "Her combination of impeccable scholarship and lyrical prose make *The Grass Crown* a pleasant orgy indeed—extremely satisfying but leaving plenty of room for more" (Ann Hume Wilson 1991). Others, however, are less able to cope with the deluge of information. A largely complimentary review of *The First Man in Rome* in the *Sunday Times* admits ruefully that "as it is over eight hundred pages long with more than one hundred pages of notes, diagrams, maps and illustrations . . . one could be forgiven for mistaking it for a textbook" (Eskine 1990). One English newspaper tersely summarized *The First Man in Rome* as obese and flatulent, while a reviewer for the London *Times* said: "A classical education, as everyone knows, equips you for everything. Indeed, one nineteenth-century doctor argued that reciting Demosthenes was a splendid means for strengthening the chest. Readers of *The First Man in Rome*, however, will need more than rock-hard pectorals to grapple with *Thorn Birds* McCullough's new 800 page blockborer. While a small hoist could come in handy simply to negotiate the pages (the book is almost cubic), nothing less than a serious piece of prose-moving equipment is needed to get through the story . . . Unable to absorb information about the past into her creative imagination, McCullough resorts instead to dumping inert sackloads of it over the plot" (Jones 1990).

Mass Marketing Romans

Despite the sneers of her critics, McCullough's classical studies have borne fruit: each of the books in the series to date has risen immediately to the *New York Times* list of top ten best-selling novels. As bestsellers, they are generically required to boast eye-catching jackets, and it is instructive to compare the effect of the publishers' jackets, with their colorful pictures and blurbs, to McCullough's stated goal of historical authenticity.

The hardback edition of the first of the novels, *The First Man in Rome*, has a cover with a somber, unsensational tone. The dust jacket reproduces a painting of the *Ara Pacis*, or Altar of Peace; all the figures on it are men. The relief on the altar looks, in the painting, more fragmentary than it really is, as if the appearance of a ruin must lend some authenticity to the historical backdrop of the novel. This "ruinized" *Ara Pacis* is also an anachronism: the Altar of Peace was not yet constructed in the time of Marius and Sulla, the major protagonists of the first novel. (It was built some decades after the events that unfold in *The First Man in Rome* by Augustus Caesar.) Nevertheless, as a representative monument, it presides over the cover of the hardbound edition. The predominant colors are gray and black on a cream ground; the effect is static and monumental. The paper is also embossed so that the figures in the painting stand out slightly from the page, reproducing the effect of the relief on the original monument. The title appears in bold Roman capitals, while the author's name, in sober black, is prominent but slightly smaller than the title. It is likely that this understated image, with its representation of an authentic (if anachronistic) Roman monument, represented McCullough's own wishes for the cover design. An article from the *Orlando Sentinel Tribune* (6 January 1991) relates an incident involving cover of one of her earlier novels. The cover designer complained that McCullough was hard to please: "I had two different designers working on covers for *A Creed for the New Millennium*, so she would have a choice. One was stark and somber, the other was soft and feminine. Of course, she chose the wrong cover, the downbeat one, and there was no talking her out of it."

In rather striking contrast, the paperback cover of the second book in the series, *The Grass Crown*, presents a vision of Rome more likely to appeal to a mass-market audience.[13] McCullough's name is far larger than the title—*she* is now what is being sold—and is printed in a less classical, more "feminine" font. The color scheme is far more lurid, with a blond, bronzed Sulla, looking more like a California surfer than a Roman dictator, crowning himself in front of what appears to be a Mardi Gras parade, complete with a peculiar fellow wearing a bird mask and an Ann-Margret look-alike doing an exotic dance with a tambourine. The static, toga-clad *patres* of the first cover are reduced now to tiny, agitated men in white who swarm over the equestrian monument on the book's spine.

The mass-market paperback version of *Fortune's Favorites*, printed in 1994, continues this trend. On the front cover, any Roman content is almost entirely effaced, replaced by the iconography of a women's romance novel: a masculine sword balances an open rose blossom on its blade against a backdrop of shining gold. The trend towards feminizing McCullough's name continues as well; it now appears above the title in flowing purple italics. The title and the author's name are in the same-sized type. There is more to this cover than meets the eye immediately, however. Inside is a second cover: a fresco-style painting of a noble, blond, Roman dignitary wearing an oak crown and a voluptuous dark-haired woman clearly in the grip of powerful emotion. On the floor behind them lies a purple rose, presumably the one from the front cover. The implication is clearly that the novel is the chronicle of a love story, which is actually far from the case. In fact, it is difficult to figure out which two characters from the novel might be represented by the cover figures. A blurb helpfully offers a bit of background, trumpeting "a brilliant and beautiful boy whose ambition was unequaled, whose love was legend, and whose glory was Rome's. A boy they would one day call 'Caesar.'" McCullough, who has obviously done her research into Roman nomenclature and knows that Caesar is a family name and not a title, must have winced at this clumsy bit of publicity.

Like *The First Man in Rome*, the cover of the hardbound edition of *Caesar's Women* incorporates a modern rendition of ancient art, this time a pseudo-fresco done in panels, portraying Roman men and women (a man and a woman on the front, a man and a woman on the back, a girl on the spine). Again, the cover suggests a romance plot that the book does not in fact contain, and it is hard to identify the figures with any precision. The handsome man on the front cover must be Caesar, but the identity of the others is unclear, except for the young girl who appears on the spine, who presumably represents Caesar's daughter Julia. Like the cover of *The First Man in Rome*, this evokes an ancient work of art, but whereas *First Man*'s cover "antiqued" an authentic Roman artifact, the *Ara Pacis*, this painting is a complete fabrication, albeit done in a "Roman" style. *First Man*'s drab colors have given way to glowing Pompeian hues, and the tiny parade of Roman *patres* has been replaced by large, colorful individuals with a ratio of three women to two men. The hardcover edition of *Caesar's Women* is a tasteful blend of an urge to convey the classical respectability of the project and the need to appeal to mass-market readers with bright colors, prominently featured females, and the suggestion of romance.

Author, Author!

McCullough's Roman novels appeal to readers, perhaps especially women readers, because they market a fantasy, a chance to identify with characters caught up in dramatic historical events against a colorful backdrop. McCullough herself shares in her readers' identification with the series' characters, as we have seen ("when I was writing, I *was* a

Roman"). The reader gets the chance to respond in different ways to an array of characters in different situations: sympathetically, up to a point, and then censoriously to the frustrations of the impassioned Julilla, whose love earns her only her man's disgust; sadomasochistically to the desires of Servilia, a *dominatrix* who enjoys the mastery of Caesar; with equal parts of empathy and disgust to the entertainingly deviant Sulla. Of the female characters, it is certainly Aurelia with whom McCullough identifies the most. Her pragmatic business sense reflects that of her creator, who said in one interview: "I'm logical, pragmatic, sensible; I'm not a romantic, all things the Romans were, which is why I identify with the period so strongly" (Kidder 1990). The figure of Cleopatra has yet to be unveiled, but she promises to be an equally powerful object of identification, sharing Aurelia's brains and self-control, if not her good looks. McCullough has said she will not be the usual Nilotic beauty, but a serious player in world politics, with a nose and a chin that could double as a nutcracker (Shinkle 1996). But both of these women, although powerful characters in their own right, are ancillary to McCullough's ultimate hero, Julius Caesar, who combines brilliance, beauty, ruthlessness, and discipline with a true love of Rome. Readers can indulge either in the fantasy that they *are* Caesar, endowed with superhuman attributes and possessed of unlimited power, or in the fantasy that they might, like Servilia or Cleopatra, *have* Caesar, at least temporarily.

While Colleen McCullough identifies with the pragmatic Romans, her readers are meant to identify with her as well as with her characters. If the characters enable readers to live out vicarious fantasies of mastery, so, too, does their author's own life story, which has become a major part of the highly pragmatic marketing campaign for the series. Like Danielle Steel, McCullough has a large and devoted following, and her books sell because of the public's immediate recognition of her name. Despite the variety of subgenres McCullough has mastered (the family saga, the futuristic sci-fi novel, and the historical novel), there is a substratum that is recognizably "McCullough" in all of them. Indeed, she herself frequently refers to her novels generically, as she does in one interview where she regrets that she doesn't have a larger male audience for *The First Man in Rome*: "I've always thought that if men could be persuaded to read my books, they would like them. And they'd really like this one. This is one McCullough that they won't have to feel bashful about reading in public" (Pate 1990).

The conflation between the author and her product is not casual. A key feature of the many interviews and publicity stories published about her since the beginning of the series is her own life story, which, not co-incidentally, reads like the plot of a women's novel. Her family left New Zealand for New South Wales, where she grew up with a domineering father, a sugar cane cutter who despised her as ugly and lazy. Fat and un-attractive, but intelligent, she took refuge as a child in writing novels, though she had no intention of publishing them. She wanted to study medicine, but an allergy to soap together with a lack of money dissuaded her. She left Australia in 1963 and studied neurophysiology in London, then eventually moved to the United States where she became a research assistant to a professor in the Yale College of Medicine. Unwilling to submit to the drudgery of hard work for little money, she pondered her options and decided to try to change her life, realizing that she did not want to be one of a "group of women who were grossly underpaid for what they did. So I said to myself, 'Coll, ol' gal, you better try writing or you're going to be a very poor old spinster'" (Shinkle 1996).

Her first novel, *Tim*, about an older woman who has a love affair with a mentally retarded young man, was quite successful, but it was the family saga *The Thorn Birds* that catapulted her into the big leagues of best-selling novelists. The television mini-series made from *The Thorn Birds* was a major viewing event, and she made enough money from it to be able to do, quite literally, whatever she liked for the rest of her life. Delighted to leave her poorly paid research job at Yale, unenthusiastic about life in New Haven, and unnerved by all the attention her success was attracting in the United States, she retreated to the South Seas. Nor-folk Island, where she now lives, is only three miles wide by five miles long; it lies roughly one thousand miles from the coast of Australia and is populated largely by the descendants of Fletcher Christian and the Bounty mutineers.

Living in a tropical paradise with unlimited financial resources and no time constraints, McCullough decided that she was at last free to live out a youthful fantasy: she would devote herself to the study of classics. Earlier in her life, while she was pursuing a practical undergraduate de-gree in science at the University of Sydney, she had in fact begun to study classics as an elective, out of a concern that she "had never acquired much culture" (Mehren 1990). To the young McCullough, as to so many in the English-speaking world, classics had come to signify cultural re-spectability; its study was a form of self-improvement, a way to move up the ladder both intellectually and socially. She took it up again after mak-ing her fortune because, she said, she thought it would be an appropri-ate study for a single, middle-aged woman: "Life being serious when you are a spinster and expecting to remain a spinster" (Mehren 1990). It may be true as well that the attainment of the education she had been unable to afford in her youth represented for her the final escape from the harsh, emotionally unrewarding, and financially precarious existence she knew as a child.

The fantastic attainment of wealth, a South Sea island retreat, and the acquisition of one of the world's largest private libraries of classics reference material are only the backdrop to the culmination of McCullough's career, however. In interview after interview, she stresses the romantically satisfying tale of her unexpected late romance and marriage to Cedric Robinson, a man thirteen years her junior, whom she met while he was painting her house on Norfolk Island. Relishing the difference in their ages, she jokes, "I am Mrs. Robinson," referring to another notorious older woman, the character Anne Bancroft played in *The Graduate*. She describes her husband as "a real man with all that implies, including the chauvinism," a "princely looking man, a colonial aristocrat," and (presumably with respect to his innate wisdom) as "much older than I am, a patriarchal figure."[14] An ideal marriage indeed, between partners who have both achieved the status usually granted to dominant males: he has manliness (including the chauvinism), youth endowed with the wisdom of maturity, and the characteristics of a natural aristocrat; she has experience, worldwide fame, and vast wealth. Fully as ambitious and driven as the Great Men she admires and chronicles, occupying what seems to be a permanent position on the best-seller list, earning enough to support a life in Paradise, with all the resources of modern scholarship at her command, and a trophy husband at her side, McCullough has in her own way achieved the total mastery her heroes struggle to attain.

Black Cigars

McCullough's rags-to-riches story, with its compelling trajectory from exploited lab worker to best-selling novelist, has given her little sympathy for those at the bottom of the power pyramid, including her readership, which consists mainly of women. The world of Roman women as depicted in this series is unenviable. The misogyny that is so rampant in the *Masters of Rome* series may be part of McCullough's relentless quest for historical authenticity; certainly it would be hard to argue that it was not a significant feature of Roman culture. However, there are indications that it reflects her own worldview as well. Her frequent references in interviews to the sad condition of spinsterhood, her recognition of the class of exploited female employees, and her childhood experience as the unattractive and unappreciated daughter of a violent father would give her ample reason to internalize the notion that women are inherently weaker and powerless in comparison to men. This conservatism is certainly part of her mass-market appeal: her Rome exemplifies power and strength. She makes no attempt to use the decadence and corruption of late republican Rome as a way of critiquing modern society, as, for example, Naomi Mitchison used the fate of early Christians in Rome in *The Blood of the Martyrs*, or the failed Spartan revolution of Agis and Cleomenes in *The Corn King and the Spring Queen* as part of her socialist critique of Britain, or as Henry Sienkiewicz used the romantic fate of his Christian heroine and her Roman lover as a way to promote Christian values and Polish nationalism in *Quo Vadis?*[15] Nor does McCullough adopt the strategy of presenting a worm's eye view of the Roman world from the point of view of the poor and the downtrodden. Instead, she outspokenly identifies with the worldview of the Roman aristocratic male. "I'm loving writing about an exclusively male society," she said in one interview, "By temperament, I think I am a Roman" (Kidder 1990).

Much of the appeal of McCullough's books to women lies in her recognition of the desire of many women to identify with the successful male, a desire she openly shares. Indeed, she presents herself in interviews *as* a man. Called a Renaissance woman by one reporter, she replied, "but I'm not, I'm a Renaissance man. Renaissance woman sat around doing embroidery and trying to please her man" (Vincenzi 1990). In a telling remark in the same interview, she predicts what she will be like at age eighty: "I plan to terrify everyone to death, smoking black cigars and sitting with my legs apart wearing pink bloomers. It is not my intention to be a sweet old lady." In this pre-Lewinsky cigar fantasy, McCullough manages to have it all. She retains and highlights her female sexuality (the pink bloomers), while attaining the perks (black cigars) and adopting the posture (legs apart) of the male: a perfect androgyny that renders her, like some fantastic mythical composite, self-sufficient and terrifying to all.

McCullough's Rome reveals some of the tensions that characterize her attempt to balance the writing of serious historical fiction with her need to appeal to mass culture. Despite the author's fundamental conservatism, the novels reveal no narrative based on redemption, as was typical of earlier historical novels with a Roman setting, such as *Ben-Hur* or *Quo Vadis?* in which narratives of Christian resistance to imperial decadence offered readers a chance to identify with cherished social values such as freedom, innocence, and Christianity. Instead, McCullough's

Rome is a playground for the id, an arena where men (and the occasional woman) compete for power, and cruelty and death are part of the spectacular appeal. McCullough's claim to "seriousness" rests not on any improving moralism, but rather on her genuine respect for and enthusiastic study of classics, which still retains its ability to bestow cultural prestige even in this mass-market guise. As we can see from the marketing of the book, from McCullough's accounts of her own life story, and from the often strained mismatch between the apparatus of scholarship in the notes and text and the sensational events of the novels, a rhetoric of historical accuracy and diligent scholarship plays itself out against a powerful appeal to fantasies of wealth, total power, and self-indulgence. McCullough's idiosyncratic formula in this series, in which she combines the promise of blockbuster entertainment with the claim to complete historical accuracy, has allowed her, through her mastery of classics, to acquire the "black cigar" of money, status, and educational achievement— but she is not about to drop her mass-market pink bloomers.

Notes

This is a revised version of an essay that first appeared in D. Konstan, N. Felson, T. Falkner, eds., *Contextualizing Classics: Ideology, Performance, Dialogue* (Rowman & Littlefield 1999); I thank Rowman & Littlefield for giving me permission to reprint it and the editors of this volume, especially Sandra Joshel, for their improving comments.

1. The fifth novel in the series, *Caesar: Let the Dice Fly*, appeared too late for me to include it in my discussion, which is limited to the first four novels. McCullough is finding it hard to let the character of Caesar go: she has also written a related book, not part of the series: *Caesar: A Novel* (William Morrow & Co.).

2. Gerhart and Groer 1996. I thank Judith Hallett for drawing this story to my attention.

3. Perhaps Gingrich was moved to collaborate by McCullough's style, which brought the following image to the mind of one reviewer: "To sum it up in blurb-speak, *The Grass Crown* is in the grand tradition of the Congressional Record, masses of gassy morass with a nugget of interest here and there" (Jennings 1991).

4. The existence of—and Sulla's marriage to—the younger Julia (called Julilla) are McCullough's own invention, as she acknowledges in her glossary entry "Julilla" (McCullough 1990.824–25), where she discusses her reasons for creating the character.

5. Cleopatra is yet to come, but from interviews it seems that McCullough intends her, too, to be an immensely appealing figure (Shinkle 1996).

6. The translation is my own.

7. Caesar notes the line of fur at their first meeting: "Though she was irre-

proachably covered up as her class and status demanded, the back of her robe had sagged . . . and there, like a finely feathered track, a central growth of black fuzz traveled down from her head to disappear into the depths of her clothing . . ." He follows up six pages later: "His breath cooled her neck like a breeze on wet skin, and it was then she understood what he was doing. Licking that growth of superfluous hair that she hated so much, that her mother had despised and derided until the day she died. Licking it first on one side and then the other, always toward the ridge of her spine, working slowly down, down, down" (McCullough 1996.45).

8. Much has been written on this subject lately. For gender construction in satire, see Richlin 1984 and 1992a, Gold 1998, and Walters 1998. In general, Keuls 1985; Halperin, Winkler, and Zeitlin 1990; Konstan and Nussbaum 1990; Winkler 1990; Gleason 1995; Hallett and Skinner 1997; and Clarke 1998 offer an entry into the complicated area of ancient sexuality and gender construction.

9. As one testy British reviewer noted: "She thinks that a fellator irrumates and vice-versa, which does not give one much confidence in her 'scholarship' either" (Jones 1990).

10. See Persius 1.15–25, for a portrait of an effeminate poet seducing his audience, and 4.33–41, for a description of a young aristocratic male who depilates his groin.

11. Juvenal 2.93–101. Translated by Peter Green (Penguin Books, third edition, 1998).

12. Mehren 1990. My emphasis.

13. There is evidently a difference in marketing strategies for paperback versus hardcover sales. Of the four covers I discuss here, two (*The First Man in Rome* and *Caesar's Women*) are hardcover and two (*The Grass Crown* and *Fortune's Favorites*) are paperback. The paperback covers are more generic and less revealing of the series' Roman content: they rely more on the author's name and on sensational graphics to sell the book to impulse buyers. The more sober historical appeal of the hardcovers seems designed to reassure the reader that the $25.00 or so he or she will spend is actually an investment in a serious work.

14. Kidder 1990 ("real man with all that implies"); Donohue 1990 ("colonial aristocrat"); Vincenzi 1990 ("patriarchal figure").

15. Naomi Mitchison's many novels include *The Blood of the Martyrs*, in which the Christians persecuted in Rome are proto-socialists, and the extraordinary tale of a barbarian brother and sister swept into the corrupt and confusing world of Hellenistic power politics, *The Corn King and the Spring Queen* (also published in this country under the title *The Barbarian*). For a discussion of both the novel and the film versions of *Quo Vadis?* see Wyke 1994.

Shared Sexualities

Roman Soldiers, Derek Jarman's *Sebastiane*, and British Homosexuality

Maria Wyke

Roman soldiers forge a link between Hollywood's Roman histories and that of the British film *Sebastiane*, which was co-directed by
Derek Jarman and Paul Humfress and released to mixed critical response
in 1976.[1] Like the Marcus Superbus of Paramount's *Sign of the Cross*
(1932, Cecil B. DeMille, director) or the Marcus Vinicius of MGM's *Quo
Vadis* (1951, Mervyn LeRoy, director), the hero of this independent
production is a Roman soldier who rebels against the authority of a
Roman emperor in defense of persecuted Christians. Even within the
British film's Latin narrative, another Roman soldier refers back to the
golden age of his youth as a time when "Cecilli Mille" used to lay on excellent orgies and chariot races. Yet Jarman's film constitutes a subver-
sion of Hollywood's earlier representations of ancient Rome, a revision
of Hollywood's Cold War ancient histories, shaped to suit wholly other
purposes.

Sebastiane opens with a riotous party held by Diocletian on December 25, 303 C.E. to celebrate the birth of the sun and to honor Sebastian
as captain of the palace guard and the emperor's favorite. Sebastian, however, protests against the subsequent execution of Christians at the imperial party and is therefore banished to a remote outpost of the empire.
There he is treated with suspicion by almost all of his fellow soldiers for
his Christian mysticism and renunciation of the flesh and develops a
sadomasochistic relationship with his commanding officer that leads to
his torture and eventual death. Unlike the elaborate, widescreen blockbuster productions of a spectacular Rome by the Hollywood studios in
the 1950s and early '60s, this 1970s account of Roman soldiery was shot
in three and a half weeks, on 16mm, following a semi-improvisatory pro-

cedure by a professional crew but largely nonprofessional cast, on a measly budget of some thirty thousand pounds (Jarman 1984.140–67; cf. Rayns 1976.236). In terms of narrative, whereas the Hollywood epics of Neronian Rome culminate in individual conversion to Christianity and the spiritual triumph of religion over pagan decadence and tyranny, *Sebastiane* begins where those epics end—with a soldier whose conversion to Christianity leads only to his banishment and loss of place among the heady sexual pleasures available at the imperial court at Rome. Hollywood's soft-focus, heterosexual romances between star-crossed Roman soldiers and their Christian beloveds are replaced by a slow-motion sensual embrace between two members of the Roman military. Stylistically, Roman history is not domesticated, glamorized, commodified, and rendered somehow familiar. Instead, attention is focused on the elsewhere of Roman history: barren barracks life on the edges of empire. Dialogue is delivered not according to Hollywood's War-of-Independence paradigm of American and English accents, but in terms of a guttural, aggressive Latin translated into English subtitles. Painterly image substitutes for action. The cinematic convention of parades, races, battles, and games is replaced by a narrative listlessness in which ancient Roman life is rendered both dislocated and disturbing.

At least on their surface, most Hollywood epics of the 1950s dress present anxieties about the Cold War in the ancient costume of a momentous struggle between Christianity and godlessness, liberty and tyranny, heterosexual morality and polymorphous perversity. Pulled in both directions, the Roman soldier finally turns to his beloved and her God. History, spectators are reassured, must repeat itself. Another pagan empire will fall and victory (this time) will be granted to the American faithful (Wyke 1997b, esp. 22–23 and 142–44). Jarman's *Sebastiane*, however, celebrates pagan Rome for its exuberant expression of homoerotic desire and punishes early Christianity for the repression of that desire. Designed as an assault on British society and its cruel treatment of homosexuals and homosexual behaviors, this independent film projects ancient Rome not to reassure audiences of a shared religiosity, but to challenge them with a shared sexuality. Pondering what might be the benefits of exploring history, Jarman declared in one of his autobiographies: "An orgasm joins you to the past. Its timelessness becomes the brotherhood; the brethren are lovers; they extend the 'family.' I share that sexuality. It was then, is now, and will be in the future" (Jarman 1993.31). The purpose of this chapter, therefore, is to set Jarman's film apart from Hollywood's visions of imperial Rome, to explore its conception of a sexuality shared with antiquity, and to analyze the multiple ways in which it challenged (and continues to challenge) British attitudes to homosexuality. Although, in some contexts, *Sebastiane* might be considered a work of high culture, an art-house film made by a painter who inhabited the London counterculture of the early 1970s, the film's commercial distribution justifies an analysis of it in this present volume.

In a later autobiography, Jarman retrospectively established a specific historical context for and urgent purpose to the making of *Sebastiane:* the film was designed to open to young British men a door into another world, one away from their own in which to be a homosexual was frequently to be a social outcast and, until as recently as 1967, a criminal (Jarman 1993.29). On the opening pages of the same work, the director catalogued the hardships he had experienced as a homosexual who had been born in Britain in 1942 (Jarman 1993.4):

> For the first twenty-five years of my life I lived as a criminal, and the next twenty-five were spent as a second-class citizen, deprived of equality and human rights. No right to adopt children—and if I had children, I could be declared an unfit parent; illegal in the military; an age of consent of twenty-one; no right of inheritance; no right of access to a loved one; no right to public affection; no right to an unbiased education; no legal sanction of my relationships, and no right to marry. These restrictions subtly deprived me of my freedom. It seemed unthinkable it could be any other way, so we all accepted this.
>
> In ancient Rome, I could have married a boy; but in the way that ideals seem to become their shadows, love came only to be accepted within marriage. Since we could not be married, we could not fall in love. Since we could not fall in love, we were not loved.

Jarman here draws on a rich tradition begun in nineteenth-century Europe, whereby arguments for the acceptance of homosexuality were frequently troped in terms of ancient Greek and (less frequently) Roman analogies (Weeks 1977.51, Halperin 1990.3–4, Dyer 1993.25–29). While current academic studies of Roman sexualities agree that the degree of same-sex eroticism acceptable within Roman society often exceeded modern limits (until, perhaps, more recent times), they are substantially more circumspect in their depiction of the types of eroticism that were accepted (e.g., Craig Williams 1999, esp. 245–52 on marriage between men). Nonetheless, for a large part of the nineteenth and twentieth centuries, ancient Greece and Rome have operated as ideal worlds of sexual liberalism. *Sebastiane* accordingly opens with a riotous party at Diocletian's court. Lascivious dancers frantically "masturbate" huge phalluses as they circle around their chorus leader, who eventually collapses to the floor and, in extreme close-up, exhibits his relish at the ejaculations with which his face is now spattered.[2] The sexual liberalism that Jarman perceived in the culture of Graeco-Roman antiquity was for him a revelation and an inspiration to read between the lines of history, to hunt for forebears who might validate his existence as a homosexual in contemporary Britain, and to pose a question: "Was Western civilisation Queer?" (Jarman 1993.46).[3] *Sebastiane* was thus the first of Jarman's cinematic forays into the queering of history.

Jarman's *Sebastiane*, both at the time of its release in 1976 and in subsequent histories of lesbian and gay cinema, has generally been regarded as an innovative work that, unusual for a commercially released British film of the period, broke with the classical style of film narration to offer a sustained, homoerotic celebration of the male body. After the intricately choreographed, frantic, and orgasmic dance sequence which opens the film at the court of the emperor Diocletian, a series of relatively static set pieces puts on display the erotic beauty of the male nude. As soon as the film narrative shifts to the remote imperial outpost, day dawns over Sebastian who washes himself in the courtyard of the barracks, watched at a distance by his commander Severus. Repeatedly the commander's lustful gaze is counter-cut with slowed-down shots in extreme close-up of Sebastian's naked body, so that its fragmented parts move in a languorous and sensual slow motion in the eye of the film's internal—and, by extension, external—beholder (O'Pray 1996.87). The English subtitles, which, at this point, overlay Sebastian's glistening body on screen and translate his voiced-over Latin hymn to the god of the sun, detail nature's amorous response to the god's awakening and thus suggest an identification between the latter's stimulating beauty and that of the awakened Sebastian: "Hail, messenger of dawn. The young God has arisen . . . The reeds sigh when the young God rises. The waters sing when the young God rises. Mankind awakens from sleep. The scarlet cock struts when the young God rises." A central, extended sequence of the film depicts two of Sebastian's fellow soldiers, the lovers Antony and Adrian, stroking and kissing each other by the seashore. According to the approving description of this scene of "untrammelled eros" in Richard Dyer's discussion of lesbian and gay cinema, "slow-motion photography caresses their limbs and, in the pool, shows mesmerising streams of water drops glancing off and haloing their bodies" (1990.169).[4] Again, in a later sequence set in the bathhouse of the barracks, the camera in close-up moves smoothly over the naked bodies of the Roman soldiers as they wash and then scrape their oiled skin with strigils (O'Pray 1996.89).[5] And, in the final, culminating moments of the film, after Sebastian's comrades have tied his body to a stake, according to the contemptuous review of the British newspaper the *Evening News*, they proceed to "zing those arrows into him—in the same kind of slow, tender motion that is used to show the centurions sodomising each other" (5 November 1976).[6]

For Jarman, who began his career as a painter and set designer, the fundamental source and validation of this eroticized depiction of Saint Sebastian's martyrdom lay not in the historiographic traditions of the early Christian Church at Rome but in the regular appropriation and frequent deployment of the sacred subject by artists from the Renaissance to the present day: "As one stands in the catacomb in front of his tomb, one can dream of the artists who have rescued him from the darkness. To Bernini, whose sculpture is in the catacomb, he is a hero who gazes into the sunlight next to him. Georgetti [whose sculpture is in the basilica above Sebastian's crypt] has sculpted him as a youth captured in the ecstasy of death. But through all these and many other interpretations one thought is shared. The arrows are laid on Sebastian as lightly as a caress."[7]

The martyred body of Saint Sebastian is certainly shrouded in darkness where the historical record is concerned.[8] So meager is the ancient evidence concerning Sebastian—the saint, for example, possesses no "authentic" *Acts*—that it has led some scholars of the early Church to question whether he even existed. The initial, foundational hagiographic recital of Saint Sebastian's deeds and death is the anonymous *Passio S. Sebastiani* whose composition is attributed to the period 432–40 c.e.[9] According to it, Sebastian was a most Christian man of outstanding virtue who was so greatly regarded by Diocletian that he was elevated to the command of the first cohort. He was revered like a father by the soldiers and held in dearest affection by all, since he was a true venerator of God and, therefore, necessarily lovable. At Rome, Sebastian variously encourages, cures, and converts until he is denounced to the emperor. Faced with the soldier's claim that succor can only come from the one God of heaven, Diocletian orders him to be taken into a field and shot with arrows. Sebastian, however, does not die, but is taken into the care of a widow. Once healed, he seeks out Diocletian in order to bear witness against the persecutor of the Christians and is accordingly clubbed to death on the Palatine. The saint now appears to a matron in a dream and orders her to find his body and bury it in the Catacombs. A church is soon built there over his relics.

Except for brief references to the regard, affection, and love in which the Roman soldier was universally held, the legend of Saint Sebastian, as Jarman himself intimates, does not provide promising ground on which to build a homosexual martyrdom (cf. Kaye 1996.89). The *Passio* belongs rather to the theater of militant Christianity of the fifth to ninth centuries, when the text would have been read out regularly by clerics on the saint's feast day, since the martyrdom of a Roman soldier, in particular, demonstrated the victory of faith in Christ and his Church over a citizen-soldier's loyalty to his emperor. Sebastian became an immensely popular figure for devotion in the medieval cult of the saints as a result not only of the wide diffusion of his *Passio* but also from the power widely attributed to him of hindering the plague which then regularly decimated Europe. Seeing in the wounded body of the saint a symbol of their own sick bodies, sufferers assumed that Sebastian could combat the plague's "arrows" because he had, himself, been healed. Thus the iconographic type first developed to suit the saint's status as both militant soldier of Christ and thaumaturge has Sebastian appear as a pastor: elderly, bearded, and severe, dressed in a tunic under which can be glimpsed golden armor and grasping in his hand the crown of martyrdom.[10] From the thirteenth century, given Saint Sebastian's continuing function as intercessor against the plague, artists began to represent him most often at the very moment of his torment, bound and pierced by arrows. His body, having ultimately triumphed over the arrows' bite, was rendered beautifully intact: an index of Sebastian's incorruptible saintliness and, for the faithful, an invitation to patience and the hope of victory over their own suffering. So in Andrea Mantegna's *Saint Sebastian* (dated to the period 1481–88), the saint appears bound to the ruins of an imperial arch and a Corinthian column, his careworn features expressing the pain of sagittation which his heavily muscular, manly body endures. He displays the robustness appropriate to a Roman soldier, but one who is now learning the better fortitude of martyrdom. Sebastian's body here bears witness to the triumph of Christianity and the decline of brutal empire.[11]

Historians of Christian iconography, however, have observed that, from the fifteenth century, the Italian Renaissance more commonly rejected the depiction of Saint Sebastian in terms of a muscular and mature masculinity in favor of the alignments of an exquisite youth. The Roman soldier becomes a beardless adolescent of Apollonian beauty, a naked ephebe. The most frequently deployed explanation for this development grounds it in aesthetics: the representation of Saint Sebastian's martyrdom provides an opportunity to imitate and to challenge antiquity in the glorification of the beauty of the male nude.[12] Margaret Walters, among others, has added a further explanation: "The martyr is often no more than an excuse to paint a luscious classic nude; he also provides an outlet for usually suppressed homosexual fantasies. The arrows signify pleasure *and* punishment, the nude saint is a focus for growing delight in the flesh, *and* for guilt at being seduced by the grace of the body" (1979.82).[13] Appropriations of the classical male nude for the representation of martyrdom provided the painters of the Italian Renaissance with an opportunity to subvert the puritanism of traditional Christian iconography, for such nudes carried the charge of a culture in which the male body appeared to be freely admired as an object of beauty and of sexual desire (Walters 1979.99, Cooper 1994.2). In particular, the martyred body of Saint Sebastian provided a ready site on which to convey a classicizing male eros. As Derek Jarman himself observed, "The arrows which pierce the passive adolescent are as overt a symbol as any Freudian could wish for."[14]

Play with the signs of gender could further mark Sebastian's sagittation as the tacit delineation of a forbidden sexual act. *The Martyrdom of Saint Sebastian*, attributed to a collaboration between the brothers Antonio and Piero Pollaiuolo and dated to 1475, exhibits a carefully balanced composition. The viewer observes in the center a young and nude Sebastian tied high up on a tree trunk, below and around whom six archers are grouped in a contrapuntal arrangement of poses. Together the six executioners provide a complete record, in fine anatomical detail, of the strenuous actions an archer must perform. Against these tough and vigorous athletes, Sebastian performs a passive, feminine role. Young, gracefully nude, soft of flesh, and beautifully fragile, the martyr submits to his suffering with seeming resignation.[15] So gendered, the act of penetration is also sexualized. As Richard Dyer notes, sexuality (which has no equivalents to the biological markers of sex and race) is often conflated with gender roles in acts of representation in order to make the invisible visible (Dyer 1993.19–25, 42–44). In the iconography of the Italian Renaissance, therefore, the nude body of Sebastian is regularly configured as, in some sense, feminine: passive, submissive, and receptive to penetration by brute, masculine force.[16]

Furthermore, masculine penetrators do not need to be present in a painting for Sebastian's martyrdom to be rendered sexually suggestive and homoerotic. In many examples, such as the multiple versions produced by Pietro Perugino towards the end of the fifteenth century or that of Guido Reni at the beginning of the seventeenth, Sebastian appears as an isolated languorous ephebe. Nonchalantly posed, nude, fragile, and alone, bound to his post and delicately pierced by a few arrows, his uplifted face is transfixed by an ecstasy that speaks of loss of self, erotic abandon, the *desire* to be penetrated.[17] Here, and in the blatantly sensual seventeenth-century sculptures by Bernini and Georgetti which Jarman was able to see at the Catacomb of Saint Sebastian, the bodily metaphors of passion, which had earlier been deployed by mystics to express the soul's joyful ravishment by and ecstatic union with God, regain their literalism and materiality as Sebastian takes orgasmic delight in his suffering (Kraehling 1938.37, 41, Margaret Walters 1979.177–79, 183–87).

In his study of Sebastian's tradition as a homosexual icon, Richard A. Kaye suggests that the representation of Sebastian's self-absorbed detachment which had been developed in the Renaissance possessed a particular utility towards the end of the nineteenth century: "The crux of the saint's mythic power for writers and artists of the last century comprises an evolving dynamic of the self in isolation, in which a young, accomplished soldier announces a 'true' self and is therefore punished for his self-incriminating candour. Sebastian thus could stand for homosexual self-revelation as opposed to homosexual affection, and, as such, he was a splendid vehicle for a new conception of same-sex desire, which, as numerous historians of sexuality have suggested, encompassed a shift from a stress on homosexual *acts* to an emphasis on homosexual *identity*" (Kaye 1996.91). This new suggestiveness for Saint Sebastian partially accounts for the virulence with which the Catholic Church condemned a performance of *Le martyrdom de Saint Sébastien* staged in Paris in 1911. A "mystery" in five acts, it starred the famed Russian dancer Ida Rubinstein in the lead role crying "Encore! Encore!" during her execution by arrows (Forestier 1983.156–63, Kaye 1996.88). The apparent perversity of allotting the martyr's role to a woman, of rendering Sebastian a decadent, androgynous icon, may have been exacerbated by the current medicalization of homosexuality as a congenital abnormality, a distinctly feminine illness, which lead to a widely circulated definition of the homosexual as a female mind trapped in a male body.[18]

During the course of the twentieth century, Saint Sebastian came to represent the formation and self-formation of the modern male homosexual in quite explicit terms. Thus a *Saint Sebastian* of 1934 painted by Albert Courmes playfully transfers the martyr to the modern setting of a French harbor and converts him from soldier to "camp" sailor. Posed with his hands placed lightly behind his head, Sebastian's profile appears before a partially glimpsed full moon that stands in for a sanctifying halo. Dressed in a sailor's costume only from head to waist, he displays that part of his body which was conventionally hidden in Renaissance iconography. The arrows pierce his skin only from calf to waist and in directions which lead the viewer's eye directly upward to his genitals provocatively on display center frame (Kaye 1996.87, Dyer 1993, fig. 6.5).

The Japanese writer Yukio Mishima even configured his own erotic awakening and his very body in terms of the martyrdom of Saint Sebastian (Black 1991.200–01, 206–07, Kaye 1996.91, 93–94, 101). He gave an initiatory significance to his discovery as a boy of a reproduction of the painting by Guido Reni in one of his father's art books, claiming that it stimulated his first ejaculation. The martyr came to dominate Mishima's narrative of adolescent homosexual self-awakening. In his autobiographical *Confessions of a Mask*, published in Japan in 1949, the narrator describes his intense fascination with Saint Sebastian's apparently fatal eroticism and finds himself adopting the saint's gestures as they had been represented in Reni's painted version: "Ever since becoming obsessed with the picture of St. Sebastian, I had acquired the unconscious habit of crossing my hands over my head whenever I happened to be undressed. Mine was a frail body, without so much as a pale shadow of Sebastian's abundant beauty. But now once more I spontaneously fell into the pose. As I did so my eyes went to my armpits. And a mysterious sexual desire boiled up within me" (Kaye 1996.94). In gruesome anticipation of his own suicide by *seppuku* in 1970, Mishima posed four years earlier for a series of photographs taken by Kishin Shinoyama entitled "Death of a Man." One such scene was a recreation of Saint Sebastian's martyrdom, where Mishima is seen to copy closely the attire and gestures of Reni's depiction, down to the location of the three arrows which pierce the flesh.[19] Reading the iconography of the martyr's sagittation as an image of an intense erotic pleasure in excruciating death, Mishima drew on Saint Sebastian as an aesthetic embodiment of extreme sadomasochistic eroticism that required duplication completely.

This, then, is the aesthetic tradition to which Derek Jarman laid claim for his homoerotic celebration of Roman soldiery in *Sebastiane:* "Sebastian. Renaissance. Pretty boy smiles through the arrows on a thousand altar pieces—plague. Saint. Captain of Diocletian's guard. Converted, stoned, and thrown into the sewers. Rescued by a Holy Woman. Androgyne icon banned by the bishop of Paris. Danced by Ida Rubinstein. Impersonated by Mishima. In love with his martyrdom" (1984.142).[20] *Sebastiane* itself is a painterly film that contains numerous references to the martyr's homoerotic iconography. Jarman's cinematic style here has been well-documented: slow-motion techniques foreground the static, pictorial quality of the film's compositions; the frequently frontal orientation of those compositions slide into lingering *tableaux vivants;* the absence of significant character development and the employment of only brief amounts of dialogue delivered in Latin both draw the attention of spectators away from the film's narrative drive and toward its presentation of spectacle.[21] In particular, Sebastian's invocations of and identifications with the god of the sun—the beautiful and beloved Apollo—during the course of the film and the composition of his final martyrdom evoke the multiple Apollonian Sebastians of the Italian Renaissance (fig. 8.1). The arrangement of the six executioners around the martyr in the closing sequence of *Sebastiane* recalls that in the painting by the Pollaiuolo brothers. The actor who plays the Roman soldier, Leonardo Treviglio, is posed with both hands tied above his head and with one arrow in his armpit in imitation of the Reni Sebastian which so possessed Mishima, while the arrow piercing his neck and his uplifted expression of ecstatic agony are suggestive of works by Perugino (cf. Nash 1985.31, Dyer 1990.169). It is precisely through such evocations that Jarman's cinematic representation of Saint Sebastian as a homosexual martyr gains a feeling of credibility and much of its aesthetic effectiveness.

But, in the homoerotic sheen *Sebastiane* casts over ancient Rome, the film can also be positioned in close relation to another, pornographic, tradition. As Richard Dyer has observed, from the nineteenth century, classicism had regularly been utilized as a means of imaging homoerotic desire for men as well as of arguing for it to the world (1993.25). Shot on location in Sardinia, the pictorial images of glistening, nude or seminude Roman soldiers in *Sebastiane* recall the iconographic pattern of desire laid out in the photographs taken by Baron Wilhelm von Gloeden at the end of the nineteenth century. Distributed to an established clientele throughout Europe, they comprised scenes of nude Sicilian boys classically posed with vaguely classical props in the open air, before a rocky landscape, bathed in strong Mediterranean sunlight (Waugh 1996.72–102, Margaret Walters 1979.288). Von Gloeden included in his repertoire portraits of boy saints and martyrs, while, for a similar community of consumers, the American aesthete F. Holland Day photographed the potential eroticism of religious ecstasy in a series of photographs of Saint Sebastian (Waugh 1996.95–96).

Figure 8.1 The martyrdom of Sebastian, from Derek Jarman's *Sebastiane* (1976).

Closer in time to the production of Jarman's film, such classicizing forms of homoerotic desire entered into mainstream popular culture during the 1950s and '60s, when physique magazines and mail-order photographs circulated through a vast international network images of male nudes posed often as Greek athletes or Roman soldiers. The rhetoric of classicism, most evidently in this context, provided a rationalization for the pleasurable contemplation of the male nude in terms of both aesthetics and history (Waugh 1996.176–283, Wyke 1997a.59–63). Short films were also circulated widely throughout the gay community in the 1950s and early 1960s for private consumption in which the ancient world continued to be used to justify the pleasures of the homoerotic gaze. Even before Jarman's own revision of Hollywood's Roman histories, these physique films sometimes subverted the strategies of the extravagant Hollywood epics currently running in local cinemas. One such film entitled *The Captives* (c. 1959, Dick Fontaine, director) plays out a narrative in which two men are taken prisoner while on their way to Rome to pay tribute to an unspecified Caesar. Their Roman captor chains one prisoner to a pillar, removes some of the prisoner's clothing, and examines the hardness of his pectoral muscles. Impressed by the bravery of his captives, the official declares—in a humorous parody of the grandiose style of Hollywood epics—"You have won your people's freedom, go in peace." The spectator then witnesses the happy couple's departure, one still clad only in his posing strap (Waugh 1987.87–91 and 1996.267–68, Wyke 1997a.62).[22] More delightfully still, as a mischievous appropriation of Hollywood's epics for homoerotic purposes and as a signal of the homoerotic pleasures available even from Hollywood's ancient Rome, *Ben-Hurry* (c. 1960, Dick Fontaine, director) actually contains as its characters three bodybuilders taking a break from playing gladiators in a feature film that is imagined as currently being shot offscreen. After much horsing about against the backdrop of a self-evidently inauthentic Roman villa, the extras hear the call: "All girls and gladiators on set please!" Reluctantly they restore their discarded gladiatorial skirts and head off to play at being Romans, as one admonishes "Ben, hurry!" (Waugh 1987.87, 91, Wyke 1997a.62–63).

This pornographic tradition for rendering homoeroticism Roman was acknowledged by Derek Jarman (although only indirectly) when he noted, for example, that, at the time of the commercial release of *Sebastiane*, there was only one porn cinema in central London catering to a gay clientele—its name was The Spartacus (1993.83). Yet many of the film's British reviewers regarded it as fit only for just such a cinema. According to the *Sunday Times* for October 31, 1976, the film was "a piece of homosexual soft-porn detailing the gradual humiliation, torture, and eventual destruction of St. Sebastian—a kind of gay version of 'The Story of O,' or perhaps 'The Story of Oh! Oh! Oh!'"

Consequently, at the time of the release of *Sebastiane* in 1976, its celebration of the male body from a distinctly homoerotic perspective made the film a cause célèbre in Britain and elsewhere (O'Pray 1996.8). Responses varied wildly from expressions of discomfort or condemnation to unqualified praise. When first screened at the Locarno film festival in June 1976, it was barracked by the audience, whereas it gained record attendances when later premiered in London at the Gate, Notting Hill (Jarman 1984.156, 159). Many of the reviews in mainstream British newspapers were quick to reassure readers that the film could be of no interest to a heterosexual spectator: "It is, however, more geared to attract chaps who like chaps, lying and stretching and fainting in tormented, bronzed coils, than your family audience . . . The film positively encourages the restive hetero to resist it" (*New Statesman*, 29 October 1976). Yet it was the commercial release of *Sebastiane* and its correspondingly wide distribution that constituted one of the film's distinctions. As Jarman himself later recalled: "*Sebastian* [*sic*] didn't present homosexuality as a problem and this was what made it different from all the British films that had preceded it. It was also homoerotic. The film was historically important; no feature film had ventured here" (1993.83).[23]

Both Jarman and historians of cinema have read *Sebastiane* as a contribution made to the British politics of gay liberation—a movement stressing openness, defiance, pride, and identity—that had developed rapidly after the partial decriminalization of homosexual acts in 1967.[24] Part of the film's polemical value was seen to lie in its public revelry in what had, until the successful passage of Leo Abse's Sexual Offences Bill, been both private and illegal. And, for this, it was warmly embraced by the gay community, as a review of the period in *Gay News* suggests: "Very occasionally there appears a film of such power and authority that one emerges from the cinema feeling somewhat shaken and disoriented . . . *Sebastiane* is a very special, and indeed, a quite remarkable film that represents a milestone in the history of gay cinema" (O'Pray 1996.83; cf. Parkes 1996.143–44 and Lippard 1996.3); "A gorgeously evangelistic vision of homosexuality" (*Financial Times*, 29 October 1976). *Sebastiane*, in terms of its narrative structure, also constituted a critique of the British society in which homosexuality need assert its existence (O'Pray 1996.92). The filmic representation of the torment and martyrdom of Saint Sebastian comprised an indictment of both the long-standing oppression of male homosexuals in Britain and the fixity of notions of gender which had accompanied it. Designed for the public pleasure of the gay community, *Sebastiane* also offered a challenge to what Jarman customarily labeled the dominant culture of "Heterosoc."[25]

In his cinematic rereadings of history, Derek Jarman constantly used the past to color polemical examinations of contemporary British society (O'Pray 1996.7–8, Parkes 1996.141–43). In this respect, his exploration of imperial Rome in the time of Diocletian was no different. Exhibiting a gallery of faces familiar from the London "countercultural" scene of the 1960s and early 1970s—the painter Robert Medley as Diocletian, Lindsay Kemp and Troupe as court dancers, the punk figure Jordan as imperial guest—the opening of *Sebastiane* draws explicit attention to its presentist interests. Jarman later recalled the preparations and outcome of shooting the opening sequence as if it were a London party in classical dress: "During August we painted Andrew Logan's studio upstairs at the Wharf as Diocletian's palace, and we festooned the place with gold material. Christopher gilded a caryatid—everyone was invited for nine in the morning and asked to dress Roman . . . Lindsay Kemp and a gang of boys danced a lascivious dance with barber-pole cocks and ended it with a condensed milk orgasm. Modern London winked at ancient Rome" (1984.151). Throughout the film, humorous contemporary references abound, transposed into Latin dialogue, from self-reflexive comments on the earlier cinematic depictions of ancient Rome directed by Cecil B. DeMille and Federico Fellini, to the categorization of the moral campaigner Mary Whitehouse (in the Latin guise of Maria Domus Alba) as "the terror of civilisation" (Rayns 1976.236, Gardner 1996.55–56, O'Pray 1996.86). This latter reference discloses the film's central narrative concern with British assaults on the expression of homosexual desire, here epitomized by the right-wing, evangelical Festival of Light, which, in the era of gay liberation, had been set up by Mary Whitehouse to campaign against precisely such "permissiveness" as well as against pornography (Weeks 1977.205, O'Pray 1996.54).

Beyond the opening celebration of homosexual acts in *Sebastiane*, the film's subsequent and sustained motif of martyrdom has a long-standing history in Britain as a means of expressing the male homosexual's painful experience of institutional victimization. After his notorious trial and imprisonment, Oscar Wilde wrote during the 1890s: "I have no doubt we shall win, but the road is long, and red with monstrous martyrdoms" (Weeks 1977.115). In Jarman's film, the execution of Saint Sebastian is thus available to be read as an angry indictment of the repressive apparatus of Heterosoc's economy, his torture and death at the orders of his military commander a hyperbolic articulation of the violence with which the British state regularly treated those citizens deemed not to conform to its regimes of the sexual (Parkes 1996.138–40). Displacing the narrative of Sebastian's martyrdom to a lonely outpost of the Roman empire, the film establishes a self-contained, entirely male community where Sebastian embodies a challenge to the authority of the soldiers' world, expressed frequently in terms of a transgression of gender. The sexually voracious soldier Max acts as a brutal and hypocritical guardian of the community's heterosexual morals. His constant condemnation of homosexuality as a perverse decline into the feminine adheres to the traditional deployment in this century of gender, rather than sexual orientation, to define homosexual identity (Weeks 1977, Dyer 1993), while his obsessive concern to perform and to instate in others an aggressive masculinity at the same time as he involves himself in violent sexual horseplay suggests the fragility of that definition and the moral bankruptcy of its proponents. For Max, the commander's desire for his subordinate

Sebastian represents a potential breakdown of the community's order, and its source therefore requires violent elimination (Dyer 1990.168–69, O'Pray 1996.85–92).

Given the date of its release, however, *Sebastiane* reflects on homosexual experience in Britain both prior to and *after* the possibilities afforded by decriminalization and gay liberation, and thus it renders the Roman soldier's martyrdom ambivalently as simultaneously heroic *and* unnecessary.[26] Sebastian's desire for the earthly Apollonian commander Severus has been understandably stifled and displaced, as a result of his sadistic persecution and developing Christian mysticism, onto an idealized unworldly love object—his beloved God of the sun. As a homosexual under a state of siege, Sebastian is sympathetically portrayed despite the feminine religious passivity into which he retreats when confronted by masculine military aggression (O'Pray 1996.84–85).[27] The spectator is offered several opportunities, for example, to identify with Sebastian's bodily suffering. When he is staked out in the hot sun, the camera looks up into its glare as seen from the martyr's point of view and, in the last lingering shot of the whole film, a wide-angled lens is employed to distort the image into a curving horizon filled with six executioners who face *us*—a perspective never depicted in Sebastian's Renaissance iconography. Yet *Sebastiane* also characterizes the martyr's renunciation of the flesh as perverse precisely because it also celebrates the new possibilities available for homoerotic self-expression.

In the opening sequence of the film, the marginal is now central and the central marginal. Countercultural London and its sexual liberalism have become an imperial court from which Christian sexual sublimation can be banished. Within the community of Roman soldiers to which Sebastian is exiled, an entire taxonomy of male eros is elaborated that allows significant space to the lovers Antony and Adrian, whose sensual lovemaking in a central and extended sequence of the film was later described by Jarman himself as "ecstatic" (1993.84) (fig. 8.2). The Renaissance iconography of Sebastian's homoerotic, mystical self-absorption is here ousted by the mutual, fleshly embrace of a pair (whose names are perhaps designed to recall another famous Roman precedent for homosexual desire: the lovers Hadrian and Antinous).[28] The centrality of this sequence in *Sebastiane* would appear to argue that, in the post-liberation climate of mid-1970s Britain, there should be no further need for homosexual martyrs. Or, as Jarman put it more vigorously in a later reflection on his film: "Sebastian, the doolally Christian who refused a good fuck, gets the arrows he deserved. Can one feel sorry for this Latin closet

Figure 8.2 Antony and Adrian make love, from Derek Jarman's *Sebastiane* (1976).

case? Stigmata Seb who sports his wounds on a thousand altars like a debutante. All fags liked a good Sebastian. Mishima tried him on like leather chaps" (Jarman 1993.83).

In the years since 1976, moreover, several significant developments in the politics of British homosexuality have seemed to call for yet further revisions of the martyrdom of Saint Sebastian and Jarman's cinematic representation of it. In conclusion, I will concern myself briefly with two of them, namely the debates that have arisen since the late 1970s concerning the value of sadomasochistic practices and the renewed gay activism of the late 1980s and 1990s necessitated by the AIDS epidemic. In an analysis of how film critics have come to interpret the sadomasochistic representation of homosexuality in Jean Genet's *Un chant d'amour*, Richard Dyer has noted that, under the influence of the writings of Michel Foucault, it is no longer understood as an allegory for, or evidence of, the distasteful state oppression of gay men but as a discourse on the rituals of sexual pleasure. According to this account, through the dynamic play of domination and submission and the allocation of heavily marked gender roles to the penetrator and penetrated, sadomasochism can explore and interrogate the social relations of power that are the essence of sexuality and thus dismantle utopian visions of caring, romantic intimacies. Gay male sadomasochism can thus both reclaim conventional masculinity and, perhaps more important, empower and render appealing the passivity and self-renunciation traditionally marked as both feminine and demeaning (Dyer 1990.70–99).[29] Those critics, like Michael O'Pray, who, in turn, interpret the associations of sex and ritual violence in *Sebastiane* as a covert discourse on sadomasochism's pleasures have accordingly reread the depiction of Adrian and Antony's lovemaking as "stylised, idealised, and ultimately unworldly and unconsummated" (1996.89) and sensed in the film a certain admiration for Max as a character "who recognises lust for what it is and refuses to sublimate or idealise it" (1996.93), but have yet to redeem the martyrdom of Sebastian as a dramatization through pain of the potential erotic ecstasy of self-renunciation. And this despite Derek Jarman's own repeatedly published statement on the question of his attitude to masculinity: "Until I'd enjoyed being fucked I had not reached balanced manhood. When you overcome your fear, you understand that gender has its own prison. When I meet heterosexual men, I know they have experienced only half of love" (Jarman 1993.32).

In an essay on the contemporary image of Saint Sebastian, Richard A. Kaye details how the symbolic importance of the martyr has undergone a transformation and taken on greater intensity in the late 1980s and 1990s. In the time of AIDS, his legend as a thaumaturge able to ward off the "arrows" of plague has been revived as of consoling value, and his status as a Roman soldier who nonetheless resists the state has been appropriated as emblematic of the militant, politicized homosexual who must combat government neglect and social persecution (1996.86–87, 98, 101–02). Given that, from the early 1980s, Derek Jarman emerged center stage in Britain as a persistent defender of gay rights, as an HIV positive activist engaged in the politics of ACT UP, Queer Nation, and Outrage!, it is perhaps no surprise that in the title of his 1993 autobiography *At Your Own Risk: A Saint's Testament*, in his public account of his canonization by the Sisters of Perpetual Indulgence (when he was crowned with a halo woven of celluloid film), and in the obituaries published on his death from AIDS in February 1994, the metaphor of martyrdom was appropriated for the director himself.[30] But here martyrdom regained the significance it had had at the turn of the century when, for example, the sexologist Havelock Ellis talked of the perilous attempt to change public attitudes to homosexuality as "the pursuit of the martyr's crown" (Weeks 1977.65).[31]

Notes

This chapter is a revised version of "Playing Roman Soldiers: The Martyred Body, Derek Jarman's *Sebastiane*, and the Representation of Male Homosexuality," which appeared as Wyke 1998 (used with permission of Oxford University Press). I am very grateful to Jonathan Walters for the helpful and enthusiastic suggestions he made when I began my research on Saint Sebastian. I would also like to express my thanks to Dominic Montserrat and Helen Morales for their comments on an early draft. I was able to undertake the original research thanks to the generosity of the British School at Rome where I held a Balsdon Fellowship in 1997.

1. Although *Sebastiane* was co-directed by Paul Humfress and co-scripted by James Whaley, it has since taken up a place in the analysis of Jarman's *oeuvre* as his first feature film. For the purposes of this chapter, which analyzes the film in conjunction with Jarman's own writings and his public persona, I shall take the liberty of referring to it hereafter as Jarman's work.

2. My description of the sequence follows that of O'Pray 1996.86–87.

3. For Jarman's distinctive use of the term *queer* see Lippard 1996.9 n. 2. For a more general discussion of its usage see, for example, Horne and Lewis 1996.1–2.

4. Cf. O'Pray 1996.89 and Jarman's own comments (1993.83–84).

5. Cf. Jarman's account of the erotic charge attached to the Roman strigil by the actor Ken Hicks (1984.143).

6. On the erotic symbolism of this last scene see Kaye 1996.98.

7. In item 3 of the production documents on *Sebastiane* in the British Film Institute's Derek Jarman Collection. Cf. the similar press release put out by Jarman's production company Megalovision at the time of the film's initial screenings.

8. Saint Sebastian's historical record and early legend are conveniently catalogued in the *Bibliotheca Hagiographica Latina Antiquae et Mediae Aetatis* (ed. Socii Bollandiani, Brussels 1900–01) and presented in greater detail in *Acta Sanctorum Januarii* 2 (ed. Johannes Bollandus, Venice 1734), 257–96. See further Delehaye 1934.33–37, Forestier 1983.27–33, Ferrua 1990.33, Giubelli 1992.2–16. And for a summary of this material see Wyke 1998.247–50.

9. For the Latin text of the *Passio S. Sebastiani* see *Patrologia Latina*, ed. J. P. Migne, vol. xvii (1845), col. 1021–58. An approximate English summary can be found in Rev. S. Baring-Gould, *The Lives of the Saints*, January, vol. i.300–05 (Edinburgh 1914²).

10. On the veneration of Saint Sebastian and his early iconography see Kraehling 1938.10–16, Réau 1959.1191–94, Geary 1978.45–48, Forestier 1983 passim, Ferrua 1990.23–27, 34–38, Giubelli 1992.18–28.

11. On Mantegna's painting see Kraehling 1938.29 and pl. 12, Margaret Walters 1979.97–98, Lightbown 1986.134–36, 420–21, and catalogue no. 22.

12. Kraehling 1938.25–35, Réau 1959.1192–93, Ferrua 1990.34, Giubelli 1992.30–33. Cf. Margaret Walters 1979.78–79, 94, 96, Cooper 1994.1.

13. Cf. Dyer 1993.43–44, Cooper 1994.xvii, 1, Kaye 1996.88–89.

14. In item 2b of the production documents on *Sebastiane* in the British Film Institute's Derek Jarman Collection. Cf. Kaye 1996.88–89.

15. On the painting by the Pollaiuolo brothers see further Kraehling 1938.28–29 and pl. 15; Ettlinger 1978.49–50, 139–40, and pls. 83–89, Margaret Walters 1979.102, 113–14. Cf. Jarman's comments on this painting in item 2b of the production documents on *Sebastiane* in the British Film Institute's Derek Jarman Collection.

16. On the gendered iconography of male martyrs in the Italian Renaissance cf. also Margaret Walters 1979.10, Cooper 1994.6–9, Kaye 1996.88–89.

17. On representations of Sebastian's serenity or erotic ecstasy see Kraehling 1938.29 and pls. 17, 39, 40, Réau 1959.1194, Castellaneta and Camesasca 1969.6, Walters 1979.82, Kaye 1996.88–89.

18. See Kaye 1996.87, 89, for the relationship between Sebastian's modern representations and the medicalization of homosexuality. On the latter, more generally, see Weeks 1977, esp. 26–27.

19. Black 1991 helpfully juxtaposes a reproduction of Reni's painting with Mishima's enactment of it.

20. Cf. Jarman's detailing of Sebastian's artistic *Nachleben* in the various production documents for *Sebastiane* in the British Film Institute's Derek Jarman Collection.

21. See further, Nash 1985.31–32, Dyer 1990.168, Lippard and Johnson 1993.282, Biga 1996.23, Hawkes 1996.105, 108, O'Pray 1996.9–10, 67, 82.

22. I am very grateful to Richard Dyer for having shown me this and related physique films.

23. Cf., with only slight qualification of Jarman's claims, Dyer 1990.168, O'Pray 1996.11, 83.

24. For the development in Britain of the gay liberation movement after 1967 see Weeks 1977.185–237 and Jarman's own account which forms a constant thread through *At Your Own Risk*. Weeks's book was published only a year after the release of *Sebastiane*, suggesting that as the tenth anniversary of decriminalization approached, the achievements (and the future) of the gay liberation movement were undergoing significant scrutiny.

25. For Jarman's notion of Heterosoc see Quinn-Meyler 1996.

26. The film's ambivalent characterization of Sebastian was recognized by Jarman himself in a Megalovision press release and in some contemporary newspaper reviews, as well as in later critical accounts.

27. Cf. Parkes 1996.142–43 for a similar reading of the besieged homosexual in other films directed by Jarman, and Dyer 1993.84, 89, on the typology of "the sad young man" (popular in the 1940s to 1960s) as a means to express the melancholy of gay existence under oppression.

28. For this reading see esp. Dyer 1990.168–69. On Hadrian and Antinous see Boswell 1980.84–85 and Craig Williams 1999.60–61.

29. See further Bersani 1995.77–112, who expresses some reservations concerning Foucault's enthusiastic advocacy of sadomasochistic sex.

30. For Jarman's involvement in gay political activism in the 1980s and 1990s see Jarman 1993 passim, Parkes 1996.137–40, O'Pray 1996.7–15, 174–207. See also the substantial obituary by Colin MacCabe in the British newspaper the *Independent* on 21 February 1994.

31. On martyrdom as metaphor for Jarman's political activism cf. Gardner 1996.40–41.

9 Living like Romans in Las Vegas

The Roman World at Caesars Palace

Margaret Malamud
and Donald T. McGuire, Jr.

When Caesars Palace opened on August 5, 1966, it set a new standard of luxury for the Nevada casino-resort industry (fig. 9.1). The owner and chief designer, Jay Sarno, tired of Wild West themes, went for "a little true opulence" in the form of a recreation of the Roman empire in the age of the Caesars.[1] A Las Vegas newspaper trumpeted its opening with the headline: "Golden Age Returns: Roman Empire Reborn in Las Vegas"; and the three-day grand opening established a mood of excess and extravagant consumption (*Las Vegas Review*, 4 August 1966). Over a thousand guests were invited, including Nevada Governor Grant Sawyer and Jimmy Hoffa, whose International Brotherhood of Teamsters had lent ten million dollars toward the cost of building the Palace. Hoffa was the guest of honor at the opening floor show at the Circus Maximus Supper Club and, according to one employee, his presence added "a little Greco-Roman class to Vegas" (*New York Times*, 14 August 1966). At the grand opening, 50,000 glasses of imported champagne were poured, 2 tons of filet mignon and 300 pounds of Maryland crabmeat consumed, and the largest order of Ukrainian caviar ever delivered to a single party eaten. In the Caesars Forum Casino, guests gambled and were served free cocktails by employees dressed as gladiators and goddesses, they drank and danced at Cleopatra's Barge Nightclub (a floating cocktail lounge and disco in the shape of an Egyptian ship afloat in a miniature Mediterranean Sea), and they lounged in the landscaped "Garden of the Gods" with a marble pool in the shape of a Roman shield. Andy Williams opened the show at the Circus Maximus Supper Club, its booths in the shape of Roman chariots and its walls decorated with

Figure 9.1 Caesars Palace 1966.

Roman shields. Heralded by eight Roman soldiers, the curtains parted to reveal "Rome Swings," a stage full of swinging, gyrating Cleopatras.[2]

The spectacle of Caesars Palace rising from the desert sands of Las Vegas is enough to evoke wonder in the spectator. Why recreate the Roman world at all? Why on such a scale? And what images of the Roman empire are conjured up and fabricated in the built environment of Las Vegas? Most studies of the impact of the Roman world on American architecture focus on its influence on monumental and public architecture;[3] our interest, however, is in how Roman references and representations of the Roman empire take popular and commercial shape in the entertainment architecture of Las Vegas. While some architectural historians have discussed Caesars Palace in the context of American vernacular architecture, our focus is on how its interior design and architectural features invoke and manipulate images of imperial Rome in American culture.[4]

We argue that the architecture and design of the Caesars Palace complex play with and profit from a long-established tradition in American architecture of using monumental Roman architecture to signify grandeur and civic magnificence. In Las Vegas, Roman architectural references are deployed to signify the pleasures and benefits of imperial power and plenty, and they give a legitimating veneer of classical culture to the pleasures of conspicuous consumption. More important, Caesars capitalizes on the cultural force of the myth of a decadent and opulent Rome, a myth the Hollywood film industry helped disseminate into American popular culture. Owner Jay Sarno's vision of Rome was primarily inspired by the material splendor and excesses of the cinematic Rome of Hollywood spectacular films. The Rome at Caesars Palace is the Rome of Hollywood's late republic and empire—the Rome of powerful rulers, bread and circuses, and lavish and extravagant displays of wealth and consumption. In translating a cinematic Rome into a marble gambling palace in the deserts of Nevada, Sarno also drew on the design techniques and strategies of the glamorous movie theaters that once showcased Hollywood films. Sarno perfected what the movie "dream palaces" had offered patrons: an immersive, luxurious, simulated environment that encouraged fantasy and identification with the glamorous stars on the screen. Caesars Palace's guests are meant to feel that they have passed through to the other side of the movie screen to become stars in a Hollywood-inspired projection of ancient Roman opulence and decadence.

We begin with a tour of Caesars Palace, emphasizing the original 1966 casino-resort, and starting with a description of the various street entrances. We follow the most popular of those entrances into the 1992 Forum Shops, a Roman-themed shopping mall, and from there proceed into the Palace itself. In the second part of the chapter, we analyze how Roman references are utilized at the Palace and situate them within the context of the 1960s, the decade in which the original Caesars was built.

Tour of Caesars Palace

Any tour must begin with the original sign (fig. 9.2). Like all signs in Las Vegas, it is visually arresting, as Thomas Wolfe pointed out: "One can look at Las Vegas from a mile away on Route 91 and see no buildings, no trees, only signs. But such signs! They tower. They revolve, they oscillate, they soar in shapes before which the existing vocabulary of art history is helpless. I can only attempt to supply names— Boomerang Modern, Palette Curvilinear, Flash Gordon Ming-Alert Spiral, McDonald's Hamburger Parabola, Mint Casino Elliptical, Miami Beach Kidney" (Wolfe 1965.8). Similarly, after a road trip, Umberto Eco observed that, in the urban American west, "Eyes are something to focus, at a steady driving speed, on visual-mechanical wonders, signs, constructions that must impress the mind in the space of a few seconds" (Eco 1990.26). And in 1972, architect Robert Venturi and his colleagues noted in their essential work on the vernacular architecture of Las Vegas,

Figure 9.2 1966 Caesars Palace sign.

Learning from Las Vegas, that Las Vegas, like much of the west, catered to an automotive culture: architecture was experienced primarily from the vantage of an automobile passing along Las Vegas Boulevard; the buildings were generally low and nondescript, distinguished from each other only by signs that beckoned at curbside (Venturi et al. 1972.34–72).

The Young Electric Sign Company, *the* neon sign company of the day, designed Caesars Palace's sign as an Ionic temple, drawing on familiar elements of classical architectural vocabulary, but stretching the idiom to a new context, neon roadside signs, and grafting local components of popular culture onto the idiom. When Young's designers bought some toy Roman centurions at a local Woolworths to indicate scale in a mock-up of the planned sign, Sarno loved the look so much he insisted that life-size fiberglass centurions and alluringly clad Roman maidens stand by the finished construction (Hess 1993.86–87). Now the once striking sign on Las Vegas Boulevard no longer serves as the chief magnet to attract passersby. It has been dwarfed by the expansion of the Caesars Palace complex and by the tremendous increase in the number and size of the other casinos along the Strip. Although the original 1966 entrance that takes guests into the main lobby of the Palace is still usable, most visitors are now whisked into the complex on "people-movers," that is, moving sidewalks: one leads to hotel registration, one directly to the casinos, and the grandest (and newest) through the 1992 Forum Shops complex to the Palace.

The "people-movers" are noteworthy for two reasons. First, they are one-way conveyors, moving only inward, without any exit along the way, toward the ultimate objectives: the shops and casinos. Second, it is with the people-movers that we first see one of the strategies that underlies the planning of Caesars Palace, namely the multiplicity of emperors invoked, for it is clear during a visit that more than one emperor is conjured up by the design elements and decorations throughout the complex. Marking the start of the earliest people-mover (1972) is a *tholos*-type structure housing an equestrian statue (fig. 9.3). The statue is a copy of the equestrian statue from the Capitoline Hill in Rome of Marcus Aurelius, but the *tholos* clearly refers to a different Caesar: with its oculus and dome, it invokes the architectural vocabulary of Hadrian's Pantheon. Caesars collapses the historical specificity of individual Roman emperors into one mega-emperor; what matters is the category "emperor" rather than any particular ruler.

Similarly, a pastiche of allusions to the people, places, and events that make up the popular conception of Rome prepares guests to enter a luxurious Roman world in which they will be treated like emperors. On the second of the three people-movers, visitors first pass the "Prima Porta Augustus," a copy of the famous statue of Augustus found at the gate of his wife Livia's palace, and then move into The World of Caesar, a rotunda designed to resemble a Roman temple (fig. 9.4). The World of Caesar contains a miniature city of Rome "as it might have looked two thousand years ago" (Caesars Palace press kit). Inside the rotunda is a diorama of ancient Rome that includes holographic images of Julius Caesar and Cleopatra, the Colosseum, the Forum, and the Palatine Hill. Visitors can even experience the sights and sounds of a Roman bacchanalia that takes place inside one of the miniature buildings. Fiber optics, laser-powered sound, simulated holography, and other special effects combine, in the words of the press kit, to "recreate the feeling of guests approaching a celebration at a mighty emperor's palace." The scenarios portrayed at The World of Caesar, though popularly associated with imperial Rome, in fact, conflate different aspects and eras of Roman culture.

At the third entrance, the quadriga statue—four gold-leaf horses and a charioteer—beckons Caesars visitors to pass through a series of five

Figure 9.3 Marcus Aurelius.   **Figure 9.4** The World of Caesar.

consecutive triumphal arches of increasing scale into the Forum Shops and Olympic Casino, one of the casinos of Caesars Palace. Roman triumphal arches were signs of Roman conquest and were erected to honor generals who had won important battles. At Caesars, visitors pass beneath the arches as if they were conquering generals, and the Roman triumphal arch is deployed to celebrate modern consumer culture, now figured as conquests to be achieved through spending at Gucci and Dior and at the craps tables and slot machines (fig. 9.5).

Today the most frequently used route takes visitors through the Forum Shops, a set of shops designed to recreate downtown ancient Rome, into the Olympic Casino.[5] The progression is mediated, appropriately, by a giant, twenty-five-foot statue of the goddess Fortuna. Adjacent to the Olympic Casino is the original 1966 Caesars Forum Casino. Sarno believed oval shapes were conducive to relaxation, and Caesars Forum is a sunken, circular casino set below the lobby-registration area. An enormous chandelier in the shape of a Roman medallion, made of 100,000 handmade and hand-polished crystals, hangs overhead. Ringing the casino, which originally housed 30 gambling tables and 250 slot ma-

Figure 9.5 Triumphal arches leading into the Caesars Palace complex.

chines, are a series of 20 black Italian marble columns trimmed with white marble and gold leaf. Classical statuary and friezes on the walls depicting scenes from Roman history adorn the Casino: Roman military conquests and women as booty are frequently repeated motifs (fig. 9.6). Caesars Forum was the heart of the original Palace: radiating out from this center were the Circus Maximus Supper Club, where patrons could see Hollywood stars perform, the Bacchanal Restaurant, and Cleopatra's Barge nightclub.

At the casino, employees dressed as gladiators (fig. 9.7) and goddesses offer guests free drinks. In the 1960s, the goddesses were instructed to say "I am your slave" and to respond to drink orders with "Yes, master." The costumes of the cocktail waitresses are the same today as those designed by Jay Sarno in 1966 (fig. 9.8): white, off-the-shoulder mini-tunics and high-heeled Roman sandals. According to Sarno's wife, Joyce Sarno, he deserves credit for this innovation in Las Vegas casino-resort gimmicks: "Jay was the first one to put a cute costume on the cocktail waitresses" (Barrows 1994.10). There are also private facilities for high-stakes gambling: the Emperors Club, decorated with por-

Figure 9.6 Frieze of Roman rapine and conquest.

traits of the imperial Caesars, offers privileged guests a private space for gambling and other round-the-clock services.

Although gambling is the key attraction and focus of the Palace, it also offers food, lodging, and entertainment to its guests. Caesars, in addition, has facilities for private parties: guests can arrange their own banquets, including toga parties. In 1986, the annual Teamsters convention was held in Las Vegas, and the Eastern Conference of Teamsters hosted a lavish party at Caesars. The cost of the party was around $650,000, and several thousand Teamsters and their guests enjoyed an open bar and tables loaded with caviar, crab claws, roast beef, and fifteen different desserts. Jackie Presser, who had extensive ties to the Mafia and the FBI, was running for president of the Teamsters and staged a grand entrance. Four weight lifters, dressed as Roman centurions with red-plumed helmets, carried Presser into the party on a gold litter (Presser weighed over three hundred pounds). As he entered waving at the assembled Teamsters from his litter, an amplified voice boomed, "Hail, Caesar!" (Neff 1989.416).[6]

For non-Teamsters, the grandest dinner experience is provided in the Bacchanal Restaurant, one of the original components of the resort. The restaurant was designed to recreate the garden of a luxurious Roman villa in Pompeii. The beamed ceiling is blue so that the innermost portion of the room appears to be open to the sky, a huge grape arbor loops from beam to beam, and the walls are frescoed with bucolic scenes and views of the Mediterranean. In the center is a long pool with a statue of a naked Vestal Virgin pouring water, a striking contrast to real Roman

Figure 9.7 Gladiator.   **Figure 9.8** Cocktail waitress.

priestesses, who were required to remain sexually pure and were always covered from head to foot. Here guests are treated to an imperial banquet. Sarno, who knew that the Romans offered sacrifices, intended to start off the feast each night with one. In his original plans, he wanted to throw a live pig into the pool filled with piranhas, but he was dissuaded from this novel idea, and the nightly banquets now proceed along more traditional lines. Dinner guests are served a seven-course meal by waiters dressed as Roman centurions, and their wine glasses are kept full by scantily clad "wine goddesses." The banquet evokes a Roman orgy, something mandatory in cinematic representations of imperial Rome, and, in keeping with Hollywood's depictions of a Roman orgy, the wine goddesses, dressed like extras from a Cecil B. DeMille epic, massage male customers' backs. During the meal, some of the wine goddesses perform a Las Vegas version of a Middle Eastern belly dance along the edge of the pool; their costumes and dance conflate Hollywood's Rome with orientalist images of the Middle East.

Caesar and Cleopatra make an appearance every night at the Bacchanal and greet all of the guests (fig. 9.9). Their costumes fuse Holly-

Figure 9.9 Caesar and Cleopatra.

wood spectacular with Las Vegas showtime: Cleopatra, for example, wears an extravagant gold bead– and jewel-encrusted dress and an elaborate plumed headdress. Not surprisingly, there is a higher turnover for the role of Cleopatra than for Caesar. The current requirements for the job of Cleopatra include "exotic" looks and the ability to fit into the $10,000 costume.

The emperors Augustus and Nero are also popular at the Palace. Augustus's statue appears in several forms and locations, most notably in two copies of the "Prima Porta Augustus" (fig. 9.10). His sober and pious figure in the Olympic Lounge offers a contrast to the statue of Nero and his lyre with which it is paired (fig. 9.11). Nero's presence is felt at every turn. A popular steakhouse bears his name, and his notorious burning of Rome seems to be recalled in the Palace's stationery, the edges of which are treated to appear burned. Nero as the persecutor of Christians, an image popular in such Hollywood films as *Quo Vadis* (1951), is absent; instead, Caesars celebrates Nero as the embodiment of sensual pleasure and excess.[7] This is the Nero of popular legend: the emperor who lived a wild and decadent life, who thought of himself as an artist, and who played music while Rome burned and then rebuilt the city in marble splendor. The representations of the two emperors offer patrons two competing images of imperial Rome: the decadent but exciting Rome of Nero and the well-ordered and sober Rome of Augustus. Jay Sarno

Figure 9.10 The Prima Porta Augustus.   **Figure 9.11** Nero with lyre.

may well have identified himself with both emperors—with the indulgence and excess associated with Nero together with his sumptuous rebuilding of Rome, and with the achievements of Augustus, especially Augustus's imperial building projects. Augustus claimed to have found Rome a city of brick and left it a city of marble, and Sarno built a marble palace and casino empire in the sands of Las Vegas.

Luxurious hotel suites offer another place to view lavish reconfigurations of Rome and to measure the favor afforded different Romans. Each of the fourteen so-called Villa Suites is named after a notable Roman: Romulus and Remus, the founders of Rome; ten of the twelve emperors whose biographies were written by the second-century Roman author Suetonius; Marcus Aurelius, who ruled after Suetonius died; and Mark Antony, who was neither a founder nor an emperor. Here famous Roman figures are invoked to name places where guests experience what they can imagine are Roman luxuries. The art deco, Hollywood *moderne* decor creates a sumptuous atmosphere where guests can lounge on round beds under mirrored ceilings, sip wine at a private bar, or soak in sculpted "Mae West" bathtubs. The Villa Suites

Figure 9.12 Roman Fantasy Suite.

are set around the main pool area known as the Garden of the Gods.[8] This oasis in the Nevada desert is landscaped with flowering vines, trees, classical statuary, fountains, and a huge pool in the shape of a Roman shield. Water is the Olympian element in the deserts of Nevada, and huge displays of water are part of the spectacle of Caesars Palace; the casino-resort uses more than 240,000,000 gallons of water a year.

The Roman Fantasy Suites, the last site on our tour, vividly articulate Augustus's prime position among the Caesars. Destiny and power are associated with Augustus, the first emperor, and each suite specifically invokes him, as each suite's living room ceiling is equipped with a fiber-optic display, designed to "re-create the night sky as it is believed to have looked on the evening of the birth of Caesar Augustus" (Caesars Palace press kit) (fig. 9.12). These suites are located on top of the Olympian Tower and are accessible by the wonderfully didactic elevators that teach waiting passengers about the various "Olympians" who stay in the Fantasy Suites on the twenty-second floor. The brass doors of these elevators are engraved with representations of the Olympian gods and inscribed with their names and functions.

The ten Fantasy Suites are two-story, 4,500-square-foot apartments reserved exclusively for Caesars Palace's most important guests (in the words of the press kit: "celebrities, members of the royal families, casino customers, and the like"). Each suite cost one and a half million dollars to build, and close to that amount to renovate in 1989, and each is now filled with up-to-date electronics (nine TVs, a karaoke machine, elaborate sound systems, over ten thousand feet of cable per suite), commissioned artwork, and recreations of the components of classical architecture. It is clear that Caesars Palace spares no effort to keep its highest rollers in tune with both the harmony of the cosmos and destiny's mighty potential.

Caesars Palace and Sixties Popular Culture

Si non oscillas, noli tintinnare (If you don't swing, don't ring!)
—*Carved above the entrance to Hugh Hefner's Chicago Playboy Mansion (Wolfe 1968.4)*

A *New Yorker* columnist writing shortly after the opening of Caesars Palace noted that the imperial Roman world was invoked in a variety of ways in 1960s popular culture. Roman things, he commented, "are in vogue in many unexpected forms, from salads to motels, and in many unexpected places, from Rockefeller Center to Palo Alto . . . Surely the most preposterous example of this classical revival has just manifested itself in the most preposterous setting: a gambling casino-night club-restaurant-hotel called Caesars Palace" (*New Yorker*, 20 August 1966.25–26). Interest in classical Rome was strong enough for *Life* magazine to publish a seven-part series entitled *The Romans* in 1966, the same year Caesars opened. Burt Shevelove and Larry Gelbart's musical comedy, *A Funny Thing Happened on the Way to the Forum*, opened in 1962 and ran for years on Broadway. Romans were popular in outer space too. The *Star Trek* television series featured Roman-themed episodes, and Isaac Asimov's *Foundation* trilogy focused on a galactic empire that was consciously modeled on the decline and fall of the Roman empire. (In 1966, Asimov was awarded the Hugo Award by the World Science Fiction Convention for the best series ever published.)

Perhaps the best indication of the American fascination with imperial Rome in the 1960s is the spate of Hollywood movies set in ancient Rome: Stanley Kubrick's *Spartacus* (1960), Joseph Mankiewicz's *Cleopatra* (1963), Anthony Mann's *The Fall of the Roman Empire* (1964), and Richard Lester's cinematic adaptation of the Broadway comedy *A Funny Thing Happened on the Way to the Forum* (1966) (Futrell, Winkler, Margaret Malamud in this volume; Wyke 1997b, Solomon 1978, Elley 1984, Hirsch 1978). Each of these movies spoke to the era in different ways. *Spartacus* contemplated the many shapes of totalitarianism and the concerns and anxieties of the Cold War, while *The Fall of the Roman Empire* stood at least in part as a meditation on the assassination of President John F. Kennedy. *A Funny Thing Happened on the Way to the Forum* satirized 1960s America by conflating it with ancient Rome and, at the same time, parodied the heavily moralizing "sword-and-sandal" Hollywood epics of the 1950s. All of these films, however, focused on the opulence of ancient Rome and the decadence of the late republic and empire. In Mann's film, the Romans themselves, not the barbarians, are responsible for the fall of Rome: the Romans' failure to live up to their own ideals brought about their demise. At the end of the film, the voice-over warns: "A great civilization is not conquered until it has destroyed itself from within." Mann's assessment echoes the views of Roman historians and their successors on the fall of the Roman republic and the problems of empire, and the films and their audiences drew parallels between the excesses and ills of contemporary American society and those of ancient Rome.[9] What captured the popular imagination was the image of a civilization that destroyed itself through corruption, intrigue, and political and moral decline.

Although representations of Rome in Hollywood films and at Caesars Palace signify luxury, power, and, above all, extravagant consumption, the films present Roman corruption and decadence as ultimately destructive, while Caesars Palace celebrates them. At Caesars, visitors are encouraged to emulate the supposed lifestyles of decadent Romans. Absent from Caesars Palace is any hint of the uplifting moralism of earlier 1950s films like *Quo Vadis* (1951), *The Robe* (1953), *Demetrius and the Gladiators* (1954), and *Ben-Hur* (1959), where Romans are depicted as the "other," as the depraved, evil oppressors of early Christians and Jews. As contributors to this volume and others have shown, these films articulated tensions precipitated by post–World War II American expansionism abroad and domestic and economic restructuring at home (Wyke 1997b; Fitzgerald, Futrell, and Winkler in this volume). Sarno's Palace promotes instead the boom-time prosperity, the shifts in sexual attitudes, and the loosening of restraints on self-gratification and the pursuit of pleasure that characterized the 1960s, rather than the triumph of Judaeo-Christian values over Roman decadence popular in the 1950s cinematic representations of the Roman world.

The architecture and interior design of the Palace encouraged fantasy and promoted excess of all kinds. As founder Jay Sarno admitted, "Complete authenticity we don't have . . . my approach is to guess what the public will like" (*Los Angeles Herald-Examiner*, 24 July 1966). The design of the casino owes a debt to the architecture, interior decor, and marketing strategies of the glamorous theaters that showcased and promoted Hollywood films. The 1966 Palace built on the success of the movie "dream palaces" first popular in the 1920s and 1930s and in use through the mid-1960s. Like Sid Grauman, the owner of two of the earliest and most influential of these luxurious movie theaters (the Egyptian Theater and the even more famous Chinese Theater), Jay Sarno understood the power of showmanship and the desire of patrons for glamour (Beardsley 1983). The elaborately designed and decorated theaters offered patrons a lavish and exotic environment where they were pampered by costumed employees.

Jay Sarno, like Grauman and other theater managers and designers, was fond of spectacle, stunts, and gimmicks, and he and his successors used some of the same strategies the Hollywood studios used when promoting their spectacular epics set in the ancient world. At Caesars, as at the dream palaces, "the show started on the sidewalk," with Caesars' sign and its fiberglass Roman soldiers and maidens. Like the theaters with their elaborate canopied and carpeted entries, the Palace was set far back from the street: the long, spectacular entrance was lined with imported Italian cypress trees and led patrons past towering fountains and a huge reflecting pool. Copies of classical statuary stood in front of the fountains near the boulevard, including a copy of Giovanni Bologna's *Rape of the Sabine Women* in front of the original entrance. This reference to a Roman legend of rapine and conquest (which appears again in a frieze inside the Palace), located at the entrance to Caesars, invites fantasies of sexual and monetary conquests.

Caesars borrowed from Hollywood promotional techniques and at times coordinated its activities with the openings of films. At many theater premieres, employees were dressed in costumes appropriate to the film being shown. At the premiere of *Quo Vadis*, for example, ushers were dressed as Praetorian Guards and usherettes as Roman "hostesses" and, in one theater, as Vestal Virgins.[10] When *A Funny Thing Happened on the Way to the Forum* premiered in 1966, United Artists ran a chariot race from Caesars Palace to the Fine Arts Theater in Los Angeles; and when it premiered in Rome, a party was held at the Colosseum (*Hollywood Reporter*, 8 September 1966). When Caesars opened, Sarno hired a plane to fly in from "ancient" Rome employees dressed as Roman goddesses, gladiators, centurions, and Caesar and Cleopatra to greet and serve guests.[11]

Visits to movie palaces and attendance at gala premieres, like a visit to the Palace-casino, offered the public vicarious access to a sumptuous realm of desire.[12] As Hollywood director William DeMille, brother of Cecil B. DeMille, pointed out in the 1930s, the meaning of a premiere lay in the public's wish to identify with and celebrate "those who have helped them find their dream-selves" (DeMille 1939.89). Movie stars attended the grand premieres, and their attendance drew large crowds. The presence of real-life stars at the luxurious and fantastical theaters offered patrons glamour and a chance to "become part of the show."

Celebrities were showcased at the Palace, and the chance to glimpse real stars was part of the appeal of the casino-resort to the general public. Caesars attracted Hollywood stars like Elizabeth Taylor and Richard Burton as guests and entertainment stars like Dean Martin and Frank Sinatra (called "the noblest Roman of them all") as performers at the Circus Maximus Supper Club: the publicity office promoted their visits in advertising displays. Against a backdrop of Roman luxury, patrons were pampered and served as if they were stars. Surrounded by opulence, excess, and luxury, they were encouraged to identify with the powerful and hedonistic elites of the imperial Roman and Hollywood worlds, elites whose images were made glamorous and attainable at the Palace.

The conflation of Hollywood stars and the Roman imperial elite is strikingly illustrated in the publicity about and avid public interest in the production of the 1963 film *Cleopatra*. Many patrons of the original Caesars had seen or at least heard about Joseph Mankiewicz's *Cleopatra*. Mankiewicz's film set the love affair between Cleopatra and Julius Caesar and her passionate romance with Mark Antony against the backdrop of Roman splendor and power. The film was famous for its expenditures, repeated setbacks, and, most of all, for the love affair between its two stars, Elizabeth Taylor and Richard Burton. Newspapers and magazines covered in detail the filming of the movie, particularly the romance. There was a deliberate conflation by the media and the public of the historical romance between Antony and Cleopatra with the off-screen romance between Burton and Taylor. As Vivian Sobchack has noted, the epic repeated its narrative outside the film: the illicit "extratextual" romance of the stars mimicked the historical text they were performing. Moreover, the casting of such famous stars lent magnitude to the film (Sobchack 1990.35).[13] The publicists and producers of the film knew that the conflation of Cleopatra and Antony with Taylor and Burton was good business: "I think the Taylor-Burton association is quite constructive," said producer Darryl Zanuck; and the publicist, Nathan Weiss, said, "Everybody, but everybody, will go to see this picture to say that they can see on screen what's going on off it" (Hughes-Hallett 1990.292).

Representations of the Egyptian queen have varied from era to era (Hughes-Hallett 1990, Hamer 1993, Wyke 1997b.73–109). In the 1917 *Cleopatra*, for example, Theda Bara played her as a vamp and an exotic femme fatale, and advertisers used her to signify luxury and sexual power. In Cecil B. DeMille's *Cleopatra* (1934), Claudette Colbert makes Cleopatra witty, sophisticated, and someone who fully enjoys her sexuality. In the big-spending era of the 1960s, Taylor's Cleopatra signifies conspicuous consumption and sexual power: the film features a sumptuous and extravagant lifestyle at Cleopatra's court in Alexandria and in Rome, and both Caesar and Antony enjoy prodigious pleasures with the Egyptian queen. Publicity and press about the making of the movie and the lives of its stars mirrored the film's depiction of Roman opulence and excess (Hughes-Hallett 1990.287). Even before the shooting of *Cleopatra* started, the production was notorious for its high costs. Elizabeth Taylor's fee was a million dollars plus expenses; her pleated, gold lamé costume used 24-carat-gold thread; and the huge Roman Forum that was constructed in the Cinecittà studios in Rome was reported by the film's publicist to be "bigger than the original and about a hundred times as expensive" (Hughes-Hallett 1990.287).

The life Taylor and Burton led together during and after the movie was "publicly understood to be a perpetual debauch," and they were cast as "moderation's antithesis" (Hughes-Hallett 1990.288–91). Like Cleopatra, Taylor was reputed to lead an extravagant life. Newspapers and magazines reported that she lived in a villa in Rome faced in pink marble; every evening the cigarette holders, matchbooks, candles, flowers, and tablecloths were changed to match her dress. It was said that she brought three hundred dresses with her to Rome and threw each away after one wearing. Richard Burton bought her fabulous diamonds and a private plane about which he commented: "I bought it so we could fly to Nice for lunch" (Hughes-Hallett 1990.291).

Jay Sarno wanted every visitor to his Palace to feel like a Caesar or a Cleopatra. This, in fact, is the reason there is no apostrophe in Caesars. He believed the possessive would signify a place for only one Caesar, whereas he wanted every visitor to feel sovereign: "It's not a palace of one Caesar. It's a palace for all the Caesars, and a palace for all of the people. We wanted to create the feeling that *everybody* in the hotel was a Caesar" (Barrows 1994.12). Howard Hughes, owner of the Desert Inn, the Frontier, the Silver Slipper, and the Landmark offered this comment in 1966 about Las Vegas: "I like to think of Las Vegas in terms of a well-dressed man in a dinner jacket and a beautifully jeweled and furred female getting out of an expensive car. I think that is what the public expects here—to rub shoulders with VIPs and stars" (Hess 1993.88–89). At Caesars, guests not only rubbed shoulders with stars, they were encouraged to imagine that they *were* stars. In Las Vegas, the experience of living like the Romans was informed and mediated through an assimilation of Hollywood's representations of the lives of Roman elites with the lifestyles of the glamorous stars who played them.

In his analysis of Hollywood epics set in the ancient world, Michael Wood suggested that the lavish expenditures and displays of excess in these films are a metaphor for Hollywood itself, in particular, for Hollywood's capacity to duplicate and rival past splendors (1975.167–73).[14] Similarly, Caesars Palace demonstrates Las Vegas's and Jay Sarno's ability to conjure up and supersede the fabled magnificence and decadence of Hollywood's Roman empire in the deserts of Nevada. By 1966, Las Vegas entertainment entrepreneurs could claim victory over Hollywood in the arena of spectacle. Caesars Palace animated cinema's Roman empire and offered its patrons an immersive, simulated environment where they could act out Hollywood-inspired fantasies of Roman opulence and decadence.

Caesars neatly encompasses and capitalizes on a key tension in American society between the egalitarian ideals of democracy and the fact of economic difference. Jay Sarno's populist rhetoric ("everybody is a Caesar") speaks to one version of the American Dream: it offers each guest the chance to transcend economic constraints and class barriers; and the design, facilities, and amenities at the Palace not only promise but allow the fulfillment of desire, wealth, and power. At Caesars Palace, every person can be Caesar for a day, a peculiarly American conflation of democracy and aristocracy. Like the movie palaces, Caesars democratized luxury and the experiences associated with the lifestyles of rich and famous elites, real or fictional.[15]

Caesars also capitalizes on what the historian of American advertising T. Jackson Lears has called "fantasies of utopian abundance," by which he means the desire for freedom from the obligation to work, for effortless plenty, and for transformation through consumption.[16] All are made to seem accessible to the privileged guests of the casino-resort. The principal designer of the resort's Fantasy Suites, Aram Stepanian, said about them: "I wanted to design a suite that could trigger the imagination, transferring a guest through time and space. For a few hours, you feel that you have been chosen by the gods" (Caesars Palace press kit). Surrounded by the promotion and promise of opulence and luxury, visitors are encouraged to spend and lose their money; the obliteration of reality makes spending money pleasurable. In Las Vegas, the experience of Roman luxury and decadence is translated into a particular economy of spending, and participation in Roman conquest and the enjoyment of the pleasures of empire are experienced through the guests' own consumption and expenditures.

In the end, Caesars Palace is about America, and casinos like Caesars—and Las Vegas itself—are celebrations of consumption, excess, and showmanship. Casino developers, like Hollywood moguls and, indeed, like the ancient Romans themselves, are big builders whose colossal building projects express an imperial self. Like Hollywood spectaculars, much of the casino's appeal emanates from the excess and wastefulness of Hollywood and Vegas as well as from the land of plenty revealed in the architecture and its decoration.[17] The Roman Palace that Las Vegas has built and continues to renovate is a monument to itself: to the "magic" of the entertainment industry and American capitalistic enterprise, and to feats of production presumed to be possible nowhere else. Many visitors in the late 1960s might well have shared the sentiments of the *New Yorker* columnist who attended the spectacular opening of Caesars Palace in 1966: "We think of Nero in Hades, shaking his head in wonder and envy. Rome—*his* Rome, which he rebuilt with broad streets and splendid villas—was never a patch on Vegas" (20 August 1966.26).

Notes

This article grew out of a joint presentation, "Caesars Palace in Las Vegas: Rome in American Consumer Culture," given at the 1995 meeting of the International Society for the Classical Tradition at Boston University; an expanded version was given at the 1995 annual meeting of the American Philological Association in San Diego. We thank Jay C. Sarno for sharing memories and written materials about his father and Caesars Palace in the 1960s. Margaret Malamud thanks the staff at Caesars Palace, especially Margaret Kurtz and Lori Krogel, for arranging a private tour of the Palace, allowing her to photograph, and providing materials from the archives. She would also like to thank Toni (Antonya) Nelson for her enthusiastic participation in the first research trip to Caesars Palace and her insistence that we eat at the Bacchanal Restaurant, and Scott Bukatman for company and fun on subsequent research trips to Las Vegas. Finally, Scott Bukatman, Ken Hammond, Sandra Joshel, Martha Malamud, Deborah Steiner, and Maria Wyke all offered perceptive comments and suggestions.

1. Jay Sarno conceived the design for the Palace and Miami architect Melvin Grossman was the chief architect of the casino-resort.

2. Descriptions of the gala opening can be found in "Roman Splendor to Amaze Hotel Guests," *Las Vegas Sun*, 5 August 1966, and in Hevener 1991.20–21.

3. For a study of the impact of Rome on American writers, architects, and artists see Vance 1989; for a survey and discussion of Roman-influenced architecture in America see Galinsky 1992 and Chaitkin 1979.

4. See the influential work by Venturi, Scott Brown, and Izenour 1972. On changes in American strip architecture since the 1968 visit of Venturi, Scott Brown, and Izenour see Izenour and Dashiell 1990.46–51. See also Holden 1991.62–66, Rugoff 1995.3–9, and Hess 1993.

5. For an analysis of the Rome fabricated at the 1992 Forum Shops see Malamud 1998.

6. Thanks to David Myers for this reference.

7. For a survey of representations of Nero from antiquity to the present see Elsner and Masters 1994; for the image of Nero in film see Wyke 1997b.110–46.

8. The Garden of the Gods was reconstructed and enlarged in 1997. Its garden design and entertainments are said to have been inspired by the Baths of Caracalla in Rome.

9. The theme of moral decline as an explanation for the ills of Roman society is a common *topos* in the writings of a number of Roman historians, including Livy, Sallust, and Tacitus. And, as Martin Winkler has pointed out, the words also "echo [Edward] Gibbon's verdict that, with the establishment of the imperial system of government, 'the enemies of Rome were in her bosom; the tyrants and the soldiers' (Gibbon 1:216)," Winkler 1995.151.

10. The MGM press book for *Quo Vadis* contains a number of pictures and instructions for theater managers on how to stage openings. Margaret Malamud thanks Ned Comstock of the USC Film Library for gathering materials for her. For usherettes as Vestal Virgins see Babington and Evans 1993.9.

11. We thank Jay Sarno's son, Jay C. Sarno, for this anecdote about the opening stunt. He described his father as "a P. T. Barnum kind of guy."

12. For a recent study of the architectural history of the movie theater (with an extensive bibliography) see Valentine 1994. See also Nasaw 1993.221–40 and May 1980.151–63.

13. As Sobchack put it: "Consider how Taylor and Burton's illicit extratextual romance—and their magnitude as stars—mimicked the historical situation of the text in which they were imitating Cleopatra and Antony and extended the produced History of the past into the present moment of historical production" (1990.35).

14. Wood notes the pure excess expended in the production of the epics that he calls "a ritual expression of lack of need"—something he sees as part of the American way of life: "The planned prodigality, spectacular waste, waste as a way of life: glass skyscrapers and cars that give you seven miles to the gallon" (1975.180–81).

15. According to architect George Ramp, the movie palaces were "shrines

to democracy." Lloyd Lewis agreed, saying: "The royal favor of democracy it is: for in the 'de luxe' house every man is a king and every woman a queen" (Nasaw 1993.230, 239).

16. Lears charts a broad shift, beginning in the 1880s, from the values of production to the values of consumption in American society—a shift that accompanied a movement from an economy organized around production to one organized around consumption and leisure. Lears discusses the movement from an ethic of self-discipline and self-control and "relentless production" to one of self-gratification and personal pleasure, and he documents this change as it was displayed in changes in advertisements (Lears 1994.1–133, 1983.1–38).

17. Compare with: "What is happening here is something like the reverse of mimesis. This is not an imitation of life but a complete replacement of life by a life-size simulacrum: a full-scale model of the Exodus makes the real Exodus seem pale by comparison. The real Exodus, after all, was not conceived and executed by a single movie producer (unless we think of God in that role) solely as a form of mass entertainment" (Wood 1975.170).

Bibliography

Abraham, R. 1989. *Rosa Luxemburg: A Life for the International*. Oxford.

Allen, Robert C. 1985. *Speaking of Soap Opera*. Chapel Hill.

———, ed. 1992a. *Channels of Discourse, Reassembled*. Chapel Hill.

———. 1992b. "Introduction to the Second Edition, More Talk about TV," in Allen 1992a.1–30.

———. 1992c. "Audience-Oriented Criticism and Television," in Allen 1992a.101–37.

———, ed. 1995a. *To Be Continued: Soap Operas Around the World*. New York.

———. 1995b. "Introduction," in Allen 1995a.1–26.

Anderson, Benedict. 1991. *Imagined Communities*. London.

Anderson, Margaret. 1998. "'Stop Messing About!' The Gay Fool in the *Carry On* Films," *Journal of Popular Cinema* 1.37–47.

Anderson, Warren D. 1971². *Matthew Arnold and the Classical Tradition*. Ann Arbor.

Asimov, Isaac. 1977. "*I, Claudius*," *TV Guide*, 12 November. 32–33.

"A Touch of Murder," *Variety*, 29 September 1976.55.

Babington, Bruce, and Peter William Evans. 1993. *Biblical Epics: Sacred Narrative in the Hollywood Cinema*. Manchester.

Balsdon, J. P. V. D. 1979. *Romans and Aliens*. London.

Barrett, Wilson. 1895. *The Sign of the Cross*. London.

Barrows, Jay. 1994. "Jay Sarno . . . The Man Who Dreamed Las Vegas and Blazed the Trail for Others to Follow," *Las Vegas Style*, May. 10.

Barthes, Roland. 1972. *Mythologies*, trans. Jonathan Cape. New York.

Batley, Edward Malcolm. 1990. *Catalyst of Enlightenment: Gotthold Ephraim Lessing*. Bern.

Beard, Mary. 1993. "Casts and Cast-offs: The Origins of the Museum of Classical Archaeology," *Proceedings of the Cambridge Philological Society* 39.1–29.

——— and John Henderson. 1995. *Classics: A Very Short Introduction*. Cambridge.

Beardsley, Charles. 1983. *Hollywood's Master Showman: The Legendary Sid Grauman*. New York.

Berland, Jody. 1992. "Angels Dancing: Cultural Technologies and the Production of Space," in Lawrence Grossberg, Cary Nelson, and Paula A. Treichler, eds., *Cultural Studies*. New York. 38–55.

Bernal, Martin. 1987 and 1991. *Black Athena: The Afroasiatic Roots of Classical Civilization*. New Brunswick, N.J.

Bersani, Leo. 1995. *Homos*. Cambridge, Mass.

Bhabha, Homi. 1984. "Of Mimicry and Men: The Ambivalence of Colonial Discourse," *October* 28.125–33.

Biga, Tracy. 1996. "The Principle of Non-Narration in the Films of Derek Jarman," in Lippard 1996.12–30.

Bird, Robert Montgomery. 1919. "The Gladiator," in Foust 1919.297–440.

Biskind, Peter. 1983. *Seeing Is Believing: How Hollywood Taught Us to Stop Worrying and Love the Fifties*. New York.

Black, Joel. 1991. *The Aesthetics of Murder: A Study in Romantic Literature and Contemporary Culture*. Baltimore.

Bondanella, Peter. 1987. *The Eternal City: Roman Images in the Modern World*. Chapel Hill.

Bordwell, David, Janet Staiger, and Kristin Thompson. 1985. *The Classical Hollywood Cinema*. New York.

"Boston Worried about Boise and Cuts from *I, Claudius*," *New York Post*, 21 November 1977.50.

Boswell, John. 1980. *Christianity, Social Tolerance, and Homosexuality: Gay People in Western Europe from the Beginning of the Christian Era to the Fourteenth Century*. Chicago.

Bourdieu, Pierre. 1998. *On Television and Journalism*, trans. Pricilla Parkhurst Ferguson. London.

Bradley, Keith. 1987. *Slaves and Masters in the Roman Empire*. New York.

———. 1989. *Slavery and Rebellion in the Roman World, 140 B.C.–70 B.C.* Bloomington, Ind.

———. 1994. *Slavery and Society at Rome*. Cambridge.

Brantlinger, Patrick. 1983. *Bread and Circuses: Theories of Mass Culture as Social Decay*. Ithaca.

Breen, Myles, and Farrell Corcoran. 1982. "Myth in the Television Discourse," *Communication Monographs* 49.2.127–36.

Brennan, Timothy. 1987. "Masterpiece Theatre and the Uses of Tradition," in Donald Lazere, ed., *American Media and Mass Culture: Left Perspectives*. Berkeley. 373–83.

Briggs, Asa. 1995. *The History of Broadcasting in the United Kingdom, Volume V: Competition*. Oxford.

Brown, Les. 1977. "TV's *I, Claudius* Will Test the Boundaries of Public Broadcasting," *New York Times*, 6 November. 1, 35.

Brownlow, Kevin. 1968. *The Parade's Gone By . . .* New York (reprinted Berkeley 1976).

Brunsdon, Charlotte. 1981. "*Crossroads*: Notes on Soap Opera," *Screen* 22.4.32–37.

Bubuscio, Jack. 1977. "Camp and the Gay Sensibility," in Dyer 1977.40–58.

Bücher, Karl. 1874. *Der Aufstand der unfreien Arbeiter 143–129 v. Chr.* Frankfurt.

Buckingham, David. 1987. *Public Secrets: EastEnders and Its Audience.* London.

Bulwer-Lytton, E. G. 1834. *The Last Days of Pompeii.* London.

Callow, Simon. 1995. *Orson Welles: The Road to Xanadu.* New York.

Cameron, Ian, and Mark Shivas. 1969. "Interview with Richard Lester," *Movie* 16.16–27.

Canfora, Luciano. 1980. *Ideologie del classicismo.* Turin.

Capra, Frank. 1971. *The Name Above the Title: An Autobiography.* New York (reprinted New York 1981).

Carcopino, Jerome. 1940. *Daily Life in Ancient Rome.* New Haven.

Carter, Angela. 1978. *The Sadean Woman and the Ideology of Pornography.* New York.

Castellaneta, Carlo, and Ettore Camesasca. 1969. *L'opera completa del Perugino.* Milan.

Ceplair, Larry, and Steven Englund. 1979. *The Inquisition in Hollywood.* Garden City, N.Y.

Chaitkin, William. 1979. "Roman America," *Architectural Design* 49.8–9.8-15.

Clarke, Gerald. 1977. "Romans and Countrymen," *Time*, 14 November. 54.

Clarke, John R. 1998. *Looking at Lovemaking: Constructions of Sexuality in Roman Art 100 B.C.–A.D. 250.* Berkeley.

"Close Up" in *TV Guide*, 6 November 1977.A-41.

"Close Up" in *TV Guide*, 12 November 1977.A-27.

Cohan, Steven, and Ina Rae Hark, eds. 1993. *Screening the Male: Exploring Masculinities in Hollywood Cinema.* London.

Cohen, Sarah Blacher. 1983. *From Hester Street to Hollywood: The Jewish-American Stage and Screen.* Bloomington, Ind.

Colley, Linda. 1992. *Britons: Forging the Nation, 1707–1837.* New Haven.

Collins, Richard. 1988. "Wall-to-Wall *Dallas*: The U.S.-U.K. Trade in Television," in Cynthia Schneider and Brian Wallis, eds., *Global Television.* Cambridge. 79–93.

Cooper, Duncan. 1991a. "Dalton Trumbo vs. Stanley Kubrick," *Cineaste* 18.3.34–37.

———. 1991b. "Who Killed Spartacus?" *Cineaste* 18.3.18–27.

———. 1996. "Spartacus: Still Censored After All These Years," *The Kubrick Site* Online, 7 November 1997.

——— and G. Crowdus. 1991. "Resurrecting Spartacus: An Interview with Robert Harris," *Cineaste* 18.3.28–29.

Cooper, Emmanuel. 1994². *The Sexual Perspective: Homosexuality and Art in the Last 100 Years in the West.* London.

Core, Philip. 1984. *Camp: The Lie that Tells the Truth.* London.

Croft, Stephen. 1995. "Global *Neighbours*?" in Allen 1995a.98–121.

Cullmann, Oscar. 1962. *Peter: Disciple, Apostle, Martyr,* trans. Floyd V. Filson. Philadelphia.

Dahl, Curtis. 1963. *Robert Montgomery Bird*. New York.

Davis, Russell, ed. 1993. *The Kenneth Williams Diaries*. London.

Delehaye, Hippolyte. 1934. *Cinq leçons sur la méthode hagiographique* (Subsidia Hagiographica 21). Brussels.

DeMille, William. 1939. *Hollywood Saga*. New York.

Diderot, Denis J. 1779–1782. *Encyclopédie, ou, Dictionnaire raisonné des sciences, des arts et des métiers*. Lausanne. S.v. "Esclavage: droit naturel."

Dienst, Richard. 1994. *Still Life in Real Time: Theory After Television*. Durham.

Donohue, D. 1990. "McCullough's Road Leads to Rome," *USA Today*, 29 November.

Douglas, Kirk. 1988. *The Ragman's Son*. New York.

Douglas, Lloyd C. 1942. *The Robe*. Boston.

Dumont, Jean Christian. 1987. *Servus: Rome et l'esclavage sous la République*. Rome.

Dyer, Richard, ed. 1977. *Gays and Film*. London.

———. 1986a. *Stars*. London.

———. 1986b. *Heavenly Bodies*. New York.

———. 1990. *Now You See It: Studies on Lesbian and Gay Film*. London.

———. 1993. *The Matter of Images: Essays on Representations*. London.

Eco, Umberto. 1990. *Travels in Hyperreality*. New York.

Edwards, Catharine. 1996. *Writing Rome: Textual Approaches to the City*. Cambridge.

———, ed. 1999. *Roman Presences: Receptions of Rome in European Culture, 1789–1945*. Cambridge.

Elley, Derek. 1984. *The Epic Film: Myth and History*. London.

Ellis, John. 1982. *Visible Fictions: Cinema, Television, Video*. New York.

Elsner, Jas, and Jamie Masters, eds. 1994. *Reflections of Nero: Culture, History, and Representation*. Chapel Hill.

Enloe, Cynthia. 1990. *Bananas, Beaches, and Bases: Making Feminist Sense of International Politics*. Berkeley.

Eskine, Barbara. 1990. "Marriage Italian Style," *Sunday Times*, 4 November. London.

Ettlinger, Leopold D. 1978. *Antonio and Piero Pollaiuolo*. Oxford.

"Every Cough and Orgy," *Horizon*, September 1977.

Ewen, Stuart, and Elizabeth Ewen. 1982. *Channels of Desire*. New York.

Faludi, Susan. 1992. *Backlash: The Undeclared War Against American Women*. New York.

Fast, Howard. 1944. "History in Fiction," *New Masses*, 18 January. 7–9.

———. 1950. *Literature and Reality*. New York.

———. 1951. *Spartacus*. New York.

———. 1957. *The Naked God: The Writer and the Communist Party*. New York.

———. 1990. *Being Red: A Memoir*. Boston.

Ferrua, Antonio. 1990. *La basilica e la catacomba di S. Sebastiano*. Vatican City.

Feuer, Jane. 1983. "The Concept of Live Television: Ontology as Ideology," in
   E. Ann Kaplan, ed., *Regarding Television—Critical Approaches: An Anthology.*
   Frederick, Md. 12–22.
———. 1986. "Narrative Form in American Network Television," in Colin
   MacCabe, ed., *High Theory/Low Culture: Analyzing Popular Television and
   Film.* New York. 101–14.
Finley, Moses I. 1980. *Ancient Slavery and Modern Ideology.* New York.
Flitterman-Lewis, Sandy. 1992. "Psychoanalysis, Film, and Television," in
   Allen 1992a.203–46.
Ford, Dan. 1979. *Pappy: The Life of John Ford.* Englewood Cliffs, N.J.
Forestier, Sylvie. 1983. *Saint Sébastien: Rituels et figures.* Paris.
Foust, Clement Edgar. 1919. *The Life and Dramatic Works of Robert Montgomery
   Bird.* New York.
Freeman, E. 1988. "From Raynal's 'New Spartacus' to Lamartine's *Toussaint
   L'Ouverture*: A Myth of the Black Soul in Rebellion," in E. Freeman and
   William D. Howarth, eds., *Myth and Its Making in the French Theatre.*
   Cambridge. 136–57.
Frommer, Myrna Katz, and Harvey Frommer. 1991. *It Happened in the Catskills:
   An Oral History in the Words of Busboys, Bellhops, Guests, Proprietors, Comedi-
   ans, Agents, and Others Who Lived It.* San Diego.
Fuller, Robert C. 1995. *Naming the Antichrist: The History of an American Obses-
   sion.* New York.
Futrell, Alison. 1997. *Blood in the Arena: The Spectacle of Roman Power.* Austin.
Gabler, Neal. 1988. *An Empire of Their Own: How the Jews Invented Hollywood.*
   New York.
Galinsky, Karl. 1992. *Classical and Modern Interactions: Postmodern Architecture,
   Multiculturalism, Decline, and Other Issues.* Austin.
Gans, Herbert J. 1979. *Deciding What's News.* New York.
Gardella, Kay. 1977. "Roman Holiday," *Daily News*, 6 November. 11, 17.
Gardner, David. 1996. "Perverse Law: Jarman as Gay Criminal Hero," in Lip-
   pard 1996.31–64.
Geary, Patrick J. 1978. *Furta Sacra: Thefts of Relics in the Central Middle Ages.*
   Princeton.
Geist, Kenneth. 1978. *Pictures Will Talk: The Life and Films of Joseph L.
   Mankiewicz.* New York (reprinted, with corrections, New York n.d.).
Gelbart, Larry. 1996. "The Funny Thing Was How Old Humor Is," *New York
   Times*, 7 April. 4, 6.
———. 1998. *Laughing Matters: On Writing M*A*S*H, Tootsie, Oh God!, and a
   Few Other Funny Things.* New York.
——— and Burt Shevelove. 1985. *A Funny Thing Happened on the Way to the
   Forum and The Frogs.* New York.
Gell, William. 1824. *Pompeiana: The Topography, Edifices, and Ornaments of Pom-
   peii.* London.

Geraghty, Christine. 1991. *Women and Soap Opera: A Study in Prime Time Soaps.* Cambridge.

Gerhart, Ann, and Anne Groer. 1996. "The Reliable Source: Two Birds of a Feather," *Washington Post,* 18 January.

Gibbon, Edward. 1993. *The History of the Decline and Fall of the Roman Empire,* 6 vols. New York (first published 1776–88).

Giubelli, Lucia. 1992. *Sebastian: Roman Martyr.* Milan.

Gleason, Maude. 1995. *Making Men: Sophists and Self-Presentation in Ancient Rome.* Princeton.

Gold, Barbara. 1998. "'The House I Live in Is Not My Own': Women's Bodies in Juvenal's *Satires,*" *Arethusa* 31.369–86.

Goscinny, Rene, and Albert Uderzo. 1965. *Asterix et Cleopatra.* Paris.

Grant, B. K., ed. 1995. *Film Genre Reader II.* Austin.

Graves, Robert. 1989a [1929]. *Good-bye to All That.* New York.

———. 1989b [1934]. *I, Claudius.* New York.

———. 1989c [1935]. *Claudius the God.* New York.

Green, Peter, trans. 1998. *Juvenal: The Sixteen Satires.* New York.

Grillparzer, Franz. 1892. *Grillparzers Samtliche Werke,* ed. August Sauer, vol. 11: *Spartakus.* Stuttgart.

Gwyn, William B. 1991. "Cruel Nero: The Concept of the Tyrant and the Image of Nero in Western Political Thought," *History of Political Thought* 12.421–55.

Hagedorn, Roger. 1995. "Doubtless to Be Continued: A Brief History of Serial Narrative," in Allen 1995a.27–48.

Halberstam, David. 1993. *The Fifties.* New York.

Hall, Peter. 1993. *Making an Exhibition of Myself.* London.

Hall, Stuart, and Lawrence Grossberg, eds. 1996. "On Postmodernism and Articulation: An Interview with Stuart Hall," in David Morley and Kuan-Hsing Chen, eds., *Stuart Hall: Critical Dialogues in Cultural Studies.* New York. 131–50.

Hallett, Judith P., and Marilyn B. Skinner, eds. 1997. *Roman Sexualities.* Princeton.

Halliwell, Leslie. 1995[11]. *Halliwell's Filmgoer's and Video Viewer's Companion,* ed. John Walker. New York.

Halperin, David M. 1990. *One Hundred Years of Homosexuality and Other Essays on Greek Love.* New York.

———, John J. Winkler, and Froma I. Zeitlin, eds. 1990. *Before Sexuality: The Construction of Erotic Experience in the Ancient Greek World.* Princeton.

Hamer, Mary. 1993. *Signs of Cleopatra: Histories, Politics, Representation.* London.

Hark, Ina Rae. 1993. "Animals or Romans: Looking at Masculinity in *Spartacus,*" in Cohan and Hark 1993.151–72.

Harper, Sue. 1994. *Picturing the Past: The Rise and Fall of the British Costume Film.* London.

Harris, Robert. 1959. "A Young Dramatist's Diary: The Secret Records of R. M. Bird," *Library Chronicle* 25.8–24.

Hawkes, David. 1996. "'The Shadow of This Time': The Renaissance Cinema of Derek Jarman," in Lippard 1996.103–16.

Heath, Melville. 1952. Review of *Spartacus* by Howard Fast, *New York Times*, 3 February. 22.

Heath, Stephen, and Gillian Skirrow. 1977. "Television: A World in Action," *Screen* 18.7–59.

Herman, Jan. 1995. *A Talent for Trouble: The Life of Hollywood's Most Acclaimed Director, William Wyler*. New York.

Hess, Alan. 1993. *Viva Las Vegas: After Hours Architecture*. San Francisco.

Hevener, Phil. 1991. "Caesars Turns Twenty-Five," *Nevada*, September/October. 20–21.

Hibbin, Sally, and Nina Hibbin. 1988. *What a Carry On: The Official Story of the Carry On Film Series*. London.

Higham, Charles. 1973. *Cecil B. DeMille*. New York (reprinted New York n.d.).

———. 1993. *Merchant of Dreams: Louis B. Mayer, M.G.M., and the Secret Hollywood*. New York.

Hill, William. 1992. *Titter Ye Not: The Life of Frankie Howerd*. London.

Hirsch, Foster. 1978. *The Hollywood Epic*. South Brunswick.

Hitchens, Christopher. 1990. *Blood, Class, and Nostalgia: Anglo-American Ironies*. New York.

Hodgson, Godfrey. 1978. *American in Our Time*. New York.

Holden, Anthony. 1991. "Where Kitsch Is King," *World Magazine* 54.62–66.

Hopkins, Keith. 1978. *Conquerors and Slaves*. Cambridge.

Horne, Peter, and Reina Lewis, eds. 1996. *Outlooks: Lesbian and Gay Sexualities and Visual Cultures*. London.

Howerd, Frankie. 1976. *On the Way I Lost It*. London.

Hughes-Hallett, Lucy. 1990. *Cleopatra: Histories, Dreams, and Distortions*. New York.

Hunt, Leon. 1993. "What Are Boys Made of? Spartacus, El Cid, and the Male Epic," in Pat Kirkham and Janet Thumin, eds., *You Tarzan: Masculinity, Movies, and Men*. New York. 65–83.

Huston, John. 1980. *An Open Book*. New York.

Hynes, Samuel. 1982. *The Auden Generation*. Princeton.

Izenour, Steven, and David Dashiell III. 1990. "Relearning from Las Vegas," *Architecture* 79.46–51.

Jarman, Derek. 1984. *Dancing Ledge*. London.

———. 1993². *At Your Own Risk: A Saint's Testament*, ed. Michael Christie. London.

Jenkins, Henry. 1992. *What Made Pistachio Nuts? Early Sound Comedy and the Vaudeville Aesthetic*. New York.

Jennings, Gary. 1991. "Roman Scandals," *New York Times*, 6 October.

Jivani, Alkarium. 1997. *It's Not Unusual: A History of Lesbian and Gay Britain in the Twentieth Century*. London.

Johnson, Geoffrey. 1993. "In Medias Res: Colleen McCullough's Latest Take on Rome," *Chicago Tribune*, 31 October.

Jones, Peter. 1990. "Titter Not, O Aves Spinae," *Times*, 1 November.

Joshel, Sandra. 1997. "Female Desire and the Discourse of Empire: Tacitus's Messalina," in Hallett and Skinner 1997.221–54.

Joyrich, Lynne. 1991–92. "Going Through the E/Motions: Gender, Postmodernism, and Affect in Television Studies," *Discourse* 14.1.

Karlin, Fred. 1994. *Listening to Movies: The Film Lover's Guide to Film Music*. New York.

Kaye, Richard A. 1996. "Losing His Religion: Saint Sebastian as Contemporary Gay Martyr," in Horne and Lewis 1996.86–105.

Kelly, Katie. 1977. "Two Mini-Series: One Good and the Other a Loser," *New York Post*, 4 November. 78.

Kennedy, Duncan. 1999. "A Sense of Place: Rome, History, and Empire Revisited," in Edwards 1999.19–34.

Kersnowski, Frank, ed. 1989. *Conversations with Robert Graves*. Jackson.

Keuls, Eva. 1985. *The Reign of the Phallus: Sexual Politics in Ancient Athens*. New York.

Kidder, Gayle. 1990. "Roman Epic Not Written in a Day," *San Diego Union-Tribune*, 10 October.

Kitman, Marvin. 1991. "*I, Claudius*: Pure Decadent Pleasure," *TV Guide*, 15 June. 16.

Klingaman, William K. 1996. *Encyclopedia of the McCarthy Era*. New York.

Konstan, David, and Martha Nussbaum, eds. 1990. *Sexuality in Greek and Roman Society* (= *Differences* 2.1).

Koppes, Clayton R., and Gregory D. Black. 1987. *Hollywood Goes to War: How Politics, Profits, and Propaganda Shaped World War II Movies*. New York (reprinted Berkeley 1990).

Kostof, Spiro. 1973. *The Third Rome 1870–1950: Traffic and Glory*. Berkeley.

Kozloff, Sarah. 1992. "Narrative Theory and Television," in Allen 1992a.67–100.

Kraehling, Victor. 1938. *Saint Sébastien dans l'art*. Paris.

Kreidl, John Francis. 1977. *Nicholas Ray*. Boston.

Kreutzner, Gabriele, and Ellen Seiter. 1995. "Not All 'Soaps' Are Created Equal: Toward a Cross-Cultural Criticism of Television Serials," in Allen 1995a.234–55.

Krupnick, Jerry. 1991. "Gore and Glory of Ancient Rome Revisited," *Sunday Star Ledger: TV Time*, 9 June. 1, 8.

Leaming, Barbara. 1985. *Orson Welles: A Biography*. New York (reprinted New York 1986).

Lears, T. J. 1983. "From Salvation to Self-Realization: Advertising and the Therapeutic Roots of the Consumer Culture, 1880–1930," in Richard Wightman and T. J. Jackson Lears, eds., *The Culture of Consumption: Critical Essays in American History, 1880–1980*. New York. 1–38.

———. 1994. *Fables of Abundance: A Cultural History of Advertising in America*. New York.

LeRoy, Mervyn, and Dick Kleiner. 1974. *Mervyn LeRoy: Take One*. New York.

Lessing, Gotthold Ephraim. 1970. *Gotthold Ephraim Lessing Werke*, ed. Karl Eibl and Herman Georg Gopfert. Munich.

Levick, Barbara. 1990. *Claudius*. New Haven.

Levine, Lawrence. 1988. *Highbrow/Lowbrow: The Emergence of Cultural Hierarchy in America*. Cambridge.

Liebknecht, Karl. 1958–1971. *Gesammelte Reden und Schriften von Karl Liebknecht*, ed. Wilhelm Peck, vol. 9: "Trotz Alledem!" Berlin.

Lightbown, Ronald. 1986. *Mantegna*. Oxford.

Lippard, Chris, ed. 1996. *By Angels Driven: The Films of Derek Jarman*. Trowbridge.

——— and Guy Johnson. 1993. "Private Practice, Public Health: The Politics of Sickness and the Films of Derek Jarman," in Lester Friedman, ed., *Fires Were Started: British Cinema and Thatcherism*. Minneapolis. 278–93.

Liversidge, Michael, and Catherine Edwards, eds. 1996. *Imagining Rome: British Artists and Rome in the Nineteenth Century*. London.

Lorenz, Alfred, ed. 1938. *Richard Wagner: Ausgewählte Schriften und Briefe*, vol. 2. Berlin.

Luxemburg, Rosa. 1974. *Rosa Luxemburg: Gesammelte Werke*, ed. Georg Adler, vol. 4: "Die Krise der Sozialdemokratie (Junius Pamphlet)." Berlin.

MacDonald, Andrew. 1996. *Howard Fast: A Critical Companion*. Westport, Conn.

MacKenzie, Robert. 1977. "Review: *I, Claudius*," *TV Guide*, 31 December. 33.

Malamud, Margaret. 1998. "As the Romans Did? Theming Ancient Rome in Contemporary Las Vegas," *Arion* 6.12–40.

———. 2000. "The Imperial Metropolis: Ancient Rome in Turn-of-the-Century New York," *Arion* 7.3.64–108.

Manfull, Helen, ed. 1970. *Additional Dialogue: Letters of Dalton Trumbo, 1942–1962*. New York.

Mannes, George. 1991. "Latest Tape Releases," *Video Review*, September. 56.

Margulies, Stan, ed. 1960. *Spartacus: The Illustrated Story of the Motion Picture Production*. St. Louis.

Martin, Jean-Pierre. 1982. *Providentia deorum: Recherches sur certains aspects religieux du pouvoir impérial romain*. Rome.

Marx, Karl. 1975. *Karl Marx, Frederick Engels: Collected Works*, ed. Richard Dixon et al. New York.

Masterpiece Theatre's Promotional Material for *I, Claudius*, from Frank Goodman Associates, 1776 Broadway, New York, N.Y. 10019.

May, Larry. 1980. *Screening Out the Past: The Birth of Mass Culture and the Motion Picture Industry*. Oxford.

Mayer, David, ed. 1994. *Playing Out the Empire:* Ben-Hur *and Other Toga Plays and Films, 1883–1908: A Critical Anthology*. Oxford.

McBride, Joseph. 1992. *Frank Capra: The Catastrophe of Success*. New York.

McConachie, Bruce. 1992. *Melodramatic Formations: American Theatre and Society 1820–1870*. Iowa City.

McCullough, Colleen. 1974. *Tim: A Novel*. New York.

———. 1978. *The Thorn Birds*. New York.

———. 1990. *The First Man in Rome*. New York.

———. 1992. *The Grass Crown*. New York.

———.1994. *Fortune's Favorites*. New York.

———.1996. *Caesar's Women*. New York.

———.1997. *Caesar: A Novel*. New York.

———.1999. *Caesar: Let the Dice Fly*. New York.

McGinn, Bernard. 1994. *Antichrist: Two Thousand Years of the Human Fascination with Evil*. San Francisco.

Medhurst, Andy. 1986. "Music Hall and British Cinema," in Charles Barr, ed., *All Our Yesterdays: Ninety Years of British Cinema*. London.

Mehren, Elizabeth. 1990. "A Writer in Paradise," *Los Angeles Times*, 22 October.

Meissner, August Gottlieb. 1800. *"Masaniello" and "Spartakus."* Mannheim.

Meyer, Hershel D. 1958. *History and Conscience: The Case of Howard Fast*. New York.

Miller, Lillian B. 1966. *Patrons and Patriotism: The Encouragement of the Fine Arts in the United States 1790–1860*. Chicago.

Mills, C. Wright. 1953. *White Collar: The American Middle Classes*. New York.

Momigliano, Arnaldo. 1934. *Claudius: The Emperor and His Achievements*. Oxford.

———. 1963. "Christianity and the Decline of the Roman Empire," in Arnaldo Momigliano, ed., *The Conflict between Paganism and Christianity in the Fourth Century*. Oxford. 1–16 (reprinted with corrections, Oxford 1964).

"MPC Buys U.S. Rights to Pair from BBC," *Variety*, 16 January 1980.81.

Müller, Eugen. 1905. *Spartacus und der Sklavenkrieg in Geschichte und Dichtung*. Salzburg.

Mumford, Laura Stempel. 1995. *Love and Ideology in the Afternoon: Soap Opera, Women, and Television Genre*. Bloomington.

Murolo, Priscilla. 1984. "History in the Fast Lane," *Radical History Review* 31.22–31.

Muszkat-Muszkowski, Jan. 1909. "Spartacus: Eine Stoffgeschichte." Ph.D. diss., Universität Leipzig.

Naremore, James. 1989². *The Magic World of Orson Welles*. Dallas.

Nasaw, David. 1993. *Going Out: The Rise and Fall of Public Amusements.* New York.

Nash, Mark. 1985. "Innocence and Experience," *Afterimage* 12.31–35.

Navasky, Victor S. 1980. *Naming Names.* New York (reprinted Harmondsworth 1981).

Neff, James. 1989. *Mobbed Up: Jackie Presser's High-Wire Life in the Teamsters, the Mafia, and the FBI.* New York.

Negrine, Ralph. 1998. *Television and the Press since 1945.* Manchester.

Nettl, J. P. 1966. *Rosa Luxemburg.* Oxford.

Nochimson, Martha. 1993. *No End to Her: Soap Opera and the Female Subject.* Berkeley.

Norton, Paul F. 1977. *Latrobe, Jefferson, and the National Capitol.* New York.

O'Connor, John J. 1977. "TV: Tour of Rome with *I, Claudius,*" *New York Times,* 3 November. 21.

O'Haire, Patricia. 1996. "A Beautiful Thing," *Daily News,* 5 May. 3.

Olivova, Vera. 1980. "Spartacustradition," *Eirene* 17.89–99.

O'Pray, Michael. 1996. *Derek Jarman: Dreams of England.* London.

O'Prey, Paul. 1982. *In Broken Images: Selected Letters of Robert Graves 1914–1946.* London.

Parker, Holt. 1998. "Loyal Slaves and Loyal Wives: The Crisis of the Out-sider-Within and the Roman *Exemplum* Literature," in Sandra R. Joshel and Sheila Murnaghan, eds., *Women and Slaves in Greco-Roman Culture: Differential Equations.* New York. 152–73.

Parkes, James Cary. 1996. "Et in Arcadia . . . Homo: Sexuality and the Gay Sensibility in the Art of Derek Jarman," in Roger Wollen, ed., *Derek Jarman: A Portrait.* London. 137–45.

Pate, Nancy. 1990. "Australian Author's Epic Plans," *Orlando Sentinel Tribune,* 21 October.

Pepper, Frank S. 1985. *Dictionary of Biographical Quotations.* London.

Perin, Bernadotte, trans. 1918. *Plutarch's Lives Vol. VII.* London.

———, trans. 1920. *Plutarch's Lives Vol. IX.* London.

Perkins, Pheme. 1994. *Peter: Apostle of the Whole Church.* Columbia, S.C.

PM: See Masterpiece Theatre.

Quartermaine, Luisa. 1995. "'Slouching towards Rome': Mussolini's Imperial Vision," in Tim Cornell and Kathryn Lomas, eds., *Urban Society in Roman Italy.* London. 203–15.

Quinn-Meyler, Martin. 1996. "Opposing 'Heterosoc': Derek Jarman's Coun-terhegemonic Activism," in Lippard 1996.117–34.

Raynal, Guillaume Thomas François. 1770. *Histoire philosophique et politique des établissements et du commerce des Européens dans les deux Indes.* Amster-dam.

Rayns, Tony. 1976. "Sebastiane," *Monthly Film Bulletin* 43.514.235–36.

Réau, Louis. 1959. *Iconographie de l'art chrétien,* vol. 3.2. Paris.

Richlin, Amy. 1984. "The Invective Against Women in Roman Satire," *Arethusa* 17.167–80.

———. 1992a. *The Garden of Priapus: Sexuality and Aggression in Roman Humor,* revised edition. New York.

———, ed. 1992b. *Pornography and Representation in Greece and Rome.* New York.

Roddick, Nick. 1980. "A Funny Thing Happened on the Way to the Forum," in Frank Magill, ed., *Magill's Survey of Cinema.* Englewood Cliffs, N.J. 592–95.

de Romilly, Jacqueline. 1977. *The Rise and Fall of States According to Greek Authors.* Ann Arbor.

Ross, Robert, 1996. *The Carry On Companion.* London.

Rubinsohn, Wolfgang Zito. 1993. *Die grossen Sklavenaufstände der Antike.* Darmstadt.

Rugoff, Ralph. 1995. "Gambling with Reality: The New Art of Las Vegas," in Ralph Rugoff, ed., *Circus Americanus.* London. 3–9.

Russo, Vito. 1987. *The Celluloid Closet: Homosexuality in the Movies,* revised edition. New York.

Ryan, Michael, and Douglas Kellner. 1990. *Camera Politica: The Politics and Ideology of Contemporary Hollywood Film.* Bloomington, Ind.

Saurin, Bernard-Joseph. 1821. In *Répertoire général du théâtre français: Théâtre du second ordre, tragédies,* vol. 5: *Spartacus.* Paris. 71–134.

Schwoch, James, Mimi White, and Susan Reilly. 1992. *Media Knowledge: Readings in Popular Culture, Pedagogy, and Critical Citizenship.* Albany.

Secrest, Meryle. 1998. *Stephen Sondheim: A Life.* New York.

Segal, Erich. 1987². *Roman Laughter.* Oxford.

———, trans. 1996. *Plautus: Four Comedies.* Oxford.

Sellar, W. C., and R. J. Yateman 1930. *1066 and All That: A Memorable History of England, Comprising All the Parts You Can Remember . . .* London.

Seymour, Miranda. 1995. *Robert Graves: Life on the Edge.* New York.

Seymour-Smith, Martin. 1995. *Robert Graves: His Life and Work.* London.

Sharpe, Jenny. 1989. "Figures of Colonial Resistance," *Modern Fiction Studies* 35.137–55.

Shinkle, Florence. 1996. "Romance for McCullough: Never Happily Ever After," *St. Louis Post-Dispatch,* 6 February.

Sienkiewicz, Henryk. 1896. *Quo Vadis.* Boston.

Simon, Erika. 1986. *Augustus: Kunst und Leben in Rom um die Zeitenwende.* Munich.

Sinyard, Neil. 1985. *Films of Richard Lester.* Totowa, N.J.

Smallwood, E. Mary. 1981. *The Jews under Roman Rule: From Pompey to Diocletian: A Study in Political Relations.* Leiden (reprint, with corrections, of the 1976 edition).

Smith, J. P. 1989. "A Good Business Proposition: Dalton Trumbo, *Spartacus,* and the End of the Blacklist," *The Velvet Light Trap* 23.75–100.

Sobchack, Vivian. 1990. "'Surge and Splendor': A Phenomenology of the Hollywood Historical Epic," *Representations* 29.24–49.

Solomon, Jon. 1978. *The Ancient World in the Cinema.* New York.

Sontag, Susan. 1961. *Against Interpretation and Other Essays.* New York.

Sordi, Marta. 1983. *The Christians and the Roman Empire*, trans. Annabel Bedini. London.

Stanev, N. 1981. "Un heros condamné: configurations à l'appreciation de la posterité," in Aleksandur Fol, ed., *Spartacus: Symposium Rebus Spartaci Gestis Dedicatum 2050 A.* Sofia. 95–101.

Stray, Christopher. 1998. *Classics Transformed: Schools, Universities, and Society in England, 1830–1960.* Oxford.

Sullivan, J. P., trans. 1986. *Petronius/The Satyricon and Seneca/The Apocolocyntosis.* London.

Swanson, Vern G. 1977. *Sir Lawrence Alma-Tadema: The Painter of the Victorian Vision of the Ancient World.* London.

Syme, Ronald. 1939. *The Roman Revolution.* Oxford.

"Talking About *I, Claudius,*" *Plays and Players* 1972.19.11.18–21.

Tarr, Judith. 1991. "Empire Building: Part Two of McCullough's Sprawling Epic of Rome," *Washington Post*, 21 October.

Theweleit, Klaus. 1989. *Male Fantasies*, vol. 2: *Male Bodies: Psychoanalyzing the White Terror.* Minneapolis.

Thompson, Bruce. 1981. *Franz Grillparzer.* Boston.

Took, Barry. 1992. *Star Turns: The Life and Times of Benny Hill and Frankie Howerd.* London.

Traister, Daniel. 1995. "Noticing Howard Fast," *Prospects: An Annual of American Cultural Studies* 20.525–41.

Trotnow, Helmut. 1980. *Karl Liebknecht: Eine politische Biographie.* Cologne.

Truchet, Jacques. 1974. *Théâtre du XVIIIe siècle.* Paris.

Trumbo, Dalton. 1949. *Time of the Toad: A Study of the Inquisition in America by One of The Hollywood Ten.* Hollywood.

———. 1957a. "Blacklist = Black Market," *Nation*, 4 May. 383–87.

———. 1957b. "Dalton Trumbo Gags 'Rich' Tale," *Variety*, 3 April. 1, 87.

———. 1991. "Report on Spartacus," *Cineaste* 18.3.30–33.

Tulloch, John, and Manuel Alvarado. 1983. *Doctor Who: The Unfolding Text.* London.

Unger, Arthur. 1977. "*I, Claudius*: Mirror of Rome's Decline," *Christian Science Monitor*, 4 November. 26.

Ustinov, Peter. 1977. *Dear Me.* Boston.

Vahimagi, Tise. 1996[2]. *British Television: An Illustrated Guide.* Oxford.

Valentine, Maggie. 1994. *The Show Starts on the Sidewalk: An Architectural History of the Movie Theatre, Starring S. Charles Lee.* New Haven.

Vance, William. 1989. *America's Rome*, 2 vols. New Haven.

Van Horne, Harriet. 1977a. "Harriet Van Horne Looks at the TV Week," *New York Post*, 5 November. 22.

———. 1977b. "Harriet Van Horne Looks at the TV Week," *New York Post*, 12 November. 22.

Varis, Tapio. 1988. "Trends in International Television Flow," in Cynthia Schneider and Brian Wallis, eds., *Global Television*. Cambridge. 95–107.

Venturi, Robert, Denise Scott Brown, and Steven Izenour. 1972. *Learning from Las Vegas*. Cambridge, Mass. (revised edition 1977).

Vidal, Gore. 1961. "Barry Goldwater: A Chat." *Life*, 9 June (reprinted in Vidal 1993.827–40).

———. 1976. "Who Makes the Movies?" *New York Review of Books*, 25 November (reprinted in Vidal 1993.1166–79).

———. 1992. *Screening History*. Cambridge, Mass.

———. 1993. *United States: Essays 1952–1992*. New York.

———. 1995. *Palimpsest: A Memoir*. New York.

Vincenzi, Penny. 1990. "Renaissance Man Revisited," *Times*, 29 October.

Vogt, Joseph. 1974. *Ancient Slavery and the Ideal of Man*. Oxford.

Voltaire, François Marie Arouet. 1974. *Les oeuvres complètes de Voltaire*, ed. Theodore Bestermann. Banbury.

Von Hoffman, Nicholas. 1977. "Advertising on the Petroleum Broadcasting System," *San Francisco Examiner*, 27 November.

Wald, Alan M. 1992. *The Responsibility of Intellectuals: Selected Essays on Marxist Traditions in Cultural Commitment*. Atlantic Highlands, N.J.

Wallace, Lew. 1959 [1880]. *Ben-Hur: A Tale of the Christ*. New York.

Walters, Jonathan. 1998. "Making a Spectacle: Deviant Men, Invective, and Pleasure," *Arethusa* 31.355–67.

Walters, Margaret. 1979². *The Nude Male: A New Perspective*. Middlesex.

Wanger, Walter, and Joe Hyams. 1963. *My Life with Cleopatra*. New York.

Ward, Cyrenus Osborne. 1888. *The Ancient Lowly: A History of the Ancient Working People from the Earliest Known Period to the Adoption of Christianity by Constantine*. Chicago.

Waugh, Thomas. 1987. "Hard to Imagine: Gay Erotic Cinema in the Postwar Era," in *Homosexuality, Which Homosexuality?* International Conference on Gay and Lesbian Studies, vol. 1. Amsterdam. 78–93.

———. 1996. *Hard to Imagine: Gay Male Eroticism in Photography and Film from Their Beginnings to Stonewall*. New York.

Weeks, Jeffrey. 1977. *Coming Out: Homosexual Politics in Britain from the Nineteenth Century to the Present*. London.

Weingrad, Jeff. 1977. "Rome's Tangled Web Due as Royal Import," *New York Post*, 4 November.

Welles, Orson, and Peter Bogdanovich. 1998². *This Is Orson Welles*, ed. Jonathan Rosenbaum. New York.

Wexman, Virginia Wright. 1993. *Creating the Couple*. Princeton.

White, Mimi. 1992. "Ideological Analysis and Television," in Allen 1992a.161–202.

Whitfield, Stephen J. 1991. *The Culture of the Cold War*. Baltimore.

Wilken, Robert L. 1984. *The Christians as the Romans Saw Them*. New Haven.

Williams, Craig A. 1999. *Roman Homosexuality: Ideologies of Masculinity in Classical Antiquity*. New York.

Williams, Douglas. 1997. "The Eagle or the Cross: Rome, the Bible, and Cold War America." Ph.D. diss., University of California at San Diego.

Williams, Geoffrey, and Ronald Searle. 1954. *How to Be Topp* . . . London.

Williams, Raymond. 1975. *Television: Technology and Cultural Form*. New York.

Wilson, Ann Hume. 1991. "Roman Saga Offers Orgy of Perfect Prose," *Atlanta Journal and Constitution*, 6 October.

Wilson, Edmund. 1950. *Classics and Commercials*. New York.

Winkler, John J. 1990. *The Constraints of Desire: The Anthropology of Sex and Gender in Ancient Greece*. New York.

Winkler, Martin M. 1995. "Cinema and the Fall of Rome," *Transactions of the American Philological Association* 125.135–54.

Wolcott, James. 1977. "I, Klutzius," *Village Voice*, 7 November. 43.

———. 1978. "Nearer My Claudius to Thee and More Lewd Remarks," *Village Voice*, 23 January. 60.

Wolfe, Tom. 1965. "Las Vegas (What?) Las Vegas (Can't Hear You! Too Noisy) Las Vegas!!!!" in *The Kandy-Kolored Tangerine-Flake Streamline Baby*. New York. 3–28.

———. 1968. "King of the Status Dropouts," in *The Pump House Gang*. New York. 61–79.

Wood, Michael. 1975. *America in the Movies: Or "Santa Maria, It Had Slipped My Mind."* New York.

Wood, Robin. 1977. "Ideology, Genre, Auteur," *Film Comment* 13.46–51.

Wright, Judith H. 1974. "Genre Films and the Status Quo," *Jump Cut* 1.1, 16, 18.

Wright, Rosemary Muir. 1995. *Art and Antichrist in Medieval Europe*. Manchester.

Wyke, Maria. 1994. "'Make Like Nero!' The Appeal of a Cinematic Emperor," in Elsner and Masters 1994.11–28.

———. 1997a. "Herculean Muscle!: The Classicizing Rhetoric of Bodybuilding," *Arion* 4.3.51–79.

———. 1997b. *Projecting the Past: Ancient Rome, Cinema, and History*. New York.

———. 1998. "Playing Roman Soldiers: The Martyred Body, Derek Jarman's *Sebastiane*, and the Representation of Male Homosexuality," in Maria Wyke, ed., *Parchments of Gender: Deciphering the Bodies of Antiquity*. Oxford. 243–66.

——— and Michael Biddiss, eds. 1999. *The Uses and Abuses of Antiquity*. Bern.

Yanni, Nicholas. 1977. "Imperial Soap," *Soho Weekly News*, 3 November. 58.
Zaniello, Tom. 1996. *Working Stiffs, Union Maids, Reds, and Riffraff.* Ithaca.
Zinn, Howard. 1984. *The Twentieth Century: A People's History.* New York.

Filmography

Androcles and the Lion. 1952. Directed by Chester Erskine. 98 mins. RKO.

Barabbas. 1962. Directed by Richard Fleischer. 144 mins. Dino De Laurentiis Cinemotografica.

Ben-Hur: A Tale of the Christ. 1925. Directed by Fred Niblo. 141 mins. MGM.

Ben-Hur: A Tale of the Christ. 1959. Directed by William Wyler. 212 mins. MGM.

Ben-Hurry. 1960. Directed by Dick Fontaine.

Caligula. 1979. Directed by Tinto Brass et al. 115 mins. GTO/Felix/Penthouse.

The Captives. 1959. Directed by Dick Fontaine.

Carry On Cleo. 1964. Directed by Gerald Thomas. 92 mins. Anglo-Amalgamated.

Un chant d'amour. 1951. Directed by Jean Genet. 26 mins.

Cleopatra. 1917. Directed by Charles L. Gaskill. Helen Gardner Picture Plays.

Cleopatra 1934. Directed by Cecil B. DeMille. 102 mins. Paramount.

Cleopatra. 1963. Directed by Joseph Mankiewicz. 243 mins. Twentieth Century Fox/Walter Wanger.

Demetrius and the Gladiators. 1954. Directed by Delmer Daves. 101 mins. Twentieth Century Fox.

The Fall of the Roman Empire. 1964. Directed by Anthony Mann. 183 mins. Bronston-Roma Productions/Paramount.

Fellini Satyricon. 1970. Directed by Frederico Fellini. 138 mins. P.E.A. (Rome)/ Les Productions Artistes Associés (Paris).

A Funny Thing Happened on the Way to the Forum. 1966. Directed by Richard Lester. 99 mins. United Artists/Quadrangle.

Gladiator. 2000. Directed by Ridley Scott. 154 mins. Dreamworks.

The Greatest Story Ever Told. 1965. Directed by George Stevens. 196 mins. George Stevens Productions/United Artists. Originally released at 260 mins. (version unavailable).

Julius Caesar. 1953. Directed by Joseph L. Mankiewicz. 120 mins. MGM.

The King of Kings. 1927. Directed by Cecil B. DeMille. 115 mins. Pathe Exchange, Inc.

King of Kings. 1961. Directed by Nicholas Ray. 168 mins. Samuel Bronstein Productions/MGM.

The Last Days of Pompeii. 1935. Directed by Ernest B. Schoedsack. 96 mins. RKO.

Quo Vadis. 1951. Directed by Mervyn LeRoy. 171 mins. MGM.

The Robe. 1953. Directed by Henry Koster. 135 mins. Twentieth Century Fox.

Sebastiane. 1976. Co-directed by Derek Jarman and Paul Humfress. 90 mins. Megalovision et al.

The Sign of the Cross. 1932. Directed by Cecil B. DeMille. 124 mins. (original version). Paramount.

Sign of the Pagan. 1955. Directed by Douglas Sirk. 92 mins. Universal.

Spartacus. 1960. Directed by Stanley Kubrick. 196 mins. (version restored in 1991). Bryna Productions.

Triumph of the Will. 1935. Directed by Leni Riefenstahl. 110 mins. Leni Riefenstahl Studio-Film.

Up Pompeii! 1971. Directed by Bob Kellet. 90 mins. EMI/Associated London Films.

Why We Fight. 1942–45. Supervised by Frank Capra. 7 parts, 424 mins. U.S. War Department.

Index

Abbott, George, 192, 193
Abse, Leo, 241
Academy of Motion Picture Arts and
    Sciences, 97
Adrian, Max, 181
Aeneid, 23, 27, 29, 215–16
Agnew, Spiro, 128
Agrippina (Agrippinilla), 122–23, 127, 143
Allen, Woody, 200
Alma-Tadema, Sir Lawrence, 27, 169
American Legion, 98
The Ancient Lowly (Ward), 89, 91
Androcles and the Lion (film; 1952), 34,
    48n21, 186n4
Antonius, Marcus. *See* Antony, Mark
Antony, Mark: and Caesars Palace, 259,
    264; in *Carry On Cleo*, 17, 162, 163,
    168, 170, 172, 175–76, 177, 187n9; in
    Cleopatra, 28, 46; in *Julius Caesar*, 58,
    59; McCullough on, 219
Antony and Cleopatra (Shakespeare), 197
Appian, 80, 81, 82–83
Argonautica (Apollonius), 216
Asimov, Isaac, 261
Askey, Arthur, 166
At Your Own Risk: A Saint's Testament
    (Jarman), 245
Augustus: and Caesars Palace, 253, 258–59,
    260; in *I, Claudius*, 126, 133–34, 143,
    144, 146, 147, 150; in *King of Kings*, 63
Aurelia (in *Masters of Rome* series), 16,
    214–15, 220, 223
Aurelius, Marcus, 30, 33, 40, 44–45, 46,
    253, 259

banquets, 3, 8, 18, 92–93, 256–57
Bara, Theda, 265
Barabbas (film; 1962), 31, 43–44
Barrett, Wilson, 5, 47n19
Barrie, Amanda, 163, 168
BBC (British Broadcasting Corporation),
    163, 171, 180–81, 182, 185

Beard, Mary, 209
Ben-Hur (film; 1925), 65, 70–71
Ben-Hur (film; 1959): and camp comedy,
    169, 185, 204; and Christian actors, 64;
    and Christianity, 23; Currie in, 30; and
    fascism, 59, 65–69; fatherhood in, 44,
    45; and merchandising, 21; oppression
    in, 53; power in, 68, 69–72; public *vs.*
    private spheres in, 32–33; relations be-
    tween men in, 37–39, 40, 41; romance
    in, 38; Rome in, 5, 27, 57
Ben-Hur (Wallace), 5, 25, 38, 70–71, 226
Ben-Hurry (film; c. 1960), 240
Benny, Jack, 193
Berle, Milton, 197, 199, 201
Bible, 23, 25, 37, 184
Bird, Robert Montgomery, 5, 87–88, 96
bisexuality, 38, 52, 105–6. *See also* homo-
    sexuality
Blessed, Brian, 119, 154, 155n1
The Blood of the Martyrs (Mitchison), 226,
    228n15
Bogdanov, Michael, 184
Bologna, Giovanni, 263
Bondanella, Peter, 8, 119
Borscht Belt, 191–92, 197–200
Boyd, Stephen, 37–38, 40
The Boys from Syracuse (Rodgers and
    Hart), 193, 200
The Brave One (film; 1957), 97
Brennan, Timothy, 21, 161n44
Brenton, Howard, 184
Brice, Fanny, 197
Britain: and empire, 12–13, 17, 124–25; as
    Greece, 167–68; and homosexuality,
    164, 230–31, 241–44; as Pompeii, 182;
    and Rome, 2–3, 7, 9, 18, 87, 154, 162–
    63, 175; and sexuality, 161n44; and
    United States, 17, 20, 50, 163
British camp comedy. *See* camp comedy
Brooks, Mel, 184, 193
The Brothers Menaechmi (Plautus), 193

Credits